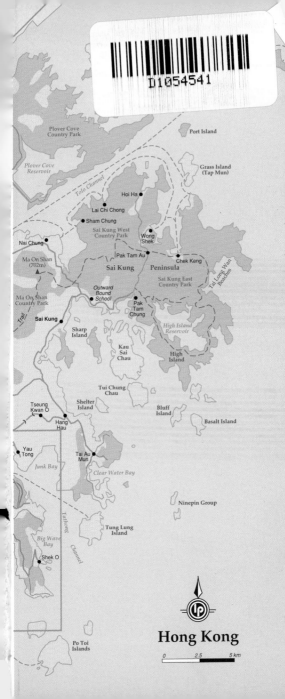

Hong Kong

0   2.5   5 km

Hong Kong

a Lonely Planet city guide

Nicko Goncharoff

Hong Kong
1st edition

Published by
Lonely Planet Publications
Head Office: PO Box 617, Hawthorn, Vic 3122, Australia
Branches: 155 Filbert St, Suite 251, Oakland,
CA 94607, USA
10 Barley Mow Passage, Chiswick,
London W4 4PH, UK
71 bis rue du Cardinal Lemoine,
75005 Paris, France

Printed by
Colorcraft Ltd, Hong Kong

Script Typeset by
Kam Y Lau, Lushan Charles Qin

Photographs by
Glenn Beanland, Nicko Goncharoff, Tony Wheeler,
Hong Kong Tourist Association (HKTA), The Peninsula

Front cover: Tin Hau Temple, Yaumatei (Glenn Beanland)

First Published
September 1996

Although the authors and publisher have tried to make the information as accurate as possible, they accept no responsibility for any loss, injury or inconvenience sustained by any person using this book.

National Library of Australia Cataloguing-in-Publication Data

Goncharoff, Nicko
Hong Kong.

1st ed.
Includes index.
ISBN 0 86442 426 4.

1. Hong Kong – Guidebooks. I. Title.
(Series: Lonely Planet city guide).

915.125045

text & maps © Lonely Planet 1996
photos © photographers as indicated 1996

Nicko Goncharoff

Nicko Goncharoff grew up in New York, found his true home while attending university in Colorado, and promptly left it upon graduating for a brief stint in Asia. He ended up staying eight years, first living in Taiwan for nearly three years and then in Hong Kong. After writing for several magazines and a news wire service, Nicko joined the Lonely Planet team to work on the 5th edition of *China*. He now calls Boulder, Colorado, his home, even if he's not there that often.

From the Author

Thanks first and foremost to Byron, Chris Taylor, Chris and Hope, Dan and Kirsten, Murray, Neal, Rieko, Winnie and Winny: I know you've heard it before, but I owe you all beers. Also to the folks at KRFN, who always give me a warm welcome and a place to rest my feet. Special appreciation to Christine Jones at Phoenix, Bob Sherbin at Hongkong Bank, Peter Randall and Lynne Beattie at HKTA and Ian Haynes at Delaney's, who all took time out to help me with my research. Thanks also to David Solloway at United Airlines, who helped me change my ticket at the worst time of the year. And lastly, a tip of the hat to the kind folks at *HK Magazine*.

From the Publisher

This first edition of *Hong Kong* was edited by Megan Fraser and designed and laid out by Chris Love. Chris also drew the maps for this new book. Greg Alford was responsible for proofreading, Simon Bracken and David Kemp designed the front cover and gatefolds and Louise Keppie created the title page. Dan Levin was the mind behind the Cantonese fonts and Kerrie Williams compiled the index.

Thanks especially to Sally Steward, Lou Callan, Ian Ward, Kam Y Lau and Lushan Charles Qin for their help with the Chinese script sections. Thanks also to Eve Melmon for her portrait photo of the author.

Warning & Request

Things change – prices go up, schedules change, good places go bad and bad places go bankrupt – nothing stays the same. So if you find things better or worse, recently opened or long since closed, please write and tell us and help make the next edition better. Your letters will be used to help update future editions.

We greatly appreciate all information that is sent to us by travellers. Back at Lonely Planet we employ a hard-working readers' letters team to sort through the many letters we receive. The best ones will be rewarded with a free copy of the next edition or another Lonely Planet guide if you prefer. We give away lots of books, but, unfortunately, not every letter/postcard receives one.

Lonely Planet books provide independent advice. Accredited Lonely Planet writers do not accept discounts or payment in exchange for positive coverage.

Contents

Maps

HKTA

Introduction

Even though Hong Kong can now be counted among the world's most modern cities, its name still has an exotic ring to it. The mind conjures up Chinese fishing junks sailing through the morning mist over Victoria Harbour, narrow cobbled lanes where sidewalk tailors and fortune-tellers ply their trade, and crowded streets with forests of vertical neon signs that stretch as far as the eye can see.

Despite Hong Kong's embrace of all things new and advanced, scenes like this can still be seen, though perhaps not exactly as one might imagine. Most fishing junks sport high-tech radar sets. Narrow cobbled lanes will more likely than not boast a boutique or a computer store. The tall neon signs are still there in force, but they vie with gleaming shopping malls for customers' business.

In its drive to become one of Asia's leading centres for finance, trade, shipping and telecommunications Hong Kong inevitably buries more and more signs of its past. This is how it's always been. From the start the territory was living on borrowed time, and it made sense to live for the here and now, not worry about some future that was beyond control. Though Hong Kong's return to China in 1997 closes the colonial chapter, the capricious nature of its new rulers in Beijing should preserve that air of uncertainty for some time to come.

The need to live for the moment helps explain the phenomenal level of energy in Hong Kong. Nearly everyone seems to be rushing to get something done, even during the weekend. Construction goes on 24 hours a day, taxi drivers work 15-hour shifts, the lights in office buildings burn late into the night. Even when at play, Hong Kong seems to be in a headlong rush: just watch the crowds frantically scramble to squeeze aboard the weekend ferries to the Outlying Islands.

All this action translates into a barrage of sights, sounds and smells for the visitor. Old women chatting around a park bench compete with a nearby jackhammer to see who is louder. Flower sellers and cloth merchants work side by side, oblivious to the stench of the fresh food market behind them. A young woman lights a stick of incense to honour her ancestors before going back to crooning karaoke with her friends. This collage of colours, noises and scents, rather than any particular sight or attraction, is likely to be your strongest impression of Hong Kong.

GLENN BEANLAND

Glittering Hong Kong at night

Hong Kong's crowded sidewalks, street markets and skyscrapers make for fascinating touring. Even the public transport can be fun. Board one of Hong Kong Island's rickety trams for a double-decker view of street life. The Star Ferry, long the only link between Hong Kong Island and the Kowloon peninsula, offers some of the world's best harbour views.

Despite all the energy it exudes, Hong Kong can be a pretty exhausting place to tour around. However if the city becomes too much, it's easy to seek relief in the lush green hills of the Peak area and beaches of southern Hong Kong Island. To slow things down further, take a little excursion out to the New Territories, or one of the Outlying Islands, where life moves at a much more civilised pace.

If you only have a brief time to spend in Hong Kong, try not to use it all up dashing from one sight to the next. In all honesty, some of Hong Kong's attractions aren't very special. Often it's what you see en route that makes for the total experience. Pick a few things that interest you, and give yourself time to duck into little alleys or shops along the way. Hong Kong certainly doesn't smell like roses, but it's still worth stopping every once in a while to take a sniff.

Facts about Hong Kong

HISTORY

When Hong Kong is handed over to China in 1997, it will have existed as a British colony for 156 years: not a long history for what is today one of the world's great cities. But the brevity of that timeline is part of Hong Kong's mystique. Stand amidst the forest of skyscrapers in Central and try to imagine the 'barren island with hardly a house upon it' that British naval officers surveyed as they hoisted the Union Jack over the empire's newest addition in 1841. It is difficult to picture, for in its headlong dash toward ever-greater prosperity, Hong Kong has worked hard to bury its humble origins.

Neglected Imperial Outpost

Hanging on the southern edge of Guangdong Province, the peninsula and scattered islands that would one day become Hong Kong counted only as a remote pocket in a neglected corner of the Qing Dynasty empire. Inhabitants included scattered communities of farmers and fishermen as well as pirates, who hid from Qing authorities among the rocky islands that still afforded easy access to the nearby Pearl River.

GLENN BEANLAND

Nathan Rd shopping strip, Kowloon

What society existed was dominated by five Cantonese landowning families, or clans, each with its own walled villages and communal farmland. Other Chinese races included the Hakka, who were generally looked down upon by other Chinese, and the Tanka, who mostly lived on boats and occupied an even lower social standing than the Hakka.

Though relatively isolated, the area saw a steady traffic of sampans, imperial war junks, pirate ships and cargo vessels headed to or from the Pearl River estuary. Some paused to anchor in the superb deep-water harbour at the southern tip of the Kowloon peninsula. By the early 19th century locals also began to see other, unfamiliar ships: the sleek, multi-masted schooners and brigs of the west.

Western Trade & the Opium Wars

European ships were already a regular sight in the city of Guangzhou (then known as Canton), the one port through which China maintained contact with the outside world. For centuries it had played host to traders from South-East Asia, India and the Middle East. First contact with Western Europe came via the Portuguese, who in 1557 were given permission to set up base in nearby Macau. Britain, France and Holland eventually followed. Their first overtures were haughtily rebuffed by the Chinese, who saw little profit in further trade with the 'Outer Barbarians', as all foreigners were classified. But Guangzhou finally opened to Europeans in 1685, and foreign traders were allowed to establish warehouses on the waterfront, from where they sold textiles and manufactured goods, and bought tea and silk.

Trade grew, but since the Chinese were largely self-sufficient and disdained western manufactured goods, the balance was mostly in favour of China. This was not what the western merchants had in mind, and in the late 18th century they found a solution: opium. The British, having a virtually inexhaustible supply of the drug in India, developed the trade aggressively, and opium formed the basis of most their transactions with China by the start of the 19th century.

Alarmed by the soaring increase in opium addiction within his realm, Chinese Emperor Dao Guang decreed a ban on it in 1796. But in Guangzhou, 1500 miles away from Beijing, corrupt Chinese officials helped ensure that the trade continued, and fortunes were amassed on both sides. Imports of the drug jumped further after 1834, when the British East India Company lost its monopoly on China trade, and other British firms rushed in. All this was to change in 1839 with the arrival of Lin Zexu, a mandarin of unusual integrity with orders from Beijing to stamp out the opium trade. He succeeded in destroying 20,000 chests of opium, which led to Captain Charles Elliot, Britain's chief superintendent of trade, suspending all trade with China. In London, Foreign Secretary Lord Palmerston, egged on by prominent Scottish merchants in Guangzhou, William Jardine and James Matheson, ordered the navy in Guangzhou to force open the closed doors of China trade.

The force arrived in June 1840, blockaded Guangzhou and then sailed north, occupying or blockading a number of ports and cities on the coast and the Yangtze River, ultimately threatening Beijing itself. The Chinese were forced to negotiate. Acting on his own authority, Captain Elliot demanded that a small, hilly island near the Pearl River estuary be ceded to the British 'in perpetuity'.

The place was familiar to British seamen, who had been using a waterfall on its southern shore as a source of fresh water, and knew the island as Hong Kong. The name was usually interpreted as 'fragrant harbour' or 'incense port'. As Captain Elliot saw it, from here the British Empire and its merchants could conduct all their trade with China and establish a permanent outpost, under British sovereignty, in the Far East.

The Guangzhou merchants, members of the Royal Navy and Lord Palmerston himself did not agree, however. A small barren island with nary a house on it was not the type of sweeping concession that a British victory was supposed to achieve. 'You have treated my instructions as if they were waste paper', Palmerston fumed at Elliot. British traders, in their newspaper the *Canton Press,* caustically observed that 'we now only require houses, inhabitants, and commerce to make this settlement one of the most valuable of our possessions'. Elliot was shunted off to the diplomatic backwaters of the USA, his foresight never to be acknowledged or rewarded.

On 26 January 1841 Commodore Gordon Bremmer led a contingent of naval men ashore and claimed Hong Kong Island for Queen and empire.

Sino-British tensions continued and the Chinese were forced to accept the Treaty of Nanking which, among other things, again ceded Hong Kong to the British 'in perpetuity', this time officially. Hong Kong formally became a British possession on 26 June 1843, and its first governor, Sir Henry Pottinger, lost no time in declaring the island would soon be awash in the riches of commerce. It would, but not in his lifetime.

The ending of the Second Anglo-Chinese War in 1860 gave the British another chance to expand their outpost. Along with other concessions, the Convention of Peking ceded to the British the Kowloon peninsula plus nearby Stonecutters Island.

Hong Kong made its last land grab in a moment of panic 40 years later when China was on the verge of being parcelled out into 'spheres of influence' by the western powers and Japan, all of which had sunk their claws into the country. The British army felt it needed more land to protect the colony, and in June 1898 the Second Convention of Peking presented Britain with what is now known as the New Territories. But instead of annexing the land outright, the British agreed to a 99 year lease, beginning 1 July 1898 and ending at midnight on 30 June 1997. Though those of the time likely gave it little thought, the countdown to British Hong Kong's expiration had already begun.

From Backwater to Boom Town

While merchants in Hong Kong prospered from the China trade, for decades the colony failed to live up to expectations. Fever and typhoons threatened life and property, and at first the colony attracted a fair number of criminals. However, by the end of the 19th century Hong Kong began to shape itself into a more substantial community. Gas and electrical power companies were set up, and ferries, electric trams and the Kowloon-Canton Railway finally provided a decent transport network. Nonetheless, in the years leading up to WWII, Hong Kong lived in the shadow of Shanghai, which had become the premier trade and financial centre of the Far East.

Though snubbed by its imperial masters, Hong Kong became a beacon for China's regular outflow of refugees. One of the earlier waves was sparked by the Chinese Revolution of 1911, which ousted the decaying Qing Dynasty and ushered in several decades of strife, warlordism and mass starvation. Steady numbers continued to enter the colony during the 1920s and 1930s, but the stream became a flood after Japan invaded China in 1937: an estimated 750,000 mainland Chinese sought shelter in Hong Kong between 1937 and 1939.

But Hong Kong's British status only offered brief sanctuary. On 8 December 1941, in conjunction with its attack on US forces at Pearl Harbor, Japan's military swept down from Guangzhou into Hong Kong. After a week of fierce but futile resistance, the British forces surrendered, beginning nearly four years of Japanese

GLENN BEANLAND

NICKO GONCHAROFF

NICKO GONCHAROFF

GLENN BEANLAND

Top: Apartment block, Nathan Rd, Kowloon
Middle Left: Galleria shopping mall, Central
Middle Right: St John's Cathedral, Central
Bottom: Hong Kong History Museum, Tsimshatsui

occupation. Conditions were harsh, and in the latter years Japan actually started deporting people from Hong Kong in a bid to ease a severe food shortage there.

Following the defeat and withdrawal of the Japanese, Hong Kong looked set to resume its sleepy routine. But events in China forced the colony in a new direction. The communist revolution in 1949 sent capitalists pouring into Hong Kong. The following year Beijing sided with North Korea and went to war against the US and United Nations' forces. The subsequent embargo on all western trade with China threatened to strangle the colony economically. Hong Kong had to find another way to survive, and in doing so finally came into its own. On a paltry, war-torn foundation, foreign and Chinese businesses built an immense manufacturing and financial service centre that transformed Hong Kong into Asia's most vibrant city. A steady stream of refugees from China provided an enormous pool of cheap labour, and European, American and Asian investors provided the funds needed to employ it.

Working conditions in these early years of Hong Kong's industrial revolution were often Dickensian: 16 hour days, unsafe equipment, hideously low wages and child labour were all common. Refugee workers endured, and some even earned their way out of poverty and into prosperity. The Hong Kong government, after coming under international pressure, eventually began to set and enforce labour standards and the situation gradually improved.

By the end of the 1950s Hong Kong-made textiles, watches and basic electronics were finding their way into the homes around the world. Though these products did not always carry a reputation for high quality, the money they brought in started turning the colony into an unlikely economic powerhouse.

From 600,000 in 1945, Hong Kong's population soared to three million in 1960. Most of these new inhabitants fled communist China, which for some reason had not seen fit to reclaim Hong Kong militarily.

However, China was often quick to remind Hong Kong of its tenuous position. In 1962 it suddenly opened the border gates, allowing 70,000 people to flood into the colony in a matter of weeks. In 1967, at the height of the Cultural Revolution, Hong Kong again seemed doomed when riots inspired by the Red Guards rocked the colony. Several bombs were detonated. On 8 July 1967 a militia of 300 Chinese crossed the border with automatic rifles, killed five policemen and penetrated three km into the New Territories before pulling back. Expatriates thought the end was near. Property values in Hong Kong fell sharply and panic spread through the business community. But Hong Kong's colonial masters held their ground and police gradually restored order, supported in most part by the locals.

As China went back into its shell, Hong Kong got on with the business of getting rich, which included improving infrastructure. In 1972, the cross-harbour tunnel opened, ending the reliance on ferries as the only link between Hong Kong Island and Kowloon. The next year, the first New Town was completed, paving the way towards better housing for Hong Kong's millions. By 1979 the colony even had its own subway with the opening of the first line of the Mass Transit Railway.

During the 1970s some of Hong Kong's Asian neighbours, including Taiwan, South Korea and Singapore, began to mimic the colony's success. Just as their cheap labour pools were threatening to undermine the competitive edge of Hong Kong manufacturers, China decided to emerge from nearly two decades of self-isolation. Deng Xiaoping, who took control of China in the mayhem following Mao Zedong's death in 1976, opened up the country to tourism and foreign investment in 1978.

Deng's 'Open Door' policy, designed to pull China into the 20th century, revived Hong Kong's role as the gateway to its mysterious, giant northern neighbour. Hong Kong companies gradually began shifting their factories across the border, and foreign firms came in droves seeking out Hong Kong businesses for their China contacts and expertise. Investment in China grew and trade in Hong Kong skyrocketed as it became a transhipment point for China's exports, and later on, imports. Underpinning this boom was the drive to rake in profits ahead of 1997, when Hong Kong's unpredictable new master was due to take over.

'One Country, Two Systems'

Actually, few people gave much thought to Hong Kong's future until the early 1980s, when the British and Chinese governments started meeting to decide what would happen come 1997. In theory, Britain was legally bound only to hand back the New Territories. But with nearly half of Hong Kong's population living in those same New Territories, it would be an awkward division.

More importantly, for the government in Beijing, Hong Kong remained the last reminder of foreign imperialism on mother soil (Macau is a somewhat different story, having never been formally ceded to Portugal – it is due to revert to China in 1999). As China's economy and confidence grew, a British presence in Hong Kong became intolerable.

In December 1984 the British formally agreed to hand the entire colony back to China in 1997. The agreement, enshrined in a document known as the Sino-British Joint Declaration, theoretically allows Hong Kong to retain its present social, economic and legal systems for at least 50 years after 1997. On 1 July 1997 Hong Kong will be transformed into a Special Administrative Region (SAR) of China. Beijing's catch phrase for this is 'one country, two systems', whereby Hong Kong will be permitted to retain its capitalist system after 1997, while across the border the Chinese continue with a system which they label socialist.

As a follow-up to the Joint Declaration, in 1988 Beijing published The Basic Law for Hong Kong, a hefty document not unlike a constitution. The Basic Law permits the preservation of Hong Kong's legal system; guarantees the right of property and ownership; gives residents the right to travel in and out; permits Hong Kong to remain a free port and to continue independent membership of international organisations; and guarantees continuing employment after 1997 for Hong Kong's Chinese civil servants. The rights of assembly, free speech, association, travel and movement, correspondence, choice of occupation, academic research, religious belief and the right to strike are all included.

Hong Kong's fledgling pro-democracy movement denounced the Joint Declaration as the new 'unequal treaty' and blasted Britain for selling out the best interests of Hong Kong people in order to keep good economic relations with China. And like the treaty that gave Britain Hong Kong in 1841, local residents never had any say in these agreements – the negotiations were held entirely behind closed doors.

China insists that the Basic Law is the Hong Kong people's guarantee of the good life after 1997. Indeed, Chinese officials often bristle when Hong Kong politicians or journalists raise any doubts as to China's benevolent intentions. However, Beijing's actions have consistently given Hong Kongers good cause to worry.

Chief among these was the Tiananmen Massacre of 4 June 1989, when Chinese troops used tanks and machine guns to break up pro-democracy demonstrations in Beijing. In Hong Kong, more than one million people attended rallies to protest the massacre in Beijing. Confidence plummeted – the Hong Kong stock market fell 22% in one day, and a great deal of capital headed to safer havens overseas. In the following weeks the Hong Kong government took steps to rebuild confidence, including the launch of a new HK$160 billion Airport & Port Project designed to shore up locals' faith in Hong Kong's future and lure back foreign investors.

But the signal had been sent. Hong Kong-based Chinese officials who had spoken out against the Tiananmen killings were yanked from their posts, or sought asylum in the USA and Europe. Those Hong Kongers with money and skills made a mad dash to emigrate to any country that would take them. Those that remained warned of a 'brain drain' that would cripple the economy.

In 1990, Hong Kong introduced a Bill of Rights, designed to put the colony in line with international human rights standards. Beijing responded by threatening to tear up the bill after 1997.

Sino-British ties turned still worse with the arrival in 1992 of Chris Patten, Hong Kong's newest, and probably last, British governor. A highly skilled politician, Patten immediately set out to give Hong Kong a last-minute democratic foundation. He pushed through a series of legislative reforms which eventually led to direct elections for both lawmakers and municipal officials.

Hong Kongers were by and large sceptical, with many wondering why Britain had chosen to wait until this late date to start experiments in democracy. China reached new peaks of rage, first levelling daily personal attacks on Patten, then threatening the post-1997 careers of any pro-democracy politicians or officials. When these tactics didn't work, it finally targeted Hong Kong's economy. Negotiations on business contracts straddling 1997 suddenly dragged to a halt, and Beijing boycotted all talks on the new airport programme, successfully scaring off foreign investors.

Sensing that it had alienated even its supporters in the colony, China backed off a bit, and in 1994 gave its blessing to the new airport and other Hong Kong business ventures. Its hostility toward direct elections remains, and China has vowed to throw out all democratically elected legislators come 1997, and replace them with a 'provisional legislature' until Special Administrative Region lawmakers take over.

As the 1997 handover draws near, panic seems to be giving way to pragmatism. Fears that Beijing would close the 'Open Door' after Tiananmen have proven false, and it now seems impossible that China could ever reverse its economic reforms, which have penetrated to nearly every sector of the country. Hong Kong's migrants of the early 1990s are returning (though with foreign passports in hand, just in case.) The number of foreign companies setting up shop in Hong Kong continues to increase, as does foreign investment. China itself has poured tens of billions of US dollars into the colony. While few hold out any hope for press or political freedoms in China's Hong Kong, most believe Beijing won't kill the goose that lays the golden egg. Which means Hong Kong will at the very least be able to continue doing what it does best: make money.

GEOGRAPHY

With its magnificent harbour, steep peaks and surrounding islands, Hong Kong is one of the world's more geographically interesting cities. The territory's 1084 sq km is divided into four main areas – Hong Kong Island, Kowloon, the New Territories and the Outlying Islands.

Victoria Harbour is basically Hong Kong's centre of gravity, with most of the urban areas lining either the northern or southern shores. Originally about one mile wide, the harbour is being squeezed by ambitious reclamation works on both sides.

On the south side of the harbour lies Hong Kong Island, which covers 78 sq km, or just 7% of Hong Kong's land area. Most of the commercial and residential areas are on the north side of the island, including Central, the main business, banking and government district. The southern side of the island houses mostly wealthy residents and boasts some nice beaches. The two sides are separated by a backbone of steep hills, including Victoria Peak, Hong Kong's premier scenic viewpoint.

Kowloon is a peninsula on the north side of the harbour. The southern tip of this peninsula (Tsimshatsui) is a major tourist area, and has seemingly endless blocks of shops and hotels. The areas further north and west are filled with residential and commercial towers and industrial zones that include some the most cramped and dingy parts of Hong Kong. Boundary St, which cuts across the middle of the peninsula, marks where the British-Chinese border was before Britain snatched up the rest of Kowloon along with the New Territories in 1898. Kowloon was named after a series of hills – the 'nine dragons' or *gau long* in Cantonese – that separate it from the New Territories. The name reflects the ancient Chinese belief that dragons inhabit mountains.

Sandwiched between Kowloon and the Chinese border, the New Territories occupy 980 sq km, or 91% of Hong Kong's land area. Originally Hong Kong's agricultural backyard, the New Territories now house nearly half of Hong Kong's population in the so-called New Towns, which are stark monuments to urban plan-

ning and function over form. But you can still find farms
out here, as well as white sand beaches and an impressive number of country parks.

The Outlying Islands incorporate all islands apart
from Hong Kong Island. Officially, the Outlying Islands
are part of the New Territories and make up about 20%
of Hong Kong's total land area. There are actually 234
islands and while many are tiny rocks, the largest
(Lantau Island) is nearly twice the size of Hong Kong
Island. Previously, there were 235 islands until Stonecutters Island got absorbed by reclamation off the western
shore of the Kowloon peninsula. Some of the larger
islands, including Lantau, Cheung Chau and Lamma,
are well served by commuter ferries and offer both
residents and visitors an escape from Hong Kong's blis-
tering urban pace. They are also home to some excellent
country parks.

CLIMATE

Hong Kong is perched on the south-east coast of China
just south of the tropic of Cancer, on much the same
latitude as Hawaii or Calcutta. The climate is sub-trop-
ical, but tends toward temperate for nearly half the year.
This is because the huge land mass of Asia generates
powerful blasts of arctic wind that blow from the north
during winter. In summer, the seasonal wind (monsoon)
reverses and blows from the south bringing hot, humid
tropical air.

Late October through December usually sees sunny
and dry weather with cool breezes, though for most of
November it's still warm enough to go swimming.
January and February are more cloudy and see occasional cold fronts. Temperatures can drop as low as 10°C
in the New Territories, but snow and frost are quite rare.
Not much rain falls, but when it does, it's usually a chilly,
depressing drizzle that lasts for days on end. Because of
a low cloud ceiling, the mountains are often shrouded
in mist, which often spoils visits to the Peak and other
scenic outlooks. Winter weather usually continues into
March and often ends abruptly when the arctic wind
stops blowing. Even during winter, there are windless
days when the weather gets amazingly balmy.

March through May/April are also usually pleasant,
as the scorching summer heat usually doesn't arrive
until June. But there's a higher chance of rain and humidity than in autumn.

Big thundershowers become more frequent as June
approaches. June tends to be the wettest month, with the
beginning of the summer monsoon. On into July and

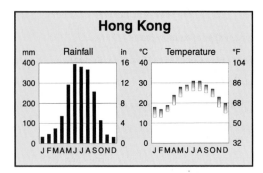

temperatures usually hover between 26°C and 34°C through the middle of September. Though there are occasional cool breezes off the water, the heat is generally oppressive.

September brings a hint of cooler weather, but is also the month during which Hong Kong is most likely to be hit by typhoons, which can really mess with your travel plans. Typhoons vary in size from tropical storms to severe super-typhoons. If the typhoon just brushes past Hong Kong, it will bring a little rain and wind that might only last for half a day. If it scores a direct hit, the winds can be deadly and it may rain for days on end. You can't go outside for very long during a bad typhoon and most businesses shut down. When a typhoon becomes a possibility, warnings are broadcast continuously on TV and radio. You can also call the Royal Observatory typhoon hotline (☎ 2835-1473).

ECOLOGY & ENVIRONMENT

After nearly 150 years of ignoring the issue, in 1989 the Hong Kong government suddenly realised that Hong Kong was in danger of becoming a vast, densely populated cesspool. Hong Kong's 'laissez-faire' stance towards business and economic growth meant that few or no measures existed to control water, waste or air pollution.

Although it's starting embarrassingly late, the government is now moving to correct what it candidly calls 'past environmental mistakes'. One of the most ambitious projects is a HK$12 billion sewage treatment system designed to clean up Victoria Harbour, which swallows up as much as 50% of the territory's untreated sewage. The system won't be ready until at least 1997,

NICKO GONCHAROFF

Tranquil gardens, Wong Tai Sin Temple, Kowloon

so swimming in the harbour will be a health hazard for some years to come.

Fortunately, the government is not stopping at the harbour. Factories, farms and restaurants in the New Territories are coming under the gun for dumping untreated waste into freshwater streams or the ocean. Unfortunately, a great deal of damage has already been done: some New Territories streams are 'no better than open sewers', the government admits.

Landfills are being opened to absorb the enormous amount of trash and solid waste generated by Hong Kong's six million inhabitants. An aggressive public service campaign is also reminding locals not to treat roads, waterways and parks as rubbish bins, though not everyone is getting the message.

One of Hong Kong's most serious problems is air pollution. Smoke-belching factories, ceaseless construction and a high proportion of diesel vehicles have made for dangerous levels of particulate matter and nitrogen dioxide. Cases of asthma and bronchial infection have soared in recent years, and doctors place the blame squarely on poor air quality. Travellers with respiratory conditions should take this into consideration if planning to stay for a prolonged period. See the Health section in the Facts for the Visitor chapter for more details.

The government has also set up a monitoring system for swimming beaches, based on the amount of disease-causing bacteria in the water. While this doesn't take into account floating trash or algae, it does give an idea of the type of health risk you face. For more information, refer to the Health section in the following chapter.

Not all of Hong Kong's land is ravaged by pollution. Around 40% of the territory's total land area is protected by 21 country parks. Watershed protection was the major reason for making these areas off limits to development and private motor vehicles – all of Hong Kong's 17 freshwater reservoirs lie within park boundaries. Nevertheless, hikers, campers, bird-watchers and other nature-lovers all benefit. Most of the country parks are in the New Territories and the Outlying Islands, but even the higher mountainous slopes of Hong Kong Island are protected.

It remains to be seen if China will pick up where the British Hong Kong government has left off. China itself is an ecological disaster zone, and Beijing is doing little to clean things up. But Hong Kong's cash-rich government can easily afford its environmental programmes, which is some cause for optimism.

FLORA & FAUNA

Back in 1841, British Foreign Secretary Lord Palmerston disparaged Hong Kong as a 'barren island with nary a house upon it'. While the lack of houses was nothing unusual, the barrenness certainly was. With abundant rainfall and a warm climate, the British might well have expected to find a dense jungle on the shores of southern China. Instead, they found Hong Kong nearly devoid of trees, a situation that persists today.

The simple reason for this is that Hong Kong's earlier inhabitants cut down all the trees. Massive tree cutting by settlers started as long ago as the Song Dynasty (960-1279) and continued until the hills were stripped bare. Green politics were not fashionable in those days, and no efforts were made at replanting. With the forests removed, heavy summer thundershowers quickly eroded Hong Kong's steep slopes, and the lack of topsoil has prevented the forests from regenerating. However, remnants of original forests can be found in steep ravines both on Hong Kong Island and in the New Territories, mostly within the boundaries of the country parks.

These days, most uninhabited regions of Hong Kong are grasslands. Somewhat ironically, the only areas of Hong Kong that have seen any reforestation efforts are those inhabited by humans. The British were never happy about the lack of shade trees during the scorching summers, and thus planted quick-growing species around their colonial residences. The Chinese have also planted groves in an attempt to please the spirits of the deceased. Trees with commercial value like bamboo have been planted in small groves in agricultural regions. However, Hong Kong today has precious little to offer in the way of forests.

The loss of so much vegetation has also meant the loss of habitat for animals, and very few large creatures survive. Weighing in at over 100 kg are wild boars, found in some rural spots and regarded as pests because they dig up crops. Much more aesthetic, and rarely seen, are barking deer (also called muntjaks) and black-and-white quilled Chinese porcupines. The latter can be found even on the high slopes of Hong Kong Island. Small mammals thought to survive include ferret badgers, otters, masked palm civets, porcupines, shrews and bats. Wild monkeys can be found but are thought to be the descendants of escaped pets. Leopards and tigers, some of which were seen in Hong Kong's initial years, were all but wiped out at the beginning of the 20th century. The last tiger seen in the New Territories was said to have been shot in 1915, though there are claims of sightings in later years. However, the Chinese leopard cat (weighing only two to five kg) is still found breeding in remote parts of the territory.

An interesting creature is the Chinese pangolin, a scaly mammal that resembles an armadillo. When attacked, it rolls itself up into an unappetising ball. Unfortunately, its existence is threatened because the Chinese regard its flesh as a tonic medicine and aphrodisiac.

On a happier note, there are more than 250 species of birds in Hong Kong, in large part due to the establishment of the Mai Po Marshes conservation site. With 380 hectares of mudflats, shrimp ponds and dwarf mangroves, it's a large safe haven for both resident and migratory birds, and not a bad place for bird-watchers either.

GOVERNMENT & POLITICS

Hong Kong has made a few belated steps toward direct elections in the past four years, but it is by no means a democracy. Given China's outrage at even these modest political reforms, there's little chance that the post-1997 Hong Kong Special Administrative Region (SAR) will be any more democratic.

Heading Hong Kong's administration is a governor, appointed by London. After 1997, the post will go to a chief executive, to be hand-picked by Beijing. While China has yet to clearly state its plans, a chief executive-designate will likely be chosen sometime before the transfer of sovereignty. Several top Hong Kong officials and business people have been rumoured as candidates, but Beijing has kept mum on the subject.

The governor presides over meetings of both the Executive Council (EXCO) and the Legislative Council (LEGCO). EXCO is technically the top policy-making body of the government. It's composed of three top officials – the chief secretary, financial secretary and attorney general – and 10 other members appointed either by the governor or on the instructions of the British government.

One rung down the ladder is LEGCO, which frames legislation, enacts laws and controls government expenditure. As a result of Governor Chris Patten's constitutional reforms, 18 out of LEGCO's 60 members are now directly elected. Another 21 come from functional constituencies, which represent economic, social and professional sectors such as tourism, real estate, health care and so on. These legislators are directly elected by workers and executives in their respective sectors, a total of 2.9 million people. The remainder of LEGCO is made up of 18 government-appointed members and the same three top officials that head up EXCO. (Isn't that convenient?)

The Urban Council is in charge of the day-to-day running of services in Hong Kong Island and Kowloon, including street cleaning, garbage collection, food hygiene, hawkers' licences, public recreation and the like. In the New Territories, the Regional Council has much the same functions as the Urban Council.

On the next rung down are the District Boards, set up in 1982 to give Hong Kong residents a degree of control over their local area. The boards consist of government officials and elected representatives from the local area. The problem is that these boards have little real power.

Voter turnout has been better for the LEGCO elections. While LEGCO has been livelier since the electoral reforms (which many of its incumbent members sharply criticised), locals still view most legislators as political weathervanes whose chief aim is to line their own pockets. Given that lawmakers roll up for LEGCO sessions in Mercedes-Benz, Jaguars, BMWs and the like, it's not hard to see why.

But China has repeatedly insisted that it will completely scrap Patten's new LEGCO on 1 July 1997 in favour of its own 'provisional' legislature that will operate until Beijing organises its own elections. It is already setting up a 'Preparatory Committee' that will run side by side with the British administration in the lead up to 1997. China's plan is to make the British Hong Kong government a lame duck at least six months before the handover.

China's strategy also has civil servants nervous. Staff in all government departments and other areas of administration are under the umbrella of the Hong Kong Civil Service which employs 180,000 people, nearly 99% of whom are local Chinese. China may try to recruit members of its Preparatory Committee from within the ranks of the civil service. Under this scenario, department heads may find themselves being questioned by deputies who have aligned themselves with Beijing in the hope of getting a promotion after 1997. Civil servant morale has plummeted.

The colonial government is generally efficient and mostly free of corruption, but it wasn't always so. Hong Kong's police and civil service were a disgrace until 1974 when the British established the Independent Commission Against Corruption (ICAC). The ICAC was given draconian powers, and within three years of its founding nearly crushed corruption in Hong Kong. To prosecute a case, the ICAC only needs to show that a civil servant has wealth disproportional to his or her income – it's not necessary to prove that the unexplained wealth was obtained illegally. Not only can it imprison the defendant, it can also force the defendant to turn over the ill-gotten gains to the Hong Kong government.

Unfortunately, China has no independent judiciary and despite recent widespread crackdowns, corruption on the mainland is as rampant today as at any time during China's 5000 year history. After 1997, many believe that the ICAC will be intimidated by Communist Party officials and corruption will once again flourish in Hong Kong.

While Chinese officials won't enter the Hong Kong government until 1 July 1997, the Chinese Communist Party has had a presence in Hong Kong since at least 1949, when the communists came to power in China. Officially the CCP is called the Hong Kong Macau Work Committee (HMWC) and has always been headed by the director of the PRC's Xinhua news agency's Hong Kong branch, which is Beijing's official mouthpiece in the territory.

ECONOMY

This is Hong Kong's heart and soul. Where other societies find identity in their cultural history or political system, Hong Kong looks to its robust economy. For proof, pick up any newspaper, walk through any neighbourhood or eavesdrop on a lunchtime conversation. Making money, and making a lot of it, is what it's all about.

Hong Kong has proven remarkably good at it. The place is a capitalist's dream: free enterprise and free trade, low taxes, a hard-working labour force, a world-class seaport and airport facilities, excellent telecommunications and a government famous for its hands-off approach to private business.

With the opening of China during the 1980s, Hong Kong shifted away from manufacturing and toward services. Most producers moved their factories north of the border to take advantage of lower labour costs. Some large service firms, such as Hongkong Telecom, have even moved backroom administrative operations north to Guangdong Province.

China's roaring economic growth helped spark a boom in Hong Kong service industries like shipping, telecommunications, banking and insurance. Service industries, including import and export trade, employ more than 75% of Hong Kong's workforce and make up nearly 80% of its GDP.

Much of this growth in the services sector is underpinned by trade, which has expanded 37-fold over the past two decades. As entrepot for the flood of goods into and out of China, Hong Kong has become the world's eighth-largest trading entity. The total annual value of visible trade (which excludes trade in services) had risen to more than US$300 billion by 1995. Domestic exports, or products made and sent out from Hong Kong, only amount to around 20% of total exports, reflecting the shrinking number of domestic factories. The bulk of goods sent out from Hong Kong are re-exports: semi-finished and finished goods imported into the territory for additional processing or simply transhipment, which are then exported to their final destination overseas.

Being almost entirely dependent on imported resources to meet the needs of its six million inhabitants, Hong Kong is also a prodigious importer. In fact imports often outweigh exports, meaning the territory habitually posts a trade deficit. However this is usually offset by Hong Kong's robust exports of business, finance and trade-related services, which give the colony a sustained surplus in so-called 'invisible trade'.

Not surprisingly, China has become Hong Kong's largest trading partner, supplying the territory with around one-third of its total imports, and taking about one-third of its re-exports. China and the USA each take about 25% of Hong Kong's domestic exports, while the USA also accounts for around 20% of Hong Kong's re-exports. Other large export markets for Hong Kong goods are Japan, Germany, the UK, Taiwan and Singapore.

This steady stream of trade and business has allowed Hong Kong to maintain average GDP growth of around 5% during the first half of the 1990s. While enviable, such healthy growth in Hong Kong's climate of limited land and resources has kept consumer price inflation persistently high, and the leading CPI (A) indicator can be found hovering at between 8% and 10% at any given time. Though it doesn't enjoy the notoriety of Tokyo, Hong Kong's property prices are often on a par with those in the Japanese capital.

Traditionally, labour has also been scarce in Hong Kong, and for years the unemployment rate was locked between 1.5% and 2%. Imported workers from the Philippines and, increasingly China, are brought in to help meet demand for manual labour, such as domestic help and construction. Hong Kong felt a mild shock in 1995 as unemployment 'shot up' to 3.5%. Local trade unions were quick to castigate the foreign workers, who they'd never really liked anyway. But government studies showed that most of those out of work had lost their jobs due to a downturn in the financial markets: the finance sector employs around 15% of Hong Kong's workforce.

Most of those employed in the finance world need not fear for their jobs however. Hong Kong can rightfully claim to be one of Asia's most important financial centres, along with Tokyo. Of the world's top 100 banks, 85 have operations in Hong Kong. The territory's stock market, once ridiculed as no more than an upmarket casino, complete with shady dealers, now ranks among the world's top ten in terms of market capitalisation. In

1995 Hong Kong's banks and deposit-taking institutions held around US$600 billion in external assets, about 8% of the world total.

In line with this image, the Hong Kong government keeps its own finances in good order, in a way that most western developed countries can only dream about. Despite keeping the maximum rate of personal income tax at 15%, and corporate profits tax capped at 16.5%, the Hong Kong government had posted 11 consecutive annual budget surpluses as of 1995.

Although Hong Kong still gets jittery over 1997, foreign investors don't seem to be too worried. The number of foreign companies setting up offices or even regional headquarters in Hong Kong is on the rise. Perhaps most importantly, China has become the number one investor in town, having pumped billions of US dollars into the local economy in the first half of the 1990s.

Chinese firms have become major players in the property and financial markets, and long-time Hong Kong blue-chip firms, such as Hongkong Telecom and Swire Pacific, now count companies from the mainland among their key shareholders. Obviously someone in Beijing is still expecting Hong Kong to stay profitable for quite some time yet.

Hong Kong's Economy at a Glance	
GDP growth year-on-year	5.0%
Per capita GDP	US$21,600
Consumer price inflation (A) index	8.7%
Exchange fund (foreign reserves)	US$59.5 billion
Total value of imports	US$192.6 billion
Total value of domestic exports	US$29.9 billion
Total value of re-exports	US$143.7 billion
Source: Hong Kong Census and Statistics Bureau	
Note: All figures are annual for 1995	

POPULATION & PEOPLE

Hong Kong's population is just over six million, making it one of the most densely populated places in the world. The overall density of the population works out to about 5000 people per sq km, but this figure is deceiving since there is a wide variation from area to area. The urban areas of Hong Kong Island and Kowloon pack in over 25,000 people per sq km, compared with only 2860 in the rural New Territories.

GLENN BEANLAND

Fishing for the three-eyed mullet, Victoria Harbour

About 98% of Hong Kong's population is ethnic Chinese, most of whom have their origins in China's Guangdong Province. About 60% were born in the territory. About 33% of the population lives in Kowloon, 22% on Hong Kong Island, and 45% in the New Territories, with around 2% of the latter living in the Outlying Islands.

If any groups can truly claim to belong to Hong Kong, they are the Tanka, the nomadic boat people who have fished the local waters for centuries, and the Hakka, who farmed the New Territories long before Charles Elliot thought about running the Union Jack up a flagpole. The Hakka are a distinct group which emigrated from northern to southern China centuries ago to flee persecution. Hakka means 'guest'. Hakka women can be recognised in the New Territories by their distinctive spliced-bamboo hats with wide brims and black-cloth fringes.

As of December 1995, around 446,000 foreign expats permanently resided (legally) in Hong Kong, up more than 40% from just three years earlier. There are also an unknown number of illegals who usually don't stay for long. In descending order, the breakdown of legal resident expats in Hong Kong is: Filipinos 143,000; Americans 35,700; British 29,000; Canadians 28,900, Thai 26,000; Indonesians 25,500; Japanese 23,900; Australians 21,800; Indians 21,500; Malaysians 14,600; others 76,100.

Amazingly, China still has yet to say what will happen in 1997 to 'foreigners' who were born in Hong Kong and hold Hong Kong passports. Some are half or quarter Chinese, but Beijing has indicated that citizenship can only be endowed on those Hong Kongers of pure

'Chinese descent'. In other words, race is the deciding factor, not place of birth. This also poses a problem for other nationalities, such as Hong Kong's long-standing Indian residents, stateless in 1997. The Indians, looked down upon by many Hong Kong Chinese, fear that Beijing may harbour a similar attitude and expel them. Even if they're allowed to stay, many doubt China will allow them to travel freely outside Hong Kong.

In addition to would-be residents, expatriates who are just in Hong Kong for several years on working visas have no idea how they will be treated after 1997. The Hong Kong and UK governments have pressed Chinese officials for at least a hint of what official policy will be. But with less than 18 months to go before the handover, China remains silent on the issue. It could be that it honestly has no clue what to do. But more likely is that China is following past precedent and making a show of force by keeping Hong Kong on edge over its future.

ARTS

Mention art in relation to Hong Kong, and the term 'cultural desert' will likely soon grace the conversation. It's not an altogether fair description, and is usually uttered by jaded residents who have lost the energy to look for what's out there. Granted, in a city where some people proudly declare that making money is the most important thing in life, the arts tend to take a back seat. But there's still a good deal on offer, especially in the performing arts. There are both philharmonic and Chinese orchestras, Chinese and modern dance troupes, a ballet company, several theatre groups and numerous art schools and organisations. Government funds also allow local venues to bring in top international performers. Hong Kong also hosts international art and folk festivals annually, which showcase both local and overseas artists and works.

On a more grassroots level, local street opera troops occasionally pop up around the city to lay siege to neighbourhoods for several days with their armoury of clashing cymbals, gongs and high-pitched warbling. Both local and mainland Chinese opera troupes can also sometimes be seen in more formal venues.

Despite being next door to China and its venerable 5000 year cultural heritage, Hong Kong comes up a bit short on visual arts. At one it time was scorned for having the worst museums in the British Empire. It has tried to make amends, and now there are 16 museums of various types throughout the territory, though some would be hard pressed to justify their existence. Of the

16, only five can really be considered art museums. Along with a few galleries here and there, there are enough paintings and sculpture (and even a few ceramics and bronzes) to keep one interested, but to savour the true genius of Chinese art you must head to either Beijing or Taipei.

Some exquisite works do make their way to Hong Kong, but mostly en route to the auction block. Art auctions are big business in Hong Kong, and both Christie's and Sotheby's do a brisk trade. Their intermittent auctions are worth attending for sheer spectacle.

Architecture

With the exception of a few buildings in and around the central business district, Hong Kong's architecture is not all that exciting. Looking down from the Peak, or from the Tsimshatsui promenade, the city's forests of skyscrapers make for spectacular views. But taken individually, most structures are uninspiring.

A look through any coffee-table book of old Hong Kong will show this was not always the case. Over the years the colony has played host to scores of Chinese temples, walled villages, Qing Dynasty forts, Victorian mansions and Edwardian hotels. But few structures have survived Hong Kong's ceaseless cycle of destruction and rebuilding.

About the only examples of pre-colonial Chinese architecture left in urban Hong Kong are temples: the Tin Hau temples in Tin Hau (near Causeway Bay), Shaukeiwan and Aberdeen date from the mid-1800s. Government-run museums in Chai Wan and Tsuen Wan have preserved a few buildings left over from Chinese villages that predate the arrival of the British. But for anything more substantial, one has to go to the New Territories or the Outlying Islands, where walled villages, fortresses and 18th century temples can be found.

Colonial architecture is also in fairly short supply. Most of what is left can be found on Hong Kong Island, including the Legislative Council building (formerly the Supreme Court) in Central, the old police station in Stanley and an old sanatorium near Caine Lane in Sheung Wan. The Hong Kong Antiquities & Monuments Office (☎ 2721-2326), itself housed in a 1900 British schoolhouse on 136 Nathan Rd in Kowloon, has information and occasional exhibits on current preservation efforts.

Hong Kong fares better when it comes to modern architecture. Central boasts several world-class structures, such as Norman Foster's Hongkong and Shanghai

Bank Building, Remo Riva's Exchange Square and the Bank of China Tower, designed by IM Pei. Other buildings, such as the oddly adorned Central Plaza and the Hopewell Centre (both located in Wanchai) may not be in the same class, but add dazzle to Hong Kong's justly famous skyline.

Chinese Opera

For nearly a thousand years, Chinese opera has given voice to the moral dilemmas, folk legends and romantic aspirations of China's people. With its garish costumes, shrill singing, sharp percussion and martial arts displays, Chinese opera may seem a world away from its western counterpart. But the themes are pretty much the same: mortal heroes battle overwhelmingly powerful foes; legendary spirits defend the world against evil; lovers seek escape from domineering and disapproving parents.

For those used to western music, Chinese opera performances may take some getting used to. Both male and female performers sing in an almost reedy falsetto designed to pierce through crowd noise, and the instrumental accompaniment often takes the form of drumming, gonging and other non-melodic punctuation. And even with today's 'shortened' performances, an average opera lasts around three hours. But even if you don't fall in love with it, Chinese opera is worth seeing at least once, to appreciate an art form that has remained in many ways unchanged for thousands of years.

NICKO GONCHAROFF

Colourful Chinese opera posters

There are three types of Chinese opera performed in Hong Kong. Top of the line among Chinese culture buffs is reckoned to be the Beijing variety, a highly refined style which uses almost no scenery but a variety of traditional props. This is usually where you can find the acrobatics and swordplay. More 'music hall' is the Cantonese variety, usually with a 'boy meets girl' theme, and often incorporating modern and foreign references. The most traditional is Chiu Chow, now the least performed of the three. It is staged almost as it was in the Ming Dynasty, with stories from Chiu Chow legends and folklore.

Operas are usually categorised as 'civil' or 'martial': the latter may be more interesting to newcomers, as they are full of 'battles' that give the actors a chance to demonstrate their martial arts skills.

Much of the meaning in a Chinese opera can be derived from costumes, props and body language, so a little homework beforehand may make things easier to understand and enjoy. The Hong Kong Tourist Association (HKTA) offers a handout entitled *Hong Kong's Musical Heritage – Chinese Opera* that gives a good summary of the origins, symbols and workings of performances.

Dance

There are three professional dance companies in Hong Kong. The Hong Kong Dance Company focuses on Chinese traditional and folk dances as well as full-length dance dramas based on local and Chinese themes. The City Contemporary Dance Company stages modern dance performances that include new commissions and past works, often choreographed by locals. Both companies frequently work with artists from China, and sometimes with those from other Asian countries.

Hong Kong also has its own ballet company. Founded in 1979, the Hong Kong Ballet regularly performs both classical and modern pieces, and tours overseas each year.

One Chinese tradition that still lives on in Hong Kong is that of the lion dance. A group of dancers/martial artists takes position under a elaborately painted costume of a mythical Chinese lion. To the accompaniment of blazing firecrackers and banging cymbals, the lion leaps its way around the crowd, giving the dancers a chance to demonstrate their acrobatic prowess. Lion dances are now most commonly seen at the openings of new businesses or buildings. The Urban and Regional Councils, along with the Hong Kong Chinese Martial

Arts Association, also usually sponsor an annual lion dance tournament in December.

Film

Though foreign movies are always popular with local audiences, Hong Kong itself has a very vibrant film industry. Despite its small size, the territory now produces around 600 films per year, second only to India. In addition to their home market, most of these films are targeted at countries throughout Asia and sometimes further afield.

While profitable, Hong Kong film producers are saddled with a reputation for churning out mindless action films, nonsense comedies and sickening romances. In many cases this is well earned. Popular actors and actresses will sometimes work on several films simultaneously, as do film crews, with the result that quality on nearly all productions suffers. Films that do well at the box office invariably spawn a slew of imitations, so that locals soon face a glut of movies about unbeatable gamblers or double-fisted gunmen, for example. The international success of the (admittedly higher than average quality) film *Rumble in the Bronx*, starring the legendary Jackie Chan, gives an idea what to expect.

But in recent years some productions have helped Hong Kong earn a bit more respect by focusing on society and individuals rather than kung-fu fights and bimbos. In particular, the success of *Farewell, My Concubine*, a story about a Chinese opera troupe, at the 1993 Cannes Film Festival helped open eyes around the world to Hong Kong's potential. Directed by mainland Chinese director Chen Kaige, the film was a joint project between Chinese and Hong Kong producers. These joint-ventures are the kind of films to look out for: China's influence seems to bring new cultural and creative depth to the productions.

The annual Hong Kong International Film Festival, started in 1976, brings in hundreds of films from around the world, and is now billed as one of the world's major non-competitive film festivals.

Music

Hong Kong's music scene is dominated by 'Canto-pop', basically a synergy of Cantonese Chinese lyrics with western pop music. There is an entire constellation of local stars that, while perhaps known in Asia, are all but unheard of in the west. Some are movie stars who like the idea of cutting a record, while others are genuine musicians and songwriters. The latter tend to turn out more original compositions, often blending western rock-n-roll or pop with traditional Chinese melodies or rhythms. Many younger Hong Kongers pay homage to their favourite stars by crooning their tunes at karaoke bars, which are by far Hong Kong's most popular musical venues, sadly enough.

However, classical music is also alive and well in Hong Kong. The city boasts a Chinese orchestra, as well as a philharmonic, sinfonietta and chamber orchestra. Overseas performers of world repute frequently make it to Hong Kong, sometimes even giving performances in the New Territories as well as the city centre. The number of foreign performances soars during the Hong Kong Arts Festival, held in February/March every year.

Jazz, rock and other forms of modern music are hit or miss. The lack of decent venues often discourages major international acts from passing through and the local music scene is still underdeveloped. With all the karaoke and Canto-pop, local musicians have a tough time generating enough support. The bright spots in the bleak landscape are the Jazz Club, which books top musicians year after year, and the Fringe Club, which encourages the development of local music and organises an annual arts and music event, the Festival Fringe. See the Entertainment chapter for more details.

Theatre

Probably because of Hong Kong's colonial history, nearly all theatre is western in form, if not content. But most productions are staged in Cantonese, and a large number are new plays by Hong Kong writers. Leading the pack is the Chung Ying Theatre Company, which stresses locally produced plays and also takes part in government-sponsored education programmes. Smaller groups, such as the Nonsensemakers, Exploration Theatre, Actor's Family and Sand & Bricks, also give young Hong Kong writers a chance to stage their own works. The plays often provide an insightful and sometimes humorous look at contemporary Hong Kong life. In a way, Hong Kong may be home to the most progressive theatre in contemporary Chinese culture. It is certainly more interesting than China, where the state still ensures productions are bland and politically correct.

More conservative is the Hong Kong Repertory Theatre, which tends toward larger scale productions of both original works on Chinese themes or translated western plays. Actors in many of the local companies are graduates of the Hong Kong Academy for the Performing Arts, which also stages some interesting student shows, most of which are Cantonese versions of well-known western plays.

English-language theatre in Hong Kong is mostly the domain of expatriate amateurs, who perform in groups with names like the Not So Loud Theatre Company and the Breakaleg Theatre Company. Plays are more often than not scripted by local writers. The Hong Kong Cultural Centre and Academy for the Performing Arts also host foreign productions, ranging from lavish western productions like *Les Miserables* to the spartan Japanese *kyogen* plays.

Painting & Sculpture

Painting in Hong Kong falls into three broad categories: modern local, classical Chinese and western. Paintings by local Hong Kong artists often echo their angst-filled counterparts in the west. Styles and techniques tend to differ of course, as Hong Kong painters often seek new ways to blend east and west. There are also locals who are dedicated to preserving such classical Chinese disciplines as calligraphy and landscape *(shanshui)* painting. Many of these have spent years studying in China, and their work tends to reflect current trends in classical painting there. While Hong Kong does not have a great deal of homegrown western-style art, exhibits from abroad are regularly on display at the Hong Kong Museum of Art in Tsimshatsui.

Most of Hong Kong's sculpture seems to be located in public places. The deep pockets of Hong Kong's land developers have allowed them to adorn their flagship properties with some prestigious pieces. So in front of Central's Exchange Square, one can find Henry Moore's large bronze *Oval with Points*, and *Taichi* by Taiwanese artist Chu Ming. Inside the Chater Rd entrance of the Mandarin Oriental Hotel are two copper reliefs by noted Chinese artist Cheung Yee. More of Cheung's work can be found on the walls of the nearby Prince's Building and the Landmark shopping mall. Across the harbour in Tsimshatsui, near the Hong Kong Cultural Centre, stands *The Flying Frenchman* by Cezar, a gift by a French company. This unusual piece was not all that well received by the local media, but people have learned to live with it.

East of the Cultural Centre, the Salisbury Garden, which had yet to open at the time of writing, will contain a number of large sculptures by local artists. There are some more pieces by younger Hong Kong artists at Kowloon Park's Sculpture Walk, some of which may leave viewers scratching their heads. At the northern end of Sculpture Walk crouches Eduardo Paolozzi's bronze sculptural embodiment of William Blake's etching *Concept of Newton*. What Newton is doing in Kowloon is anybody's guess, but then again the man was always more concerned with himself than his surroundings, falling apples notwithstanding.

SOCIETY & CONDUCT

Traditional Culture

While Hong Kong is very westernised, many old Chinese traditions persist. Whether people still believe in all of them, or are in some cases just going through the motions, is hard to say. The British colonial government largely tried to keep its nose out of Hong Kong Chinese culture. Even polygamy was legally sanctioned for the Chinese community until 1971. The extent that traditions have survived, perished or been watered down has been mainly determined by Hong Kongers themselves.

Superstitions Southern Chinese culture embraces a wealth of guidelines on controlling the amount of good or bad luck in one's life. Many of these ideas live on in Hong Kong in varying degrees. Despite what tourist pamphlets and coffee table books may tell you, not everyone believes in all these superstitions. But there are certain ones that still affect people's daily lives.

One of the most prevalent is the belief in the power of numbers. In Cantonese, which has several tones but a limited number of consonant-vowel combinations, many words share the same pronunciation: the difference is marked by the tone the word carries. This gives rise to numerous homonyms. The number three sounds like 'life', nine like 'eternity' and the ever-popular number eight like 'prosperity.' Lowest on the list is four, which has the same pronunciation as the word for 'death'.

Thus companies or homebuyers will shell out extra money for an address that contains one or more number eights. Each year the Hong Kong government draws in millions of dollars for charity by auctioning off automobile licence plates containing lucky numbers: the bidding always reaches ridiculous heights. Dates and prices are affected too. The Bank of China Tower was opened on 8 August 1988 – a rare union of the prosperous numbers. Many restaurants will price set dinners at

HK$88. And of course gamblers at the horse-racing track will lean toward the luckier numbers, though the more sophisticated punters have long gone over to the machinations of random theory. A few buildings around the city are missing their 4th or 14th floors, but overall people seem able to live with the number four, despite its ominous overtones.

Some foods are also luckier than others. During birthdays, celebrants may eat noodles, as the long strands symbolise longevity. Sea moss, which in Cantonese has the same sound as 'prosperity' is always an auspicious ingredient. Peach juice is believed to be a life-giving elixir, while garlic and ginger can protect babies against evil.

As the God of Longevity rides on the back of the deer, parts of this animal are often used in Chinese medicine to cure ailments and prolong life. Similarly, the long life of the tortoise can be absorbed through a soup made from it. The carp, which lives longer than humans, is among the most prized possessions in a wealthy household's fishpond.

Chinese Zodiac Astrology has a long history in China and is integrated with religious beliefs. As in the western system of astrology, there are 12 zodiac signs. However, unlike the western system, your sign is based on the year rather than the month in which you were born. Still, this is a simplification. The exact day and time of birth are also carefully considered in charting an astrological path.

If you want to know your sign in the Chinese zodiac, look up your year of birth in the chart below. However, it's a little more complicated than this because Chinese astrology goes by the lunar calendar. The Chinese Lunar New Year usually falls in late January or early February, so the first month will be included in the year before.

It is said that the animal year chart originated when Buddha commanded all the beasts of the earth to assemble before him. The names of the years were established according to the first 12 animals' order of arrival. There is no cat year: apparently the rat tricked the cat into arriving late.

Being born or married in a particular year is believed to determine one's fortune. In this era of modern birth-control techniques, Chinese parents will often carefully manipulate the birth times of their children. The year of the dragon sees the biggest jump in the birth rate, closely followed by the year of the tiger.

Traditionally, the Chinese calculate age differently to most other cultures. Believing that life begins at the moment of conception, Chinese would consider a baby already one year old when it leaves the mother's womb.

So older people or those from rural communities may quote you an age that is actually one year older than that according to the western calendar.

The Chinese zodiac also plays a key role in almanacs, which people will consult to choose auspicious dates for weddings, household moves, business openings and so on. These guides even advise when to cut one's hair or to sweep: one wouldn't want to brush one's good luck away due to ill timing!

Chinese Zodiac							
Rat	1924	1936	1948	1960	1972	1984	1996
Ox/Cow	1925	1937	1949	1961	1973	1985	1997
Tiger	1926	1938	1950	1962	1974	1986	1998
Rabbit	1927	1939	1951	1963	1975	1987	1999
Dragon	1928	1940	1952	1964	1976	1988	2000
Snake	1929	1941	1953	1965	1977	1989	2001
Horse	1930	1942	1954	1966	1978	1990	2002
Goat	1931	1943	1955	1967	1979	1991	2003
Monkey	1932	1944	1956	1968	1980	1992	2004
Rooster	1933	1945	1957	1969	1981	1993	2005
Dog	1934	1946	1958	1970	1982	1994	2006
Pig	1935	1947	1959	1971	1983	1995	2007

Fortune-Telling If you're of a mind to have your destiny laid out for you, you'll not lack for choice in Hong Kong. You can go to a temple and consult the gods and spirits, have your palm or face read, or consult an almanac.

Probably the most popular method of divination in Hong Kong is using the 'fortune sticks'. The altar of a temple, whether Buddhist or Taoist, is usually flanked by stacks of the wooden sticks (*chim*), which are housed in bamboo canisters. The routine is to ask the spirits or gods a question and shake the canister until one stick falls out. Each stick bears a numeral, which corresponds to a printed slip of paper in a set held by the temple keeper. That slip of paper should be taken to the temple's fortune-teller, who can interpret its particular meaning for you. The fortune-teller will also study your face and ask your date and time of birth. Kowloon's Wong Tai Sin Temple is one of the best places to get your fortune told. It's usually also easy to find fortune-tellers at Tin Hau temples in Wanchai and Yaumatei.

If you are just seeking a simple 'yes' or 'no' to a question, and wish to bypass the fortune-teller, you may turn to two clam shaped pieces of wood called *bui*

Colour & Custom

There's more to a colour than meets the eye, at least for the Chinese. White is the colour of death, and mourners at traditional Chinese funerals will often wear white cloaks, sometimes with a black ribbon. Black on white is traditionally associated with funerals, and if you ever see a large circular flower board in black and white, it denotes someone's passing. It used to be that sending a white sheet of paper with black writing on it was a bad omen, but in these days of typewriters and laser-jet printers, that belief has gone by the wayside.

Red is a far happier colour, symbolising (you guessed it) prosperity. In traditional Chinese weddings the bride would wear red, though today the red gown is usually reserved for the wedding reception: tuxedos and western-style white wedding dresses are the norm in Hong Kong. Restaurants, temples and other places where people congregate are often decked out in red. However, it is not considered good form to write notes, letters or sign one's name in red ink. Hong Kongers don't seem too clear on why this is, but Taiwanese say that it implies the writer lacks intelligence.

Yellow, which was always the colour of the emperor, was believed to repel evil spirits, which is why temple fortune papers are printed on yellow paper. Black also supposedly stands for treachery, but this idea wilted under the forces of fashion – black clothing was all the rage among stylish young women in Hong Kong during the mid-1990s. ■

(which means 'shell' in Cantonese). The way they fall when thrown in the air in front of the altar indicates the gods' answer to your query. One side of each piece of wood is *yang*, or positive; the other side is *yin*, which is negative. If both pieces land with the same side up, the answer is negative. But if they land with different sides up, it indicates a balance of yin and yang, and denotes a positive answer.

Palm-readers usually examine both the lines and features of the hand. Palms are thought to be emotional – their lines changes in tune with one's life, and can reveal the past and what the future may hold depending on what actions one takes. Readings for men are taken from the left palm, those for women from the right.

To augment their study, palmists will examine one's facial features: there are 48 recognised eye patterns which reveal character and fortune, and eight basic facial shapes. Clues are also provided by the shape of your ears, nose, mouth, lips and eyebrows. For example, people with small earlobes are considered less likely to become wealthy. As with the fortune-stick seers, you will also probably be asked to provide the date and time of your birth. Palmists can be found near street markets, including Temple St in Yaumatei, their trade identified by palmic charts on large signs or cards. The longer the line, the better chance the palmist has a good reputation.

Some Chinese families turn to almanacs for do-it-yourself fortune-telling. Based on the Chinese zodiac, these volumes identify the good and bad aspects for each day of the year, enabling the reader to pick dates for special occasions. The books also give instructions for more indepth self-help fortune-telling.

Fung Shui The Chinese term *fung shui* literally means 'wind-water', and it always pops up in any mention of Chinese traditions in Hong Kong. As a result it's become fairly clichéd, but that doesn't diminish its role in life and business in the territory.

Fung shui, or geomancy as it's called in the west, aims to balance the elements of nature to produce a harmonious, prosperous environment. It's based on ancient classical Chinese writings, has been in practice since the 12th century AD, and continues to play a role in the design and construction of buildings, highways, parks, tunnels and grave sites, among other things. Not everyone believes in fung shui, but at the same time, few dare flout its dictates. To do so may invite business failure, ill health or a decline in family fortunes.

Before construction or remodelling begins, fung shui experts, or geomancers, are called in. The Hongkong and Shanghai Bank Building, the Bank of China Tower and Citibank Plaza are just some of the towering monuments to modernity that have taken fung shui into account in their design. The two lions that guard the entrance to the Hongkong and Shanghai Bank Building were positioned at the precise place and time dictated auspicious by a respected geomancer. This way they would be sure to protect the bank (and its depositors) against waterborne spirits in Hong Kong harbour. When building its new headquarters, Hang Seng Bank had to tear down a newly constructed walkway over Connaught Rd when a geomancer pronounced it ill-positioned. The walkway was rebuilt a few meters to the right, at a cost of several million Hong Kong dollars.

To guard against evil spirits, who can only move in straight lines, doors to the outside will sometimes be positioned at an angle. For similar reasons, sofas or beds cannot face doorways. Ideally homes and businesses should have a view of calm water, as this allows one to see their good fortune floating on calm seas. In the absence of a sea view, which commands an exorbitant price in land-scarce Hong Kong, a properly positioned indoor fishtank will do. Corporate heads are not supposed to have offices that face west: otherwise their company profits will go the same direction as the setting sun. If a business runs into bad times, a geomancer may be called in to search for any evil spirits lurking about. If the bad luck persists, a Taoist priest may have to come and perform an 'exorcism'.

Trees can house spirits, so some villages and temples in the New Territories still have fung shui groves to provide a place for the good spirits to live. Attempts to cut down fung shui groves to construct new buildings or public works have sometimes led to massive protests and even violent confrontations – the solution may be a large cash payment to the village to 'placate the spirits'. Even then, it's a delicate situation and the help of a professional geomancer will undoubtedly be required to avoid trouble.

In the rural areas, and sometimes in the city, you may come across little octagonal mirrors on doorways or windows. That's fung shui at work again: the mirrors are designed to reflect away any evil demons trying to slip indoors.

Taijiquan Formerly spelled *taichichuan*, this form of slow motion shadow-boxing has been popular in China for centuries. It is basically a form of exercise, but it's also an art form.

Taijiquan is very popular among old people and also with young women who believe it will help keep their bodies looking good. The movements are supposed to develop the breathing muscles, promote digestion and improve muscle tone. It seems to work: there are some pretty sprightly old men and women to be found practising out there.

The Chinese traditionally do this exercise at the crack of dawn, usually in public parks or gardens. The most popular park for taijiquan is Victoria Park in Causeway Bay. Other popular venues include the Zoological & Botanical Gardens in Central, and Kowloon Park in Tsimshatsui.

Appearance & Conduct

Public Etiquette Hong Kong is an international city in many ways, and there are few things travellers can do that will really faze locals. It may be good to keep in mind though that Hong Kong is no longer a great place to bargain. In many places where prices are clearly marked, such as department or chain stores, trying to talk the price below what's listed will only get you a frustrated salesperson. The rip-off camera and electronic shops of Tsimshatsui are another matter: they expect bargaining, and often mark their prices up so tourists will start negotiating from a higher price level.

Sometimes Hong Kong salespeople can be rude and annoying without you having done anything. This is really a no-win situation, as they obviously don't care much about your patronage. The best thing to do is try some other place, which is pretty easy to do in this retail-crazed city.

If you visit someone's home, it's best to bring a gift of some kind. Fruit or chocolates will do, and alcohol such as brandy or whisky is usually OK too. Even if the host doesn't drink, sooner or later he or she will have guests that do. One quirk of gift-giving here regards clocks: if for some reason you should think of giving one as a present, think again. To more traditional Chinese the clock symbolises mortality, so giving one is akin to a harbinger of death, not the most cheery of gifts.

The Chinese are on the whole quite casual when it comes to table manners, but there are some rules that should be observed when eating. For details see under Food Etiquette in the Places to Eat chapter.

Fashion is taken quite seriously in Hong Kong, but at the same time you can go to most restaurants and hotels in casual dress. Sadly, even The Peninsula allows high-tea drinkers to wear jeans and tennis shoes, though some other hotels, notably the Mandarin Oriental, enforce a stricter dress code. This relaxed attitude does not extend to the business world, where dark suit and tie or conservative skirt and blouse rule supreme.

If you go to the beach, keep in mind that in Hong Kong, as in most Asian societies, nude or topless sunbathing is considered rude and offensive.

One last point. Hong Kong is a frightfully expensive place. Hotel rooms can easily cost US$300 per night, a beer at a bar US$7. If you make or have any Hong Kong friends, try and spare them endless complaints about how much everything costs. They're already well aware of it.

The Group When it comes to leisure, the more the merrier. In general Hong Kongers love to hit the shopping malls, movies or hiking trails in large groups. Despite the infiltration of many western ways into Hong Kong society, the idea of solo recreation is almost as alien here as in China and Taiwan. It's not surprising on a country hiking trail to run across 20 to 30 Hong Kongers raising a ruckus, screaming at each other via walkie-talkie and seemingly ignoring the nature around them. It's the same scene while eating, drinking or singing – having a large group ensures a festive atmosphere. This doesn't mean that you won't find single hikers, or someone enjoying a good book at a cafe. Every city has its loners. And of course, the group mentality stops short at romance: a stroll along the Tsimshatsui promenade at night will show that double-dating is not in style.

Face Much is made of the 'mysterious' Oriental concept of face, which is roughly equivalent to status or respect. Sinologists, writers and other observers love to point to the lengths which Chinese people will go to 'gain face'. Truth be told, this hardly sets the Chinese apart from other cultures. Westerners or other Asians have also been known to buy ridiculously expensive clothing, jewellery or cars for the sake of impressing those around them. It is true that getting into a loud argument with, for instance, a shopkeeper in front of a crowd will probably get you nowhere: he or she will do their best not to knuckle under and lose face. But again, this is hardly an attitude that is unique to Chinese, or Asia for that matter. If you want to help people gain face, treat them with respect and consideration for their culture.

Money Some visitors to Hong Kong will have already heard of the city's obsession with money. As any foreign speaker of Cantonese can tell you, most conversations you hear on the bus, subway or street are about prices, incomes, rents or debts. And while Hong Kong people are more discreet than their compatriots in China, occasionally they will shock foreign visitors by asking point-blank about salaries, costs and other financial affairs that many westerners consider conversational taboo.

Actually it's not all that surprising. Hong Kong has long been a haven for refugees from China, and for many, memories of poverty and chaos are just a few decades or one generation away. Making money is the best way to protect oneself and one's family against any future misfortune. This is worth keeping in mind if a Hong Konger matter-of-factly tells you that the prime goal of life is to make money. In the context of Hong Kong, this is an honourable goal.

Of course it's not just about refugees and saving for the future. Hong Kong is without a doubt one of the world's most materialistic societies. The city has a stunning number of luxury retail stores and shopping malls, and don't think they survive on tourist dollars alone. One of the main reasons to make money is in order to buy things which show other people how much money you make. This attitude can extend to relationships: 'no flat, no car, no mobile phone – no chance' Hong Kong women have been heard to say of prospective suitors.

Not everyone buys into it: many of Hong Kong's young songwriters and playwrights often take aim against this love of money in their work. For now however, their voice remains in the minority.

GLENN BEANLAND

Stone guardian, Man Mo Temple, Sheung Wan

RELIGION

Buddhism and Taoism are the dominant religions in Hong Kong, though Confucianism, ancestor worship and ancient animist beliefs have also been incorporated into the milieu. The number of active Buddhists is estimated at 650,000 to 700,000. This figure probably also includes a good number of Taoists.

On a daily level the Chinese are much less concerned with the high-minded philosophies and asceticism of Buddha, Confucius or Laozi than they are with the pursuit of worldly success, the appeasement of the dead and the spirits, and the seeking of hidden knowledge about the future.

It can be difficult to distinguish the lines between religion, superstition and traditional practices such as fung shui. All three come into play when trying to influence the course of luck and fortune. Gods have to be appeased, bad spirits blown away and sleeping dragons soothed to keep luck on your side.

Visits to temples are usually made to ask the gods' blessings for specific issues: a relative's health, family prosperity, the success of a business, even a lucky day at the horse track! Fung shui and the Chinese zodiac also play key roles in choosing dates for funerals, and sites for graves and ancestral shrines.

Hong Kong has approximately 600 temples, monasteries and shrines, most of which are Buddhist or Taoist. Of Hong Kong's hundreds of temples, more than 40 are public ones maintained by the Chinese Temples Committee, which gets its income from donations by worshippers. Temples are usually dedicated to one or two deities whose images can be found in the main hall. Side halls house images of subsidiary gods. Since Buddhism and Taoism are both accepted as traditional Chinese religions, deities from both are often honoured within the same temple. The majority are tiny but there are some enormous ones such as the Po Lin Monastery on Lantau Island, the Temple of Ten Thousand Buddhas at Shatin and Wong Tai Sin in Kowloon.

Aside from the Chinese religions, there are several other denominations represented in Hong Kong's cosmopolitan population. There are about 500,000 Christians, about 51% of whom are Protestant and 49% Catholics. Due to the zeal of lay Christians and missionaries, the number of independent Protestant churches has steadily risen since the 1970s, and now includes around 950 congregations.

The Roman Catholic Church established its first mission in Hong Kong in 1841, when the British took possession. The present bishop, John Baptist Cheng-chung Wu, was made a Cardinal in 1988. The majority of services at the 62 parishes are conducted in Chinese, though a few churches provide services in English.

Hong Kong is also home to around 50,000 Muslims. More than half are Chinese, the rest either locally born non-Chinese or hailing from Pakistan, India, Malaysia, Indonesia, the Middle East or Africa. Four principal mosques are used daily for prayers. The oldest is the Jamia Mosque on Shelley St, in the Mid-Levels, which was established in the late 19th century and rebuilt in 1915. The Masjid Ammar and Osman Ramju Sadick Islamic Centre in Wanchai is considerably newer, having opened in 1981, and houses a mosque, library, medical clinic and classrooms. Over in Kowloon, stands the Kowloon Mosque and Islamic Centre, a white marble structure that has become somewhat of a Tsimshatsui landmark. There are also around 12,000 Hindus in Hong Kong, as well as smaller Sikh and Jewish communities.

Religious Services

The following places either offer services or will tell you when and where they are held. Check the *Yellow Pages* for a more comprehensive list of Hong Kong churches and other places of worship.

Anglican – St John's Cathedral, 4-8 Garden Rd, Central (☎ 2523-4157)

Bahai – Flat C-6, 11th floor, Hankow Centre, Middle Rd, Tsimshatsui (☎ 2367-6407)

Christian Scientist – 31 MacDonnell Rd, Central (☎ 2524-2701)

Hindu – Wong Nai Chung Road, Happy Valley (☎ 2572-5284)

Jewish – Synagogue Ohel Leah, 70 Robinson Rd, Mid-Levels (☎ 2801-5440)

Methodist – 271 Queen's Rd East, Wanchai (☎ 2575-7817)

Mormon – Church of the Latter Day Saints, 7 Castle Rd, Mid-Levels (☎ 2559-3325)

Muslim – Islamic Union, 40 Oi Kwan Rd, Wanchai (☎ 2575-2218)

Quaker – Society of Friends, 3rd floor, Conference Room, Mariners Club, Middle Rd, Tsimshatsui (☎ 2697-7283)

Roman Catholic – St Joseph's, 37 Garden Rd, Central (☎ 2552-3992)

Sikh – 371 Queen's Rd East, Wanchai (☎ 2574-9837)

LANGUAGE

Along with English, Hong Kong's official language is Cantonese, a southern Chinese dialect that originated in neighbouring Guangdong Province.

While in Hong Kong Cantonese is used in everyday life, English dominates commerce, banking and international trade, and is also used in the law courts. However, as 1997 draws near, many have noticed a sharp decline in the level of English-speaking proficiency. Those Hong Kong Chinese who speak excellent English are usually the most educated and wealthiest, and thus can emigrate most easily. In addition, today's younger Hong Kong Chinese don't seem to be as interested in learning English as the previous generation was.

On the other hand, many Hong Kongers have started to study Mandarin, the national language of the PRC and the most widely spoken Chinese dialect. There has been a fair number of Mandarin speakers in Hong Kong since the 1950s because so many refugees fled from China. But until recently, the younger generation has generally not bothered studying Mandarin, preferring instead English as a second language. The new political realities are now changing attitudes. Despite China's promises that virtually nothing will change after 1997, most Hong Kongers believe that Mandarin will soon be the official language. And, as many business executives have found out, Mandarin is vital to doing business with China: few mainlanders will bother to learn Cantonese, which many view as a barbarous southern dialect.

Short-term visitors can get along fine in Hong Kong without a word of Cantonese. There are still plenty of English speakers, especially in the tourist zones. All signs on streets and public transport are bilingual, so there is no problem getting around. About the only time you'll have a real problem is when visiting cheap noodle shops, many of which don't have English menus. Here you'll probably have to resort to the international language – pointing at what others are eating.

Spoken Chinese

Cantonese differs from Mandarin as much as French does from Spanish. Speakers of both dialects can read Chinese characters, but pronounce many words quite differently. For example, when Mr Ng from Hong Kong goes to Beijing the Mandarin speakers will call him Mr Wu.

Chinese has a fairly limited number of consonant-vowel combinations. Thus many words have the same pronunciation. The Cantonese word for 'silk' sounds just like the words for 'lion', 'private', 'master' and 'affair'. What distinguishes each word from the other is its tone. If you get your tones mixed, you can say something entirely different from what was intended. This is particularly true of Cantonese, which is said to have seven tones, compared with only four for Mandarin. To make matters worse, Cantonese is particularly rich in profanity, meaning that it's quite easy for the beginner to unknowingly let fly some real filth. Don't worry though: chances are you'll be keeping some people highly amused.

Written Chinese

Officially, written Chinese has about 50,000 pictographs or characters which symbolise objects or actions. Most of these have become archaic, but about 5000 remain in common use. There are at least 2000 essential characters which you would need to know to read a newspaper.

The written language allows Chinese from all around the country to overcome the barrier posed by the more than 200 different dialects. Both Cantonese and Mandarin speakers can understand the same newspaper, though if they read it aloud it would sound like two different tongues. However, Hong Kong, long separated from China, has developed around 150 new characters which are solely used to represent colloquial Cantonese words. These are not understood by speakers of other dialects, or even some Cantonese speakers from the mainland.

Hong Kong, like Taiwan, uses original 'complex' characters as opposed to the system of simplified characters adopted by China in the 1950s in a bid to increase literacy. The result is that many of the characters you'll see in Hong Kong are written quite differently from the same ones in China.

In Hong Kong, Chinese characters can be read from left to right, right to left, or top to bottom. In China the government has been trying to get everyone to read and write from left to right.

Cantonese Pronunciation

The following romanisation system is a simplified version designed to help you pronounce the Cantonese words and phrases in this book as quickly and easily as possible. As such it glosses over some aspects of pronunciation that you would need to know if you plan to seriously study the language. But it should be sufficient for a few days or weeks in Hong Kong.

a	like 'a' in 'father'
ai	like 'i' 'find'
au	like 'ow' in 'crowd'

e	like 'e' in 'let'
ei	like 'a' in 'say'
eu	like 'e' + 'ur' in 'urn' (this is one of the hardest sounds both to describe and learn)
i	like 'ee' in 'see'
iu	like 'yew'
o	like 'o' in 'hot'
oi	like 'oy' in 'boy'
oo	like 'oo' in 'soon'
ou	like 'o' in 'so'
u	like 'u' in 'sun'
ue	like 'ew' in 'dew'
ui	like 'oy' + 'ee'

Consonants are generally pronounced as in English, with the following troublesome exceptions:

j	sounds like 'dz'
ch	sounds like 'ts'
ng	sounds like 'ng' as in 'sing'

Cantonese Tones

Learning tones from a book is not really possible. You must hear them yourself, ideally from a teacher who takes the time to distinguish between each tone. This is merely a brief introduction to the Cantonese tonal system.

Cantonese is said to have anywhere from six to nine tones. The most commonly accepted number is seven, as the eighth and ninth are used to represent minute variations on the preceding tones. In the system outlined below (using the consonant 'm' with the vowel 'a' as an example), the first and seventh tones are denoted by the same symbol, as they are basically interchangeable, especially for beginning speakers.

The tones span three pitch ranges – high, middle and low – with rising tones in between the various levels.

First tone – highest pitch, either a sound which is long and lingering or which drops slightly; marked by falling symbol on first vowel (mà)

Second tone – middle pitch rising to highest pitch; marked by rising symbol on first vowel (má)

Third tone – level tone on middle pitch level; marked by a line over the first vowel (mā)

Fourth tone – low pitch falling to lowest pitch; no symbol on vowel

Fifth tone – low pitch rising to middle pitch; marked by double rising symbol on first vowel (mǎ)

Sixth tone – level tone on low pitch level; marked by double lines over first vowel (m̄a)

Phrase List

Although Hong Kong is easy accessible to English speakers, knowing a few Cantonese phrases can be fun and sometimes useful. Don't be discouraged if some Hong Kongers scuttle your attempts at Cantonese by replying in exasperated English. For each one of those there is someone who will be pleased by your attempts to learn their difficult dialect. Following are some phrases that may come in handy. For a more comprehensive guide, you can refer to Lonely Planet's *Cantonese phrasebook*. Many Hong Kong bookshops also sell Cantonese study kits for beginners.

Pronouns

I	*ngőh*	我
you	*néi*	你
he/she/it	*kűi*	佢
we/us	*ngőh dēi*	我哋
you (plural)	*néi dēi*	你哋
they/them	*kűi dēi*	佢哋

Greetings & Civilities

Hello, how are you?	*néi hó mā?*	你好嗎?
Fine.	*géi hó*	幾好
Fine, and you?	*géi hó, néi nè?*	幾好, 你呢?
So so.	*ma má déi*	麻麻地
Good morning.	*jó san*	早晨
Goodbye.	*bàai bāai, jōi gīn*	拜拜/再見
See you tomorrow.	*tìng yǎi jōi gīn*	聽日再見

Requests, Thanks & Apologies

Please wait a moment.
   chéng dáng yàt jǎn   請等一陣
Excuse me. (calling someone's attention)
   m gòi   唔該
Please hurry up.
   m gòi fāai dì   唔該快啲
Please slow down.
   m gòi mǎan dì   唔該慢啲
Can you please help me take a photo?
   hóh m hóh yǐ bòng ngőh yíng jèung séung ā?
   可唔可以幫我影張相呀?
Is it OK to take a photo?
   hóh m hóh yǐ yíng séung ā?   可唔可以影相呀?
Thanks. (for a gift or special favour)
   dòh jē   多謝

Thanks. (when making a request or purchase)
m gòi 唔該
Thank you very much.
dòh jě sāai, m gòi sāai 多謝晒/唔該晒
You're welcome.
m sái hāak hēi 唔駛客氣
Excuse me. (after bumping into someone)
dūi m jŭe 對唔住
Sorry.
m hó yī sī 唔好意思
Don't worry about it.
m gán yīu 唔緊要

Small Talk

Do you speak English?
něi sìk m sìk góng yìng mán ā? 你識唔識講英文呀?
Do you understand?
něi ming m ming ā? 你明唔明呀?
I don't understand.
ngóh m ming 我唔明
I understand.
ngóh ming 我明
Can you repeat that please?
chéng jōi góng yāt chī? 請再講一次
What is this called?
nì gōh gìu màt yé ā? 呢個叫乜嘢呀?
What is your surname? (polite)
chéng mǎn gwāi sīng? 請問貴姓?
My surname is ....
síu sīng .... 小姓...
My name is ....
ngóh gìu .... 我叫...
This is Mr/Mrs/Ms (Lee).
nì wái hǎi (léi) sìn sàang/tāai táai/síu jé
呢位係(李)先生/太太/小姐
Glad to meet you.
hó gò hīng yǐng sìk něi 好高興認識你

Getting Around

bus stop	*bà sí jǎam*	巴士站
airport	*gèi cheung*	機場
subway station	*děi tīt jǎam*	地鐵站
pier	*mǎ tau*	碼頭
north	*bàk*	北
east	*dùng*	東
south	*naam*	南
west	*sài*	西

I'd like to go to ....
ngőh séung hūi ....   我想去…
Where is the ....?
.... hái bìn dő ā?   …喺邊度呀?
Does this (bus, train etc) go to ....?
hūi m hūi .... ā?   去唔去…呀?
How much is the fare?
géi dòh chín ā?   幾多錢呀?
I want to get off at ....
ngőh séung hái .... lők chè   我想喺…落車
Stop here please. (taxi, minibus)
m gòi, nì dő yấu lők   唔該,呢度有落
How far is it to walk?
haang lő yīu géi női ā?   行路要幾耐呀?
Where is this address please?
m gòi, nì gőh děi jí hái bìn dő ā?   唔該,呢個地址喺邊度呀?
Please write down the address for me.
m gòi sé gőh děi jí béi ngőh   唔該寫個地址俾我

GLENN BEANLAND

'That's my final price, take it or leave it' – Central silk shop

Accommodation

Do you have any rooms available?
yấu mő fóng ā?   有冇房呀?
I would like a (single/double) room.
ngőh séung yīu yàt gàan(dàan yan/sèung yan) fóng
我想要一間(單人/雙人)房
I would like a quiet room.
ngőh séung yīu yàt gàan jĭng dì gē fóng
我想要一間靜啲嘅房
How much per night?
géi dòh chín yàt mấan ā?   幾多錢一晚呀?

Can I get a discount if I stay longer?
   jūe nōi dì yǎu mǒ jīt kāu ā?   住耐啲有冇折扣呀?

Food

Do you have an English menu?
   yǎu mǒ yìng mán chàan páai ā?   有冇英文餐牌呀?
Can you recommend any dishes?
   yǎu màt yé hó gāai sīu ā?   有乜嘢好介紹呀?
I'm a vegetarian.
   ngǒh sǐk jàai   我食齋
I would like the set menu please.
   ngǒh yīu gōh tō chàan   我要個套餐
Please give me a knife and fork.
   m gòi béi ngǒh yàt fǒo dò chà   唔該俾我一副刀叉
Please bring the bill.
   m gòi, maai dàan   唔該,埋單

Shopping

How much is this?
   nì gōh géi dòh chín ā?   呢個幾多錢呀?
That is very expensive.
   hó gwāi   好貴
Can you reduce the price?
   peng dì dàk m dàk ā?   平啲得唔得呀?
I'm just looking around.
   ngǒh sìn tái yàt tái   我先睇一睇

Health

I am sick.
   ngǒh yǎu běng   我有病
My friend is sick.
   ngǒh pang yǎu yǎu běng   我朋友有病
I need a doctor.
   ngǒh yīu tái yì sàng   我要睇醫生
I want to see a female doctor.
   ngǒh yīu wán yàt wái nǔi yì sàng
   我要揾一位女醫生
It hurts here.
   nì dǒ m sùe fǔk   呢度唔舒服
I have asthma.
   ngǒh hàau chúen   我哮喘
I have diarrhoea.
   ngǒh tǒ ngòh   我肚痾
I'm allergic to antibiotics/penicillin.
   ngǒh dūi (kōng sàng sō/poon nei sài lam) gwōh mán
   我對(抗生素/盤尼西林)過敏

Emergencies

Help!	*gāu mēng ā!*	救命呀!
Watch out!	*síu sàm!*	小心!
Thief!	*chéung yé ā!*	搶嘢呀!
Call the police!	*gīu gíng chāat!*	叫警察!
Call an ambulance!	*gīu gāu sèung chè!*	叫救傷車!

Numbers

0	*ling*	零
1	*yàt*	一
2	*yī (léung)*	二(兩)
3	*sàam*	三
4	*sēi*	四
5	*nḡ*	五
6	*lūk*	六
7	*chàt*	七
8	*bāat*	八
9	*gáu*	九
10	*sāp*	十
11	*sāp yàt*	十一
12	*sāp yī*	十二
20	*yī sāp*	二十
21	*yī sāp yàt*	二十一
30	*sàam sāp*	三十
100	*yàt bāak*	一百
101	*yàt bāak ling yàt*	一百零一
110	*yàt bāak yàt sāp*	一百一十
112	*yàt bāak yàt sāp yī*	一百一十二
120	*yàt bāak yī sāp*	一百二十
200	*yī bāak*	二百
1000	*yàt chìn*	一千
10,000	*yàt māan*	一萬
100,000	*sāp māan*	十萬
112,000	*sāp yàt māan yī chìn*	十一萬二千
1,000,000	*yàt bāak māan*	一百萬

Facts for the Visitor

WHEN TO GO

In terms of weather, October-November and April-May are probably best. Temperatures are moderate, and there's a good chance of clear skies and sun. December through March tend to see a lot of rain, and from June through September the sweltering heat and humidity make for sweaty sightseeing. For more details, see the climate section in the Facts about Hong Kong chapter.

Hong Kong hotels have two high seasons: September through January, and March through June. During this time rates go up, and rooms are often hard to find. Airfares to Hong Kong are also usually higher around these times.

Travel in and out of Hong Kong can be difficult during Chinese New Year, which falls around late January/early February. Planes are usually full, and the border with China becomes a living hell as millions (yes, millions) of locals flood to the mainland to visit relatives. On the other hand, the crowds that can make Hong Kong a tiring place to visit are absent during this time, and more and more shops and restaurants only close for one day during the holiday, instead of the traditional three to seven-day break.

If you're planning to leave Hong Kong for Australia, the UK or the USA in August, book your flight early. You will be competing for seats with tens of thousands of Hong Kong students going back to universities abroad.

ORIENTATION

Surprisingly, a good deal of Hong Kong's 1084 sq km is made up of mountains, sparsely inhabited islands and country parks. The city itself is crammed into a relatively small area centred around Victoria Harbour. Hong Kong Island lies to the south, the peninsula of Kowloon to the north. The urban area basically runs from the north side of Hong Kong Island to the Kowloon Hills, which mark the effective border between the peninsula and the New Territories.

Urban Hong Kong is divided into numerous districts. The main business, banking and government district is

Central, on Hong Kong Island directly across from Tsimshatsui, which lies at the tip of the Kowloon peninsula. Going west from Central will take you through the districts of Sheung Wan and Kennedy Town, which have some of Hong Kong's oldest residential neighbourhoods.

To the east of Central lies Admiralty, which is basically a group of commercial and government office blocks, and then Wanchai, home to scores of little family-run shops, some good restaurants and pubs and a modest strip of girlie bars. Next is Causeway Bay, one of Hong Kong's major shopping and entertainment areas. Nestled behind Wanchai and Causeway Bay, at the foot of the hills, is Happy Valley, an upmarket residential area as well as site of one of Hong Kong's two horse-racing tracks. East of Causeway Bay you will find the districts of Tin Hau, North Point, Tai Koo, Shaukeiwan and Chai Wan where the mix becomes more residential/industrial. Towering above it all is the Peak, the exclusive district that has been home to Hong Kong's upper crust since the territory was founded.

On the Kowloon side, Tsimshatsui, and the districts of Jordan and Yaumatei to the north, are home to the bulk of the colony's hotels and retail shops. Tsimshatsui also boasts numerous restaurants, bars and clubs. Mongkok, north of Yaumatei, is another major shopping area, though mostly for locals as opposed to tourists. The eastern side of the peninsula, which includes districts like Hunghom, Homantin and To Kwa Wan, is mainly residential or industrial. One exception is Tsimshatsui East, where you will find a few hotels, shopping plazas, office blocks and night clubs.

Most of these districts are relatively compact, making Hong Kong a great place to explore on foot. Sheung Wan and Wanchai, on Hong Kong Island, and Yaumatei and Mongkok, on the opposite side in Kowloon, all offer good possibilities for strolling around and checking out the local lifestyle. The Peak not only has spectacular views of Hong Kong, but a series of tree-lined walkways and trails as well. And if your feet get tired, Hong Kong's outstanding public transportation network will help get you to your destination quickly and, for the most part, comfortably.

MAPS

Good maps are easy to get in Hong Kong. The Hong Kong Tourist Association (HKTA) hands out free copies of its *Official Hong Kong Map* booklet at its offices at Kai Tak airport, the Star Ferry Terminal in Tsimshatsui and

Jardine House in Central. Maps are divided by district, have both English and Chinese script, list hotels and shopping centres and are easy to read. Similar maps can be found at the back of *The Official Hong Kong Guide* and *Hong Kong This Week*, both of which are put out by the HKTA, and are usually available in hotels as well as the HKTA offices.

A series of excellent free maps has been recently introduced by The Map Company Ltd (☎ 2537-7605). In addition to an overall *Map of Hong Kong* there are separate and quite detailed maps of the main centres. These maps can usually be found at hotels, some bars and Oliver's Super Sandwich shops. If you can't locate one, call the company.

If you're looking for even greater detail and topographical accuracy, the *Hong Kong Official Guide Map* (put out by the government) has both overall and district maps and sells for HK$35 in bookstores. The government also sells a series of countryside maps that are extremely useful if you plan to go hiking in the hills. These are available at the Government Publications Office (☎ 2537-1910) located in the Government Office Building, Queensway Government Offices, 88 Queensway, Admiralty (Map 5). The office is open 9 am to 4 pm daily, and 9 am to 1 pm on Saturdays. You may also like to check out *Hong Kong Map – Arrival, Survival,* which sells in bookstores for HK$40.

Unfortunately there is no good bus map for the city. Your best option here may be Universal Publications' *Hong Kong Guidebook,* which costs HK$60 in bookstores. This book has extremely detailed district and neighbourhood maps, and roads with bus route numbers. There is a listing of most bus routes in the back of the book, but only in Chinese. The Hong Kong Transport Department also publishes a hefty tome entitled *Public Transport in Hong Kong – A Guide to Services.* For HK$40 you get a comprehensive rundown of every bus, minibus, ferry and rail route in the territory – quite a bit more info than you need unless you're planning a long-term stay. The book is sold at the Government Publications Office.

TOURIST OFFICES

The Hong Kong Tourist Association (HKTA) is a government-sponsored organisation dedicated to promoting Hong Kong tourism and dealing with any inquiries visitors may have. It has several local offices and telephone inquiries lines, and produces reams of useful pamphlets and publications. It also runs an extensive network of overseas offices.

Information Centres

The HKTA runs three information centres with helpful staff to answer questions. They also provide maps and a wide variety of literature on sights, hotels, food, local customs, tours and so on. Though mostly free, some of their publications must be purchased. You will find the three centres at:

Star Ferry Terminal, Tsimshatsui – open 8 am to 6 pm Monday through Friday, and from 9 am to 5 pm weekends and holidays

Shop 8, Basement, Jardine House, 1 Connaught Place, Central – open 9 am to 6 pm weekdays, and 9 am to 1 pm on Saturdays

Buffer Hall, Kai Tak airport, Kowloon – open 8 am to 10.30 pm daily (information is provided for arriving passengers only)

The HKTA also has an extensive collection of editorial features that give more detailed information on various aspects of Hong Kong life and Chinese culture. The information centres should have a master list, but you may have to wait for the features to be mailed or faxed to you from the head office, where they are stocked. Alternatively, you can go in person to HKTA's head office (☎ 2807-6543), which is located at 11th floor, Citicorp Centre, 18 Whitfield Rd, North Point.

Telephone & Fax Services

The HKTA runs a telephone hotline (☎ 2807-6177) to handle tourist queries. Multilingual staff are on hand from 8 am to 6 pm from Monday to Friday, or from 9 am to 5 pm on weekends and holidays.

If you have access to a fax, you can take advantage of the HKTA fax information service. The data available includes HKTA member hotels, restaurants, places to shop and so on. To do this, if your fax machine has a handset, pick it up first and dial (☎ 177-1128); if the machine has no handset, set it to polling mode before dialling. After you connect you'll receive a list of available topics and the appropriate fax numbers to call to receive the data. You can call this service from abroad and there is no additional charge beyond what you pay for an international phone connection. If calling from within Hong Kong, the local phone company tacks on a charge of HK\$2 per minute between 8 am and 9 pm, reduced to HK\$1 from 9 pm to 8 am.

Overseas Offices

The HKTA's offices abroad include the following:

Australia
Level 5, 55 Harrington St, The Rocks, Sydney
(☎ (02) 9251-2855)

Canada
347 Bay St, Suite 909, Toronto, Ontario M5H 2R7
(☎ (416) 366-2389)

France
Escalier C, 8ème étage, 53 Rue François 1er, 75008, Paris (☎ (01) 47.20.39.54)

Germany
Humboldt Strasse 94, D60318 Frankfurt am Main
(☎ (069) 95 91 290)

Italy
c/o Sergat Italia srl, Via Monte dei Cenci 20, 00186 Roma (☎ (06) 6880-1336)

Japan
4th floor, Toho Twin Tower Building, 1-5-2 Yurakucho, Chiyoda-ku, Tokyo 100
(☎ (03) 3503-0731)
8th floor, Osaka Saitama Building, 3-5-13 Awaji-machi, Chuo-ku, Osaka 541
(☎ (06) 299-9240)

Korea
c/o Glocom Korea, Suite 1006, Paiknam Building, 188-3 Eulchiro 1-ka, Chung-gu, Seoul (☎ (02) 778-4403)

New Zealand
PO Box 2120, Auckland
(☎ (09) 520-3316)

Singapore
13th floor, 13-08 Ocean Building, 10 Collyer Quay, Singapore 0104 (☎ 532-3668)

South Africa
c/o Development Promotions Pty Ltd, 7th floor, Everite House, 20 De Korte St, Bramamfontein 2001, Johannesburg
(☎ (011) 339-4865)

Spain
c/o Sergat Espana SL, Pau Casals 4, 08021 Barcelona
(☎ (3) 414-1794)

Taiwan
9th floor, 18 Chang'an E Rd, Section 1, Taipei
(☎ (02) 581-2967)

UK
5th floor, 125 Pall Mall, London, SW1Y 5EA
(☎ (0171) 930-4775)

USA
610 Enterprise Dr, Suite 2000, Oak Brook, IL 60521
(☎ (708) 575-2828)
5th floor, 590 Fifth Ave, New York, NY 10036-4706
(☎ (212) 869-5008)
10940 Wilshire Blvd, Suite 1220, Los Angeles, CA 90024-3915
(☎ (310) 208-4582)

NICKO GONCHAROFF

Tourist junk making the rounds of Victoria Harbour

DOCUMENTS

Visas

Tourist Visas Most visitors to Hong Kong don't need a visa. The exception is for countries that have or had communist regimes: Hong Kong has always made it difficult for nationals from such countries to enter its borders, and despite the end of the Cold War things have been slow to change.

Chances are that most of the rules will stay the same after China takes possession of Hong Kong in 1997, though perhaps some of the restrictions will be eased on nationals from communist or former communist states. What exactly will transpire is difficult to say, as the Chinese government had not revealed its intentions at the time of writing.

Currently, British citizens (or Commonwealth citizens who were born in the UK or in Hong Kong) can normally stay for up to 12 months without a visa, and it's possible to stay longer. Australians, Canadians and New Zealanders get a visa-free stay for three months. Citizens of most Western European countries are also permitted to stay for three months without a visa, depending on which country they're from. Americans, Germans, Japanese and South Africans can stay for one month without a visa, as can visitors from most South American countries.

Officially, visitors have to show that they have adequate funds for their stay and that they have an onward ticket or a return ticket to their own country. In practice, this rule is seldom enforced, except in the case when a visa is required. Visitors from the following countries *must* have a visa: Afghanistan, Albania, Bulgaria, Cambodia, China, CIS (former USSR), Cuba, Czech Republic, Hungary, Iran, Iraq, Laos, Lebanon, Libya, Mongolia, Myanmar (Burma), North Korea, Oman, Romania, Slovakia, Somalia, Sudan, Syria, Taiwan, Tonga, Vietnam and Yemen.

If you do need a visa, apply at any British embassy, consulate or high commission.

Visitors are not permitted to take up employment, establish any business or enrol as students. If you want to enter for employment, education or residence you must have a work visa unless you are a UK citizen, and even then you officially have to show means of support in Hong Kong.

Work Visas You need a company on your side to get a work visa for Hong Kong. The Hong Kong Immigration Department requires proof that you have been offered employment, usually in the form of a contract. The prospective employer is also obligated to show that the work you plan to do cannot be performed by a local. Usually, visitors must leave Hong Kong in order to obtain a work permit, returning only when it is ready. Exceptions are made however, especially if the company explains that it urgently needs to fill a position. Work visas are generally granted for between one and three years. Extensions should be applied for a month before the visa expires.

Overseas, applications for work visas can be made at any British embassy, consulate or high commission. For more information in Hong Kong, contact the Hong Kong Immigration Department (☎ 2824-6111), 2nd floor, Immigration Tower, 7 Gloucester Rd, Wanchai (Map 6).

Visa Extensions Visa extensions are not usually granted unless there are special circumstances such as a cancelled flights, illness, registration in a legitimate course of study, marriage to a local and so on. If you accidentally overstay your visa, upon leaving you will likely be detained at immigration, asked to fill out an extension form and then cough up HK$150 for the service fee. The extension only allows you to leave the territory legally: it doesn't entitle you to a longer stay.

One way to get a de facto extension is to leave Hong Kong for a few days in Macau or China. Upon returning you will get another month or three months, depending on your nationality. It's probably not a good idea to try this too many times: immigration officers are wise to this scam.

For further information about extensions, contact the Immigration Department.

Identity Cards

Anyone staying in Hong Kong for more than three months is required to have a Hong Kong Identity Card. These are obtained at the Immigration Department. In any event, all visitors and residents are supposed to carry identification at all times in Hong Kong. It doesn't need to be a passport – anything with a photo on it will do. This is because the immigration authorities do frequent spot checks to catch illegal workers and those who overstay their visas.

If you're planning a prolonged stay in Hong Kong and are using your passport as ID, it's wise to register it with your consulate – this makes the replacement process much simpler in case it gets lost.

Travel Insurance

A travel insurance policy covering health, property theft, flight cancellations and so on is always a good idea. Though basic medical treatment is reasonably priced in Hong Kong, more involved procedures can get quite expensive, so it's probably best to opt for a policy that covers higher expenses. Travel insurance needs to be purchased in advance: you can't get it in Hong Kong unless you can furnish proof of local residence, and even then the insurance is only valid for travel outside the territory. Consult your travel agent or local insurance agent for information on policies.

Hopefully you won't need medical care, but do keep in mind that any health insurance policy you have at home is probably not valid outside your country. The usual procedure with travellers' health insurance is that you pay in cash first for services rendered and then later present the receipts to the insurance company for reimbursement after you return home. Other policies stipulate that you call collect to a centre in your home country, where an immediate assessment of your problem is made.

Driver's Licence

If you're planning on renting or borrowing a car in Hong Kong, an overseas licence will do: it's not necessary to furnish an international driver's licence, though it can't

NICKO GONCHAROFF

Foundation stone, French Misson Building, Central

hurt to have one in case you're journeying beyond Hong Kong. Most rental car agencies also require at least one credit card. If you plan to stay in Hong Kong for the longer term, you must turn in your own licence for a Hong Kong one within 12 months. For details, check with the Transport Department (☎ 2829-5258) which has four licensing offices spread throughout the territory.

Health Certificates

Hong Kong is a good place to get vaccinations for onward destinations in Asia. For this reason, as well as in case you need medical treatment, it's not a bad idea to bring an International Health Certificate, which carries a record of any vaccinations you've had, and any other salient health details. These can also be issued in Hong Kong for travel in other countries.

Hostelling International Card

Hong Kong's seven hostels require guests to be members of the International Youth Hostels Federation, so it would be wise to organise this at home. Some hostels will let you stay subject to a HK$25 nightly surcharge, known as a 'welcome stamp'. Six welcome stamps would be the equivalent of an IYHF membership, which is valid for 12 months. For more information, contact the Hong Kong Youth Hostels Association (☎ 2788-1638), Room 225-226, Block 19, Shek Kip Mei Estate, Kowloon.

NICKO GONCHAROFF

Old street sign in Central

Student Cards

Student cards will get you small breaks on admission fees to museums and sights in Hong Kong, but that's about it.

An International Student Identity Card (ISIC) entitles the holder to a number of discounts on airfares, trains, museums etc. To get this card, inquire at your home campus. These can also be issued by the Hong Kong Student Travel Bureau.

Photocopies

It's never a bad idea to have photocopies of all one's vital documents kept in a separate place from one's wallet, handbag or money belt. These would include copies of passport data pages, birth certificate, employment documents, education qualifications and a list of travellers cheque serial numbers. You may even consider putting an emergency cash stash in with these items. For complete peace of mind, leave a set with someone back home as well.

CONSULATES

Below are some of the diplomatic missions in Hong Kong. There's a complete list in the *Yellow Pages Commercial/Industrial Guide*. It's best to call and check on opening times – some of those consular officials take pretty long lunch breaks. Some smaller countries are represented by honorary consuls who are normally business people employed in commercial firms: it's advisable to phone beforehand to find out if they're available.

Australia
23rd & 24th floors, Harbour Centre, 25 Harbour Rd, Wanchai (☎ 2827-8881)

Austria
13th floor, Diamond Exchange Building, 8-10 Duddell St, Central (☎ 2522-2388)

Canada
11th-14th floors, Tower One, Exchange Square, 8 Connaught Place, Central (☎ 2847-7420)

China
Visa Office of the People's Republic of China, 5th floor, Lower Block, 26 Harbour Rd, Wanchai (☎ 2827-9569)

Denmark
Room 2402B, Great Eagle Centre, 23 Harbour Rd, Wanchai (☎ 2827-4555)

Finland
Room 1818, Hutchison House, 10 Harcourt Rd, Central (☎ 2525-5385)

France
26th floor, Tower Two, Admiralty Centre, 18 Harcourt Rd, Admiralty (☎ 2529-4351)

Germany
21st floor, United Centre, 95 Queensway, Admiralty (☎ 2529-8855)

India
16th floor, United Centre, 95 Queensway, Central (☎ 2528-4028)

Indonesia
6-8 Keswick St, Causeway Bay (☎ 2890-4421)

Israel
Room 701, Tower Two, Admiralty Centre, 18 Harcourt Rd, Central (☎ 2529-6091)

Italy
Room 805, Hutchison House, 10 Harcourt Rd, Central (☎ 2522-0033)

Japan
47th floor, Tower One, Exchange Square, 8 Connaught Place, Central (☎ 2522-1184)

Korea (South)
5th floor, Far East Finance Centre, 16 Harcourt Rd, Central (☎ 2529-4141)

Malaysia
24th floor, Malaysia Building, 50 Gloucester Rd, Wanchai (☎ 2527-0921)

Myanmar (Burma)
Room 2421-2425, 24th floor, Sung Hung Kai Centre, 30 Harbour Rd, Wanchai (☎ 2827-7929)

Nepalese Liaison Office
c/o HQ British Forces, HMS *Tamar*, Prince of Wales Building, Harcourt Rd, Central (☎ 2588-3255)

Netherlands
3rd floor, China Building, 29 Queen's Rd, Central (☎ 2522-5127)

New Zealand
Room 3414, Jardine House, Connaught Rd, Central (☎ 2525-5044)

Norway
Room 1502, Great Eagle Centre, 23 Harbour Rd, Wanchai (☎ 2587-9953)

Pakistan
Room 3806, 38th floor,
China Resources Building,
26 Harbour Rd, Wanchai
(☎ 2827-1966)

Philippines
Room 602, 6th floor, United
Centre, 95 Queensway,
Admiralty (☎ 2866-8738)

Portugal
Room 905, Harbour Centre,
25 Harbour Rd, Wanchai
(☎ 2802-2584)

Russia
Room 2932-2940, 29th floor,
Sun Hung Kai Centre, 30
Harbour Rd, Wanchai
(☎ 2877-7188)

Singapore
Room 901, Tower One,
Admiralty Centre, 18 Harcourt Rd, Admiralty
(☎ 2527-2212)

South Africa
27th floor, Sunning Plaza,
10 Hysan Ave, Causeway
Bay (☎ 2577-3279)

Spain
8th floor, Printing House,
18 Ice House St, Central
(☎ 2525-3041)

Sweden
8th floor, Hong Kong Club
Building, Chater Rd,
Central (☎ 2521-1212)

Switzerland
Room 3703, Gloucester
Tower, The Landmark, 11
Pedder St, Central
(☎ 2522-7147)

Taiwan
Chung Hwa Travel Service,
4th floor, Lippo Centre, 89
Queensway, Central
(☎ 2525-8315)

Thailand
8th floor, Fairmont House,
8 Cotton Tree Dr, Central
(☎ 2521-6481)

UK
c/o Overseas Visa Section,
Hong Kong Immigration
Department, 2nd floor,
Wanchai Tower Two, 7
Gloucester Rd, Wanchai
(☎ 2824-6111)

USA
26 Garden Rd, Central
(☎ 2523-9011)

Vietnam
15th floor, Great Smart
Tower, 230 Wanchai Rd,
Wanchai (☎ 2591-4510)

CUSTOMS

Even though Hong Kong is a duty-free port, there are
still items on which duty is charged. In particular, there
are high import taxes on cigarettes and alcohol. The
duty-free allowance for visitors is 200 cigarettes (or 50
cigars or 250g of tobacco) and one litre of alcohol. Apart
from these limits there are no other import tax worries,
so you can bring in reasonable quantities of almost
anything without paying taxes or obtaining permits. An
exception is ivory, which requires a bureaucratic tangle
of permits.

Fireworks are illegal to bring into Hong Kong. Hong
Kongers returning from Macau and China are often
vigorously searched for this reason. Firearms are strictly
controlled and special permits are needed to import one.

Penalties for illegal drug importation are severe, including long jail terms and steep fines. It makes no difference whether it's heroin, opium or marijuana – the law makes no distinction.

MONEY

Currency

The local currency is the Hong Kong dollar, which is divided into 100 cents. Bills are issued in denominations of HK$20 (grey), HK$50 (blue), HK$100 (red), HK$500 (brown) and HK$1000 (yellow). Coins are issued in denominations of 10 cents, 20 cents, 50 cents, HK$1, HK$2, HK$5 and HK$10. There is also an HK$10 note (green) but it is now being phased out in favour of the HK$10 coin.

Interestingly, Hong Kong currency is issued by three local banks, rather than by the government as in most other economies. The Hongkong and Shanghai Bank (often shortened to Hongkong Bank) and Standard Chartered Bank have long been Hong Kong's two designated note issuers. Though the bills issued by each share the same colours, their design is different. In May 1994 the Bank of China became the third note-issuing bank. In a further bow to 1997, the two British banks have stopped issuing notes carrying references to the British monarchy, instead switching to designs that are more palatable to the Chinese government. There are still plenty of the older notes in circulation, but most should be withdrawn in time for the hand-over of sovereignty.

Exchange Rates

Since 1983, the Hong Kong dollar has been pegged to the US dollar at a rate of US$1 to HK$7.80, though it is allowed to fluctuate within a narrow range of this level. This move was aimed at deterring rampant speculation in the currency that had been threatening the local economy. The 'peg', as it's called, frequently comes under attack by analysts, as it limits Hong Kong's fiscal policy options. But it does make for a fairly stable currency, and China has hinted that it intends to keep the system in place after 1997. The Hong Kong dollar generally moves against other currencies in line with the direction of the US dollar.

The following exchange rates were current at the time of writing:

Australia	A$1	=	HK$5.75
Canada	C$1	=	HK$5.67
China	Y1	=	HK$0.93
France	Ffr1	=	HK$1.56
Germany	DM1	=	HK$5.35
Japan	¥100	=	HK$7.34
New Zealand	NZ$1	=	HK$5.12
Singapore	S$1	=	HK$5.43
Switzerland	Sfr1	=	HK$6.65
Taiwan	NT$1	=	HK$0.29
Thailand	B1	=	HK$0.31
UK	£1	=	HK$11.96
USA	US$1	=	HK$7.73

Changing Money

There are few places on earth where it's easier to change money than Hong Kong. Most banks have foreign exchange counters, and tourist areas are also littered with private moneychanging shops. Banks and moneychangers can exchange all major trading currencies and many minor ones as well. Due to Hong Kong's lack of exchange controls, there is no foreign currency black market.

Cash Banks generally offer the best rates, the money-changing counters at the airport the worst.

However some banks charge a commission. Hong-kong Bank and Standard Chartered Bank, for instance, respectively levy fees of HK$30 and HK$50 for each transaction. Hang Seng Bank also charges a HK$50 commission. If you're changing several hundred US dollars or more you'll be given a better rate, which makes up for the fee. Hong Kong is saturated with the branches of all three banks, so you should have little trouble finding one.

Your best bet is probably Dao Heng Bank, which not only gives a slightly better rate than most other banks, but also does not charge a commission. One of Dao Heng's most convenient locations for visitors is its foreign exchange counter on the main floor of Towers One and Two, Exchange Square, 8 Connaught Rd, Central.

Licensed moneychangers, such as Thomas Cook and Chequepoint, are abundant in tourist areas like Tsimshatsui. Their chief advantage is that they stay open on Sundays, holidays and late into the evening when banks are closed. They claim to charge no commission, but instead give lousy exchange rates equivalent to a 5% commission. These rates are clearly posted, though if you're changing several hundred US dollars or more you should be able to bargain for a better rate. Before the actual exchange is made, the moneychanger is required by law to give you a form to sign clearly showing the amount, exchange rate and any service charges. Of the moneychangers, the ones operating at Chungking Mansions on Nathan Rd in Tsimshatsui usually offer the best rates.

Try to avoid changing money at hotels, which offer rates that are only marginally better than the usurious airport moneychangers.

Travellers Cheques Nearly all banks will cash travellers cheques, and all charge a fee. Again, the best deal is probably Dao Heng, which charges a flat rate of HK$20. Hongkong Bank charges 0.375% of the total amount, while Standard Chartered tacks on a HK$50 commission. Licensed moneychangers don't levy a commission, but sometimes give a slightly lower rate for travellers cheques, though this can improve if you change a significant sum.

Hong Kong is a good place to buy travellers cheques if need be. Generally the fee is 1% of the total value of cheques purchased.

International Transfers

As one of Asia's leading financial centres, Hong Kong is a great place to arrange international money transfers.

The larger banks, including Hongkong Bank and Standard Chartered, can easily handle bank drafts and telegraphic transfers. Fees for these services usually range from HK$100 to HK$150. Hongkong Bank's international transfer desk is located on the 3rd floor of the main branch, located at 1 Queen's Rd, Central. Standard Chartered Bank's main branch is located right next door. When arranging a transfer, be sure to get the Hong Kong bank's address and routing number.

ATM Cards

There are basically two ATM networks in Hong Kong. Hongkong Bank and Hang Seng Bank operate one which accepts a fairly large number of international ATM systems, such as Plus System and Cirrus, as well as Visa credit and debit cards. The Jetco network, used by Standard Chartered and a host of smaller Hong Kong banks, accepts Cirrus ATM cards and MasterCard credit and debit cards. The ATM systems accepted are displayed above the ATM machines. Payment is in Hong Kong dollars only.

Using an ATM or debit card is one of the cheapest ways to get money from overseas, as the only fees levied are those by your home bank for ATM withdrawals.

Credit Cards

Credit cards are widely accepted in Hong Kong, especially since some of the industry's heavy hitters launched massive marketing campaigns several years ago to convert the locals. Many restaurants and all but the smallest shops take credit cards, though some tack on a 3% to 5% surcharge. Check first. The most commonly accepted credit cards include American Express, Diners Club, JCB, MasterCard and Visa. The main offices are:

American Express International Inc – 20th floor, Somerset House, Tai Koo Place, 979 Kings Rd, Tai Koo (☎ 2885-9366)

Diners Club International – 42nd floor, Hopewell Centre, 183 Queen's Rd East, Wanchai (☎ 2860-1888)

JCB International (Asia) Ltd – Room 507, Hong Kong Pacific Centre, 28 Hankow Rd, Tsimshatsui (☎ 2366-7203; Japanese language ☎ 2366-7211)

MasterCard International – Suite 1401-4, Dah Sing Financial Centre, 108 Gloucester Rd, Wanchai (☎ 2598-8038)

Visa International – 6th floor, Dorset House, Tai Koo Place, 979 King's Rd, Tai Koo (☎ 2823-2323)

Costs

Hong Kong is one of Asia's most expensive cities to both visit and live in. Travellers' wallets are usually hit hardest by accommodation, eating out and entertainment.

Still, there are options for the budget traveller. A room at a hostel or guesthouse will cost between HK$50 and HK$200 per night. Breakfast at a hole-in-the-wall Chinese place or an Oliver's Super Sandwich shop will run HK$20 to HK$30, lunch in a noodle shop or fast food restaurant HK$30 to HK$50. For dinner, if you have tired of noodle shops, keep an eye out for set dinner deals: sometimes you can get an appetiser, main course, dessert and coffee for around HK$100. Add in another HK$200 for transportation and extras like snacks, drinks and admission fees and you've got a daily budget of HK$400 to $HK600. Those on a very tight budget could probably cut this back to HK$200 to HK$300, though this would make for a spartan stay indeed.

If you have more to spend, it's easily done. A double room at a mid-range hotel costs around HK$700-1200 per night, and HK$1300-2500 at one of the higher-end places. Meals, once you leave the budget places behind, can also be quite expensive. Lunch at an average restaurant in Central or Tsimshatsui will usually cost HK$150 to HK$250 per person, and dinner HK$300 to HK$500 or higher. Hong Kong is a great place to live it up, but just make sure you bring plenty of money to do it.

One of the easiest ways to empty your wallet is to visit Hong Kong's bars. Prices for beer and cocktails are on a par with those in Tokyo. A beer usually costs HK$30 to HK$50, and cocktails slightly more. One way around these prices is to target bars' happy hours, usually held between 4 and 7 pm, when prices are generally halved.

Public transportation in Hong Kong is generally quite affordable. The trams and the Star Ferry, at HK$1.20 and HK$1.70 respectively, are bargains. At the other end of the spectrum, the subway, or MTR, is relatively pricey: a single ride can cost anywhere from HK$4 to HK$11. For your money however, you get a clean, fast ride. Taxi rides are not unreasonably priced.

GLENN BEANLAND

Drying lime peel, Kowloon

Tipping & Bargaining

Tipping is somewhat haphazard in Hong Kong. In restaurants, locals often only leave several Hong Kong dollars in coins. Many restaurants levy a 10% service charge, though whether this money ever gets to the waiter or waitress is doubtful. If you appreciated the service you received, it doesn't hurt to leave a little more: at least your server will actually receive the money.

There is no need to tip taxi drivers unless, again, you feel they were particularly nice or helpful. Bellhops at hotels do expect at tip: HK$10-20 should do. If you use the porters at the airport, HK$2 to HK$3 per bag is the general rule.

Tipping in bars is pretty much up to you. Naturally if you expect to be sitting on that bar stool for any length of time, it might be a good idea to get the bartender on your side with a little cash persuasion.

Bargaining is expected in Hong Kong's tourist districts, but less so elsewhere. Trying to bargain something down to say, half the original price, may be counter-productive. If the shop allows it, it probably means the prices were far too high to begin with. If the shop is that dishonest (and many are, particularly in the Tsimshatsui tourist ghetto), the staff will probably find other ways to cheat you, like selling electronics with missing components, or a second-hand camera instead of a new one. Many of these rip-off shops don't post prices on their goods. In an honest shop, you shouldn't be able to bargain more than a 10% discount, if they'll bargain at all. Bargaining is definitely out in department stores and garment chain stores, such as Giordano or U2.

Taxes

There is no sales tax in Hong Kong, which has contributed to the city's (now debatable) reputation as a shopping paradise. About the only tax which visitors are likely to run into is a 5% government tax on hotel rates. Hotels add this to their own 10% service charge, making for a total surcharge of 15%.

DOING BUSINESS

There is probably no other city in Asia that makes doing business more convenient than Hong Kong. The city has excellent transport and communications infrastructure and abundant business services. Many local businesses are used to dealing with foreigners, lowering the risk of cultural misunderstandings. The Hong Kong government does its best to help overseas firms and executives link up with local suppliers or investment partners, and sweetens the pot by keeping both personal and corporate income taxes low (flat rates of 15% and 16.5% respectively).

The territory's legal system, modelled after that in the UK, gives ample recourse to the law, which has made

Hong Kong a better investment environment than most other Asian countries. Unfortunately it's difficult to say what will happen after China resumes sovereignty after 30 June 1997. Under the terms of the Sino-British Joint Declaration of 1984, Beijing has promised to keep Hong Kong's capitalist economy, currency, free-market policies and lifestyle unchanged for 50 years after 1997. How this turns out in practice may be different. China's own legal system has proven to be of little help to foreign investors embroiled in disputes with Chinese partners, and Beijing has already started playing power politics with the Hong Kong government over the makeup of the territory's new court of final appeal.

In general, however, it should remain easy to do business and make money in Hong Kong. China itself has tens of billions of US dollars invested in the territory's property and equity markets, a reassuring sign. Mainland Chinese firms are flooding into Hong Kong, which may make it easier to find business partners in China with experience in the international arena. And the change in government will hopefully not affect the efficiency of Hong Kong's business service industry, which is noted for getting things done on time with a minimum of hassle.

Trade & Business Organisations

Government Organisations The largest and most visible of these is the Hong Kong Trade Development Council, which for nearly 30 years has been promoting Hong Kong as a trading and manufacturing partner for foreign businesses. The HKTDC's most useful feature for foreign firms is its trade enquiry service, which has details of more than 50,000 Hong Kong manufacturers and trade companies along with 70,000 China enterprises and import/export firms. It also maintains a comprehensive reference library for local and foreign users. The HKTDC co-sponsors or takes part in numerous trade fairs each year and publishes a wealth of literature on Hong Kong markets and products.

In Hong Kong, trade enquiries and other questions are handled at the HKTDC head office (☎ 2584-4333), 38th floor, Office Tower One, Hong Kong Convention & Exhibition Centre, 1 Harbour Rd, Wanchai (Map 6). The council also has an Internet World Wide Web site at http://www.tdc.org.hk and more than 40 representative offices in 32 countries.

The Hong Kong Industry Department offers information and assistance to overseas investors at its One-Stop Unit (☎ 2727-2434), 14th floor, Ocean Centre,

5 Canton Rd, Tsimshatsui. Apart from the HKTDC, another source for trade information, statistics, government regulations and product certification is the Hong Kong Trade Department (☎ 2398-5645), 700 Nathan Rd, Mongkok.

Chambers of Commerce Hong Kong is well served by both local and overseas chambers. The largest among the locals is the Hong Kong General Chamber of Commerce (☎ 2529-9229), 22nd floor, United Centre, 95 Queensway, Admiralty. It has more than 4000 members and boasts 10 offices throughout the territory. In addition to its various member services, the chamber offers a host of services for foreign executives and firms such as translation, serviced offices, secretarial help and printing.

The Chinese General Chamber of Commerce (☎ 2525-6385), more oriented towards local firms, is authorised to issue Certificates of Hong Kong origin for trade purposes. Its address is 7th floor, Chinese General Chamber of Commerce Building, 24-25 Connaught Rd, Central. So is the Chinese Manufacturers' Association (☎ 2545-6166), which also operates testing laboratories for product certification. It is located on the 3rd floor, CMA Building, 64-66 Connaught Rd, Central.

For a complete listing of both local and overseas chambers check the *Yellow Pages Commercial/Industrial Guide*.

Business Services

There are literally hundreds of companies offering services for either visiting executives or small firms that need to contract out various tasks. It pays to check around and compare not only prices but the extent of services offered. Below are brief descriptions and addresses of some business service firms. Complete listings can be found in either Yellow Pages' *Buying Guide* or *Commercial/Industrial Guide*. With the exception of banking, the Hong Kong General Chamber of Commerce (see above) also offers many services for visiting business people.

The two major banks for business and traders are the Hongkong and Shanghai Bank (☎ 2822-1111) at 1 Queen's Rd Central in Central, and Hang Seng Bank (2825-5111) at 83 Des Voeux Rd, Central. Both offer extensive corporate services and trade financing. For business with China, you may have to go through the Bank of China (2826-6888) at 1 Garden Rd, Central,

NICKO GONCHAROFF

Worshippers at Wong Sai Tin Temple, Kowloon

though service at one of the Hong Kong banks is likely to be better.

In Hong Kong, secretarial services often include accounting, so check carefully to see what you might be paying for. Another alternative is to rent a serviced office, where secretarial services are generally provided. The further from Central, the less expensive these services get, though they are all pretty pricey.

For printing, Tappan Printing (☎ 2561-0101) has a good reputation for high quality, large-scale printing work, and is a favourite of many Hong Kong magazine publishers. For smaller jobs, Alphagraphics (☎ 2525-

5568) has English-speaking staff, and handles desktop publishing, copying, binding, and so on.

There are many translation and interpreting companies to choose from, though it might be wise to request a sample, as some agencies can't always deliver the flawless translations they invariably promise. International firms in Hong Kong that offer simultaneous interpreting in a wide range of languages are KERN (Hong Kong) Ltd (☎ 2850-4455) and the Asian Translation Centre (☎ 2533-9572).

POST & COMMUNICATIONS

Post

Hong Kong's postal system is generally fast and quite reliable. Postage rates are on a par with most developed countries. Mail boxes and post offices are clearly marked in English. Unfortunately mail boxes can be hard to find – you may end up holding on to your mail until you reach a post office.

On the Hong Kong Island side, the General Post Office (GPO) is on your right as you alight the Star Ferry in Central (Map 5). If there are long lines there, you can try the post office at the government offices west of Exchange Square along the elevated walkway. On the Kowloon side, one of the most convenient post offices is at 10 Middle Rd, east of Nathan Rd in Tsimshatsui (Map 16). Another good post office (and less crowded) is in the basement of the Albion Plaza, 2-6 Granville Rd, just off Nathan Rd, Tsimshatsui. All post offices are open Monday to Saturday from 8 am to 6 pm, and are closed on Sunday and public holidays.

Airmail The Hong Kong postal service divides the world into two distinct zones. Zone 1 is China, Japan, Taiwan, South Korea, India, Indonesia and South-East Asia generally. Rates for letters and postcards are HK$2.10 (Zone 1) and HK$2.60 (Zone 2) for the first 10g; and HK$1.10 and HK$1.20 respectively for each additional 10g. Aerogrammes are HK$2.10 for both zones.

Parcels Parcel and surface mail service is also divided into two main zones, but not the same as for airmail. Area 1 is China, Macau and Taiwan. Area 2 is all other countries. Rates vary widely depending on the destination country. Shipping by surface takes weeks or months, but is about half the cost of airmail. Post offices also sell different sized cardboard boxes, allowing you to pack and send on the spot.

Speedpost Rates for the postal service's international express mail facility varies widely according to destination, but there is little relation to actual distance. For example, a 250g Speedpost letter to Australia costs HK$85 but to China it's HK$90 and to Singapore HK$65! The main factors seem to be the availability of air transport and efficiency of mail handling at the destination country. Speedpost is usually at least twice as fast as regular airmail, and is usually cheaper than using private express mail companies such as DHL or Federal Express.

Courier Services Private companies offering rapid document and small parcel service (32 kg limit) include DHL (☎ 2765-8111), Federal Express (☎ 2730-3333) and TNT Express (☎ 2389-5279). All three companies have numerous pickup points, so call for the one nearest you.

For larger items, you will need the services of a freight forwarder. Foremost in this market is United Parcel Service (UPS), at the World Finance Centre in Canton Rd, Tsimshatsui. UPS also offers small parcel courier service, so ring them (☎ 2735-3535) for pickup.

Receiving Mail There are poste-restante services at the GPO and other large post offices. Mail will generally be held for two months. Simply address an envelope c/o Poste Restante, GPO Hong Kong, and it will go to the Hong Kong Island side. If you want letters to go to the Kowloon side, they should be addressed c/o Poste Restante, Tsimshatsui Post Office, 10 Middle Rd, Tsimshatsui.

Telephone

Hongkong Telecom, a joint-venture more than 50% owned by Britain's Cable & Wireless, for decades enjoyed a total monopoly over all phone services (but not pagers). Since 1994 other companies have been permitted into the local market, but the lucrative long-distance monopoly will continue until the year 2006. Monopolies usually charge high rates for poor service, but Hongkong Telecom is something of an exception – service is good and long-distance rates, while no bargain, are among the lowest in Asia.

All calls made within Hong Kong are local calls and therefore free, except for public pay phones which cost HK$1 per local call with no extra charges for chatting a long time. The pay phones normally accept HK$2 coins but do *not* give change, though you can make a second call by pressing the 'FC' (Follow-on Call) button before hanging up.

There are free public phones in the arrival area of the airport. You can find public pay phones in the airport, ferry terminals, post offices and hotel lobbies. On the street they are relatively rare, though perhaps the new competition will cause an increase.

International Calls If you want to phone overseas, it's cheapest to use an IDD (International Direct Dialling) telephone. You can place an IDD call from most phone boxes, but you'll need a stack of HK$5 coins handy if your call is going to be anything but very brief. An alternative is to buy a 'Phonecard', which comes in denominations of HK$50, HK$100 or HK$250. You can find Phonecards in shops, at all 7-Eleven stores, on the street or at a Hongkong Telecom office. Phones that take the cards can be frustratingly scarce: you can find them at some 7-Elevens, Hongkong Telecom Service Centres and occasionally among groups of public phones.

To make an IDD call from Hong Kong, first dial 001, then the country code, area code and number. If you're using someone else's phone and you want to know how much the call cost, dial 003 instead of 001 and the operator will call back to report the cost.

If you go to Hongkong Telecom, there are three options for overseas phone calls: operator-connected calls (paid in advance with a minimum of three minutes); IDD which you dial yourself after paying a deposit (the unused portion of your deposit is refunded); and reverse charges (which requires a small deposit refundable if the charge is accepted or if the call doesn't get through). You can place international calls at the following Hongkong Telecom Service Centres (listed more-or-less in order of convenience for travellers):

Hong Kong Island

> Shop B, lower ground basement, Century Square, 1-13 D'Aguilar St, Central (Map 5) – open 24 hours daily, including public holidays
>
> 3 Hennessy Rd, Wanchai (Map 6) – open 9 am to 6 pm Monday to Saturday, closed public holidays
>
> 3rd floor, Jusco Department Store, Kornhill Plaza South, 2 Kornhill Rd, Quarry Bay – open 10 am to 10 pm daily, including public holidays

Kowloon

Hermes House, 10 Middle Rd, Tsimshatsui (Map 16) –
open 24 hours daily, including public holidays

Unit D-37, Passenger Terminal Building, Kai Tak Airport
– open 8 am to 11 pm daily, including public holidays

Shop 4, Northern Paid Concourse, Kowloon-Canton
Railway Terminus, Hunghom (Map 16) – open 9 am to 6
pm Monday to Saturday and public holidays

New Territories

Shop 7, Paid Concourse, Tsuen Wan MTR Station, Tsuen
Wan – open 9 am to 6 pm Monday to Saturday, closed
public holidays

Shop 12, Commercial Complex, Shatin – open 9 am to 6
pm Monday to Saturday, 10 am to 5 pm Sundays and
public holidays

International Dialling Codes

Country	Direct Dial	Home Direct
Australia	001-61	800-0061
Canada	001-1	800-1100
France	001-33	800-0033
Germany	001-49	800-0049
Indonesia	001-62	800-0062
Italy	001-39	800-0039
Japan	001-81	800-0181
Korea	001-82	800-0082
Malaysia	001-60	800-0060
Netherlands	001-31	800-0031
New Zealand	001-64	800-0064
Singapore	001-65	800-0065
Spain	001-34	800-0034
Sweden	001-46	800-0046
Taiwan	001-886	800-0886
Thailand	001-66	800-0066
UK	001-44	800-0044
USA	001-1	800-1111*

** Through AT&T; you can also dial 800-1121 (MCI) or
800-1877 (Sprint), and for Hawaii you can dial 800-1188*

Another option is to make use of the home direct service,
which takes you straight through to a local operator in
the country dialled. You can then make a reverse-charge
(collect) call or a credit-card call with a telephone credit
card valid in that country. Home direct dialling codes for
some countries are listed in the table. Some places,
including Kai Tak airport, some hotels and shopping
centres, have home direct phones where you simply
press a button labelled USA, UK, Canada, or wherever,
to be put through to your home operator. For details call

☎ 013. You may want to check whether your home telephone company supports home direct services before leaving for Hong Kong.

To phone Hong Kong from overseas, use your country's international dialling code plus Hong Kong's country code – 852 – followed by the local eight-digit number.

Useful Phone Numbers & Prefixes If you're wanting to call cities or regions in mainland China, your best bet is to ring ☎ 012 (China dialling assistance) or ☎ 013 (international dialling assistance). Other useful numbers include:

Ambulance, fire & police	☎ 999
Credit-card calls	☎ 011
Crime reports & police matters	☎ 2527-7177
Directory enquiries	☎ 1081
Information hotlines	☎ 1000 (general)
	☎ 1028 (business)
Reverse billing	☎ 010
Taxi complaints	☎ 2527-7177
Time & weather	☎ 18501

Phone Directories Currently, there are four types: the *Yellow Pages Buying Guide* (three volumes, all bilingual); the *Yellow Pages Commercial/Industrial Guide* (one volume, English only); the *Business Telephone Directory* (one volume each in English and Chinese); and *Residential Directories* (three volumes each in English and Chinese).

If you're staying any length of time in Hong Kong, you should at least pick up the *Business Telephone Directory* and the *Yellow Pages Buying Guide*. These are available through the CSL shops operated by Hongkong Telecom.

Cellular Phones & Pagers Hong Kong boasts the world's highest per capita usage of cellular phones and pagers. These things have become an integral part of Hong Kong urban life. You can rent this equipment, which may come in handy if you're staying for a long period. Cellular phones can be rented from Rentel (☎ 2828-6600), 5th floor, Allied Kajima Building, 138 Gloucester Rd, Wanchai. Hongkong Telecom does not rent cellular phones, but will happily sell you one.

Pagers can be rented from a wide variety of sources. Hongkong Telecom charges a fairly low monthly fee, but tacks on usage fees and a deposit. Other companies that rent and sell pagers include ABC Communications, Hutchison Paging and Star Paging.

Fax, Telex & E-mail

Hongkong Telecom offers fax services at its service centres. Per-page rates range from HK$10 to HK$50, depending on the destination country. You can also receive faxes for HK$10 per page. Most hotels and even many youth hostels allow their guests to send and receive faxes. The surcharge for sending is usually 10% above cost, and receiving is normally HK$10 per page. If dialling your own fax for an overseas transmission, use the international prefix 002 (for a data line) rather than 001 (for a voice line).

Though rapidly becoming outmoded, telex service is still available at Hongkong Telecom Service Centres. You can send telexes from most centres, but the one at 3 Hennessy Rd, Wanchai is the only centre where you can pick up any incoming telexes.

For those who want or need to stay in touch via electronic mail, Hong Kong is a good place to log on. CompuServe and America Online, two of the world's largest online services, both have nodes in Hong Kong. There is a fairly hefty fee for using them, usually around US$12 to US$15 per hour, in addition to normal online charges. Members should check with their respective services in advance to find out the telephone numbers for the nodes, as these can change from time to time. If you want to dial direct to overseas' online services, you can try Datapak – Hongkong Telecom's packet switching network. For more information, call Hongkong Telecom.

If you're staying in Hong Kong for an extended period, you may want to look into Hong Kong Internet & Gateway Services (☎ 2527-4888; e-mail aaron@hk.net), which charges an initial fee of HK$100, and a monthly subscription rate of HK$100. The online fee is HK$20 per hour.

BOOKS

Hong Kong's British heritage has left it with a number of well stocked English-language bookstores. Whether you're looking for books about the territory, literature, paperback fiction or textbooks, you stand a good chance of finding it in Hong Kong. Unfortunately books in Hong Kong are very expensive. For information on specific bookshops, see the Shopping chapter.

Most books are published in different editions by different publishers in different countries. As a result, a book might be a hardcover rarity in one country while it's readily available in paperback in another country. Fortunately, bookstores and libraries search by title or author, so your local bookstore or library is best placed to advise you on the availability of the following recommendations.

Culture & Society

For a rundown on the customs, manners and etiquette of Hong Kong Chinese, try *Cantonese Culture* (Asia 2000, 1995) by Ingram and Ng. Anthony Lawrence, a former BBC correspondent and resident of Hong Kong for nearly 40 years, takes a fairly upbeat look at Hong Kong attitudes and superstitions in *The Fragrant Chinese* (University of Hong Kong, 1993). Along the same lines, *Games Hong Kong People Play* (TAAHK Publications, 1992) is a light-hearted examination of Hong Kong habits, morals and chicanery. In *Letters from Hong Kong* (Bookmark, 1989), Isabel Taylor Escoba gives a biting yet humorous view of Hong Kong through the eyes of a resident Filipino.

City of Darkness – Life in the Kowloon Walled City (Watermark, 1993) by Girard & Lambot uses photos and text to tell the story of the now-demolished tenement fortress in Kowloon that was off limits to Hong Kong police and government.

Those interested in local artists may want to look at *Hong Kong Artists* (Hong Kong Museum of Art/Urban Council, 1995), which includes samples of work from the museum. The museum also has several collections of catalogues from past and present exhibits.

History

Hong Kong's brief but colourful history makes for good reading. One of the best ways to tour it is through Jan Morris' *Hong Kong – Epilogue to an Empire* (Penguin, 1988). The book is excellently written and seamlessly moves between past and present Hong Kong in an effort to find what has made it so unique among the possessions of the British empire.

Long considered the definitive history of the territory, *A History of Hong Kong* (Oxford University Press, 1964) by GB Endacott is a detailed but very dry account of Hong Kong's progress, researched largely from official documents. The second edition dates from 1974, and thus lacks any account of the last two tumultuous

GLENN BEANLAND

'Here be dragons' – Man Mo Temple, Sheung Wan

decades. The foregoing is not to be confused with *A History of Hong Kong* (HarperCollins, 1993) by Frank Welsh. This monumental hardback is more recent and while thorough, makes for easier reading than Endacott's work. Form Asia, which has numerous books on Hong Kong, takes an interesting look at the territory's structural past in *Building Hong Kong – A History of the City Through its Architecture* (1989).

Maurice Collin's *Foreign Mud* (Faber & Faber, 1946) tells the sordid story of the Anglo-Chinese opium wars. *The Potent Poppy* (Form Asia, 1992) by Michael Robson is a more updated version of the same story, in coffee-table format with colour photos. *The Taipans – Hong Kong's Merchant Princes* (Oxford University Press, 1981) tells the story of the British and Scottish merchants who profited from the opium wars and founded the trading houses that would dominate Hong Kong's business world for the next century.

A rare and extremely detailed look at Hong Kong between world wars can be had in *Hong Kong Under Imperial Rule 1911-1941* (East Asian Historical Monographs, 1987) by Norman Miners. WWII buffs may be interested in *The Lasting Honour – The Fall of Hong Kong, 1941* (Hamish Hamilton, 1978), in which Oliver Lindsay takes a professional look at the failed defence of Hong Kong against the Japanese Imperial Army.

Business

There is no shortage of guides to doing business in Hong Kong, though none of them will likely be able to tell you where the profits lie. *Establishing a Company in Hong Kong* (Longman, 1993) by Stephen Terry walks you through the bureaucratic steps needed to set up shop in the territory. Basic facts on Hong Kong's government, markets, residential and business services and establishing a company are laid out in Fiona Campbell's *Setting Up in Hong Kong* (FDC Services, 1994). For a look at local business etiquette, try *Hong Kong Business: The Portable Encyclopedia for Doing Business with Hong Kong* (World Trade Press, 1994), which also has sections on taxation, the economy and financial institutions, among others.

GLENN BEANLAND

'I'm in two minds about this one' – Kowloon Park sculpture

Language

Interested in tackling one the world's most difficult languages (as the Cantonese are proud to proclaim)? *Cantonese – A Complete Course for Beginners* (NTC Publishing, 1992) promises to have you chatting comfortably with locals after 26 lessons. Easier said than done, but perhaps worth a try. Lonely Planet publishes a *Cantonese phrasebook* that should see you through any excursions out to the night market, or the New Territories. For a simple list of phrases and a pronunciation guide, try *Instant Cantonese* (Bradshaw Publishing) by Bill Loh & Nick Theobold.

Fiction

Unfortunately Hong Kong does not seem to have inspired many good novelists, but there are a few good tales worth reading. The most famous must be Richard

---

Tickling China's Funny Bone

American cartoonist Larry Feign became famous in Hong Kong for his sardonic strip *The World of Lily Wong* which ran for years in the *South China Morning Post*. No one was spared the comic wrath of Feign's pen and ink, whether it be pontificating local politicians, arrogant expats or cocky Hong Kongers. But China's repressive government came under the heaviest fire. By taking aim at Chinese Premier Li Peng, Feign may have gone too far. In a chilling portent of things to come in Hong Kong, in May 1995 the *South China Morning Post* abruptly pulled *The World of Lily Wong* after one of its characters referred to Li Peng as a 'fascist murderous dog'.

The paper declined to give any explanation to readers, and steadfastly refused to publish a critical response from Martin Lee, a well known pro-democracy legislator. As the title of his most recent book states, Feign was 'banned' in Hong Kong.

Fortunately, much of the world of Lily Wong is intact in a series of books published by Macmillan (HK) Ltd, including the *The World of Lily Wong*, *The Adventures of Superlily* and *Postcards from Lily Wong*. Feign has also penned several other non-Lily works that poke fun at life in Hong Kong, including a collaborative effort with another noted Hong Kong wit, Nury Vittachi, entitled *Execute Yourself Tonite!* For the last of Lily, and Feign's account of the *South China Morning Post's* bow to Beijing, check out *Banned in Hong Kong* (Hambalan Press, 1995). Ironically enough, you can pick up copies at *South China Morning Post* bookstores. ■

Mason's *The World of Suzie Wong* (Pegasus Books, 1994; new edition). Written in 1957, this delightful tale of a British painter who falls in love with a Hong Kong prostitute still makes an excellent read. It was made into a film starring William Holden and Nancy Kwan in 1960.

Spy-thriller author John Le Carre's *The Honourable Schoolboy* (Coronet Books, 1974) is set against the backdrop of early 1970s Hong Kong and Indochina, and is considered one of his better works.

James Clavell, who made his name writing about Japanese samurai in *Shogun*, has produced two entertaining Hong Kong novels. *Tai-Pan* (Dell, 1986) is a racy version of Hong Kong's early merchant days. The protagonists' descendants then appear in the epic-length *Noble House* which is set in the 1960s and 1970s. Also set in Hong Kong and China are Robert Elegant's *Dynasty* (McGraw-Hill, 1977) and *Mandarin* (Hamish Hamilton, 1983), though these don't read as well as Clavell's offerings.

For historical accuracy, sharp humour and a rip-roaring read, pick up a copy of George MacDonald Frasier's *Flashman and the Dragon* (Plume Books, 1985). Though most of the story takes place in China, Flashman – the most decorated, womanising, bullying, witty poltroon of Victorian England – gets a fine start in Hong Kong that gives a good perspective on English attitudes during the opium wars.

Guides

There are some good books available for those who want to delve deeper into Hong Kong. *The Hong Kong Leisure Guide* (Silver Press, 1994) gives brief descriptions, addresses, phone numbers and other vital statistics for all sorts of leisure and recreational activities in the territory, from batik to mahjong to parachuting. It's well worth picking up if you plan to stay in Hong Kong for a prolonged period. For a guide to Hong Kong's mid-range and expensive restaurants, you can try *Hong Kong's Best Restaurants* (Illustrated Magazine Publishing, 1995), which is published annually by *Hong Kong Tatler Magazine*. Better still is the annual restaurant guide put out by *HK Magazine*, which includes cheaper places and is a lot more fun to read.

Though it has a bit of an American slant, *Living in Hong Kong* (American Chamber of Commerce, 1992) has loads of useful information for anyone planning to move to Hong Kong.

If you're interested in checking out the New Territories or the Outlying Islands, Lonely Planet's *Hong Kong,*

Macau & Guangzhou can show you where to go. If you have a lot of time on your hands and want to learn about country hikes in detail, try Stella L Thrower's *Hong Kong Country Parks*, which is published by the Hong Kong government and is available at the Government Publications Office.

APA's *Hong Kong Insight Guide* has some excellent photos, and makes for good background reading on the territory. Lonely Planet also publishes several guides to the region, including *North-East Asia on a shoestring*, *South-East Asia on a shoestring* and *China – travel survival kit*.

NEWSPAPERS & MAGAZINES

Hong Kong has long been a bastion of media freedom in Asia. This will almost certainly change after 1997, as China has little patience for any media criticism with which it doesn't agree. Some Hong Kong newspaper publishers and television stations have already started exercising self-censorship to avoid ruffling feathers in Beijing. The situation has not had as great an impact as one might think. Most journalism in Hong Kong focuses on economics, business and finance, and hence can usually skirt sensitive issues. But not always. In 1994 a Hong Kong reporter working in Beijing was jailed for 12 years after he wrote a story on interest rates and central bank gold sales, which China (after the fact) deemed state secrets. And in January 1996, China announced new controls on foreign wire services disseminating economic and financial news in China, Hong Kong, Macau and (arrogantly enough) Taiwan.

But for the time being, Hong Kong is a great place to catch up on the news. There are three local English-language newspapers: the *South China Morning Post*, *Hong Kong Standard* and *Eastern Express*. The *South China Morning Post* is the most widely read, and is also the world's most profitable newspaper, due to classified advertisement sales.

Three international newspapers produce Asian editions which are printed in Hong Kong. These are the *Asian Wall Street Journal*, *USA Today* and the *International Herald Tribune*. At the time of writing, a new Asian paper, the *Asia Times* had just hit local newsstands amid controversy over whether it was entering a saturated market. Hong Kong also has its share of news magazines, including *Asiaweek*, the *Far Eastern Economic Review* and a slew of Asian-focused business magazines.

All this is a drop in the bucket compared with the local Chinese-language print media. There are nearly 50

GLENN BEANLAND

Inside tips or insider trading? – Kowloon Park

Chinese-language newspapers in Hong Kong, giving the city the world's highest per capita ratio of newspapers. Most of these cover general news, although there are five or six devoted solely to finance, and more than a dozen that report nothing but horse-racing!

If you want to see what's happening in Hong Kong entertainment and nightlife, pick up a copy of *HK Magazine*. It's published weekly and is available free in bars, some restaurants, Oliver's Super Sandwich shops and hotels. In addition to music, cinema and performing arts listings, *HK Magazine* carries lively articles on current trends in the city, reviews of restaurants and bars, and a classified ad section that makes for pretty interesting reading. Also worth checking out is *BC Magazine*, a monthly guide to Hong Kong's entertainment and partying scene. One of the most useful features of this publication for visitors is its complete listing of bars and clubs throughout the territory. It is also free and can usually be found alongside *HK Magazine* racks.

The HKTA has several free information publications, including the monthly *Official Hong Kong Guide, Hong Kong This Week* and the weekly *Hong Kong Diary* which has listings of cultural events. These are available at HKTA information centres, hotels and shopping malls.

RADIO & TV

Government-funded Radio Television Hong Kong operates three English-language radio stations. Radio 3 (AM 567 kHz) has a mix of news, documentaries and entertainment; Radio 4 (FM 97.6 to 98.9 mHz) offers classical music in a bilingual format; and Radio Six (AM 675 kHz) relays the BBC World Service. Commercial Radio's Quote 864 (AM 864 kHz) is an all music station with mainly English-language music. Another private operator, Metro Broadcast, operates Hit Radio (FM 99.7 mHz) which plays pop music for younger people, and FM Select (FM 104 mHz), aimed at listeners age 25 and up. The English-language newspapers publish a daily guide to radio programmes.

Hong Kong's terrestrial TV channels are run by two companies: Television Broadcasts Ltd (TVB) and Asia Television Ltd (ATV). Each company operates one English-language and one Cantonese-language channel, making a total of four stations in Hong Kong. The two English channels are TVB Pearl (channel 3) and ATV World (channel 4), the Cantonese channels TVB Jade (channel 1) and ATV Home (channel 2). The programme schedule is listed daily in the English-language newspapers. Pearl and World may cease after 1997, when it is likely the government requirement to provide English-language programming will be scrapped.

Hong Kong's own satellite television station STAR TV has a total of five channels, is available at most hotels and is free for anyone who owns a satellite dish. STAR broadcasts across Asia, and can even be seen in China, though only its sports, music and Chinese drama channels are generally allowed. Other regional broadcasters based in Hong Kong include NBC, TBS and sports channel ESPN.

As if this city-state of 6 million people needed more, Wharf Cable entered the scene in 1993. Started up by local conglomerate Wharf Holdings, the station currently offers 12 channels and has plans to go to 40 by the end of 1996. Whether this venture will succeed is questionable: Hong Kong people aren't used to paying for TV, and generally seem satisfied with TVB, ATV and STAR. In a way it would be a pity if Wharf failed: the cable layers have been serenading locals with jackhammers for years now. Hardly fair if it was all for naught.

PHOTOGRAPHY & VIDEO

With all the tourists, photographers and photo-journalists in this city, there's little problem in getting cameras, film and supplies. The best place to go for equipment and accessories is Stanley St in Central. See the Camera & Film section of the Shopping chapter for more information.

Developing costs around HK$30-40 per roll of 36 colour exposures. Slides cost HK$18-20, or HK$55-60 if you want them mounted. Some shops offer cheaper developing if you first buy the film from them. Color Six Laboratories (☎ 2526-0123) at 18A Stanley St does an excellent job on both prints and slides, and can even do the latter in one day.

If you are bringing along a camcorder or the like, bear in mind that Hong Kong uses the PAL standard. If you use NTSC or SECAM you may want to bring some extra cartridges, though you should be able to find some in Hong Kong.

There's little problem in taking photos anywhere in Hong Kong, aside from some security-sensitive areas at Kai Tak airport. When walking about, think before you take photos. Places like pawn shops and mahjong parlours want to keep low profiles: aiming your camera at them could invite an angry response. Many older Chinese people strongly object to having their picture taken, so be please considerate. If you're headed up to the Peak to catch stunning views of Hong Kong on film, the late afternoon is the best time to go, when the sun is shining down on the city.

TIME

Hong Kong Standard Time is eight hours ahead of GMT/UTC. Thus when it is noon in Hong Kong it is 8 pm the previous day in Los Angeles; 11 pm the previous day in New York; 4 am in London; noon in Singapore; and 2 pm in Melbourne. Hong Kong does not have daylight-saving time.

ELECTRICITY

The standard is 220V, 50 Hz (cycles per second) AC. Electrical shops in Hong Kong and elsewhere sell handy pocket-sized transformers which will step down the electricity to 110V, but most mini-transformers are only rated for 50 watts.

Hong Kong's plug and socket system is a nightmare. Some electric outlets are designed to accommodate three round prongs, others are wired for three square pins of the British design and others still for two-prong plugs! Not surprisingly, inexpensive plug adaptors are widely available in Hong Kong supermarkets, though this is not much comfort when you find you can't plug in your coffee machine in the morning. Remember that adaptors are *not* transformers. If you ignore this warning and plug a 110V appliance into a 220V outlet, it will be sparks and fireworks.

LAUNDRY

Laundry services are pretty easy to find in Hong Kong, with the exception of the business district of Central. Most hotels, and even the cheap youth hostels, have a laundry service. Prices at private laundromats are normally HK$28 for three kg, HK$7 for each additional kilo. If it's less than three kg, you still pay the same, so you might want to throw in your clothes together with a friend's.

Dry-cleaners are easy to spot as well, and some laundromats offer the service. Dry-cleaning a shirt costs around HK$15, a skirt HK$30 and trousers $HK35-40.

WEIGHTS & MEASURES

The international metric system is in official use in Hong Kong. In practice, traditional Chinese weights and measures are still common.

If you want to shop in the local markets, become familiar with Chinese units of weight. Things are sold by the *leung*, which is equivalent to 37.5g, or in *catty*, where one catty is about 600g. There are 16 leung to the catty.

Gold is sold by the *tael* which is exactly the same as a leung, and you will find many banks selling gold in Hong Kong: the tael price is displayed right alongside the international ounce price.

HEALTH

Looking after one's health in Hong Kong should pose few problems. While not such a healthy place to live in the longer term, there are only a few areas that visitors need be aware of. Access to health care is convenient, standards are generally high and English-speaking doctors abound. Medical costs are a bit lower than in many developed countries, especially the USA.

No special vaccinations are required for Hong Kong. However, it would be wise to consider both hepatitis A and B, tetanus and influenza (during winter). Hong Kong is also a good place to get vaccinations for onward travel to other countries in Asia. For these, try a public hospital if you don't mind a longer wait, or a private hospital or doctors' office if you can afford a higher bill.

While Hong Kong's public hospitals provide low-cost care to residents, visitors and other non-Hong Kong taxpayers are usually asked to pay more. Thus it is advisable to take out some travel insurance – see the Documents section earlier in this chapter.

You can buy almost any medication across the counter in Hong Kong or get it by prescription. Even so, a small medical kit is a good thing to carry, especially if you plan on going hiking in the New Territories. Your kit could include:

- Aspirin (or acetominophen in the USA) – for pain or fever
- Antihistamine (such as Benadryl) – useful as a decongestant for colds, allergies, to ease itch from insect bites and help prevent motion sickness
- Kaolin preparation (Pepto-Bismol), Imodium or Lomotil – for stomach upsets
- Antiseptic and antibiotic creme or powder – for cuts and grazes
- Calamine lotion – to ease irritation from bites or stings
- Bandages and band-aids – for minor injuries
- Scissors, tweezers and a thermometer – mercury thermometers are prohibited by airlines
- Rehydration salts – for heat exhaustion
- Insect repellent, sunscreen and chapstick

If you wear glasses, bring a spare pair of glasses and your prescription. If you are using a particular medication take an adequate supply as there is a chance it may not be available locally. Take the prescription with the generic name rather than the brand name: brand names vary from country to country, but all doctors or pharmacists should recognise the generic name.

Oral contraceptives are widely available, though it is still preferable to bring your own supply. Condoms are easy to find as well. It's best to buy a western brand, as the local and Japanese brands are not known for their reliability.

Medical Problems

Air & Water Pollution Hong Kong's air quality is abysmal. In January 1996, only six months after setting up a monitoring index, the government issued a day-long health alert warning people with respiratory ailments or heart conditions to stay indoors. The cause is the large number of diesel vehicles and factories and endless construction which kicks up clouds of dirt and concrete dust. People with asthma may find it difficult to breath and easy to contract chest infections, and should have plenty of medication on hand. It may also be wise to start using an asthma suppressant several weeks before arriving in Hong Kong.

Water pollution is also quite bad, and the Hong Kong government has set up a system to monitor the quality of water at Hong Kong's beaches. The index is based on

Chinese Medicine

Hong Kong offers a good opportunity to try Chinese medicine. Chinese doctors and pharmacies are easy to find, and some speak English. Some cures may work for you, but it's generally best to keep your experiments limited to minor health problems. And make sure the doctor you see clearly understands what you're saying: using the wrong remedy may leave you sicker than you were to begin with.

Chinese herbalists claim to have all sorts of treatments for stomach aches, headaches, colds, flu and sore throat as well as long-term problems like asthma. While some of these remedies may be effective, it seems to vary from person to person. What they can do for more serious illnesses like cancer and heart disease is far less certain. For potentially life-threatening conditions such as chest pains or appendicitis, it's best to see a western doctor.

Most herbal medicines are fairly safe, and produce few side effects. However there have been a few cases in recent years where people have died from taking too much of a certain herb, or using it under the wrong conditions. Notable among these is *chan su*, a brown rock-like substance that includes dried toad secretions and steroids found in teas made from the oleander shrub and the foxglove. Used in some aphrodisiacs, the herb sparked irregular heartbeats and eventually fatal heart attacks in four men in the USA in 1995. Other herbs to steer clear of are: encommiae ulmoide or tree bark (which, depending on the dosage, can raise or lower blood pressure) and arsenolite (which is given in external doses of less than 0.03g to treat asthma – take it internally and it will kill you). These are the exception rather than the rule, and chances of this type of problem are low.

the amount of disease-causing bacteria present in the water, which indicates levels of faecal pollution. Water quality is divided into categories of good, fair, poor and very poor. Water ratings of Hong Kong's beaches are usually published in the local newspapers, especially during warmer months.

Drinking Water & Food The Hong Kong government says it's perfectly safe to drink the tap water. This said, many residents boil it anyway just to be on the safe side: the sewer system is fairly old. Hong Kong's old plumbing also means tap water may have a high lead content, so if you can afford it, stick with bottled water. If you go hiking in the countryside do not drink from any stream or pond – it is likely contaminated by fertiliser, cow dung or waste chemicals.

A small number of Chinese medicines make use of parts of endangered animals, such as rhino horn. As expensive as rhino horn is, it's likely that herbalists are using false advertising by slipping in water buffalo horn instead. Nonetheless, why take a chance on hastening the extinction of a species in order to cure a cold? Make sure you check what's in the herbal concoction you're about to buy.

A good place to purchase herbal medicines is Yue Hwa Chinese Products Emporium at the north-west corner of Nathan and Jordan Rds, just above Jordan MTR station in Yaumatei (Map 13). In Sheung Wan, try the Eu-Yan Sang Pharmacy, on Queen's Rd Central, just west of Peel St (Map 4). Before buying anything, explain your condition to a Chinese chemist and ask for a recommendation. They consider this part of their job.

You can also try acupuncture in Hong Kong. Getting stuck with needles might not sound pleasant, but if done properly it doesn't hurt. And it can be surprisingly effective. Often it depends on the skill of the acupuncturist and the condition being treated. While acupuncture itself is probably harmless, one should not forget that AIDS and hepatitis B can be spread easily by contaminated needles. In western countries, the use of disposable acupuncture needles has become routine, but this is not necessarily the case in Hong Kong.

The following organisations could also be worth checking: Chinese Acupuncture Association (☎ 2545-7640), Ground floor, 3 Aberdeen St, Central; and the International Acupuncture Society (☎ 2771-1066), Room 1113A, 11th floor, Champion Building, 301-309 Nathan Rd, Yaumatei. ■

Eating in Hong Kong restaurants is by and large safe: cases of upset stomach and diarrhoea do occur, but not too often. Street markets are also usually fine, but be more cautious of the street stalls selling steamed or fried dumplings – these have been known to pass on some nasty stomach bugs. Waterside restaurants sometimes have the disturbing habit of using harbour water to fill their fish storage tanks. The government is cracking down on this, but you might want to try and check all the same.

If you're hungering for shellfish, make sure it comes from somewhere other than Hong Kong waters: local clams and oysters are tasty but can be risky too. Prawns, lobster and other more deep-sea creatures are OK.

Hepatitis Though Hong Kong is not nearly as bad as China, or even Taiwan for that matter, it is still possible to catch hepatitis here, and more than 1500 cases are reported annually. Granted, many are probably contracted in China. Still, it's not a bad idea to get vaccinations for both hepatitis A and B before you leave home: the hepatitis B vaccination cycle requires 6 months, so plan ahead. Poor hygienic conditions in restaurants are a common cause of hepatitis, so try and avoid any place that looks really filthy. Unwashed fresh vegetables and shellfish are the usual culprits, along with dirty plates and utensils. Some strains of hepatitis are transmitted sexually and through dirty needles used by amateur acupuncturists and drug addicts.

Tuberculosis The infection rate for TB is surprisingly high in Hong Kong – more than 7000 cases are reported annually. While there is no reason to be unduly alarmed, if you're travelling with children it might be wise to have them vaccinated. These days, nearly all children born in Hong Kong are immunised at birth, but not so in many other countries. For adults, a skin test before and after travel, to determine whether exposure has occurred, is recommended.

Medical Assistance

Every hospital in Hong Kong has a number of English-speaking doctors and staff, and most private doctors speak English as well. Dental care is available, but fees are quite high. Public hospitals charge low fees, but Hong Kong residents pay less than foreign visitors. Private doctors' fees are often higher, so it pays to make some inquiries first. Many of the larger hotels have resident doctors.

Most pharmacies in Hong Kong are open 9 am to 6 pm, with some until 8 pm. Watson's has branches all over Hong Kong and can supply most pharmaceutical needs.

Public hospitals include: Queen Elizabeth Hospital (☎ 2710-2111), Yaumatei; Princess Margaret Hospital (☎ 2310-3111), Laichikok, Kowloon; Queen Mary Hospital (☎ 2855-4111), Pokfulam, Hong Kong Island; Prince of Wales Hospital (☎ 2636-2211), Shatin, New Territories. All have 24-hour casualty wards.

There are some excellent private hospitals in Hong Kong, but their prices reflect the fact that they must operate at a profit. Some of these include: Hong Kong Adventist Hospital (☎ 2574-6211), Wanchai; Baptist Hospital (☎ 2337-4141), Kowloon Tong, Kowloon; Canossa Hospital (☎ 2522-2181), Mid-Levels; Grantham Hospital (☎ 2554-6471), Deep Water Bay, Hong Kong Island; Hong Kong Central Hospital (☎ 2522-3141),

Central; Matilda & War Memorial Hospital (☎ 2849-6301), The Peak; St Paul's Hospital (☎ 2890-6008), Causeway Bay.

Emergencies & Counselling

In the event of a medical emergency dial ☎ 999: operators speak English. St John's offers free ambulance service in Hong Kong (☎ 2576-6555), Kowloon (☎ 2713-5555) and the New Territories (☎ 2639-2555). Some people find life in Hong Kong difficult to adapt to, especially long-term residents. There are a few places who can help out: try phoning St John's Counselling Service (☎ 2525-7207) or the Community Advice Bureau (☎ 2524-5444).

TOILETS

Though it could definitely do with more, Hong Kong does have a network of public toilets. Some areas of the city are better than others: Central, for example has five or six, while Tsimshatsui has a paltry two. In general Hong Kong Island seems better equipped on this front. Most public parks have public toilets. Others are seemingly placed at random.

Facilities are relatively clean, considering the use they get. Toilets come in both sit-down and squat versions. There is no fee for using them, and all are marked with English signs.

WOMEN TRAVELLERS

Hong Kong is by and large a safe city for women travellers. But there still are a few things to be aware of. Female travellers staying in guesthouses or other budget accommodation are sometimes approached by pleasant-mannered men offering them modelling or escort work. Don't accept these offers. These guys are basically assistant pimps whose task is to dig up western women for night clubs or brothels. Most of these rackets are run by triads (Hong Kong's equivalent of the mafia), who are not people to mess around with. Chungking Mansions seems to be a popular hunting ground for these slimy characters.

Groping and other forms of sexual harassment are not too common, but do occur, especially on crowded buses and subways. Rape is also relatively rare, and local women regularly walk alone at night. But it still does take place, and some victims have reported that after the fact local police and hospital staff can be less than sympathetic, adding to the nightmare. However, as long as you avoid darkened alleys and secluded parks or travel in pairs there should be few problems.

GAY & LESBIAN TRAVELLERS

While Hong Kong is a bit more enlightened than many other Asian cities, 'homosexuality' is still a dirty word to many here. The situation is improving: the gay community is no longer completely 'underground', but is still not very visible.

HK Magazine sometimes has information on clubs, events and associations that may be of interest. And there is a burgeoning gay bar scene – see the Entertainment chapter for details.

DISABLED TRAVELLERS

Hong Kong has made a few scattered attempts to make the urban areas more accessible to people with disabilities. Some buildings and walkways have ramps, some restaurants have special rest rooms and some subway stations have lifts for those who can't negotiate stairs or escalators.

The Hong Kong Transport Department puts out a free publication called *Guide to Public Transport Services in Hong Kong for Disabled Persons*, which gives a complete rundown of facilities on buses, subways, trains, ferries and so on. It also gives telephone numbers for the various transport operators and other services aimed at assisting disabled travellers. The booklet is available at some MTR subway stations and from the Transport Office (☎ 2829-5258), 41st floor, Immigration Tower, 7 Gloucester Rd, Wanchai.

The Hong Kong Federation of Handicapped People (☎ 2759-6412) may be able to offer some information to visitors with disabilities, though they are set up to deal mostly deal with local companies and individuals.

HONG KONG FOR CHILDREN

Hong Kong may not seem a great place to take the kids: after all, who wants to pound the pavement with their parents in search of bargains in Tsimshatsui? Fortunately there's a lot more to Hong Kong than shopping, including a number of places that should be fun for both kids and any adults they drag along.

Ocean Park, near Aberdeen on the south side of Hong Kong Island, has a number of hair-raising rides, as well as dolphin and whale shows and a really cool aquarium than includes a walkway through a shark tank. Adjacent to Ocean Park is Water World, a seasonal water amusement park with pools, giant slides and the like. On the other side of Ocean Park lies the Middle Kingdom, a somewhat cheesy re-creation of ancient China.

Back on the other side of Hong Kong, in Central, Hong Kong Park has a great aviary and, nearby, a fine playground. Opposite the park, across Garden Rd, the Hong Kong Zoological & Botanical Gardens has a surprisingly well stocked zoo and plenty of space for kids to run around and work off some nervous energy. Also nearby is the Peak Tram – the ride alone is fine entertainment, but once on top there are plenty of trails and walkways to explore. Kids also might get a kick out of the gaudy statues and figurines that cover the Tiger Balm Gardens, which are located near Causeway Bay.

Over on Kowloon, first stop is the Hong Kong Space Museum in Tsimshatsui, which has all sorts of spacecraft models, skyshows and Omnimax movies. The Hong Kong Science Museum in Tsimshatsui East is also worth a visit and has lots of hands-on exhibits to shore up flagging attention spans.

Kowloon Park has a complex of indoor/outdoor swimming pools that seems built just for kids. The park is also home to the Hong Kong Museum of History, which has life-size models of an old Chinese fishing boat and 19th century Hong Kong streets.

If you don't mind making the trip out to the New Territories, the Hong Kong Railway Museum has a pretty good collection of locomotives, carriages and other rolling stock on outdoor display, some of which can be entered. For information on this and all the above attractions, see the Things to See & Do chapter.

Of course Hong Kong also has plenty of beaches and country parks for more outdoor minded youngsters and adults. A ferry ride out to one of the Outlying Islands, with their beaches, hiking trails and fishing villages, can make for a fun day's outing. Refer to the Excursions chapter for details.

Finally if you want to let your kids plan the itinerary, there's the entertaining *Tiny Travellers in Hong Kong – The Children's Travel Guide to Hong Kong*, published by Precocious Press.

LIBRARIES

Hong Kong has a fairly extensive system of public libraries. The most useful for travellers is the main library (☎ 2922-2555) at City Hall, High Block, Central, just east

GLENN BEANLAND

Hong Kong Cultural Centre, Tsimshatsui

of the Star Ferry Terminal (Map 5). With a passport and a HK$130 deposit, foreign visitors can get a temporary library card allowing them to take out books. There is also a good reference library. The library is open Monday to Thursday from 10 am to 7 pm, Fridays from 10 am to 9 pm, Saturdays from 10 am to 5 pm and Sundays from 10 am to 1 pm. It is closed on public holidays. For locations of other libraries, call the City Hall main library: their English-speaking staff should be able to help you. The American Library (☎ 2529-9661), 1st floor, United Centre, 95 Queensway, Admiralty, has good research facilities and is open from 10 am to 6 pm.

Various cultural centres, including the Alliance Française, British Council and Goethe Institut, maintain libraries as well. See the Cultural Centres section below for telephone and address information.

CULTURAL CENTRES

Several countries have set up centres in Hong Kong to promote understanding of their culture and society. All of them offer language courses, and most show films or host seminars. A few also have libraries.

The largest of these centres is the British Council (☎ 2879-5138) located in the Easey Commercial Building, 255 Hennessy Rd, Wanchai (Map 6). Its main role is to provide English-language classes and provide community access to British expertise in science and technology, but it also sponsors cultural programmes and has a library which can be used for a small fee.

The Alliance Française (☎ 2527-7825), 2nd floor, 123 Hennessy Rd, Wanchai (Map 6), also has a library and offers a wide range of cultural activities. Dante Alighieri (☎ 2573-0343), located at 704 Trinity House, 165-171 Wanchai Rd, Wanchai, is the Italian cultural society and offers courses in language and other subjects.

If you're looking for German books, films or just the chance to meet a fellow German speaker, try the Goethe Institut (☎ 2802-0088) on the 14th floor, Hong Kong Arts Centre, 2 Harbour Rd, Wanchai (Map 6).

La Sociedad Hispanica de Hong Kong (☎ 2407-8800) offers classes in Spanish language and culture and organises Spanish meals, video evenings and so on. The address is GPO Box 11751, Hong Kong.

The Royal Asiatic Society (☎ 2551-0300), GPO Box 3864, is dedicated to helping its members or visitors learn more about the history and culture of Hong Kong. The RAS organises lectures and field trips, operates a lending library and puts out publications of its own.

DANGERS & ANNOYANCES

Hong Kong is a safe city to visit, but it does have some annoying aspects. These are mostly things that you must learn how to deal with, such as constant crowds or incessant noise. Even if you are a smoker you may find the air in Hong Kong's bars a bit rich for your lungs. A few restaurants have non-smoking areas, but the general rule in most places is 'join the cloud'.

Rudeness

Next to shopping, one of the things Hong Kong is best known for is the rudeness of its people. This is in part because most visitors deal with people in the tourist trade rather than typical Hong Kong residents. Travellers routinely run afoul of sullen salespeople who pretend you don't exist or pushy ones who hurl abuse if you don't buy the product you asked to look at.

Truth be told, rudeness doesn't end in the tourist ghettos. On the street you may find people elbowing you out of their way, refusing to step aside or blatantly jumping in front of you to steal the cab you just flagged down (they'll get it too). Hong Kong phone manners must rate among the worst on earth: it's common to have someone on the other end hang up on you in mid-query. One notable exception, however, is queuing up, which most people seem to respect.

This doesn't mean every visitor will encounter such appalling behaviour. Like anywhere, some people in Hong Kong are charming, generous and helpful. Staff in clothing stores such as Giordano or in large department stores can make shopping a pleasure. Ask a person directions, and he or she may end up showing you the whole way. It's just that Hong Kong seems to have more than its fair share of impolite individuals. Some can be mollified by a show of patience and politeness. Others are impossible. If you have the misfortune to encounter any of the latter, it's best just to laugh it off and leave them to their miserable lives.

Shopping Rip-Offs

Most Hong Kong shops are honest and give you what you pay for. However, in some areas, notably Tsimshatsui and Causeway Bay, there are shopkeepers who won't blink at selling you shoddy or used equipment at ridiculous prices. The most frequent offenders are the electronics and camera shops that don't put prices on any of their goods.

You may be able to avoid these types by looking for the logo of the Hong Kong Tourist Association, which is a red Chinese junk sailing against a white background. HKTA member shops are officially required to meet a series of ethical and operating standards. Unfortunately there are some member stores which are still pretty shady. Appliance chain stores such as Fortress or department stores are generally reliable.

For more details on potential rip-off tactics and how to avoid them, see the Shopping chapter.

Theft

Despite its obvious prosperity and low unemployment rate, Hong Kong is not free of riff-raff who choose crime as their occupation. While violent crime mostly stays within the local gangster community, theft is more common, and tourists are prime targets.

The biggest worry for travellers is probably pickpockets, who favour crowded buses, subways, ferries and shopping districts. The problem has been reduced by undercover police who specialise in catching pickpockets, but it's still a problem, so keep your cash secured in a moneybelt or inside zippered pockets.

Bag-snatchers also do well in Hong Kong. A few unfortunate souls have had their luggage nicked this way right in the airport when they wandered off for a minute to use the toilets or change money. The same principle applies in restaurants and pubs – if your bag doesn't accompany you to the toilet, don't expect to find it when you return.

If you're staying in budget accommodation, keep a close eye on your belongings, as theft occurs in these places too. Sadly, the culprit could well be a fellow traveller, some of whom arrive in Hong Kong totally broke with no prospects for employment, nor any self-respect.

Hong Kong continues to fight a persistent drug abuse problem. It is estimated that there are more than 40,000 drug addicts in the territory, with heroin as the drug of choice. Again for travellers this means being careful with your valuables. It is generally safe to walk around at night, but it's best to stick to well-lit areas. Tourist districts like Tsimshatsui are heavily patrolled by the police and there is little danger of violent crime, though theft can occur anywhere.

If you get robbed or pickpocketed, you can obtain a loss report for insurance purposes at the Central District Police Station, 10 Hollywood Rd (at Pottinger St) in Central (Map 4). There are always English-speaking staff here.

LEGAL MATTERS

Unless you do something stupid like steal from a fellow traveller, it's pretty hard to run afoul of the law in Hong Kong. Two exceptions are drug use and drunk driving. Penalties for illegal drug use are severe, ranging from deportation to long jail terms. While other countries draw a line between marijuana and more addictive substances like cocaine and heroin, Hong Kong is equally serious about all of them. Police sometimes do spot checks of bars in the Lan Kwai Fong drinking area in

Central, looking for people either using or peddling marijuana, hashish or heroin. Hong Kong's finest also sometimes pay a visit to passengers debarking the ferry at Lamma Island, home to the territory's erstwhile expat hippy community.

Drunk driving has long been overlooked in Hong Kong, but police are starting to crack down. Patrol cars are being equipped with breathalysers and penalties stiffened. The campaign is taking some time to get off the ground: one of the first problems faced by the police official in charge of it was trying to convince police station canteens to stop stocking beer! In any case, Hong Kong's outstanding public transportation system means there is no real excuse to drink and drive.

If you run into legal trouble and don't have the funds to hire a lawyer, the Legal Aid Department provides both residents and non-residents with representation, subject to a means and merits test.

BUSINESS HOURS

Office hours are Monday through Friday from 9 am to 5 or 6 pm, and on Saturday from 9 am to noon. Lunch hour is from 1 to 2 pm and many offices simply shut down and lock the door at this time. Banks are open Monday through Friday from 9 am to 4.30 pm and do not close for lunch – on Saturday they are open from 9 am to 12.30 pm.

Many Hong Kong companies still run on a 5½ day working week, but this concept is beginning to fall out of favour. Some companies use the promise of a five day week in their help wanted ads to lure new employees.

Stores and restaurants that cater to the tourist trade keep longer hours, but almost nothing opens before 9 am. Even tourist-related businesses shut down by 9 or 10 pm, and many will close for major holidays, especially Chinese New Year.

Restaurants generally open from 11.30 am to 2.30 pm for lunch and 6 to 11 pm for dinner. Of course there are many exceptions to this rule. Some pubs keep the kitchen open until 1 am and Chinese noodle shops often run from early in the morning until the wee hours. Bars generally open at noon or 6 pm and close anywhere between 2 to 6 am.

PUBLIC HOLIDAYS

Western and Chinese culture combine to create an interesting mix of holidays. Trying to determine the exact date of the Chinese holidays is a bit tricky since there are

HKTA

Central nightscape – brilliantly lit up for Chinese New Year

two calendars in use in Hong Kong – the Gregorian solar calendar and the Chinese lunar calendar. As the two calendars do not correspond exactly, an extra month is added to the lunar calendar once every 30 months. The result is that the Lunar New Year, the most important Chinese holiday, can fall anywhere between 21 January and 28 February on the Gregorian calendar.

Lunar New Year, more widely referred to as Chinese New Year, can be a bad time to fly in or out of Hong Kong, as most flights are booked solid. For four days the border with China becomes a riot zone as millions of Hong Kongers flock to their relatives on the mainland. On the other hand, Hong Kong basically shuts down for three days during this holiday, so it should be easy to find a hotel room. Although shops, supermarkets and restaurants used to shut for three days to a week, now many only take one day off, making Chinese New Year a more practical time to visit Hong Kong.

Though not as bad as Chinese New Year, Ching Ming (Tomb-Sweeping Day) is another public holiday which many people turn into a three to four day vacation. Public transport is extremely crowded and the border crossing into China once again becomes a nightmare. Christmas and Easter are the other big vacation times for locals, so again booking flights can be a bit difficult.

New Year – the first weekday in January
Chinese New Year – three days; in late January or February
Easter – three days; from Good Friday through Easter Sunday
Ching Ming (Tomb-Sweeping Day) Festival – one day; usually
    during the first week in April

Tuen Ng (Dragon Boat) Festival – one day; in June

Queen's Birthday – held on a Saturday in June; following Monday is also a public holiday

Liberation Day – the last Monday in August commemorates the liberation of Hong Kong from Japan after WWII; preceding Saturday is also a public holiday

Mid-Autumn (Moon) Festival – one day; in September

Chung Yeung Festival – one day; in October

Christmas & Boxing Day – 25 & 26 December

FESTIVALS

Many Chinese festivals go back hundreds or thousands of years, their true origins often lost in the mists of time. The reasons for each festival vary and you will generally find there are a couple of tales to choose from. The HKTA's free leaflet *Chinese Festivals: Dates* will tell you the exact dates that festivals are celebrated that year. There are a good number of them between January and October, so if you visit during that time you stand a good chance of catching one.

January-June

Chinese New Year This festival is a family one, with little for the visitor to see except a fireworks display on New Year's Eve. To start the New Year properly can determine one's fortune for the entire year. Therefore, houses are cleaned, debts paid off and feuds, no matter how bitter, are ended – even if it's only for the day.

Yuen Siu (Lantern Festival) In some ways this festival is more interesting than the Chinese New Year. At the end of the New Year celebrations, lanterns in traditional designs are lit in homes, restaurants and temples. Out in the residential areas, you'll see people carrying lanterns through the streets.

Ching Ming (Tomb-Sweeping Day) Ching Ming is a time for visiting graves, traditionally to ask ancestral spirits if they are satisfied with their descendants. Graves are cleaned and food and wine left for the spirits, while incense and paper money are burned for the dead.

Tin Hau Festival This is one of Hong Kong's most colourful occasions as Tin Hau, patroness of fishing people, is one of the territory's most popular goddesses. Junks on the water are decorated with flags and sail in long rows to Tin Hau's temples to pray for clear skies and good catches.

Cheung Chau Bun Festival One of Hong Kong's most lively occasions, this Taoist festival on the island of Cheung Chau takes its name from its huge bun towers – bamboo scaffolding covered with edible buns. If you go to Cheung Chau a week or so before the festival you'll see these huge bamboo towers being built in the courtyard of the Pak Tai Temple. In previous times, hundreds of people would

---

Important Festival Dates to the Year 2000

Chinese New Year – the first day of the first moon. Dates: 7 February 1997; 28 January 1998; 16 February 1999; 5 February 2000.

Yuen Sin (Lantern Festival) – the 15th day of the first moon. Dates: 21 February 1997; 11 February 1998; 2 March 1999; 19 February 2000.

Tin Hau Festival – the 23rd day of the third moon. Dates: 29 April 1997; 19 April 1998; 8 May 1999; 27 April 2000.

Cheung Chau Bun Festival – traditionally on the sixth day of the fourth moon, in May. Precise dates are decided by village elders on the island.

Birthday of Lord Buddha – the eighth day of the fourth moon. Dates: 14 May 1997; 3 May 1998; 22 May 1999; 11 May 2000.

Tuen Ng (Dragon Boat) Festival – the fifth day of the fifth moon. Dates: 9 June 1997; 28 June 1998; 18 June 1999; 6 June 2000.

Mid-Autumn (Moon) Festival – the 15th day of the eighth moon. Dates: 16 September 1997; 5 October 1998; 24 September 1999; 12 September 2000. ∎

---

scramble up the bun towers to fetch one of the holy buns for good luck. The third day of the festival (a Sunday) is the most interesting due to a procession with floats, stilt walkers and people dressed as legendary characters. Most fascinating are the 'floating children' who are carried through the streets on poles, as if floating over the crowd. Accommodation in Cheung Chau is heavily booked at this time and the ferries out there are always packed. The bun festival is held over four days in May.

Birthday of Lord Buddha Also known as the Bathing of Lord Buddha, this festival is rather more sedate than Taoist holidays. The Buddha's statue is taken from monasteries and temples and ceremoniously bathed in water scented with sandalwood and herbs. Later the water is drunk by the faithful, who believe it has great curative powers.

Tuen Ng (Dragon Boat) Festival This one is a lot of fun despite the fact that it commemorates the sad tale of Chu Yuan, a 3rd century BC poet-statesman who hurled himself into a river in Hunan Province to protest against the corrupt government. Onlookers raced to the scene in their boats to save him but were too late. People throw dumplings into the water to keep the hungry fish away from his body.

July-December

Birthday of Lu Pan, Master Builder A master architect, magician, engineer, inventor and designer, Lu Pan is worshipped by anyone connected with the building trade. The celebration occurs around mid to late July.

Ghost Month On the first day of the seventh moon (late August or early September), the gates of hell are opened and 'hungry ghosts' – the spirits of those who were unloved, forgotten by family or suffered a violent death – are free for two weeks to walk the earth. On the 14th day, called the Yue Lan Festival, hungry ghosts receive offerings of food from the living before returning down below. Paper cars, paper houses and paper money are burnt, and these goodies become the property of the ghosts.

Mid-Autumn (Moon) Festival This festival recalls an uprising against the Mongols in the 14th century when plans for the revolution were passed around in cakes. Moon cakes are still eaten and there are many varieties. Everyone heads for the hilltops, where they light special lanterns and watch the moon rise. For young couples, it's a romantic holiday – a time to be together and gaze at the moon.

Cheung Yeung Festival This low-key holiday commemorates the story of an Eastern Han Dynasty man who, on the advice of a soothsayer, took his family away to a high place to avoid a pending disaster. The man returned a day later to find every living thing in his village had been destroyed. Many people head to the high spots again to remember.

WORK

Legally speaking, there are only three groups of foreigners who do not need employment visas for Hong Kong: British citizens, British passport holders or registered British subjects. Such people are granted a 12-month stay on arrival, after which extensions are merely a formality.

Foreign nationals (including Australians, Americans and Canadians) must get an employment visa from the Hong Kong Immigration Department before arrival. This is not easy to arrange – you need a job skill which cannot easily be performed by a local, and your employer must be willing to sponsor you. For more details see the Documents section earlier in this chapter.

Under-the-table employment is possible to obtain, but there are stiff penalties for employers who hire foreigners illegally. These rules are vigorously enforced against employers who hire labourers from China, because of the justified fear of a tidal wave of prospective illegal immigrants from across the border. Despite the rules, plenty of westerners do find temporary illegal work in Hong Kong, but there are considerable risks.

Finding a Job

Many travellers drop into Hong Kong looking for short-term work to top up cash reserves before heading off to other destinations in Asia. Some wind up staying much longer than originally anticipated. Success in finding work depends largely on what skills you have. Those with professional backgrounds in such fields as engineering, computer programming and finance will have less trouble. If you don't have a career background, finding work is possible though more difficult, and high wages may elude you.

One of the ironies of the 1997 takeover is the effect that it's having on the job market. Many skilled and talented Chinese people are fleeing Hong Kong. Furthermore, as Mandarin Chinese gains in popularity in Hong Kong, the level of spoken English is declining rapidly. Those who could speak good English have already emigrated or soon will. All this is creating job opportunities for foreigners – businesses needing English-speaking staff are sometimes unable to find local Chinese with the necessary linguistic or technical skills.

For professional jobs, registering with Hong Kong personnel agencies or headhunters may work, and one can always check classified ads in the local newspapers. The Sunday edition of the *South China Morning Post* is particularly helpful.

For more temporary work the best course is probably door-to-door and asking. A good place to start looking is at bars and western restaurants in Lan Kwai Fong, Wanchai and Tsimshatsui. Besides finding opportunities for waitering and bar work, people in gwailo bars and restaurants may have tips on English-teaching opportunities, modelling jobs, secretarial work and so on. As in most other places, who you know can count for more than what you know.

Living expenses in Hong Kong are quite high, especially rent, so be sure to reach an agreement on salary before you begin any job. In general, unskilled foreign labourers can negotiate salaries from HK$50 to HK$80 per hour. Your nationality makes a difference – unfair as it might seem, Filipinos and Thais earn considerably less than westerners for doing the same work.

It's getting harder to find work teaching English, as more and more schools now require certification in teaching English as a second language. You may still be able to find work teaching conversational English. If you're fluent in one or more foreign languages then you might get work as a translator. Modelling is another possibility for both men and women. You can find such companies listed in the *Commercial/Industrial Guide*, but again, contacts are vital. Occasionally westerners can find work standing around as extras in Hong Kong movies (long hours and little pay). Some people even try busking, but this does not seem to be highly lucrative.

Getting There & Away

AIR

To/From USA & Canada

Direct flights to Hong Kong from the west coast take around 13 hours non-stop. Flying from the east coast will require at least one stopover, which usually stretches the flight to a mind-numbing 20 hours. Jet lag hits hard after these flights, what with a time difference of between 12 and 15 hours and a date change after crossing the international date line.

Fares vary dramatically depending on the season. Seven-day advance-purchase return fares from the west coast can be as low as US$600 in the winter, and as high as US$1100 in the high-season summer and autumn months. One-way tickets are often priced at 60% to 75% of the return fare: not good value. Tickets are usually valid for one year from the date of issue, though some are only good for six months.

If you're heading to Hong Kong during the low season, carriers like Asiana, Korean Air or China Airlines can get you there from San Francisco or Los Angeles for around US$640, not including tax. Canadian Airlines International also offers a similarly priced flight via Vancouver. Most of these flights make a stop in the carrier's home country: Asiana and Korean Air take you through Seoul, China Airlines through Taipei. This is not always such a bad thing, as it's usually easy to arrange a stopover for little or no extra charge. Though it's not always the cheapest choice within Asia, Singapore Airlines sometimes offers competitively priced fares from San Francisco.

Flights from New York start at around US$800 return during the low season, but you'll be lucky to get anything below US$1050 during peak travel times. Again, Asiana, Korean Air or China Airlines are among the cheapest, though you will be facing two stops: the first is usually Anchorage, the second Seoul or Taipei. United Airlines and Northwest Airlines offer one-stop flights via Tokyo, though travel times often work out the same. Low season prices for these flights are around US$1000.

Fares from other parts of the USA depend on whether you are flying from a major domestic airport. Flying from the large hubs of Atlanta, Chicago or Denver shouldn't be too much more than from New York. But if you're coming from somewhere off the major air routes, be prepared to pay for it.

For current low fares, check the Sunday travel sections of newspapers like the *New York Times* and the *Los Angeles Times*. Council Travel and STA Travel are two travel agencies specialising in low-cost deals. Both have branches across the USA and Canada. On the west coast, a good travel agent to try is Overseas Tours (☎ (800) 222-5292), 475 El Camino Real, Room 206, Millbrae, CA 94030. A good place for low-cost fares from the east coast is Amerasia Travel & Tours (☎ (212) 227-9224), Suite 401, 198 Canal St, New York, NY, 10013. Both seem to be quite reliable, and can arrange mail-order purchases using a credit card.

Fares from Canada are similar to those from the USA. Fares from Vancouver can often match those of San Francisco, though eastern destinations such as Toronto or Montreal tend to cost more than flying to New York. Travel Cuts offers cheap return and one-way fares to Hong Kong, and has offices in a number of Canadian cities including Vancouver, Edmonton, Toronto and Ottawa.

If you're thinking of heading to the USA or Canada from Hong Kong, return fares start at around HK$5000 to the west coast and HK$7500 to New York. Prices may be lower during October-November and May-June. One-way flights are generally priced at 55% to 60% of return airfares.

To/From Europe

Flight times between Europe and Hong Kong vary widely depending on the route taken. The most common and direct route is via the Middle East. The advent of the 747-400 and Airbus 340 has resulted in more non-stop flights to Hong Kong from Amsterdam, Frankfurt, London and Paris. However, many flights make at least one stop, often in Dubai or Bangkok. Flight times range anywhere from 14 hours for direct flights from London to 20 hours or more for cut-rate excursions on cash-hungry East European or Middle Eastern carriers.

Return economy fares average around UK£600, and are valid for 14 days to six months. Occasionally carriers such as Virgin Atlantic or Cathay Pacific offer discount fares of UK£550 or less. At the time of writing Air France had a six month return ticket for UK£440, going via Paris, so it pays to ask around. Other carriers that often

NICKO GONCHAROFF

Skating across rooftops to Kai Tak airport

have good deals from London or Manchester are British Airways, Gulf Air, Malaysian Airline System and Thai Airways. These airlines often do not charge extra if passengers want to stopover en route, and some offer stopover packages which encourage it. Just remember that in general, the cheaper the airfare the more inconvenient (or interesting) the route.

London is still one of the best places in Europe to find discount airfares. STA Travel (☎ (0171) 361-6262) at 74 Old Brompton Rd, London SW7, Trailfinders (☎ (0171) 938-3444) at 46 Earls Court Rd, London W8 7RG, and Travel Bug (☎ (0171) 835-2000, (0161) 721-4000) all offer good prices on return flights to Hong Kong and can also put together interesting Round-the-World (RTW) routes that include Hong Kong. The London entertainment weekly *Time Out* and the various giveaway papers carry ads for discount travel agents, but beware of shady outfits and prices that seem too good to be true: they often are just that. Make sure you get the tickets before you hand over the cash.

In continental Europe, Amsterdam, Brussels and Antwerp are good places for buying discount air tickets. The cheapest prices are usually on a par with those in London.

From Hong Kong, return flights to London can be as low as HK$6000, though this usually includes at least one stop. Virgin Atlantic and British Airways fares start at around HK$7500 for a six month return, though prices are higher during the peak travel times of summer and Christmas. One-way flights generally cost half that of return tickets.

To/From Australasia

Depending on where in Australia you leave from, flights to Hong Kong take between 8 and 12 hours. Although this is still a fairly long flight, there is only a two hour time change between Sydney and Hong Kong, so jet lag is not a worry.

The published fares on Qantas and Cathay Pacific usually cost A$1299 but are often discounted to around A$1200. Fares on Ansett start around A$1000 to A$1100. Other carriers, including Garuda and Philippine Airlines, may offer cheaper flights which include free stopovers in Bali and Manila for A$1050 and A$990 respectively. You can also usually get free stopovers in either Singapore, Bangkok or Kuala Lumpur if you fly with Singapore Airlines, Thai Airways or Malaysian Airline System for around A$1260 to A$1300.

The weekend travel sections of papers like the Melbourne *Age* or the *Sydney Morning Herald* are good sources of travel information. STA Travel and the Flight Centre are good places to look for discount tickets. Both have offices all over Australia: check your local phone book.

Auckland is served mainly by Air New Zealand and Cathay Pacific. Fares are similar to those for Australia, and range between NZ$1300 to NZ$1600.

If you've a mind to escape Hong Kong's urban frenzy for Australia's white beaches, a two month return ticket will cost you HK$6200 on Malaysian Airline System (low season) and HK$8550 on Ansett Airlines. Ninety day return fares to Auckland are HK$6200 on Malaysian and HK$9300 for a 30 day return on Cathay Pacific. One-way tickets are priced at around 75% of the return airfare.

To/From Asia

Hong Kong is the air transport hub linking the northern and southern parts of Asia, which makes it a great access point for almost anywhere in the region. On routes that see heavy competition, such as Hong Kong-Bangkok and Hong Kong-Taipei it's easier to find good prices. However travel to and from Tokyo and Singapore remains expensive despite an increase in the number of carriers serving both cities. Philippine Airlines usually offers the cheapest flights within Asia, as long as you don't mind flying via Manila.

China There are no bargain fares into China. The Chinese government sets the prices, and all the domestic airlines toe the line, as does Dragonair, a joint-venture airline between Cathay Pacific and the PRC's CAAC with an extensive network in China. Flights can be difficult to book due to the enormous volume of business travellers and Asian tourists, so plan ahead if possible. Some sample one year return fares are: Beijing HK$4120, Chengdu HK$4230, Kunming HK$2840 and Shanghai HK$2970. One-way fares are exactly half the return price.

Japan There is no shortage of flights to and from Japan, just a lack of affordable ones. The cheapest flights start at around ¥50,000 for a round-trip on United Airlines or Northwest Airlines. Japan Airlines and All Nippon Airways usually charge ¥60,000 to ¥75,000. Prices out of Hong Kong are lower, but only marginally so. The flight from Tokyo to Hong Kong takes around five hours.

Singapore The three hour flight to Singapore costs anywhere from HK$2220 for a 90 day return on Garuda Indonesia (three flights weekly) to HK$2900 for a 30 day return on United Airlines (daily flights). Prices out of Singapore are about the same.

South Korea Korea's Asiana Airlines usually has the cheapest flights between Hong Kong and Seoul at around HK$2800 for a 14 day return. Cathay Pacific is considerably more expensive at HK$3600 for a 17 day return ticket. Ticket prices out of Seoul are usually higher than from Hong Kong. It's approximately five hours flying time between Hong Kong and Seoul.

Taiwan There are something like 15 flights a day between Taiwan and Hong Kong, with many of the seats taken by Taiwanese businessmen shuttling to and from China. This frequency will definitely drop off if direct flights between China and Taiwan open up. The cheapest way to get to Taipei from Hong Kong is on Garuda Indonesia, which offers a 21 day return for HK$1520. However, there are only a few flights per week, and some restrictions apply. The convenience of daily flights will cost you around HK$2400 on either Cathay Pacific or China Airlines. Similar flights out of Taipei cost around NT$10,000, though there are cheaper deals available. Flying time is about 1½ hours.

Thailand Hong Kong-Bangkok offers some of the best deals in Asia. Most carriers offer 21 day return tickets for HK$2000 to HK$2200, which is not bad considering the flight takes three hours, twice as far as Hong Kong-Taipei. Prices out of Bangkok are about the same.

Other Asian Centres There are regular flights between Hong Kong and other major Asian cities including Jakarta, Kuala Lumpur, Manila, New Delhi and Ho Chi Minh City (Saigon).

To/From Other Regions

There are also flights between Hong Kong and Russia (Moscow, HK$8500 return), the Middle East (Dubai, HK$7500), Africa (Johannesburg, HK$9900 return) and South America (Rio de Janeiro, HK$14,000 return).

Round-the-World Tickets

Round-the-World fares are put together by two or more airlines and allow you to make a circuit of the world using their combined routes. A typical RTW ticket is valid for one year, allows unlimited stopovers along the way and costs about UK£1200, A$2300 or US$2000. An example, including Hong Kong, would be a British Airways/United Airlines combination flying London-New York-San Francisco-Hong Kong-Bangkok-London. A South Pacific version might take you London-New York-Los Angeles-Tahiti-Sydney-Hong Kong-London. There are many options involving different combinations of airlines and routes. Generally, routes which stay north of the equator are usually a little cheaper than routes that include destinations like Australia or South America. Most packages require you to keep moving in the same direction.

Enterprising travel agents put together their own RTW fares at much lower prices than the joint airline deals but, of course, the cheapest fares will involve unpopular airlines and less popular routes.

Airline Offices

Following is a list of major airline offices in Hong Kong. Where applicable, reservation and reconfirmation telephone numbers (Res) are followed by flight information numbers (Info).

Aeroflot
New Henry House, 10 Ice House St, Central (☎ Res 2845-4232; Info 2769-8111)

Air Canada
New Henry House, 10 Ice House St, Central (☎ 2522-1001)

Air France
21st floor, Alexandra
House, 7 Des Voeux Rd
Central, Central (☎ Res
2524-8145; Info 2769-6662)

Air India
42nd floor, Gloucester
Tower, 11 Pedder St,
Central (☎ Res 2522-1176;
Info 2769-6558)

Air New Zealand
1601 Fairmont House, 8
Cotton Tree Dr, Central
(☎ Res 2524-9041;
Info 2769-6046)

Alitalia
Room 2101, Hutchison
House, 10 Harcourt Rd,
Central (☎ Res 2543-6998;
Info 2769-6448)

All Nippon Airways
Room 2512, Pacific Place
Two, 88 Queensway, Admi-
ralty (☎ Res 2810-7100;
Info 2769-8609)

American Airlines
Room 1738, Swire House, 9
Connaught Rd, Central
(☎ 2826-9269)

Asiana Airlines
34th floor, Gloucester
Tower, 11 Pedder St,
Central (☎ Res 2523-8585;
Info 2769-7782)

British Airways
30th floor, Alexandra House,
7 Des Voeux Rd Central,
Central (☎ Res 2868-0303;
Info 2868-0768) Room 112,
Royal Garden Hotel, 69
Mody Rd, Tsimshatsui East
(☎ 2368-9255)

**CAAC (Civil Aviation
Administration of China)**
Ground floor, 17 Queen's
Rd, Central (☎ 2840-1199)
Ground floor, Mirador
Mansion, 54-64B Nathan Rd,
Tsimshatsui (☎ 2739-0022)

**Canadian Airlines Interna-
tional**
Room 1702, Swire House, 9
Connaught Rd, Central
(☎ Res 2868-3123;
Info 2769-7113)

Cathay Pacific Airways
Ground floor, Swire House,
9 Connaught Rd, Central
11th floor, Room 1126,
Ocean Centre, Tsimshatsui
Shop 109, 1st floor, Royal
Garden Hotel, 69 Mody Rd,
Tsimshatsui East (☎ Res
2747-1888; Info 2747-1234)

China Airlines (Taiwan)
Ground floor, St George's
Building, 2 Ice House St,
Central
G5-6 Tsimshatsui Centre,
Tsimshatsui East (☎ Res
2868-2299; Info 2769-8361)

Dragonair
22nd floor, Devon House,
Tai Koo Place, Quarry Bay
12th floor, Tower 6, China
Hong Kong City, 33 Canton
Rd, Tsimshatsui (☎ Res
2590-1188; Info 2769-7728)

Garuda Indonesia
2nd floor, Sing Pao Centre,
8 Queen's Rd, Central
(☎ Res 2840-0000;
Info 2769-6689)

Japan Air Lines
20th floor, Gloucester
Tower, 11 Pedder St, Central
Harbour View Holiday Inn,
Mody Rd, Tsimshatsui East
(☎ Res 2523-0081;
Info 2769-6524)

KLM Royal Dutch Airlines
22nd floor, World Trade
Centre, 280 Gloucester Rd,
Causeway Bay
(☎ 2808-2111)

Korean Air
Ground floor, St George's
Building, 2 Ice House St,
Central

11th floor, South Seas Centre, Tower II, 75 Mody Rd, Tsimshatsui East G12-15 Tsimshatsui Centre, Salisbury Rd, Tsimshatsui East (☎ Res 2368-6221; Info 2769-7511)

Lufthansa
6th floor, Landmark East, 12 Ice House St, Central (☎ Res 2868-2313; Info 2769-6560)

Malaysian Airline System
Room 1306, Prince's Building, 9-25 Chater Rd, Central (☎ Res 2521-8181; Info 2769-7967)

Northwest Airlines
29th floor, Alexandra House, 7 Des Voeux Rd Central, Central (☎ Res & Info 2810-4288)

Philippine Airlines
Room 6, Ground floor, East Ocean Centre, 98 Granville Rd, Tsimshatsui East (☎ Res 2369-4521; Info 2769-6253)

Qantas
Room 1416, Swire House, 9 Connaught Rd, Central (☎ Res 2842-1438; Info 2842-1400)

Scandinavian Airlines System
Room 1401, Harcourt House, 39 Gloucester Rd, Wanchai (☎ Res 2865-1370; Info 2769-8864)

Singapore Airlines
17th floor, United Centre, 95 Queensway, Admiralty (☎ Res 2520-2233; Info 2769-6387)

Swissair
8th floor, Tower II, Admiralty Centre, 18 Harcourt Rd, Admiralty (☎ Res 2529-3670; Info 2769-6031)

Thai Airways International
24th floor, United Centre, 95 Queensway, Admiralty Shop 124, 1st floor, World Wide Plaza, Des Voeux Road & Pedder St, Central Shop 105-6, Omni, The Hong Kong Hotel, 3 Canton Rd, Tsimshatsui (☎ Res 2529-5601; Info 2769-6038)

United Airlines
29th floor, Gloucester Tower, 11 Pedder St, Central Ground floor, Empire Centre, Mody Rd, Tsimshatsui East (☎ Res 2810-4888; Info 2769-7279)

Vietnam Airlines
Room 1206, Peregrine Tower, Lippo Centre, 89 Queensway, Admiralty (☎ Res 2810-6680; Info 2747-1234 c/o Cathay Pacific)

Virgin Atlantic Airways
41st floor, Lippo Tower, Lippo Centre, 89 Queensway, Admiralty (☎ 2532-6060)

Arriving in Hong Kong

Currently all flights touch down and take off at Kai Tak airport, which sits smack in the middle of urban Hong Kong. This location makes for one of the most exciting (or nerve-wracking) final approaches of any major airport on earth. Unless wind direction dictates otherwise, planes fly in over Kowloon, weaving their way through endless apartment blocks before making a sharp bank to the right to align with the runway. If you look carefully out the window you may be able to catch somebody hanging laundry out their window, at eye-level!

Kai Tak's single runway often qualifies as the world's busiest, with aircraft movements separated by only several minutes during peak times of the day. This can lead to long lines at immigration and customs. However, relief should arrive by 1998 when Hong Kong's mega-project, the Chek Lap Kok airport (built almost wholly on landfill just north of Lantau Island), is scheduled to open. Chek Lap Kok should be pleasant enough to use. A new subway line is being built to link it with western Kowloon and Central, as well as to the existing MTR network. Travel time will be around 45 minutes, compared with just 20 to 30 minutes for Kai Tak. But the new airport's expanded facilities may cut down waiting times at immigration, baggage claim and for departing passengers, check-in.

Lines can get long at Kai Tak but immigration officials are generally quick and efficient. Baggage claim is generally speedy, though occasionally waiting times can drag when a horde of 747s descends on the airport at once. But overall it's not uncommon to be out the front doors of Kai Tak within 30 minutes of touchdown.

After passing through customs, keep an eye out for the Hong Kong Tourist Association's information centre, located in the Buffer Hall, just before you exit into the arrival hall. The staff there can supply you with a map and heaps of information on transportation, dining, sights and a host of other subjects. The office is open from 8 am to 10.30 pm daily. On either side of the information centre are hotel booking offices run by the Hong Kong Hotels Association. If you're looking for mid-range or top-end hotel accomodation, this place can book you rooms at a cheaper rate than if you just walked in. The office does not handle hostels, guesthouses or other budget accomodation.

If you need money, try and change as little as possible at the airport moneychangers: their rates are the worst in town. If you have an ATM card you might want to try the ATM machines in the arrival hall, which support global networks including Plus System and Cirrus, and dispense Hong Kong dollars.

For information on getting from the airport into town, see the following Getting Around chapter.

Leaving Hong Kong

If you want to keep your return seat, make sure to reconfirm your onward or return ticket while in Hong Kong at least 72 hours before your flight. If you don't there's a good chance you'll get bumped from your flight. The heavy volume of traffic through Hong Kong means there's almost always someone else who wants your seat.

If you are flying either Cathay Pacific or United Airlines you can take advantage of their city check-in services, which allow you to check your bags and receive your boarding pass in advance. This is also a good way to get that window or aisle seat you've been hoping for. Cathay Pacific allows you to check-in either the day before or the same day if it's at least three hours before departure. On Hong Kong Island their city check-in is at the Pacific Place Mall in Queensway, Admiralty, and at China Hong Kong City in Tsimshatsui. United Airlines accepts city check-in at their offices in Central and at Empire City in Tsimshatsui East. It's best to call ahead and check.

Kai Tak airport levies a departure tax of HK$50 per person, so be sure to have at least this much Hong Kong currency on hand when you check-in. Charges for overweight checked baggage are also high, so check with your carrier about weight limits before you go on a serious shopping spree.

Flight boardings and departures are not announced in Kai Tak, so if you find yourself waiting in the departure hall, keep an eye on your boarding gate to make sure they're not leaving without you.

TRAIN

To/From China

The only way in and out of Hong Kong by land is through China. The most convenient mode of land transport is the Kowloon-Guangzhou express train, which covers the 182 km route in 2½ hours. There is also a high-speed train that does the trip in just two hours.

From Hong Kong you catch the train at the Kowloon-Canton Railway (KCR) terminus in Hunghom, Kowloon (Map 16). Immigration formalities are completed before boarding. To get to the station from Tsimshatsui by public transport, take the 5C bus from the Star Ferry Terminal, the 8A bus from nearby on Salisbury Rd or the No 8 green minibus from Middle Rd.

Timetables change, but current departure times from Hong Kong are 7.50 am, 9.50 am (high-speed train), 12.23 pm and 2.22 pm. Trains from Guangzhou to Hong Kong leave at 8.15 am, 10.10 am, 4.50 pm (high-speed train) and 6.15 pm. At Guangzhou railway station, trains leave from the east end of the terminal, not from the main station building.

In Hong Kong, tickets can be booked up to seven days in advance at China Travel Service (CTS – the PRC's government-owned travel agency; see below) or the KCR terminus in Hunghom. Some travel agents can handle these bookings as well. One-way tickets for ordinary express trains are HK$215. High-speed trains cost HK$235 for standard class and HK$265 for 1st class. Prices increase across the board by HK$40 during 'high-season' (meaning whenever Guangzhou hosts a major trade fair or during public holidays). CTS does not accept credit cards, so bring cash or go through a travel agent.

A cheaper but less convenient option is to take the KCR commuter railway to the station at Lo Wu, cross through immigration into the Chinese border city of Shenzhen and catch a local train to Guangzhou. There are around 20 trains to and from Guangzhou daily, and the ride takes between 2½ to three hours. Hard seats (the Chinese equivalent of 2nd class) cost anywhere from HK$92 to HK$112 depending on the type of train. Soft seats (1st class) cost between HK$103 to HK$118. Prices for locals and Hong Kong citizens are cheaper, but under China's delightful dual pricing system, foreigners and overseas Chinese pay more. (Note: to take the KCR to Lo Wu you need a special ticket – a 'common stored value' ticket will not work. For more details, see the Getting Around chapter and the railways map – Map 15.)

If you're thinking of heading into China from Hong Kong, CTS can now help book onward train connections from Guangzhou. This is worth looking into, as buying a ticket in Guangzhou (for say, Beijing or Chengdu) can be a nightmare of long lines, pickpockets and frustration. Unfortunately they can't help with trains not originating out of Guangzhou.

CTS offices in Hong Kong are open 9 am to 5 pm Monday through Friday and 9 am to 1 pm Saturday. Only the Tsimshatsui and Mongkok offices are open 9 am to 1 pm Sunday. Locations include:

Head Office – 2nd floor, 78 Connaught Rd, Central (☎ 2853-3888)

Central – Mezzanine, China Travel Building, 77 Queen's Rd (☎ 2521-7163)

Wanchai – ground floor, Southorn Centre, 138 Hennessy Rd (☎ 2832-3865)

North Point – ground floor, 196-202 Java Rd (☎ 2565-8610)

Tsimshatsui – 1st floor, Alpha House, 27-33 Nathan Rd (☎ 2315-7188)

Mongkok – 2nd floor, 62-72 Sai Yee St (☎ 2789-5970)

To/From Europe

From Europe, you can reach Hong Kong by rail, though most travellers following this route also tour China. Don't take this rail journey just to save money – a direct flight from Europe to Hong Kong works out to be about the same price or less. The idea is to get a glimpse of Russia, Mongolia and China along the way.

It's a long haul. The most commonly taken routes are from Western Europe to Moscow, then on to Beijing via the Trans-Manchurian or Trans-Mongolian Railway. From Beijing there are trains to Guangzhou, and from there express trains to Hong Kong. The minimum time needed for this journey (one way) is 10 days, though most travellers spend some time in China.

In Hong Kong, tickets for the Beijing to Moscow journey can be booked at Moonsky Star (☎ 2723-1376), 4th floor, E-Block, Flat 6E, Chungking Mansions, Tsimshatsui. Staff there can also help with visas and tailor your ticket to include stops en route. Although Moonsky has an office in Beijing, arranging trips through China and Russia can be very difficult, so make allowances if the staff have trouble getting you exactly what you want. You can also organise tickets and visas in Hong Kong through Wallem Travel (☎ 2528-6514), 46th floor, Hopewell Centre, 183 Queen's Rd East, Wanchai. It can be hard to book this trip during the summer peak season. Off season shouldn't be a problem, but plan as far ahead as possible.

A popular book about the journey is the *Trans-Siberian Handbook* by Bryn Thomas (Trailblazer Publications, distributed through Roger Lascelles in the UK).

China Visas

These can be arranged by CTS and most travel agents. If you want to save a little money and don't mind spending the time to do it yourself, you can go the the Visa Office of the People's Republic of China (☎ 2827-9569), 5th floor, Lower Block, 26 Harbour Rd, Wanchai (Map 6). At the time of writing, visas processed in two days cost HK$130, in a single day HK$260. US passport holders are charged HK$130 extra, China's response to an 1994 increase in US visa fees. You must supply two photos, which can be taken at the visa office for HK$35.

BUS

Several transport companies in Hong Kong offer bus services to Guangzhou, Shenzhen and several other destinations in Guangdong Province. The most reliable of these is Citybus, which also operates a domestic bus network in Hong Kong. There are five buses daily to Guangzhou, leaving from Citybus stations at China Hong Kong City in Tsimshatsui and Shatin City One in the New Territories. Tickets are HK$180 one way. Buses from Guangzhou to Hong Kong depart from the Garden Hotel. Citybus also runs eight buses daily to Shenzhen, including two departures from Admiralty. Tickets are HK$65 on weekdays, HK$85 on weekends. Information and credit-card ticket bookings are handled by Citybus (☎ 2736 3888), CTS (☎ 2853-3888) and MTR Travel Services Centre (☎ 2922-4800). The latter also has offices located in MTR subway stations at Central, Admiralty, Causeway Bay, Kowloon Tong, Mongkok and Tsimshatui.

CTS also runs frequent buses to Guangzhou and Shenzhen, leaving from Wanchai, Hunghom, Mongkok and Tsuen Wan. Ticket prices are similar to those of Citybus. For more information call ☎ 2365-0118.

If you take the bus, don't forget to get your visa first! For details, see under China Visas in the Train section.

BOAT

Like buses and trains, most boats leaving Hong Kong are bound for China. The only exceptions are the luxury cruise ships which sometimes pass through the territory on their worldwide journeys.

From China Hong Kong City you can board daily jet catamarans and hovercraft to destinations in neighbouring Guangdong Province, including Shenzhen, Nanhai, Huizhou, Zhuhai and Guangzhou. There is also overnight ship service to Guangzhou which leaves daily at 9 pm. The overnight journey takes eight hours, compared with about three hours for catamaran or hovercraft service. Tickets for the hovercraft to Guangzhou (over two hours) are HK$190 and for the jet catamaran (three hours) HK$130. A 3rd class berth on the overnight ship costs HK$194, 2nd class is HK$234 and 1st class is HK$304. Boats to Guangzhou aren't much faster or convenient than trains or buses, but do let you take in some nice river scenery.

The terminal at China Hong Kong City also has daily morning jet boats to Wuzhou (10 hours, HK$395) in Guangxi Province, from where you can link up with buses to Guilin, Yangshuo and Nanning. If you have time, you can even take a ship up the eastern China coast to Xiamen or Shanghai. There are usually only four to five departures monthly for each destination. There are also three to four ships a month to Haikou, Hainan Island.

Sailing times and ticket prices are subject to frequent change. For the latest information as well as bookings you can either go to the ticket windows at China Hong Kong City in Tsimshatsui (Map 16) or contact CTS (see the Train section above for contact details as well as information on visas for China).

TRAVEL AGENTS

Hong Kong is a great place to arrange onward travel in Asia, or almost anywhere for that matter. A look through the travel pages of Hong Kong's Sunday English-language newspapers will show that there are dozens of travel agents specialising in the discount ticket business. Sometimes you can get a great deal through these outfits, but it pays to be cautious. Some of the 'bucket shops', as the low-fare operators are called, promise one thing but deliver another. At worst they may even take your money, roll up shop and disappear. One way to tell is to see if they are listed in the telephone book, since fly-by-night operators don't stay around long enough to get listed.

Hong Kong does have a number of excellent, reliable travel agents to choose from. If they can't get you the ticket price you saw in the paper, it probably means it never existed.

One of the best places to go is Phoenix Services (☎ 2722-7378), Room B, 6th floor, Milton Mansion, 96 Nathan Rd, Tsimshatsui. Staff are friendly, patient and work hard to get you the best price possible. While they handle bookings for anywhere, their speciality is Vietnam. Another honest outfit that gets good reviews is Traveller Services (☎ 2375-2222), Room 1012, Silvercord Tower 1, 30 Canton Rd, Tsimshatsui.

Many travellers still use the Hong Kong Student Travel Bureau (☎ 2730-3269), Room 1021, 10th floor, Star House, Tsimshatsui. They don't offer the bargain-basement fares of earlier years, but are still worth a try. If you hold an ISIC card you can get a discount. They have several branch offices: Argyle Centre (☎ 2390-0421), Room 1812, 688 Nathan Rd, Mongkok; Wing On Central Building (☎ 2810-7272), Room 901, 26 Des Voeux Rd, Central; and Circle Plaza (☎ 2833-9909), 11th floor, 499 Hennessy Rd, Causeway Bay.

If you need a ticket quickly, Hong Kong Four Seas Tours Ltd (☎ 2722-6112) has branches all over the place. Prices usually aren't as low as the discount operations listed above, but you'll almost always get the seat you need and they will deliver your ticket to you.

When going for the cheapest possible fares, remember that the number of such seats may be limited, and there are often severe restrictions. With the cheapest tickets, you often have to pay the travel agent first and then pick up the ticket at the airport – just make sure you understand any of the limitations involved.

WARNING

This chapter is particularly vulnerable to change – prices for international travel are volatile, routes are introduced and cancelled, schedules change, special deals come and ago, and rules and visa requirements are amended. Airlines and governments seem to take a perverse pleasure in making price structures and regulations as complicated as possible. You should check directly with the airline or travel agent to make sure you understand how a fare (and the ticket you may buy) works. In addition, the travel industry is highly competitive and there are many lurks and perks. The upshot of this is that you should get opinions, quotes and advice from as many airlines and travel agents as possible before you part with your hard-earned cash. The details provided in this chapter should be treated as pointers and are not a substitute for careful, up-to-date research.

Getting Around

Hong Kong boasts one of the world's best public transportation systems. Even out in the New Territories there are very few places that aren't served by bus routes. Within the urban areas transport options are as diverse as they are efficient: minibuses, trams, subways, ferries, hovercraft, double-decker buses, taxis – take your pick. There is a wide variance in fares between the different modes, but in general it doesn't cost much to get around. Interestingly, most services are run by private companies, which make money doing it. It's enough to make a western city planner blush.

THE AIRPORT

Airport Bus

Kai Tak airport is served by six different dedicated bus routes. Though not as fast as taxis, the buses are often cheaper and still get you there fairly quickly. And if you're coming out of the airport, the line for buses is always much shorter than that for taxis.

The buses are air-conditioned and have plenty of room for luggage. Departures are every 10 to 15 minutes, except for the A20, which runs every 15 to 20 minutes. English and Chinese announcements notify passengers of hotels serviced at each stop. No change is given on any of the buses, but you can get change just outside the airport exit at the airport bus service centre, which also has route maps.

A1 Airbus – Loop route through Tsimshatsui. Stops include the Star Ferry Terminal and the following hotels: Kowloon, Holiday Inn Golden Mile, Hong Kong Renaissance, Sheraton, Hyatt Regency, Chungking Mansions, The Peninsula, YMCA Salisbury and the Kowloon Shangri-La. Runs 7 am to midnight. Fare: HK$12.

A2 Airbus – Two-way route through Wanchai, Central and Sheung Wan. Coming from the airport the bus takes Gloucester and Connaught Rds on Hong Kong Island. On the return it follows Des Voeux Rd and Queensway and then circles around the Hong Kong Convention & Exhibition Centre. Hotels serviced include the Grand Hyatt, New World Harbour View, Harbour View International House, Luk Kwok, Wharney, Furama Kempinski, Ritz-Carlton and Mandarin Oriental. Terminus is at the Macau

Ferry Terminal in Sheung Wan. Runs 7 am to midnight. Fare: HK$17.

A3 Airbus – Loop route through Causeway Bay. Hotels serviced include the Park Lane, Excelsior, New Cathay, Regal Hongkong and the South Pacific. Alight at Stop 8 for Noble Hostel and nearby guesthouses, and Stop 10 for the Causeway Bay Guest House and Phoenix Apartments. Runs 7 am to midnight. Fare: HK$17.

A5 Airbus – Loop route through Tai Koo Shing (eastern Hong Kong Island). Hotels serviced include the Park Lane, Newton, City Garden, South China and Grand Plaza. Runs 7 am to 11 pm. Fare: HK$17.

A7 Airbus – Loop route to Kowloon Tong MTR/KCR station. Primarily for access to northern Kowloon via Mass Transit Railway and New Territories via Kowloon-Canton Railway. No hotels serviced. Runs 8 am to 11 pm. Fare: HK$6.50.

A20 Airport Express – Loop route through Wanchai and Central. Stops include Exchange Square, Central MTR station (Pedder St exit) and Pacific Place Shopping Mall/Cathay Pacific Citycheck. Hotels serviced include the South Pacific, Charterhouse, Empire, Island Shangri-La, Conrad, JW Marriot, Mandarin Oriental, Ritz-Carlton and Furama Kempinski. Runs 6 am to 11.30 pm. Fare: HK$17.

Taxi

Taking a taxi is the only other public transportation option here. The taxi stand is just outside the airport exit. Although the queue is often quite long, the stand can handle up to 10 taxis at once, so things move fairly quickly. Sample taxi fares from the airport include: Central (HK$85), Tsimshatsui (HK$50) and Wanchai/Causeway Bay (HK$70). There is a luggage fee of HK$5 per bag, though not all drivers insist on this. For more information on fares, see the Taxi section later on in this chapter.

TRAIN

Mass Transit Railway (MTR)

One of the world's most modern subway systems, the MTR is clean, fast and safe. Though it costs a bit more than most other forms of public transport, it is the quickest way to most urban destinations. Trains run every two to four minutes from 6 am to 1 am daily on three lines (see Map 15). Fares range from HK$4 to HK$11. A fourth line is currently being built to link Central and western Kowloon with the new airport at Chek Lap Kok and should be finished in time for the airport's opening in mid-1998.

For short hauls, the MTR is not great value. If you want to cross the harbour from Tsimshatsui to Central, the MTR is about five times the price of the Star Ferry with none of the views, and only marginally faster. But if your destination is further away, say North Point or Tsuen Wan, the MTR is considerably faster than a ferry or a bus and about the same price. Also, it's air-conditioned, which is nice in summer. If possible it's best to skirt rush hours: 7.30 to 9.30 am and 5 to 7 pm. Some 2.4 million people use the MTR every day, most of them at these times. Joining the crowd is no fun.

Riding the MTR is dead easy – just follow the signs. Everything is automated, from the ticket vending machines to the turnstiles. Ticket machines take HK$5, HK$2, HK$1 and 50c pieces but do not give change, so feed in the right amount. If you put in a HK$5 coin for a HK$4 ticket the next person gets a HK$1 discount! There are change machines that accept coins only – notes must be changed at the ticket offices or Hang Seng Bank mini banks located in the stations. Once you pass through the turnstiles, you also only have 90 minutes to complete the journey before the ticket becomes void.

The MTR uses 'smart tickets' with a magnetic coding strip on the back. When you pass through the turnstile, the card is encoded with the station identification and time. At the other end, the exit turnstile sucks in the ticket, reads where you came from, the time and how much you paid, and lets you through if everything is in order.

You can't buy return tickets, but there are 'common stored value' tickets for making multiple journeys. These are available in denominations of HK$70, HK$100 and HK$200, and are definitely worthwhile if you use the MTR frequently. They can also be used on the Kowloon-Canton Railway except for Lo Wu station (the Chinese border station). You save a bit by buying the larger denominations – the encoded value of the HK$100 ticket is HK$103, and the HK$200 ticket is worth HK$212. Another benefit is the 'last ride bonus' – no matter how little the value remaining on the ticket, you don't have to pay extra for the final ride when the ticket is used up. You can buy these tickets at the mini banks in the MTR stations. Avoid the 'tourist ticket' which costs HK$25 but is only good for HK$20 worth of travel. For your extra HK$5 you get to keep the ticket as a second-rate souvenir.

Children aged two or under can travel free and there are special child/student tickets (for children aged three to 11) which are much cheaper than adult prices. Passengers aged 12 or over can only use the child/student tickets if they are students carrying a Hong Kong Student Identity Card – an ISIC card is not acceptable.

Smoking, eating and drinking are not permitted in the MTR stations or on the trains and violators are subject to heavy fines if caught. You are not supposed to carry large objects (like bicycles) aboard trains either, though backpacks and suitcases are OK.

Unfortunately there are no toilets in either the trains or the stations. If you leave something on the train, you might be able to reclaim your goods at the lost property office at Admiralty station between 11 am and 6.45 pm, Monday to Saturday. For other queries, call the passenger information hotline (☎ 2750-0170).

Kowloon-Canton Railway (KCR)

This is a single-line commuter railway running from Kowloon to the China border at Lo Wu. The tracks are the same as used by the Kowloon-Guangzhou express, but the trains are different, bearing more of a resemblance to subway train carriages. The KCR is a quick way to get up to the New Territories, and the ride offers some nice views as well.

Fares range from HK$3 to HK$7.80, except for the train to the border at Lo Wu which costs HK$29. Trains run about every five to 10 minutes, except during rush hour, when the interval falls to every three minutes.

You can change from the MTR to the KCR at Kowloon Tong station. The southernmost station on the line at Hunghom is easily reached from Tsimshatsui by taking green minibus No 8 from Middle Rd. If you buy a stored value or tourist ticket for the MTR you can also use it on the KCR for every station but Lo Wu, for which you must buy a separate ticket. You can't ride up to Lo Wu station unless you plan to cross the border into China (see the Getting There & Away chapter for more details).

Light Rail Transit (LRT)

This is rather like a modern air-con version of the tram. The LRT runs on the road surface and stops at designated stations. However, it's much faster than the tram, at times reaching a maximum speed of 70 km/h.

Most visitors don't ever set foot on the LRT, as it only runs in the New Territories, connecting the city of Tuen Mun with Yuen Long. There are plans to connect it with the MTR and KCR networks.

GLENN BEANLAND

Trundling along by tram

There are five LRT lines connecting various small suburbs. The system operates from 5.30 am to 12.30 am Monday to Saturday, and from 6 am to midnight on Sundays and holidays. The LRT terminus in Tuen Mun is at the hoverferry pier, from where you can catch a ferry to Central. Fares on the LRT are HK$3.20 to HK$4.70 for adults and tickets are purchased from vending machines. The system of fare collection is unique for Hong Kong – there are no gates or turnstiles and customers are 'trusted' to pay. However, that 'trust' is enforced by occasional police spot checks with fines for those who haven't purchased a ticket.

BUS

The extensive bus and minibus system offers a bewildering number of routes that will take you nearly anywhere you want to go in Hong Kong. You are most likely to use the buses to explore the south side of Hong Kong Island and the New Territories. The north side of Hong Kong Island and most of Kowloon are well served by the Mass Transit Railway.

Ordinary Bus

Most buses are of the double-decker variety, which is great for visitors. A front seat on the upper deck beats any tour bus for views. A fair number of buses are now air-conditioned. This can be a lifesaver in the summer, but temperatures are set so low you may find your extremities turning blue. They don't let up in the winter months either. Air-con buses generally cost about 40% more than their non air-conditioned counterparts.

Fares range from HK$1 to HK$34. Payment is made into a fare box upon entry, so have plenty of change handy: there are no ticket collectors. To alight, push the bell strip or button just before your stop.

Most buses run from around 6 am to midnight, though some routes end as early as 7 pm. There are a few night buses that ply the roads between midnight and 6 am, but not on routes that visitors will generally use except for the cross-harbour buses (see below).

Buses are run by three private operators. China Motor Bus (CMB) has most of the routes on Hong Kong Island, which is unfortunate, as its service is generally miserable. Far better is Citybus, which managed to win some CMB routes in the early 1990s and has since expanded. The majority of Citybuses are plush air-con coaches, and drivers tend to be a bit more sedate than their CMB counterparts. Kowloon and the New Territories are served by Kowloon Motor Bus (KMB). CMB buses are blue and white, Citybuses yellow and KMB buses red and cream.

In Central, the most important bus terminal is on the ground floor right under Exchange Square. From here you can catch buses to Aberdeen, Repulse Bay, Stanley and other destinations on the south side of Hong Kong Island. In Kowloon, the Star Ferry Bus Terminal is the most crucial, with buses to the KCR station and points in eastern and western Kowloon.

The terminals have signs listing the route number, destinations, stops served en route and fare. But if you're at a regular bus stop it can be tricky to figure out where buses go, as signs there list only route numbers, not destinations. Unfortunately there is not much in the way of good bus maps (see under Maps in the Facts for the Visitor chapter for some possibilities).

All is not lost however. Most visitors are likely to only make use of several major bus terminals. A quick browse through the signs will show you where the buses end up and what stops they make along the way. And of course all buses have destinations listed in English, as well as Chinese, on the front. What's useful to note is that any bus number ending with the letter 'K' (78K, 69K etc) means that the route connects to the KCR. Similarly, bus numbers ending with 'M' (51M, 68M etc) go to the MTR stations. Those ending with 'R' are recreational buses and normally run on Sunday, public holidays or for special events like the horse-races at Happy Valley. Buses with an 'X' are express.

If you can't find the bus you need, the HKTA has leaflets and an information hotline (☎ 2807-6177) that should get you on your way. You can also contact China Motor Bus (☎ 2565-8556), Citybus (☎ 2873-0818) or Kowloon Motor Bus (☎ 2745-4466). For buses to specific sights around Hong Kong, see the relevant section in the Things to See & Do chapter.

Cross-Harbour Bus

These buses deserve special mention, as they are pretty much the only cheap way to get from Hong Kong Island to Kowloon after the MTR shuts down at 1 am. Bus routes numbered in the 100s, 300s or 600s denote service between Hong Kong and Kowloon, or the New Territories, via the cross-harbour tunnel. A few buses use the eastern harbour crossing instead. During the day the only reasons for visitors to take a cross-harbour bus are to get a glimpse of Hong Kong and save a few Hong Kong dollars. Traffic around the tunnel is nearly always backed up. If you want to get across the harbour quickly take the MTR, which serves most of the same destinations as the cross-harbour buses.

However, if it's after 1 am and you find yourself caught on the wrong side of the harbour, you might consider the No 121 and 122 buses, which operate through the cross-harbour tunnel every 15 minutes from 12.45 to 5 am. No 121 runs from the Macau Ferry Terminal in Sheung Wan on Hong Kong Island, along Des Voeux, Hennessy and Morrison Hill Rds, through the tunnel to Chatham Rd in Tsimshatsui East and then on to Choi Hung on the east side of the airport. No 122 runs from North Point on Hong Kong Island, along King's,

Double-Decker Daredevils

Asia has it's fair share of insane bus drivers who live to strike terror into the hearts of their passengers. But Hong Kong bus drivers are a breed apart. They take no heed of their passengers' attitudes, or existence for that matter. All concentration is reserved for the mission of putting their double-decker buses through gut-wrenching turns and high speeds that would do a Grand Prix racer proud. The steep and narrow roads of Hong Kong just add flavour to the challenge: what's the point of having a guardrail or retaining wall if not to miss it by two inches?

What lies behind this behaviour is something of a mystery. Part of it, of course, is a sheer display of driving skill. But these same perfectionists routinely throw their prowess into question with braking techniques that a three year old would scorn. Just see how long you can stand in one place as the bus slows before a stop: hopefully you like the looks of your neighbour, because chances are that you'll be thrust into their arms before your driver has finished his savage brake-stomping.

In general China Motor Bus drivers are the cream of the crop: one daredevil managed to actually flip his bus on its side while negotiating a steep hill in Chai Wan a few years back. Kowloon Motor Bus drivers come a close second.

To see a Hong Kong bus driver at his best (this is still a man's world), hop on the upper deck of a bus heading down from the Peak to Central, or one from Central to Repulse Bay and Stanley. Tree branches slap against the windows, oncoming cars swerve out of the way, and the bus kindly leans over far enough to give you a good view of the cliffs alongside the road. Though it may not match Ocean Park's dragon roller coaster (which loops upside down), this ride lasts a lot longer, and gives you far more thrills per dollar. ■

GLENN BEANLAND

Get set for the ride of your life!

Causeway and Hennessy Rds, through the cross-harbour tunnel to Chatham Rd in Tsimshatsui East, and then continues up the northern part of Nathan Rd on to Laichikok and Mei Foo in north-western Kowloon. Both of these buses cost HK$10.50. Obviously getting to these bus routes may be inconvenient depending on where you are. But if you've partied away all but HK$11 and need a ride home, this is it.

Minibus

Minibuses are cream-coloured with a red roof or stripe down the side, and seat 16 people. They can be fast and convenient, but difficult to use for visitors. For one, the destination is displayed in the front in large Chinese characters: there is a smaller English translation below, but it can be hard to read.

It can also be tricky to board one. Like taxis, minibuses stop almost anywhere to pick up or let off passengers. But Hong Kong's complex traffic rules and myriad no-stopping zones make things complicated. If minibuses keep passing you by, look down to see if there's a single or double yellow line on the street next to the kerb. If there is, you are in a restricted stopping zone, and neither minibuses nor cabs will stop for you. CMB, Citybus and KMB bus stops are also off limits.

The real trick is getting off. There are no buttons or bells: you must call out the stop you wish to alight at. This is no easy trick if you're not really sure where you want to get off. Moreover, minibus drivers rarely speak English, so they may not understand you. If you call out 'stop here please' chances are pretty good they will do so, but if not try the Cantonese version, which sounds like 'yow lok'. But minibuses can be handy to go short distances such as from Central to Wanchai or Causeway Bay. Another good thing is that you always get a seat: standing passengers are not allowed by law.

Fares range from HK$2 to HK$10, but tend to increase on rainy days and at night. You pay the driver when you get off, and they can change bills for you if you don't have the exact change.

If you're in Central, the best place to catch minibuses to Wanchai and points east is at the bottom of Exchange Square. If heading west, walk up to Stanley St, near Lan Kwai Fong. There are a few buses that cross the harbour late at night, running between Wanchai and Mongkok. On Hong Kong Island, they can be found on Hennessy and Fleming Rds. In Kowloon you may have to trudge up Nathan Rd as far as Mongkok before you'll find one.

One last point. If you're in a hurry, do not jump on an empty or near-empty minibus. Drivers will sit for as long as 20 minutes waiting for passengers, and if they still don't fill up they will cruise the streets, stopping constantly to try and pull in riders. When this happens, you're better off taking the bus, MTR, or walking.

Green Minibus

These have a green stripe and operate on fixed routes and stop at designated places. They are also referred to as maxicabs. Fares vary according to distance, running between HK$1 and HK$10. You pay when you get on and no change is given. In Tsimshatsui the No 1 maxicab runs from the Star Ferry Terminal to Tsimshatsui East every five minutes or so between 7.20 am and 10.20 pm. The fare is HK$2.50. On Hong Kong Island, another useful route is from Edinburgh Place (near City Hall and the Star Ferry Terminal) to the Peak. Hours of operation are 7 am to midnight and the fare is HK$6.

TRAM

One of the world's great travel bargains, Hong Kong's trams are tall, narrow, double-decker streetcars that trundle along the northern side of Hong Kong Island.

The tram line was built in 1904 on what was then the shoreline of Hong Kong Island, which helps one appreciate just how much land Hong Kong has reclaimed from the sea. Although the tram has been in operation since then, vehicles now in service were built in the 1950s and 1960s.

The trams are not fast but they are cheap and fun. For a flat fare of HK$1.20 (dropped in a box beside the driver when you leave – no change) you can go as far as you like, whether it's one block or the end of the line. Trams operate between 6 am and 1 am. On each route they run with a frequency from two to seven minutes. If the wait is much longer then there's probably been a backup somewhere down the line, so be prepared to elbow your way through the crowd to squeeze aboard when it arrives. Try to get a seat at the front window upstairs to enjoy a first-class view of life in Hong Kong while rattling through the crowded streets.

The routes often overlap. Some start from Kennedy Town and run to Shaukeiwan, but others run only part of the way and one turns south to Happy Valley. The longest run, from Shaukeiwan to Kennedy Town, takes about 1½ hours. The eight routes are as follows:

From (west)	To (east)
Kennedy Town	Causeway Bay
Kennedy Town	Happy Valley
Kennedy Town	North Point
Kennedy Town	Shaukeiwan
Shaukeiwan	Happy Valley
Western Market	Causeway Bay
Western Market	Shaukeiwan
Whitty Street	North Point

BOAT

Hong Kong has an extensive network of ferries. As long as you aren't prone to seasickness, the boats are fun and the harbour views stunning when the weather co-operates. Fares are very reasonable, and there are discounts for children under 12. Though you'll find that many people break the rules, smoking is prohibited on all ferries and the fine for violating this is HK$5000.

Star Ferry

A ride on the Star Ferry, with its spectacular views of both Hong Kong Island and Kowloon, is a must for visitors. It is also an essential mode of transport for commuters. All the ferries have names like Morning Star, Evening Star, Celestial Star, Twinkling Star etc.

There are three Star Ferry routes, but by far the most popular is the one running between Tsimshatsui and Central. The trip takes seven minutes, enough time to knock off some great photos. Fares for the lower and upper deck are HK$1.70 and HK$2 respectively. Those 65 years of age and older ride for free. The coin-operated turnstiles do not give change. You can get change from the ticket window if you take the upper deck, but the lower deck does not have a ticket window. A special tourist ticket is available for HK$20, which allows unlimited rides on the Star Ferry and Hong Kong's trams. Seeing how cheap the normal fare is, you'd have to do at least 14 trips in four days to make this worthwhile. The Star Ferry also links Tsimshatsui with Wanchai, and Central with Hunghom. Operating hours are as follows:

Central (Edinburgh Place) – Tsimshatsui: every five to 10 minutes from 6.30 am to 11.30 pm

Wanchai – Tsimshatsui: every 10 to 20 minutes from 7.30 am to 11 pm

Central (Edinburgh Place) – Hunghom: every 12 to 20 minutes (every 20 minutes on Sundays and holidays) from 7 am to 7.20 pm

GLENN BEANLAND

The Star Ferry – for stunning views of the harbour

Hong Kong Island-Kowloon-New Territories Ferries

The Hong Kong & Yaumatei Ferry Co (HYF) operates numerous large and medium-size conventional and hovercraft ferries which serve Hong Kong Island, Kowloon, the New Territories and the Outlying Islands. Routes between Hong Kong Island and Kowloon/New Territories are as follows:

Ferry:
Central – Yaumatei (Jordan Rd): every 12 to 15 minutes from 6.15 am to midnight
North Point – Hunghom: every 20 minutes from 6.03 am to 10.40 pm
North Point – Kowloon City: every 20 minutes from 6.05 am to 10.25 pm
North Point – Kwun Tong: every 15 minutes from 6 am to midnight
Wanchai – Hunghom: Monday to Friday every 15 to 20 minutes from 6.30 am to 9.50 pm
(Note: all fares for adults are HK$4.40)

Hoverferry:
Central (Queen's Pier) – Tsimshatsui East: every 20 minutes from 8 am to 8 pm (HK$5.20 for adults)
Central (Outlying Islands ferry piers) – Tsuen Wan: every 25 minutes from 7.20 am to 5.20 pm (HK$10.50 for adults)
Central (Outlying Islands ferry piers) – Tuen Mun: every five to 15 minutes from 6.45 am to 8.30 pm (HK$19 for adults)
Central – Tuen Mun by jet catamaran (HK$25 for adults)

Outlying Islands Ferries

These are large vessels run by HYF that serve Hong Kong's more populous islands, including Lantau, Cheung Chau, Peng Chau and Lamma Island. Departures are from the Outlying Islands ferry piers, which sit on a plot of newly reclaimed land in front of Exchange Square in Central. On weekends there are a few ferries to Lantau and Cheung Chau from the Star Ferry Terminal in Tsimshatsui.

The larger boats are separated into ordinary and deluxe classes. The latter comprises an air-conditioned top deck that can induce frostbite, and a small open-air deck on the fantail. This last spot is one of the nicest places to be in Hong Kong on a warm sunny day, and is the main reason why you'd want to shell out extra for the deluxe ticket.

Fares are generally reasonable, except on weekends, when prices nearly double. From Monday through Saturday morning, ordinary adult fares are HK$8.50 or HK$9, those for children and senior citizens HK$4.30 or HK$4.50. Deluxe fares are HK$16, with no discount for children or seniors. Saturday afternoons, Sundays and public holidays ordinary fares rise to between HK$11.50 and HK$16. Deluxe fares are HK$30 across the board. Prices for children and senior citizens are about half. Beverages and snacks are available on board. If you decide to venture out to one of the islands, try and do so during the week, as boats are packed to the gunwales on weekends. For more information on the Outlying Islands, see the Excursions chapter.

Lantau is also served by ferries linking Central with Discovery Bay, a bedroom community sitting on the eastern side of Lantau Island. Ferries run every 20 minutes during the day and every hour or so throughout the night. The one-way fare is HK$20, and boats depart from the eastern side of the Star Ferry Terminal in Central.

Basic schedules for some of the major Outlying Islands ferries are listed below. Times are subject to change. For the latest information, pick up a seasonal schedule at the HYF information office located next to the Outlying Islands ferry piers in Central.

Central – Cheung Chau: approximately hourly from 5.35 am to 11.30 pm, with more frequent sailings during rush hours

Tsimshatsui – Cheung Chau: one sailing to Cheung Chau at 4 pm Saturdays; sailings to Cheung Chau at 8 and 10 am Sundays; one sailing to Tsimshatsui at 12.45 pm Sundays

Central – Lantau (Mui Wo): approximately hourly from 6.10 am to 12.20 am

Tsimshatsui – Lantau (Mui Wo): every one to two hours from 1 to 7 pm Saturdays and from 9 am to 7 pm Sundays

Central – Peng Chau: approximately hourly from 6.30 am to 12.20 am

Central – Lamma Island (Yung Shue Wan): approximately every 1½ hours from 6.25 am to 12.30 am

Central – Lamma Island (Sok Kwu Wan): every two to three hours from 6.50 am to 11 pm

Kaidos & Sampans

A *kaido* is a small to medium-sized ferry which can make short runs on the open sea. Few kaido routes operate on regular schedules, preferring to adjust supply according to demand. Kaidos run mostly on weekends and holidays when everyone tries to 'get away from it all', though some make weekday runs on more popular routes, such as Aberdeen to Lamma Island.

A *sampan* is a motorised launch which can only accommodate a few people. A sampan is too small to be considered seaworthy, but can safely zip you around typhoon shelters like Aberdeen Harbour.

Bigger than a sampan, but smaller than a kaido, is a *walla walla*. These operate as water taxis on Victoria Harbour. Most of the customers are sailors living on ships anchored in the harbour.

TAXI

Though prices continue to rise, Hong Kong taxis are still not too expensive compared with other major developed cities. And with more than 18,000 cruising the roads, they're usually easy to flag down.

When a taxi is available, there should be a red 'For Hire' sign displayed in the windscreen and the 'Taxi' sign on the roof will be lit up at night. It's important to realise that taxis cannot stop at bus stops or where a yellow line is painted next to the kerb, which denotes a restricted stopping zone.

In Kowloon and Hong Kong Island, taxis are red with silver tops. In the New Territories they are green with white tops. New Territories taxis are not permitted to pick up or put down passengers in Kowloon or Hong Kong Island. On Lantau Island, taxis are blue.

In Hong Kong and Kowloon, the flagfall is HK$14 for the first two km and HK$1.20 for every additional 0.2 km. In the New Territories, flagfall is HK$11.8 for the first two km, and HK$1.1 for every 0.2 km thereafter. There is a luggage fee of HK$5 per bag but not all drivers insist on this. Most drivers carry very little change so keep a supply of coins and HK$10 bills.

If you go through either the cross-harbour or eastern harbour tunnels, you'll be charged an extra HK$20. The toll is only HK$10, but the driver is allowed to assume that he won't get a fare back so you have to pay for his return toll as well. There is no double charge for other tunnels, tolls for which are as follows: Aberdeen HK$5; Lion Rock HK$6; Shing Mun HK$5; Tate's Cairn HK$4; Tseung Kwan O HK$3. There is no charge for the tunnel under Kai Tak airport.

It's often hard to get taxis during rush hour, when it rains or during driver shift changes (around 4 pm). Taxis are also in higher demand after midnight. Officially, there are no extra late-night charges and no extra passenger charges. Unofficially, during heavy rains and after midnight some drivers try to charge double, which is illegal – just pretend you 'don't understand' and pay the meter fare.

Many taxis have a card on which the top 50 destinations are listed in Cantonese, English and Japanese – very useful since many taxi drivers don't speak English. Even if the card doesn't list your specific destination, it will certainly have some nearby place. However, it's never a bad idea to have your destination written down in Chinese if possible.

If you feel a taxi driver has ripped you off, get the taxi number and call the police hotline (☎ 2527-7177) to lodge a complaint with the relevant details about when, where and how much.

CAR & MOTORCYCLE

Driving is on the left side of the road, the same as Australia and Britain but the opposite to China. Seat belts must be worn by the driver and all front-seat passengers. Police are strict and give out traffic tickets at the drop of a hat.

Driving in crowded Hong Kong brings little joy. Traffic often slows to a crawl and finding parking is a nightmare. On top of that, the government has deliberately made driving expensive in order to discourage it. For a local resident to get a driving licence, he or she must take an expensive driving course and wait about 18 months. The motor vehicle import tax is 100% and the petrol tax is more than 100%. Vehicle registration (based on engine size) averages about HK$8000 annually and liability insurance is compulsory.

As for foreigners, anyone over the age of 18 with a valid driving licence from their home country, or an international driving permit, can drive in Hong Kong for up to 12 months. If you're staying longer, you'll need a Hong Kong licence.

Car Rental

There's not much need to rent a car in Hong Kong, unless you are planning an excursion to the New Territories. Even then, unless the place is quite out of the way, you may do better with public transportation. It still can be fun though.

Car rental firms require either an international driver's licence or one from your home country, and a credit card deposit of HK$10,000 (the slip is torn up upon return of the undamaged vehicle). Drivers must be at least 25 years of age. Daily rates run from HK$600 for small car like a Honda Civic to HK$2500 for a high-end Mercedes or BMW model. A few of the more reputable car rental outfits in Hong Kong include: Ace (☎ 2572-7663), Happy Valley; Avis (☎ 2890-6988), Causeway Bay; and Hertz (☎ 2375-8779), Tsimshatsui.

Motorcycle

It's impossible to rent motorcycles in Hong Kong, but if you're staying for a while you can buy one. In truth, Hong Kong is not a great place to ride: traffic is fierce, exhaust fumes heavy and other drivers don't give a damn about motorcyclists. Registration is expensive and somewhat of a hassle. But when the weekend comes, all that slips away as you speed down to the beaches or up to the New Territories.

The best place to look for a motorcycle, new or used, is on Caroline Hill Rd in Causeway Bay. There is a string of shops, most of which have at least one English speaker. Unless you have a good job, you may only be able to window-shop. Hong Kong's soaring import duties make motorcycles ridiculously expensive. A Honda CB550 can cost up to HK$60,000 new and HK$35,000 used.

BICYCLE

Bicycling in Kowloon or Central is suicidal, but in quiet areas of the islands or the New Territories a bike can be quite a nice way of getting around.

Some places where you can rent bikes and ride in safety include: Shek O on Hong Kong Island; Shatin and Tai Mei Tuk (near Tai Po) in the New Territories; Mui Wo (Silvermine Bay) on Lantau Island; and on the island of

Cheung Chau. The bike rental places tend to run out early on weekends however.

WALKING

Much of Hong Kong is best seen on foot. However, walking around isn't necessarily easy or relaxing, especially in the business districts. Poorly designed crosswalks, crushing masses of people and hurtling buses can make your stroll anything but casual. But if you persevere you will be rewarded with the sights, sounds and smells that define Hong Kong.

Rural Hong Kong offers some outstanding walks and hikes. Even Hong Kong Island has a 50 km 'Hong Kong Trail' that spans the length of the island and takes you up and out of the city and into the trees and hills. If that daunts you, just stick to the 3.5 km circuit around the Peak. For more information on city and rural walks, see the Things To See & Do and Excursions chapters.

The World's Longest Escalator

Along with its other diverse forms of transport, Hong Kong is also home to the world's longest escalator. Officially dubbed the 'Hillside Escalator Link', this novel idea looks like something borrowed from Paris' Pompidou Centre. Consisting of covered escalators and moving walkways elevated above street level, the entire system is 800m long. It also has a rather strange design: it only goes one way. When the city was presented an estimate of what it would cost to build a two-way system it balked and opted for a single lane that moved down in the morning during rush hour, and up from 10 am onward.

The escalator was built to alleviate traffic in the Mid-Levels, home to many of Hong Kong's well-to-do commuters. Although it's not that far a walk to Central's business district, it's a steep one, which means a strenuous climb at the end of the day that few are willing to make.

The escalator is worth a try just for the novelty, though the Mid-Levels themselves make for fairly dull exploring. There is no fee to use it. Although the system moves at a snail's pace, many people stand, so if you want to get there quickly, you'll end up walking anyway. ∎

ORGANISED TOURS

Tourism is one of Hong Kong's main money earners, so it's no surprise that there is a mind-boggling number of tours available. Along with specialised tour outfits, hotels, bus companies, ferry operators and even the MTR all offer tours to just about anywhere in Hong Kong. Listing them all would require a separate book.

Of all the options out there, some of the best are offered by the HKTA. While it tends to sugarcoat Hong Kong somewhat, it has also done its homework. Tours take in some genuinely worthwhile sights, and are well run. If you only have a short time in Hong Kong, or are not in the mood to deal with public transportation, these may be just what you're looking for. Some tours are standard excursions covering major sights on Hong Kong Island such as Victoria Peak, or a visit to the Sung Dynasty Village, a re-creation of life in ancient China. Other tours take you on harbour cruises, out to the islands, or through the New Territories.

The HKTA also has a series of thematic tours covering subjects such as horse-racing, Chinese folk customs and lifestyles, sports and recreation, and life in Hong Kong's public housing estates, where you visit a Chinese family. Prices range from HK$130 to HK$500 per person, and there are discounts for children and seniors. The HKTA also arranges tours of Macau and Guangdong Province. For details pick up the *Hong Kong Wonders on Tour* pamphlet at a HKTA information centre or call the tour operations department (☎ 2807-6390) Monday through Saturday from 9 am to 5 pm.

Another well established outfit is Watertours (☎ 2724-2856), owned by venerable Hong Kong trading conglomerate Jardine Matheson. As the name implies, the company specialises in water-borne sightseeing, and offers nearly 20 different harbour tours, island excursions and dinner and cocktail cruises. Prices range from HK$130 for the Noonday Gun Harbour Cruise to HK$575 for the Aberdeen & Harbour Night Cruise. Prices are a bit lower for children. You can book through Watertours, a travel agent or, in many cases, your hotel.

The Star Ferry Company and Hong Kong Tramways offer daily tours on their boats and trams. There are five ferry tours a day, including the Tsing Ma Bridge Cruise which takes you out to the construction site of the massive suspension bridge that will link Hong Kong to its new airport at Chek Lap Kok. Cruises cost HK$130 to HK$150 for adults, and HK$90 to HK$100 for children 12 and under. Open-top tram tours, which use special luxury trams, leave four times daily and cost HK$125 for adults, and HK$90 for kids. For information and bookings, call MP Tours Ltd (☎ 2311-3509).

Things to See & Do

Hong Kong is not so much worth visiting for sights as for spectacle. With a few exceptions – the stunning night-time view from the Peak or the frenzy of Victoria Harbour seen from the Star Ferry – your sharpest memories are likely to be not of individual sights but the frantic fusion of colours, sounds and scents that make up this vibrant city.

Of course many of Hong Kong's attractions are still fun to visit. They are pretty spread out, but excellent public transport makes it easy to reach them. Though most visitors to Hong Kong don't do so, try and take your time. Often getting to and from a sight, or nosing around the surrounding neighbourhood, offers as much if not more than the sight itself.

Hong Kong's Top Ten

The Peak (page 166) – spectacular views of Victoria Harbour from the top of Hong Kong Island

Hong Kong Island tram ride (pages 138, 149) – a slow but picturesque trundle through the heart of Hong Kong

Sheung Wan (page 156) – a busy merchant area and a good spot to explore Hong Kong's narrow backstreets

Stanley (page 174) – a lively market and relaxing seaside getaway

Shek O (page 175) – one of the best beaches on Hong Kong Island, almost deserted during the week

Tsimshatsui Promenade (page 180) – more spectacular views, this time of Hong Kong Island's high-rises

Hong Kong Museum of History (page 179) – a great way to revisit old Hong Kong

Wong Tai Sin Temple (page 183) – a lively and colourful Taoist temple in Kowloon

Bird Market (page 183) – Hong Kong's singing street of feathered friends

Afternoon tea at The Peninsula (pages 177, 232) – as the sun sets on the British Empire...

HIGHLIGHTS

It has already become very clichéd to describe Hong Kong as a blend of old and new, tradition and modernity.

147

But this is a genuine part of the territory's appeal, and unless you stay rooted in Central for your entire stay, you're bound to notice it.

It's not a bad idea to kick off your visit with a trip up to Victoria Peak, more often referred to as just 'the Peak'. Not only do you get a spectacular view, weather permitting, but you can also acquire a good feel for the geography and layout of Hong Kong. The Peak area also has some fine walking trails that take you to shady groves of trees and yet more stunning views of the western and southern parts of Hong Kong Island.

From there it depends on what you're looking for. If you're in the mood to see Hong Kong at its modern best, take a walk through Central, stopping to peer at the Hongkong and Shanghai Bank Building and the Bank of China Tower. Or hop on the MTR to Causeway Bay, home to some of Asia's most sophisticated department stores outside of Tokyo.

To really see what urban Hong Kong looked like a century ago, you'll have to visit the Hong Kong Museum of History. But you can get a feel for the old days by wandering the streets and alleys of Sheung Wan on Hong Kong Island, or Yaumatei and Mongkok in Kowloon. A visit to one or two of Hong Kong's scattered temples offers a chance to soak up some traditional atmosphere and incense.

Tsimshatsui, Hong Kong's main tourist district, is where you throw yourself into the thick of it. Jam-packed with people at any time of day, this district throbs with hustle and bustle, and streets are lined with shady electronics shops, high-fashion clothing stores, hole-in-the-wall restaurants and bars and a hotel on nearly every block.

When you've had your fill of urban excitement, head out to the beaches and country parks on the south side of Hong Kong Island. Sun yourself on the beaches at Shek O or Repulse Bay, shop for cheap clothing and tacky trinkets at the Stanley market or go hiking in Aberdeen Country Park. If the bus ride over didn't give you enough ups and downs, try Ocean Park, Hong Kong's very own amusement park, complete with roller coaster, log flume, marine mammal shows and more, all set on a promontory overlooking the South China Sea.

HONG KONG ISLAND

Though the island makes up only 7% of Hong Kong's total land area, it is the territory's centre of gravity. This, after all was where the original settlement, Victoria, was founded. Most of the major businesses, government offices, top-end hotels and restaurants and upper crust residential neighbourhoods are here. The island is home to the governor's mansion, the stock exchange, the legislature, the territory's premier shopping district, the original horse-racing track and a host of other places that define Hong Kong's character. Not surprisingly, a good deal of Hong Kong's sights are also on the island.

Looking across from Tsimshatsui shows how unbelievably crowded the northern side of the island is. About the only natural places left to build on are the steep hills rising up behind the skyscrapers. As well as moving up, Hong Kong keeps on moving out. Reclamation along the harbour edge continues to add the odd quarter km every so often, and buildings once on the waterfront are now several hundred metres back. The latest round is altering the shorelines of the Sheung Wan, Central, Admiralty and Wanchai districts, leaving some wags to predict that the harbour will soon be completely filled.

One of greatest ways to see the north side is to jump on one of the wobbly double-decker trams that trundle between Kennedy Town and Shaukeiwan. Try and go during mid-morning or mid-afternoon, when there's a better chance of grabbing a front seat on the upper deck. The trams take their time, moving slower than almost every other form of traffic. While this may not be great for rushed commuters, if you want to sit back and get a feel for Hong Kong city life, this is just the ticket. And for HK$1.20, it's also one of the best bargains out there.

The south side of Hong Kong Island has a completely different character to the north. For one thing, there are some fine beaches here, and the water is actually clean enough to swim in. The best beaches are at Big Wave Bay, Deep Water Bay, Shek O and Repulse Bay. Incredibly expensive villas are perched on the hillsides, though these are being joined more and more by soaring, and usually ugly, multi-storey apartment blocks.

It's easy to circumnavigate the island by public transport, starting from Central and taking a bus over the hills to Stanley, then heading clockwise along the coast via Aberdeen back to the Star Ferry Terminal.

Central

Nearly every visitor to Hong Kong passes through Central (Map 5) whether for sightseeing, taking care of errands such as changing money, or en route to the bars and restaurants of Lan Kwai Fong. Many business travellers spend all their time in this district, where most of Hong Kong's larger international companies have their offices. Sights per se around here are limited mainly to some architecturally interesting buildings and a few nice parks. But taken together the overall effect is fairly impressive.

A good place from which to start exploring Central is the Star Ferry Terminal. Coming out of the terminal on the right-hand side is **Jardine House**, a 40 storey silver monolith covered with circular porthole-style windows. This is the headquarters of Hong Kong's venerable trading house-turned-conglomerate, Jardine Matheson. In honour of the building's appearance (and, some say, of the more snobbish employees working within) this structure has been nicknamed the 'House of a Thousand Orifices' though it also goes by a more off-colour epithet. Aside from this distinction, the building's basement is also where you will find the Hong Kong Island HKTA information centre, where you can pick up scores of leaflets on sights, accommodation, public transport and just about anything else relating to visiting Hong Kong.

West of Jardine House is **Exchange Square**, home to the Stock Exchange of Hong Kong and one of Central's more elegantly designed structures. The entire complex of three office towers is elevated. Access is via a pedestrian walkway network that stretches west to Sheung Wan and which also links Exchange Square to many of the buildings on the other side of Connaught Rd. The ground level is given over to the Exchange Square Bus Terminus and minibus stop. The stock exchange is located at the main entrance to towers One and Two. Tours of the stock exchange (☎ 2840-3859) are possible, but they are not really geared up for a flood of tourists, so don't be surprised if they turn you down. One floor up in the lift lobby, there is a small art gallery open to the public and a Dao Heng Bank moneychanging desk, which has some of the best rates in town.

Take the pedestrian walkway over Connaught Road and you will find yourself in the heart of Central. Most of the buildings are office towers, but those with an eye towards shopping can check out the Prince's Building and the Landmark shopping centre, both of which cater to more well-heeled consumers.

Going past the Landmark, tucked uphill a little ways is **Lan Kwai Fong** (Map 8), a densely packed cluster of bars and restaurants in Central's south. Formerly an expatriate drinking ghetto, the area has now become popular with local Chinese as well. The bars are nothing to get too excited about, but it's a fun place to do a little pub-crawling. There are a number of good places to eat too, and at lunchtime during the week Lan Kwai Fong becomes a swirling, dizzy mass of office workers trying to squeeze a decent meal into a pitifully short lunch-break. For more details, see the Places to Eat and Entertainment chapters.

Right next to the Prince's Building lies **Statue Square**, which used to display effigies of England's royalty, including Queen Victoria, Queen Alexandra, King Edward VII, King George V and the Duke of Connaught. The statues were taken down and spirited away by the Japanese when they occupied Hong Kong during WWII. Though they were found intact in Japan after the war, colonialism was on the defensive and only Queen Victoria was restored, not in Central but in Causeway Bay's Victoria Park. Fittingly the sole survivor in the square is a bronze likeness of Sir Thomas Jackson, a particularly successful Victorian-era head of the Hongkong and Shanghai Bank. He is now joined by a cenotaph, dedicated to Hong Kong residents, Chinese and expatriate alike, who died in the world wars.

Statue Square is now best known in Hong Kong as the spot where thousands of Filipino migrant workers congregate on the weekends to picnic, sing, dance and generally celebrate a respite from their often dreary jobs as domestic helpers or factory workers. The ornate colonial building on the east side of the square is the former Supreme Court, now serving as the **Legislative Council Chamber**. In the front is a blindfolded statue of the Greek goddess Themis, representing justice. This is a good place to watch Hong Kong's grassroots political movements in action: they routinely stage protests outside the east entrance. East of the Legislative Council is Chater Garden, which is a good place to watch Chinese practising *taijiquan* exercises in the early morning.

Hong Kong and Shanghai Bank Building Emblazoned on most Hong Kong dollar notes, this headquarters of the territory's most famous and powerful bank has come to symbolise modern Hong Kong: daring, innovative and frightfully expensive.

Sitting south of Statue Square, this bizarre yet graceful jumble of steel, glass and aluminium occupies the same spot as every preceding headquarters since the bank's founding in 1865. Indeed the need to fit a huge office tower on the original site is what pushed renowned British architect Norman Foster to adopt such a unique design. Most of the building's major components were assembled overseas and brought together on site, requiring an unprecedented degree of engineering and assembly precision.

By using bridge engineering techniques and locating all services in prefabricated modules hung on the east and west sides of the building, Foster eliminated the need for a central core. The result is a striking atrium that soars upward eleven stories from the ground level. A computer controlled bank of 480 mirrors hung on the south side of the building reflect natural light into the atrium, adding to the sweeping, open feeling.

Perhaps most incredibly, on orders from the bank, Foster designed the building to be expandable: the front and side sections can support a 30% weight increase in the form of additional floors and service modules. There aren't too many other buildings that can actually grow. Not surprisingly, this was not a cheap project. It cost nearly US$1 billion, making it the world's most expensive building at the time of its completion in 1985.

It's definitely worth riding up the escalator to the 1st floor to gaze at the cathedral-like atrium and the natural light filtering through. The bank does not conduct tours of its masterpiece, but staff are accustomed to tourists wandering in. The bank is open from 8.30 am to 4.30 pm Monday through Friday, and from 8.30 am to 12.30 pm Saturdays.

Bank of China Tower Vying with the Hongkong and Shanghai Bank Building for mastery of Hong Kong's skyline is the elegant Bank of China Tower, designed by Chinese-American architect IM Pei. When built it was the tallest building in Hong Kong at 74 storeys, though it has since been eclipsed by the hulking 78 floor Central Plaza in Wanchai.

Unfortunately there is no public access to the upper floors, which offer great views and excitement when the wind blows (the building is designed to sway several feet at the very top). Visitors can tour the lobby, which looks like an ancient Chinese tomb, but that's about it.

What makes this building particularly interesting is its owner. The Bank of China is the main international bank of the People's Republic of China. The construction of such a dominating Hong Kong headquarters was an undeniable symbol of things to come. Local *fung shui* experts also noted that the tower's sharp angles and corners were tantamount to a spiritual attack on its neighbours. However, despite those jitters, the fortunes of adjacent landlords Hongkong Bank, Citibank and Standard Chartered Bank don't seem to have been adversely affected. As for the governor of Hong Kong, whose residence is also within fung shui range, well...

Tsui Museum of Art The pet project of a Hong Kong tycoon, this little museum is tucked away on the 11th

NICKO GONCHAROFF

Good fung shui? The Bank of China Tower looms
over the Legislative Council building.

floor of the old Bank of China Building (not to be confused with the Bank of China Tower) at 2A, Des Voeux
Rd, next to Hongkong and Shanghai Bank. The collection is interesting though modest in size, with a good
display of *sancai* (or three colour) pottery from the Tang
Dynasty (618-907AD), bronzes from as far back as the
late Shang Dynasty (1700-1100BC) and a few paintings
and calligraphy scrolls. Admission is HK$30 for adults,
HK$15 for children; operating hours are 10 am to 6 pm
weekdays and 10 am to 2 pm Saturdays. For more information, call the museum (☎ 2868-2688).

St John's Cathedral Built in 1847, this is one of the few truly colonial structures left in Hong Kong. Criticised for marring the oriental landscape of the colony when it was built, this Anglican church is now lost in the forest of skyscrapers that make up Central.

Services have been held continuously since the church opened, save from 1942 to 1944 when the Japanese Imperial Army used it as a social club. The building was ravaged during the occupation, and the wooden front doors were rebuilt after the war, using timber salvaged from HMS *Tamar*, a British warship that used to guard the entrance to Victoria Harbour.

The church is still quite active, and in addition to weekly services runs a number of community and social services, as well as a small bookstore. Behind the cathedral is the **French Mission Building**, a charming structure dating from 1917 and now home to Hong Kong's new Court of Final Appeal. Both the cathedral and the French Mission Building are on Battery Path, a tree-lined walk that takes you back into the heart of Central.

Government House This is the residence of the governor of Hong Kong, located on Upper Albert Rd, opposite the Zoological & Botanical Gardens. The original sections of the building date back to 1858. Other features were added by the Japanese during their occupation of WWII, including the rectangular eaved tower.

Government House is closed to the public except for one day in March (always a Sunday) when the azaleas are in bloom. But even from the outside it's interesting to gaze at one the world's last stately displays of colonial administration.

Zoological & Botanical Gardens First established in 1864, the gardens are a pleasant collection of fountains, sculptures, greenhouses, aviaries, a zoo and a playground. There are hundreds of species of birds, exotic trees, plants and shrubs on display. The aviaries aren't bad, though not nearly as fun as the one in Hong Kong Park. The zoo is surprisingly comprehensive, though it's sad to see magnificent creatures like jaguars cooped up in tiny cages. This is also one of the world's leading centres for captive breeding of endangered species.

The gardens are divided by Albany Rd, with the botanics and the aviaries in the first section, off Garden Rd, and the animals in the other. If you go to the gardens at about 8 am the place will be packed with Chinese toning up with a bit of taijiquan before heading off to work. Opening hours are 6 am to 10 pm daily (6 am to 7 pm for the zoo). Admission is free.

The gardens are at the top end of Garden Rd – an easy walk, but you can also take bus No 3 or 12 from the stop in front of Jardine House on Connaught Rd. The bus takes you along Upper Albert and Caine Rds on the northern boundary of the gardens. Get off in front of the Caritas Centre (at the junction of Upper Albert and Caine Rds) and follow the path uphill to the gardens.

Hong Kong Park This unusual park seems designed to look anything but natural. Rather, the park stresses synthetic creations such as its fountain plaza, conservatory, aviary, artificial waterfall, rubber-floored playground, viewing tower, museum and Taichi Garden. For all that, the park is beautiful in its own weird way, and makes for dramatic photography with a wall of skyscrapers on one side and mountains on the other. There is a marriage registry located on the grounds, conveniently allowing newlyweds to sign the papers and get on with the all important business of wedding photos near the waterfall.

Within the park is the **Flagstaff House Museum** (☎ 2869-0690), the oldest western-style building still standing in Hong Kong, dating from 1846. The museum houses a Chinese tea-ware collection, including pieces dating from the Warring States period (473-221BC) to the present. It is open daily except Wednesday, from 10 am to 5 pm and is closed on several public holidays. Admission is free.

Perhaps the best feature of the park is the **aviary**. Home to more than 600 birds (and 30 different species), the aviary is large enough to allow free flight, and the feeling is quite unlike that of animals kept in captivity. Visitors walk along a wooden bridge suspended about 10m above ground, putting one eye-level with the tree branches, where most of the birds are to be found.

Hong Kong Park is an easy walk from either Central or Admiralty. Bus Nos 3, 12, 23, 23B, 40 and 103 will also get you there. Alight at the first stop on Cotton Tree Dr.

Li Yuen St Actually this is two streets: Li Yuen St East and Li Yuen St West, which run parallel to each other between Des Voeux and Queen's Rds, opposite the Lane Crawford Department Store. Closed to motorised traffic, these two lanes are crammed with shops selling clothing, handbags, fabrics and assorted knick-knacks. Nearby Pottinger St, with old cobbled steps and equally ancient-looking street hawkers, is also worth looking into.

Central Market You shouldn't have any trouble finding the Central Market – just sniff the air. The market is a large four storey affair between Des Voeux and Queen's Rds. It's more a zoo than a market, with everything from chickens and quail to eels and crabs, alive or freshly slaughtered. It may not merit a separate visit, but it's worth a look if you don't have time to make it to any of Hong Kong's older districts like Sheung Wan or Yaumatei. The upper floor of the market has been converted into the lower terminus of the Hillside Escalator Link, which stretches up 800m into the heart of the Mid-Levels.

Sheung Wan

This district (Map 4), lying just west of Central, once had something of the feel of old Shanghai. A steady onslaught of jackhammers and cement mixers has stripped a lot of this away, and old stairway streets once cluttered with stalls and street sellers have been cleared away to make room for new buildings. It's hard to tell, for instance, that the neighbourhood of Shek Tong Tsui (near Kennedy Town) was once the brothel centre of Victorian Hong Kong.

Nevertheless the area is still worth exploring. There aren't many sights per se: it's best to just start walking. Take a tram down Des Voeux Rd West, past all the shops selling dried seafood, Chinese medicine and flattened, preserved ducks. Get off at the terminus in Kennedy Town for a look at the barges and river boats offloading fresh vegetables, pigs and other cargo from China. Or take a stroll through the narrow alleys and backstreets of Sheung Wan, where there are still a few shops that carry on business the same way they've done for decades.

Western Market Almost directly opposite Shun Tak Centre and the Macau Ferry Terminal is the Western Market. This four storey Edwardian building, first built in 1906, was fully renovated and reopened in 1991 as, (surprise, surprise), a shopping centre. It's filled with modern but very trendy shops and restaurants. An unusual theme here is that the ground floor shops must present one-of-a-kind merchandise – the idea is to prevent the usual boring overlap of lookalike imitations so common in most Hong Kong shopping malls. The 1st floor is a 'cloth alley', similar to those outdoor markets which are fast disappearing. Some good silks can be bought here. The 2nd floor houses a restaurant specialising in traditional Cantonese dishes. The 3rd floor is a centre for performing arts and exhibits. Shops are open from 10 am to 7 pm, the restaurant from 11 am to 11.30 pm.

Man Mo Temple This temple, on the corner of Hollywood Rd and Ladder St, is one of the oldest and most famous in Hong Kong. The Man Mo – literally meaning 'civil' and 'military' – is dedicated to two deities. The civil deity is a Chinese statesman of the 3rd century BC and the military deity is Kuanti, a soldier born in the 2nd century AD and now worshipped as the God of War.

The civil deity (Man) is dressed in a red robe, holding a writing brush. Kuanti is dressed in green, a sword in hand. To the left of the main altar is Pau Kung, the black-faced God of Justice. To the right is Shing Wong, the God of the City, a kind of protector of urban dwellers.

Outside the entrance are four gilt plaques on poles which are carried at procession time. Two plaques describe the gods being worshipped and the others request quietness and respect, and warn menstruating women to keep away. Inside the temple are two antique chairs shaped like houses used to carry the two gods at festival time. The coils suspended from the roof are incense cones burnt by worshippers. A large bell on the right is dated 1846 and the smaller ones on the left, 1897.

The exact date of the temple's construction has never been agreed on, but it's certain it was already standing when the British arrived to claim the island as their own. The present Man Mo Temple was renovated in the middle of the last century.

The area around Man Mo Temple was used extensively for location shots in the film *The World of Suzie Wong*. The building to the right of the temple was used as Suzie's hotel. Actually, the real hotel in the novel (the Luk Kwok, alias the Nam Kok) was in Wanchai, several km to the east. The temple is open from 7 am to 5 pm.

Fung Ping Shan Museum This museum (☎ 2859-2114) is located on the campus of Hong Kong University, which sits on the hills above the neighbourhood of Shek Tong Tsui, west of Central. The campus is nothing special to look at, but the museum is one of the best of its kind in Hong Kong. The collection consists mainly of ceramics and bronzes, plus a lesser number of paintings and carvings. The bronzes are in three groups: Shang and Zhou Dynasty ritual vessels; decorative mirrors from the Warring States period to the Tang, Song, Ming and Qing dynasties; and Nestorian crosses from the Yuan Dynasty. A collection of ceramics includes Han Dynasty tomb pottery and recent works from the Chinese pottery centres of Jingdezhen and Shiwan in the PRC.

Take bus No 3 from Edinburgh Place (adjacent to City Hall) in Central, or bus No 23 or 103 coming from

Shueng Wan Walking Tour

Walking through the streets of Sheung Wan (Map 4) hardly takes you back in time: scores of new high-rise apartment blocks and the steady traffic keep you firmly rooted in the present. But there are traces here and there of late 19th and early 20th century Hong Kong, and if you use a bit of imagination you may get a feel for the way things used to be. If you do the whole route, this walking tour should take you a leisurely two to three hours.

Start off by taking a tram westwards along **Des Voeux Rd**. (Trams headed to either Whitty St or Kennedy Town will do, but Western Market trams stop too early.) Get off at Sutherland St, the third stop after Western Market. Take a little look around Des Voeux Rd West, sticking your head (and nose) into the occasional **dried seafood shop**. Here you can find preserved oysters, shrimp, mussels, squid and all sorts of fish. Some shops also sell preserved ducks, which have been flattened so that they look as if a truck ran over them.

Head off Des Voeux Rd West up Sutherland St to **Ko Shing St**, where there are still a few traditional Chinese **herbal wholesalers** still in action. Life moves pretty slowly behind these walls: conversation seems to be the chief activity (though they're probably at least talking about business).

Continue down to the end of Ko Shing St, briefly back onto Des Voeux Rd and turn right onto **Bonham Strand West**, which is lined with wholesale **ginseng sellers** and more Chinese medicinal herb shops. Though some of the shops have modernised, others appear to have retained equipment for decades, giving an idea of what the Chinese trading houses of 1930s Shanghai might have looked like.

Hook a left onto **Bonham Strand** and walk up to the intersection with Queen's Rd West. To the left you'll find shops selling **bird's nests** (for the soup!) as well as paper offerings. The latter are replicas of homes, cars, furniture and bank notes which are burnt at funerals to ensure the deceased doesn't head into the afterlife without the necessary creature comforts. Also at this intersection is Kaffa Kaldi Coffee, where you can recharge if your energy is flagging.

Diagonally across Queen's Rd is **Possession St**, the spot where Captain Charles Elliot first planted the Union Jack in 1841, formally annexing Hong Kong. Aside from the street name, there's nothing else to indicate the event took place here. In fact, reclamation has pushed the shoreline so far out, it's hard to believe this used to be the coast. Heading up Possession St keep an eye out for a **traditional coffin shop** on the south side of the intersection with Hollywood Rd. These guys have been doing it the way it's been done for centuries, using four logs to achieve a distinctive rounded shape that is both graceful and creepy.

Climbing Pound Lane to where it meets **Tai Ping Shan St**, look to the right to find the **Pak Shing Temple**. This shrine was built in the 1850s to hold ancestral tablets brought over from China by some of Hong Kong's first Chinese inhabitants. There are still some 3000 ancestor tablets in this diminutive structure.

Up the steps on Tai Ping Shan St is the small neighbourhood **Kuanyin Temple**, which is worth a quick look. Descend Upper Station St back to **Hollywood Rd**, where you will run into a string of Chinese **antique shops**. Here at the western end of Hollywood Rd the shops tend be a bit more suspect: prices are easily knocked down, and a lot of shopowners somehow seem to have gotten hold of the same priceless artefacts.

Continuing east on Hollywood Rd will bring you to **Man Mo Temple** (see the relevant section under Sheung Wan for details). The extremely steep flight of steps next to the temple is **Ladder St**. Well over 100 years old, this unique cobbled thoroughfare used to be one of the best remaining examples of old Hong Kong, crammed with stalls and shops. Now it's been paved over with concrete.

A short hop down Ladder St is **Upper Lascar Row**, home of the highly overrated **Cat St market** and **antique galleries**. There are a few nice pieces to be found here, but most of the stuff displayed on the pavement is trash. Most of the antique merchants have moved into the Cat Street Galleries, a four storey building on Lok Ku Rd.

Taking Ladder St all the way down will bring you to Queen's Rd again, which you can cross over to get to **Hillier St**. This narrow street has all sorts of **street stalls** selling noodles, dim sum and other snacks. Stay away from anything with too much meat in it: people have been known to get sick from eating here. Even if you don't eat, it's still fun to watch the action.

Down onto Bonham Strand, heading east you'll come across **Man Wa Lane**. This is the place to go if you want to have a traditional chop made. Chops, or seals, have long been used in Chinese to endorse documents, and the more elaborate designs are quite beautiful.

Heading further east will bring you back again to Queen's Rd. Cross over and hike up **Wellington St**, which is home to a number of **mahjong parlours** and shops selling mahjong pieces and tables. While the action in a mahjong parlour is great to watch, it's not a good idea to stop and stare too long, as players may take serious offence.

Up on **Graham St** you'll find a fresh food market set up on the cobbled steps, where it looks as if very little has changed in decades (except for the food of course). One block further, on **Cochrane St**, there are a series of street-side tailors as well as a shop selling snake blood, which is supposed to bolster strength and male virility. If you're hungry, the cooked **food market** on Stanley St is a good place to get a steaming plate of fried noodles or veggies.

Back down to Queen's Rd, head west briefly to check out **Eu-Yan Sang Pharmacy**, a Chinese medicine shop where the prescriptions are written out in a little booth in one corner of the store and then sent buzzing across a little wire-pulley system to the clerks behind the counter. It's definitely more interesting than Watson's.

To wind up the tour, cut through the narrow confines of **Wing Kut St**, where you can buy (or chuckle at) a bizarre array of **costume jewellery**, which is pretty much all they sell here. On the other side of Wing Kut St lies **Des Voeux Rd**, where you can catch a tram at the stop ahead and to the right, or head left to the MTR station. If you need to sit down and rest those weary feet, there is an Oliver's Super Sandwiches right near the MTR station. ■

GLENN BEANLAND

Ladder Street, Sheung Wan

Causeway Bay, and get off at the university campus on Bonham Rd, opposite St Paul's College. The museum is open Monday to Saturday, 9.30 am to 6 pm, and some public holidays. Admission is free.

Admiralty

Heading just east of Central brings you to Admiralty (Map 5), a clump of office towers, hotels and shopping centres. There are no sights here, but the **Pacific Place Shopping Mall** is one of the nicest in Hong Kong, with both mid-priced and expensive shops, restaurants and one of Hong Kong's biggest cinemas, the UA Queensway. You can also get to Hong Kong Park by taking the escalators up at the west side of the mall, near the pedestrian bridge spanning Queensway.

Across Queensway, the **Lippo Centre** (the work of architect Paul Rudolph) makes an interesting addition to Hong Kong's skyline. It's not all that fascinating from the inside however.

Sitting on the hill above Pacific Place are the JW Marriot, Conrad and Island Shangri-La hotels, probably the main reason why visitors make it to Admiralty.

Wanchai

To those familiar with Hong Kong, Wanchai (Map 6) still brings to mind visions of topless bars, hookers working the sidewalks and drunken sailors on the prowl. In its sleazy heyday, as an R&R destination for the US and UK naval fleets it was all that. And in many people's minds Wanchai is still *The World of Suzie Wong*, even though Richard Mason's tale of the kind-hearted Hong Kong prostitute dates back to 1957.

Though Wanchai today is mostly office towers and shopping centres, it is still a pretty interesting place to poke around. The rows of narrow streets sandwiched between Johnston Rd and Queen's Rd East harbour all sorts of interesting shops and mini factories where you can see the real Hong Kong at work: watchmakers, blacksmiths, shoemakers, printers, signmakers and so on. Nestled in an alley on the south side of Queen's Rd East, is **Tai Wong Temple**, where fortune-tellers used to do a brisk trade. It is still active, if somewhat subdued. Just east of the temple, also on Queen's Rd East, the **Hopewell Centre** is another one of Hong Kong's rather unique office towers. Basically a 40 storey cylinder, it is the flagship building of Hong Kong property and construction magnate Gordon Wu. There is a tacky revolving restaurant at the top, which is accessed by two bubble-shaped external elevators. Though it's a short trip, riding up these elevators is a great way to get an overhead view of Wanchai.

The area between Hennessy and Gloucester Rds, north of the Hopewell Centre, has become one of Hong Kong's main entertainment spots. There are a slew of good restaurants and an impressive number of bars, many of which stay open until just before sunrise. See the Places to Eat and Entertainment chapters to find out more.

Wanchai North, which lies on the other side of Gloucester Rd, is a fairly sterile group of high-rise office blocks and hotels, including the Grand Hyatt. In this strange setting you'll find the **Hong Kong Academy for Performing Arts** (☎ 2584-1500) at 1 Gloucester Rd, which often stages both local and overseas performances of dance, drama and music. The building was designed by local architect Simon Kwan. Next door at 2 Harbour Rd is the **Hong Kong Arts Centre** (☎ 2582-0200). The Pao Sui Loong Galleries on the 4th and 5th floors feature international and local exhibitions year round with an emphasis on contemporary art. Opening hours are 10 am to 8 pm daily. Admission is free.

East of the Arts Centre, looming over Wanchai like a malevolent giant ballpoint pen is the 78 storey **Central Plaza**, Hong Kong's tallest building. Across from Central Plaza, facing the harbour, is the **Hong Kong Convention & Exhibition Centre**, an enormous building that boasts the world's largest 'glass curtain', a window seven storeys high. The centre is almost constantly hosting trade shows or other major events, and it's worth darting in to see what's on. Although this is already quite a large venue, Hong Kong apparently feels it's not enough: an 'extension' that will dwarf the original centre is being built on a chunk of reclaimed land just offshore.

Housed in the Causeway Centre within the China Resources Building complex, the **Museum of Chinese Historical Relics** (☎ 2827-4692) houses cultural treasures from China unearthed in archaeological digs. Two special exhibitions each year focus on artefacts from specific provinces. It's pretty much touch and go: sometimes the exhibits are interesting; other times you'd do better wandering through the adjacent gift shop. Operating hours are 10 am to 6 pm on weekdays and Saturdays, 1 to 6 pm on Sundays and holidays.

To get to any of the above spots in Wanchai North, you can take the MTR to Wanchai station, which connects with a pedestrian walkway that crosses Gloucester Rd and brings you to Central Plaza. Alternatively, from Central take bus No 10A, 20 or 21.

Causeway Bay

Along with Tsimshatsui, Causeway Bay (Map 7) is where Hong Kong goes to shop. A cluster of Japanese department stores – Sogo, Daimaru, Matsuzakaya and Mitsukoshi – acts like a black hole, drawing in a constant mass of people. If crowds bother you, absolutely steer clear of Causeway Bay on the weekend.

Causeway Bay is referred to in Cantonese as Tung Lo Wan, meaning 'Copper Gong Bay'. In either language, the namesake has almost disappeared due to repeated reclamation. This area was the site of a British settlement in the 1840s and was once a *godown* (warehouse) area for merchants. Jardine Matheson set up shop here, which explains some of the street names: Jardine's Bazaar, Jardine's Crescent and Yee Wo St (Yee Wo is Jardine Matheson's Chinese name).

Shopping is not confined to the department stores. Jardine's Crescent, Jardine's Bazaar and the area south of there are filled with shops peddling cheap clothing, luggage and electronics. For more information see the Shopping chapter.

In addition to buying things, people come to Causeway Bay to dine out and, to a lesser extent, go drinking. The rush of consumers, diners and drinkers gives this district a vibrant feel at almost any time of day. It has also spawned a profit-driven form of urban renewal. In the past three or four years several new shopping centres have popped up south of Hennessy Rd. Chief among these is **Times Square**, an enormous retail/office complex that jars sharply with the decrepit 1950s low-rise tenements around it. Defying critics who said the location would doom the project, Times Square and its shops, restaurants, cinema and office towers have created a second centre of gravity in Causeway Bay.

One of the few remaining vestiges of the district's colonial past is the **noon day gun**, a recoil-mounted three-pounder built by Hotchkiss in Portsmouth in 1901. It stands in a small garden in front of the Excelsior Hotel on Gloucester Rd and is fired daily at noon. Exactly how this tradition started is unknown. Noel Coward made the gun famous with his satirical 1924 song *Mad Dogs and Englishmen* about colonists who braved the heat of the noon day sun while the natives stayed indoors: 'In Hong Kong they strike a gong, and fire a noon day gun, to reprimand each inmate who's in late'.

To see for yourself, you have to cross under Gloucester Rd via a tunnel that starts below the World Trade Centre. There used to be a door outside the centre on Gloucester Rd that led to the tunnel, but at the time of writing the building was being completely renovated: you might ask the staff at the Excelsior Hotel next door for directions.

The noon day gun overlooks the Causeway Bay **typhoon shelter**, a mass of junks, fishing boats, yachts and *sampans* huddling behind a large breakwater. Occasionally you can get a glimpse of the boat people, a few of whom moor their homes in the shelter. The little arm of land jutting out to the side is **Kellett Island**, which was actually an island until a causeway was built in 1956. Further land reclamation turned it into a peninsula. Now it's the headquarters of the Royal Hong Kong Yacht Club.

Victoria Park One of the biggest patches of green grass on the northern side of Hong Kong Island, Victoria Park is one of the territory's most popular parks. Football matches are played on weekends and the Urban Services League puts on music and acrobatic shows.

The best time to stroll around the park is daytime during the week. Early in the morning it's a good place to see the slow-motion choreography of taijiquan practitioners. The evening is given over to Hong Kong's young lovers. If it's between April and October you can take a dip in the Victoria Park swimming pool for HK$17. Do the backstroke and you'll get a good view of the Causeway Bay skyline.

Victoria Park becomes a flower market a few days before the Chinese New Year. The park is also worth a visit during the evening of the Mid-Autumn (Moon) Festival when people turn out en masse carrying lanterns. Other events in the park include the Hong Kong Tennis Classic and the Hong Kong International Kart Grand Prix.

Tin Hau Temple Just east of the park, dwarfed by surrounding high-rises, is a tiny Tin Hau temple on Tin Hau Temple Rd at the junction with Dragon Rd (near Tin Hau MTR station). Before reclamation, the temple to the seafarers' goddess stood on the waterfront. Staff say it has been a site of worship for 300 years, though the current structure is only about 200 years old. A painting on the outside of the temple, left of the main entrance, shows the original building as it looked 300 years ago. There is also an old bell inside dating back to the 15th century. Adjacent to the temple is a little park with a fountain and benches.

Tiger Balm Gardens Not actually in Causeway Bay but in adjacent Tai Hang district are the famous (infamous?) Tiger Balm Gardens, officially known as the Aw Boon Haw Gardens. A pale relative of the better known park of the same name in Singapore, Hong Kong's Tiger Balm Gardens are three hectares of grotesque statuary in appallingly bad taste. These concrete gardens were built at a cost of HK$16 million (and that was in 1935!) by Aw Boon Haw, who made his fortune from the Tiger Balm cure-everything medication. Aw is widely described as having been a philanthropist, though perhaps his millions could have been put to a more philanthropic use. Still his creation has at least provided amusement for untold numbers of visitors.

The gardens are just off Tai Hang Rd, within walking distance of Causeway Bay. Alternatively take bus No 11 from Admiralty MTR station or Exchange Square in Central. The gardens are open daily from 9.30 am to 4 pm and admission is free.

Happy Valley

This quiet residential suburb has one claim to fame: the Happy Valley **horse-racing track**. On race days (either Wednesday, Saturday or Sunday) it seems as though half of Hong Kong swoops down in this little hamlet to indulge in the territory's favourite sport: betting. Going to the races can be a lot of fun, especially if you win (the odds are against you). The racing season is from late September to May. For details, see the Entertainment chapter.

Across the street from the spectator stands are **cemeteries** that make for interesting history. They are divided into Catholic, Protestant and Muslim sections and date back to the founding of the colony. Their placement is somewhat ironic, as is Happy Valley's name, for the area was a malaria-infested bog that led to a fair number of fatalities before the swamps were drained.

The easiest way to Happy Valley is by tram. Trams marked Happy Valley run in both directions. Bus Nos 1 and 5 will get you here from Central.

Eastern Hong Kong Island

Sights really start to thin out east of Causeway Bay, with the landscape dominated by apartment towers and industrial blocks. **Quarry Bay**, however, has the Cityplaza Shopping Centre, one of Hong Kong's biggest malls, and the only one with an ice-skating rink. If you're out to shop this is a much more relaxed environment than Tsimshatsui. To get there take the MTR to Tai Koo station from where there is an exit leading directly into the shopping mall.

Some travellers make it out to **Shaukeiwan**, either to catch the No 9 bus to Shek O or because it's the eastern terminus of the tram line. If you do, you might consider a stroll through the Ah Kung Ngam wharf area, which is about 10 minutes walk from Shaukeiwan MTR station. This spot has long been the site of a small fishing community, though high-rise apartments and a sewage treatment plant have now invaded. But a stroll down Ah Kung Ngam Village Rd and Shaukeiwan Main St still reveals some traces of traditional lifestyle, and the area has a decided port feel to it. On Shaukeiwan Main St there's even a Tin Hau temple that in past years has welcomed both Hong Kong Governor Chris Patten and former UK Prime Minister Margaret Thatcher. Opposite Ah Kung Ngam Village Rd is access to the Shaukeiwan Typhoon Shelter. Pop down to the jetty for a glimpse of the working fishers and boat people. Sampans are constantly shuttling inhabitants or visiting sailors out to their boats, and you may be able to hire one to take you around. At the very least it's less touristed than Aberdeen. Near the jetty is Tan Kung Temple, built in 1905.

To get to Ah Kung Ngam, walk from Shaukeiwan MTR station toward Tung Hei Rd, which runs under the elevated freeway. Follow it north-east for about 10 minutes until you reach Ah Kung Ngam Village Rd on the right hand side. The jetty and temple are to the left, across Tung Hei Rd.

Chai Wan, the easternmost district on the north side of Hong Kong Island, is another forest of stark apartment towers and multi-storey factories. But if you make it out here, stop by the Law Uk Folk Museum (☎ 2896-7000), a 200 year old Hakka home that has been restored to a rather sparkling version of its original state, complete with furniture and farm tools. The museum is located at 14 Kut Shing St and is open 10 am to 1 pm and 2 to 6 pm Tuesdays through Saturdays and 1 pm to 6 pm Sundays and some public holidays. Admission is free.

The Peak

The Peak (Map 9) is one sight that truly should not be missed. You may feel like every tourist in town is going up there with you, but there's a good reason. The view is spectacular. It's also a good way to get Hong Kong into perspective. It's worth repeating the Peak trip at night – the illuminated view is something else. Bring a tripod for your camera if you wish to get some sensational night shots.

Unfortunately, developers couldn't resist throwing up an overblown, overpriced, four-level shopping plaza at the top, the **Peak Galleria**. This robbed the area of some of its charm. Not only that, but the structure doesn't really afford 360° views. However a spectacularly ugly tower being built over the Peak Tram terminus may have the sole virtue of an unobstructed viewing deck – at least the old building did. The hideous design sparked howls of protest in Hong Kong when it was unveiled, but money talks louder than aesthetics. Don't worry though. A walk around the surrounding area still rewards with great views and pretty tree-lined pathways that justify the trip up here.

The Peak has been *the* place to live ever since the British moved in. The taipans built their summer houses there to escape the heat and humidity (it's usually about 5°C cooler than down below), although they spent three months swathed in mist for their efforts. It's still the most fashionable place to live in Hong Kong, as reflected by the astronomical real estate prices: homes up here routinely sell for millions of US dollars.

The top of the tram line is at 400m elevation. The Peak Galleria is right next to the terminus. The place is designed to withstand winds of over 270 km/h, hopefully more than the theoretical maximum that can be generated by typhoons. The viewing deck is reached by taking escalators up to the 3rd level. Inside the mall you'll find a number of expensive restaurants and all number of retail shops, from art galleries to duty-free. If you're looking for a bite to eat, see if there's a free table at the Peak Cafe, which is a much better dining experience. See the Places to Eat chapter.

Just north of the mall, down Findlay Rd, is **Lions Pavilion**, a lookout point that gives a 180° perspective on Hong Kong Island, the harbour and Kowloon. It's often packed, but the view is hard to beat.

When people refer to the Peak, this generally means the Peak Galleria and surrounding residential area. The actual summit is **Victoria Peak**, about half a km to the west and 140m higher. You can hike up here by following the narrow road rising up next to the Peak Tram terminus. At the top are gardens, playing fields, benches and a little stand selling cold drinks.

Just below the summit are remains of the **old governor's mountain lodge**. The building was burnt to the ground by the Japanese during WWII, but the gardens remain and are open to the public. The views are particularly good.

If you're going to the Peak, you should go by the **Peak Tram** – at least one way. It's an incredibly steep ride, and the floor is angled to help passengers getting off at the midway stations. In the summer, packed with people, the inside of those trams can get pretty hot though.

The tram terminal is in Garden Rd, Central, behind Citibank Plaza, 650m from the Star Ferry Terminal. Once every 20 minutes there is a free shuttle bus between the Star Ferry and the Peak Tram terminal from 9 am to 7 pm (8 pm on Sundays and holidays). The tram trip takes about eight minutes and costs HK$14 one way, or HK$21 round trip (HK$4/HK$7 for children under 12). The tram operates daily from 7 am to midnight, and runs about every 10 minutes with three stops along the way. Avoid going on a Sunday when there are usually long

queues. Alternatively, bus No 15 from the Exchange
Square Bus Terminus in Central will take you on a 40
minute trip around the perilous-looking road to the top.
The trip down is even more hair-raising. Bus No 15B
runs from Causeway Bay (Yee Wo St) to the Peak. Green
minibus No 1 leaves from the HMS *Tamar* building, on
the eastern side of City Hall.

Peak Walks The best way to appreciate the Peak is to
walk around it. One particularly pleasant (and popular)
route is a 3.5 km loop on Harlech and Lugard Rds.
Harlech Rd, on the south side, takes you past a small
waterfall and offers great views of southern Hong Kong
Island and Lamma Island beyond. When you reach a

The Hong Kong Trail

The Peak is also the starting point for the 50 km Hong
Kong Trail (see Map 3), which spans the entire length of
Hong Kong Island. Obviously doing the whole thing at
once is only for the fittest of hikers. But the route is divided
into eight sections, which offer walks of varying length and
difficulty.

The trail winds through five country parks, zigzagging
along the ridgetops until it finally descends to end at Shek
O, at the south-east tip of the island. The eight sections
are divided as follows:

Section	Km	Hrs	Difficulty	Bus No
1 The Peak	7.0	2	medium	15
2 Pokfulam	4.5	1+	medium	4,7,37,40
3 Aberdeen	6.5	1	medium	7, 38, 70, 78, 95
4 Wong Chuk Hang	7.5	2	easy	15
5 Jardine's Lookout	4.0	1+	hard	6, 41, 61, 262
6 Tai Tam	4.5	1+	easy	2, 20, 21, 22, 80, 102
7 Tai Tam Bay	7.5	2	easy	14
8 Tai Long Wan	8.5	2+	hard	9

If you're attempting this or any other long hike in summer,
be sure to bring lots of water. Though humid, Hong Kong's
heat can still dehydrate. And while it's not a major concern,
do be aware that you're sharing these trails with native
inhabitants of the country parks, including snakes.

For detailed information on this hike, you can pick up
the *Hong Kong Trail* map published by the Country Parks
Authority. Another map worth picking up is *Countryside
Series Sheet No 1: Hong Kong Island*, which shows many
details of the streets and topography not on the hiking
map. Both maps are available from the Government Publications Office (see the Maps section in the Facts for the
Visitor chapter). ■

playground/barbecue area turn right onto Lugard Rd, which weaves through tropical-type forests and takes you onto a pedestrian causeway jutting out from the side of the hill that gives amazing views northward.

Another pleasant hike that is only a bit more strenuous is the Governor's Walk, which can be accessed from either the Victoria Peak summit area or near the intersection of Harlech and Lugard Rds.

For a downhill hike you can walk about two km from the Peak to Pokfulam Reservoir. This route starts at Peak Rd across from the car park exit, and winds down Pokfulam Reservoir Rd past the reservoir to the artery of Pokfulam Rd where you can get the No 7 bus to Aberdeen or back to Central.

If you're feeling energetic, you can drop off Pokfulam Reservoir Rd onto the Family Walk, which takes you through actual forests, past a small stream, several picnic tables and some very pleasant scenery. The main trail winds up at a lookout point at the end of Harlech Rd. The entire loop, back to the Peak Tram terminus, is around 6 km.

Another good walk is from the Peak to Hong Kong University. First walk to the west side of Victoria Peak by taking either Lugard or Harlech Rds. After reaching Hatton Rd on the west side of Victoria Peak, follow it down. The descent is steep but the pathway clearly marked. It eventually leads to the university and Kotewall Rd, where you can catch a minibus to Central. Alternatively walk down through the university to Pokfulam or Bonham Rds, both of which have bus stops with frequent buses to Central.

Aberdeen

Aberdeen (Map 10) is rated as one of Hong Kong's top tourist attractions, but when you get here you may wonder why. The urban area is not much more than a cluster of dingy apartments, shopping centres and industrial buildings. The main lure is **Aberdeen Harbour**, where several thousand people still live or work on junks anchored there. The other main draw is a string of three palace-like **floating restaurants**, the most famous of which is the Jumbo.

This being the case, the best way to see Aberdeen Harbour is by sampan, which can weave in and out of the rows of boats and bring you close to the action: Tanka women preparing food, racks of fish drying in the sun, kids playing in the water and so on.

Sampan tours can be arranged at the Aberdeen Promenade. You have your choice of private operators, which generally mill around the eastern end of the promenade, or full-fledged operators, like Watertours. The private sampans usually charge HK$60 per person for a 30 minute ride, though you should easily be able to bargain this down if there are several of you. If you are by yourself, just hang out by the harbour as the old women who operate the boats will leap on you and try to get you to join a tour. Watertours does a 25 minute trip around the harbour for HK$50 per person, but it's usually more fun to charter your own sampan. If you don't mind missing out on close-up shots of boat life, you can get a free 10 minute tour by hopping on one of the boats out to the floating restaurants and then riding back.

On the south side of the harbour is the island of **Ap Lei Chau**. There's not much to see there, but a walk across the bridge to Ap Lei Chau affords good views of the harbour and the few boat yards that are still in operation.

If you've got time to spare, a short walk through Aberdeen will bring you to a **Tin Hau temple**, at the junction of Aberdeen Main and Aberdeen Reservoir Rds. Built in 1851, it's a sleepy spot, but still an active place of worship. It's also one of Hong Kong's more important altars to the patron deity of Hong Kong's boat people, given Aberdeen's harbour community. Down near Aberdeen Main Rd is the Hung Hsing Shrine, a collection of ramshackle altars and incense pots.

If you're feeling vigorous, the entrance to Aberdeen Country Park and Pokfulam Country Park is about a 15 minute walk up Aberdeen Reservoir Rd. From here you can hike up to the Peak and catch the Peak Tram or the bus down to Central.

Getting to Aberdeen is fairly easy. From the Exchange Square Bus Terminus in Central, take bus No 7 or 70. No 7 goes via Hong Kong University and western Hong Kong Island, and No 70 goes via the Aberdeen tunnel, which runs from Wanchai to Wong Chuk Hang, just east of Aberdeen. The No 70 terminates at the Aberdeen bus station, the No 7 passes by there.

Ocean Park & Water World A stimulating cultural experience this is not. But these two fun parks are set in a nice location just to the east of Aberdeen and are quite entertaining. They are also good places to go see modern Hong Kong at play.

Hong Kongers are quite proud of Ocean Park, a full-fledged amusement park, complete with roller coaster, space wheel, octopus, swinging ship and other stomach-turning rides. It is also something of a marine park, with a wave cove housing seals, sea lions and penguins, daily dolphin and killer whale shows and an aquarium that features a walk-through shark tank.

The complex is built on two sides of a steep hill, and is linked by a very scenic seven minute cable car ride. The park entrance is on the 'lowland' side, which also has children's attractions like a dinosaur discovery trail, kid's world and mini-rides. The main section of the park sits on the 'headlands' and affords a beautiful view of the South China Sea and southern Hong Kong Island. This is where you'll find the rides and marine attractions. A few more rides, including a log flume and the space wheel, are tucked away on the back side of the hill, above the rear entrance to the park on Shum Wan Rd.

At the rear entrance is the Middle Kingdom, a sort of Chinese cultural village with temples, pagodas, traditional street scenes and staff dressed in period garments. There are also arts and crafts demonstrations, live theatre and Cantonese opera. This is a highly whitewashed version of ancient China, but it's harmless enough.

Entrance fees are HK$130 for adults, or HK$65 for kids aged three to 11. Opening hours are 10 am to 6 pm daily. It's best to go on weekdays: weekends are amazingly crowded.

Water World is right next to the front entrance of Ocean Park. A collection of swimming pools, water slides and diving platforms, it's a great place to go and splash around in the searing heat of summer. Water World is open from June to October. During July and August, operating hours are from 9 am to 9 pm. During June, September and October it is open from 10 am to 6 pm. Admission for adults/children costs HK$60/30 during the daytime, but in evenings falls to HK$40/20.

Probably the most convenient way to get to Ocean Park and Water World is via a special Citybus that leaves from the bus station next to Admiralty MTR station. Buses leave every half-hour from 8.30 am. Citybus sells a package ticket that includes transportation and admission to Ocean Park for HK$146 for adults, HK$73 for children. Transport alone costs HK$10 one way (HK$5 for kids). Buying the package tickets actually costs HK$6 more, but may save you a long wait in line when you arrive.

A cheaper way to get there is to catch bus No 70 (HK$3.60) from the Exchange Square Bus Terminus in Central and get off at the first stop after the tunnel. From there it's a 10 minute walk. The No 6 green minibus (HK$7) from Central's Star Ferry Terminal takes you directly to Ocean Park and Water World, but does not run on Sundays and holidays. Bus No 73 connects Ocean Park with Aberdeen to the west and Repulse Bay and Stanley to the east.

GLENN BEANLAND

Jumbo floating restaurant in Aberdeen Harbour

Deep Water Bay

This is a quiet little beach with a generous dose of shade trees located a few km east of Aberdeen. There are a few nice places to eat and have a drink and there is a barbecue pit at the east end of the beach. If you want a dip in the water, this spot is usually less crowded than Repulse Bay (see below).

To get here from Central, take bus No 6A, 260 or 262 from the Exchange Square Bus Terminus. Bus No 73 connects Deep Water Bay with Aberdeen to the west and Repulse Bay and Stanley to the east.

Repulse Bay

Repulse Bay's long, somewhat white beach is the most popular on Hong Kong Island. Packed on weekends, it's good for people watching, bad if you're hoping for solitude. In the summer even the weekdays see a big turnout. Middle Bay and South Bay, about a 10 minute and 30 minute walk along the shore to the east, also have beaches and are usually less crowded.

Toward the eastern end of Repulse Bay beach is an unusual **Tin Hau temple** popularly known as the Life Saver's Club. In front of the temple is Longevity Bridge – crossing it is supposed to add three days to your life.

Repulse Bay is also home to some of Hong Kong's rich and famous, and hills behind the beach are saturated with luxury apartment towers. One worth noting is the pink, purple and yellow monstrosity with a giant square cut out of the middle. Apparently this unique design feature was added at the behest of a fung shui expert, though in Hong Kong such a stunt might also work to push up the value of the property.

GLENN BEANLAND

GLENN BEANLAND

Top: 'Holey' apartment block, Repulse Bay
Bottom: Long lunch, Stanley

Shopping arcades and restaurants also abound. Down by the beach, the Repulse Bay Panorama has a string of ethnic eateries and beachside bars. The latter have good happy hour deals – not a bad place to sip a cold one and watch the sunset.

Bus Nos 6, 6A, 61, 260 and 262 from Central's Exchange Square Bus Terminus all pass by Repulse Bay. To get here from Aberdeen take bus No 73.

Stanley

Here lies another one of Hong Kong's top tourist destinations (Map 11). Most people come to swarm through **Stanley Market**, several covered blocks worth of cheap (and not-so-cheap) clothing, sporting goods, low grade jewellery and art, and the usual smattering of trinkets and souvenirs.

The market is fairly entertaining, at least for a little while. But it's worth visiting Stanley for the relaxed atmosphere. Wander down Stanley Main St to the waterfront restaurants for a drink or a bite to eat. Or head over to the other side of the isthmus to Stanley Main Beach and kick back on the sand. A lot of Hong Kong's wealthier commuters live here to enjoy the laid-back atmosphere: you can too.

About 2000 people lived here when the British took over in 1841, making it one of the largest settlements on the island at the time. The army set up a garrison here, a presence that continues to this very day (until 1 July 1997 that is). The colonial government also built a prison near the village in 1937 – just in time to be used by the Japanese to intern the expatriates.

From the Stanley Bus Terminal it's a two minute walk down to Stanley Market. On weekends it's bursting with both tourists and locals, so it's better to come on a weekday. The market is open daily from 10 am to 7 pm. A short walk out of town along Stanley Main St is yet another Tin Hau temple, which dates back to 1767. However, the building has undergone complete renovation, and is now a bit of a concrete hulk.

From town you can walk south along Wong Ma Kok Rd to **St Stephen's Beach**, where windsurfers, hobiecats and small sailboats are available for hire in summer. The walk takes about 25 minutes. Turn right when you finally come to a small road leading down to a jetty. At the end of the small road turn left, and walk past the boathouse to reach the beach. You can also hop on bus No 73A, which takes you close to the intersection with the small road. Opposite the bus stop is a **military cemetery** for military personnel who died during the British occupation of Hong Kong and WWII. The oldest graves date from 1843.

To get to Stanley from Central take bus No 6 or express bus No 260 from the Exchange Square Bus Terminus. The No 6 bus climbs over the hills separating the north and south sides of the island, which makes for a scenic, winding ride. Bus No 260, which goes via the Aberdeen tunnel is quicker, and perhaps better for those prone to motion sickness. From Hoi Ping Rd in Causeway Bay you can take the No 40 green minibus. If you're coming from Shaukeiwan (eastern terminus of the tram), take bus No 14 down to Stanley. Bus No 73 connects Stanley with Repulse Bay and Aberdeen.

One note of warning. If you visit Stanley during the weekend, you may have a tough time catching a bus back to Central between 5 and 8 pm, when everybody else is also trying to get home. If queues for the Nos 6 and 260 buses are too long to endure, consider the No 73 to Aberdeen. Or check the queue for the No 40 green minibus to Causeway Bay.

Shek O

Shek O, on the south-east coast, has one of the best beaches on Hong Kong Island. And because it takes around two hours to get here, it's usually less crowded than the other south island spots. On weekdays the town is sometimes almost deserted, and it's easy to spend the afternoon lazing on the beach, snacking at the open-air restaurants or gawking at the mansions dotting the Shek O headlands.

Shek O is a small village so it's easy to get your bearings. From the bus stop walk five minutes and you're on the beach. En route you'll pass a few good restaurants (see the Places to Eat chapter.) If you take the road leading off to the left you'll enter a maze of small homes, which gradually grow in size and luxury as you head up the peninsula that juts out east of the beach. This is the **Shek O headlands**, home to some of Hong Kong's wealthiest families. If you traipse down to the tip of the peninsula you'll come to a viewpoint where you can look out over the South China Sea: next stop, the Philippines.

There are some hikes around Shek O beach, though the terrain is steep and the underbrush quite thick in spots. Better yet, take advantage of the bicycle rental shops and peddle down to **Big Wave Bay**, another fine beach located two km to the north of Shek O. To get there just follow the road out of town, past Shek O Country and Golf Course, bear right at the traffic circle and keep going until the road ends.

To get to Shek O, take the MTR or tram to Shaukeiwan, and from Shaukeiwan take bus No 9 to the last stop. It's a long ride but quite scenic and, depending on your driver, exciting.

KOWLOON

Kowloon presents another face of Hong Kong, quite different from that of the former colonial outpost across Victoria Harbour. Leave the glittering hotels and shopping malls of Tsimshatsui and you begin to see where Hong Kong and China come together, culturally at least. East doesn't really meet west in Kowloon: it swallows it up. Walk down a street in Yaumatei or Mongkok. While Hong Kong Island has its share of gritty neighbourhoods, there's something in them that feels familiar to western eyes. Not so here. While English signs abound, they look decidedly secondary. Hong Kong Island is home to big business and government. Kowloon is home to shopkeepers and triads.

Kowloon's districts are best seen on foot. In a consistent theme for Hong Kong, there aren't too many fantastic sights here. It's the overall experience that's worth taking in. However, there are a few good destinations, and travelling to them should give you plenty of chance to soak up the atmosphere.

Strictly speaking, Kowloon (as annexed in 1859) is the 12 sq km extending from Tsimshatsui north to Boundary St. The remainder of the peninsula, up to the hills that form the effective border with the New Territories, is officially called New Kowloon, which the British gained in 1898. However nearly 100 years later few people note the distinction, and the entire peninsula is referred to as just Kowloon.

Tsimshatsui

Perched at the very edge of the peninsula, Tsimshatsui (Map 16) is Hong Kong's tourist ghetto. Countless clothing and shoe stores, restaurants, pubs, sleazy bars, fast-food places, camera and electronics stores and hotels are somehow crammed into a few sq km. Like its Hong Kong Island counterpart Causeway Bay, this is one of Hong Kong's key shopping districts and is also a good place to avoid on weekends if you don't enjoy dense crowds.

Next to the Star Ferry Terminal and the Hong Kong Cultural Centre is one of Kowloon's few remaining examples of colonial architecture, a 45m tall **clock tower**. This is all that has been preserved from the original

southern terminus of the Kowloon-Canton Railway
(KCR), which was built in 1916 and torn down in 1978.
The old station was a colonial-style building adorned
with columns, but it became too small to handle passenger traffic, which soared with the development of the
New Territories. The new station at Hunghom, where
travellers now begin their journey to China, is much
larger but far less appealing.

On the other side of the Star Ferry Terminal is **Ocean
Terminal/Harbour City**, a labyrinth of swanky retail
shops, hotels and office towers that seems to stretch several
km. Ocean Terminal is the long building jutting out into
the harbour, which is also Hong Kong's sole pier for cruise
liners. The sheer size and number of stores make this
mega-mall interesting, but if you're one of those people
that dislikes shopping, you'll hate this place.

A few blocks east along Salisbury Rd stands one of
Hong Kong's landmarks, the famous hotel, **The Peninsula**. Although it now has plenty of worthy competitors,
for many this is still the place to stay when in Hong
Kong. Some of its outward elegance was sacrificed when
a new 20 storey extension was added. And reclamation
has robbed the hotel of its prestigious waterfront location. But it's still worth browsing through the exclusive
shops and the main lobby, usually packed with tourists
rather than guests. Afternoon tea here is still one the best
experiences in town. For more details on The Peninsula,
see the Places to Stay chapter.

The area behind The Peninsula, including Ashley,
Hankow and Lock Rds, is a warren of cheap (and often
shady) shops, restaurants and bars. It's a fun area to
wander around, particularly in the evening. And of
course no visit to Kowloon is complete without at least
a brief stroll down **Nathan Rd**. This artery was named
after the governor of the time, Sir Matthew Nathan, who
held office at the start of this century. It was promptly
renamed Nathan's Folly, since in those times Kowloon
was sparsely populated and such a wide road was
unnecessary. The southern section is known as the
'Golden Mile', which refers to both the price of real estate
here and also its ability to suck money out of tourist
pockets.

Dominating the intersection of Nathan and Cameron
Rds is the **Kowloon Mosque & Islamic Centre**, the
largest mosque in Hong Kong. The present building was
completed in 1984 and occupies the site of a previous
mosque built in 1896 for Muslim Indian troops who were
garrisoned in barracks at what is now Kowloon Park.
The mosque is interesting to admire from the outside,
but you can't simply wander in and take photos. If you

are a Muslim, you can participate in their religious activities; otherwise you must obtain permission.

Hong Kong Cultural Centre Complex The government chose a worthy, if perhaps not very attractive, successor for the prime plot of waterfront land formerly occupied by the KCR station. The **Hong Kong Cultural Centre** (☎ 2734-2009) was built as 'a high-technology nail in the coffin of the long-dead cliché that Hong Kong is a cultural desert'. Or so the government says. It is in many ways a world-class venue, including a 2100 seat concert hall, a theatre that seats 1800, a smaller 300 seat theatre, rehearsal studios, an arts library and a pretty impressive main lobby. The concert hall even has an 8000 pipe organ, the largest in South-East Asia (how many others are there?). The advent of the Cultural Centre has enabled Hong Kong to regularly book high-profile international artists. The Cultural Centre is open 9 am to 11.30 pm daily, and 30 minute tours (HK$10 for adults, HK$5 for kids and seniors) are offered at 12.30 pm and 4 pm.

Adjacent to the Cultural Centre and grabbing one of the nicest views in town is the **Hong Kong Museum of Art** (☎ 2734-2167). It's easy to spend an afternoon wandering around here. There are six galleries exhibiting Chinese antiquities; Chinese fine arts; historical pictures, paintings and lithographs of old Hong Kong; and the Xubaizhi collection of painting and calligraphy. The sixth gallery has rotating international exhibits. The exhibits are quite tastefully displayed, giving one the feeling that funding isn't a major problem for this particular museum. When your feet are sore, take a seat in the hallway and enjoy the harbour vista. There is a gift shop on the ground level that has a commendable collection of art books and prints, including an extensive section on Chinese art. The museum is closed on Thursdays, otherwise operating hours are weekdays (including Saturdays) from 10 am to 6 pm, and Sundays and holidays from 1 to 6 pm. Admission is HK$10 for adults, HK$5 for kids and seniors.

Behind the art museum, looking like a giant golf ball, is the **Hong Kong Space Museum** (☎ 2734-2722). It's divided into three parts: the Space Theatre (planetarium), the Hall of Space Science and the Hall of Astronomy. Exhibits include ancient astronomy, early rockets, future space programmes, manned spaceflight and solar and stellar science. The displays are in general quite interesting and in many cases interactive. Though most of the spacecraft shown are models, the museum did manage to snare the Mercury space capsule piloted by astronaut Scott Carpenter in 1962. Opening times for the exhibition halls are weekdays (except Tuesdays) from 1 to 9 pm, and from 10 am to 9 pm on weekends and holidays. Admission is HK$10 for adults and kids, HK$5 for students and seniors.

The Space Theatre has several 'sky shows' daily (except Tuesdays), some in English and some in Cantonese. Headphone translations are available for all shows. The museum also shows Omnimax, or giant-screen, films. However the films are projected onto the rounded dome of the theatre, and the effect is more laughable than dramatic. Space Theatre shows generally start at 11.30 am, with the last show usually at 8.30 pm. Both skyshows and Omnimax films cost HK$28 for adults and children, HK$14 for students and seniors. To find out what's playing and when, stop by the ticket window or call the museum. Advance bookings can be made up to one hour before show time by calling (☎ 2734-9009).

Kowloon Park Once the site of the Whitfield Barracks for British and Indian troops, this area has been reborn as a park that is interesting mostly for how artificial it looks. Concrete pathways and walls crisscross and dissect the grass, birds hop around in cages, and cement towers and viewpoints dot the landscape. Still, it's not a bad place to escape the cacophony of Tsimshatsui. The Hong Kong Museum of History is here (see below), as well as an excellent indoor/outdoor pool complex complete with waterfalls. If you want to swim (between April and October when the pools are open), go in the morning or afternoon on a weekday: on weekends there are so many bathers it's tough to make out the water. There's a fee of HK$17 to use the pools. Admission to the park itself is free. Open hours are 6 am to midnight.

Hong Kong Museum of History A visit here is almost essential for anyone who hopes to gain a deeper understanding of Hong Kong. The museum (☎ 2367-1124) is located in the grounds of Kowloon Park, near the Haiphong Rd entrance. The museum takes the visitor on a walk through Hong Kong's entire existence, from prehistoric times (about 6000 years ago, give or take a few) to the present. In addition to a large collection of 19th and early 20th century photographs, there are replicas of village dwellings, traditional Chinese costumes and a re-creation of an entire street block from 1881. It's an attractive exhibit, and does a fine job of telling the fascinating story of Hong Kong. The museum is open Monday to Thursday and Saturday from 10 am to 6 pm, and Sunday and public holidays from 1 to 6 pm.

It is closed on Friday. Admission costs HK$10, HK$5 for students and seniors.

Tsimshatsui East

This triangular block of land east of Chatham Rd didn't even exist until 1980. Built entirely on reclaimed land, Tsimshatsui East (Map 16) is a cluster of shopping malls, hotels, theatres, restaurants and night clubs. Everything is new – there are none of the old, crumbling buildings of nearby Tsimshatsui. The area has a few office towers, but mainly caters to more affluent shoppers, diners and night-owls. If you get curious and decide to venture into a night club, be prepared to burn a hole in your pocket. For more information, see the Entertainment chapter.

The Promenade Along with the Peak, this waterfront walkway offers some of the best views in Hong Kong. It's a great place to stroll during the day, and a return trip at night shows the Hong Kong Island skyline in all its neon glory. Your companions will include joggers, amorous couples, fellow visitors and, believe or not, people fishing right off the Promenade. (Didn't think anything could survive in that water, did you?) The Promenade becomes a sea of people during the Chinese New Year fireworks display and again during the Dragon Boat Festival.

The Promenade officially starts at the New World Centre, though you can walk along the water starting from the Star Ferry Terminal. It goes all the way to the Hong Kong Coliseum and Kowloon KCR station. Midway along is a ferry pier, where you can catch a hovercraft across the harbour to Hong Kong Island.

Hong Kong Science Museum This is a good place to take the kids. The museum (☎ 2732-3232) is near the corner of Chatham and Granville Rds, about 10 minutes walk north from the Promenade. It's a multi-level complex with more than 500 exhibits on computers, energy, physics, robotics, telecommunications, transportation and more. About 60% of the exhibits are 'hands-on', which helps keep younger visitors interested. Admission is HK$25 for adults, HK$15 for kids, students and seniors. Operating hours are 1 to 9 pm Tuesday to Friday, and 10 am to 9 pm on weekends and holidays.

Yaumatei

In Cantonese Yaumatei means 'place of sesame plants'. The name obviously dates from years gone by. Now the only plants you'll find in this heavily urban district are sitting in planters that cling precariously to grimy, crumbling tenements. The narrow streets and alleys of Yaumatei (Map 13) are a good place to check out Hong Kong's more traditional urban society. Within the square bordered by Kansu, Woosung, Nanking and Ferry Sts you'll stumble across old pawn shops, outdoor fresh food markets, Chinese pharmacies, mahjong parlours and other retailers practising their time-honoured trades. To see some weird items, poke your nose into one of the dried food stores – fancy dried lizard on a stick? How about bat?

The best way to see this area is to just set off by foot and take whichever turns beckon. It's just a short walk from Yaumatei MTR station. If you want a detailed guided tour, pick up a copy of the HKTA's *Yaumatei Walking Tour*, available at HKTA information centres for HK$28.

Jade Market Hong Kong tourist literature really hypes up this place, but it's actually fairly dull.

There are several hundred stalls selling all varieties and grades of jade from inside a large tent. Jade is a traditional symbol of longevity for the Chinese, and this market definitely works better for locals than tourists. Some sellers are reasonable, other dishonest. Unless you really know your jade, it's probably not wise to spring for any really pricey pieces here.

The market is located near the junction of Battery and Kansu Sts under a flyover. It's open daily between 10 am and 3.30 pm, but go early as you may find the sellers packing up and leaving at about 1 pm. To get there take bus No 9 from the Kowloon Star Ferry Bus Terminal in Tsimshatsui, get off at Kowloon Central Post Office and walk down to Kansu St. You can also take the MTR and get off at either Jordan or Yaumatei MTR stations.

Tin Hau Temple East of Public Square St, a block or two to the north of the Jade Market, is a large Tin Hau temple, dedicated to the Patron Goddess of Seafarers. Off to the right as you face the main temple is a row of fortune-tellers. The temple complex also houses an altar dedicated to Shing Wong (the City God) and To Tei Kung (the Earth God). The temple is open daily from 8 am to 6 pm.

Temple St The liveliest night market in Hong Kong, Temple St is the place to go for cheap clothes, cheap food, watches, footwear, cookware and everyday items. It used to be known as 'Men's St' because the market only sold men's clothing. Though there are still a lot of men's items on sale, vendors don't discriminate – anyone's money will do.

Near the Tin Hau temple you'll usually find fortune-tellers and palm-readers, a few of whom may speak English. If you're lucky (or unlucky, depending on your tastes) you may run into a street troupe performing Cantonese opera, though this is fairly rare.

For street food, head to the section of Temple St north of the Tin Hau temple. At night you can get anything from a simple bowl of noodles to a full meal, served at your very own table on the street. There are also a few good restaurants around here.

Temple St hawkers set up at 6 pm and leave by midnight. The market is at its best in the evening from about 8 to 11 pm when it's clogged with stalls and people.

Mongkok

This district has one of the highest population densities of any place on earth, a point that hits home as soon as you hit the sidewalks. Aside from housing a ridiculous number of people in shabby apartment blocks, Mongkok (Map 13) is also one of Hong Kong's busiest shopping districts: the name in Cantonese aptly means 'prosperous corner'. But this is not a place for designer fashion, ritzy jewellery and hovering salespeople. This is where locals come to buy everyday items like jeans, tennis shoes, kitchen supplies, computer accessories and so on. This is also a good place to buy backpacks, hiking boots and other travel gear (see the Shopping chapter). Even if none of these items are on your shopping list, it's worth taking a look around.

Most of the action is east of Nathan Rd. Two blocks' walk from Mongkok MTR station, Tung Choi St throws up a nightly street market that is fun to wade through. An alter ego of the Temple St market in Yaumatei, Tung Choi St used to also be known as 'Women's St' selling only goods for females. Like Temple St, it now happily caters to both sexes.

The streets west of Nathan Rd reveal Hong Kong's seamier side, for here is where you'll find some of the city's seediest brothels. Mostly run by triads, these places are often veritable prisons for young women and teenage girls, usually brought to Hong Kong on false pretences and then forced into prostitution. The Royal Hong Kong Police routinely raid these places, but a look at the rows of brightly coloured signs shows that business goes on as usual. This is not a great part of town to hang around after midnight, though there's little risk of violent crime.

Bird Market Though it's only one block long, the bird market is one of the most interesting streets in Hong Kong. Chinese have long favoured birds as pets, especially ones that sing. The singing prowess of a bird often determines its price. Some birds are also considered harbingers of good fortune, which is why you'll see some men carrying birds to the horse races.

Aside from the hundreds of birds on display, elaborate cages carved from teak and bamboo, and ceramic water and food dishes are also on sale. The birds seem to live pretty well: the Chinese use chopsticks to feed live grasshoppers to their feathered friends, and give them honey nectar to coat the vocal cords.

The market is on Hong Lok St, an obscure alley on the south side of Argyle St, two blocks west of Nathan Rd. At one time the Hong Kong government had plans to move the bird market but as yet nothing has happened. Just in case it might be wise to check with the HKTA.

Other Kowloon Sights

Most of Kowloon's other districts, such as Shamshuipo, Kowloon City or Kwun Tong are vast tracts of featureless public housing estates, residential towers and industrial buildings. However there are a few sights worthy of mention scattered about. And though some are not that fascinating, getting there and back will definitely add to your perspective on Hong Kong.

Wong Tai Sin Temple This Taoist temple is one of the largest and liveliest in Hong Kong, and is worth visiting mainly to see the crowds. The buildings and gardens, dating from 1973 onwards, are attractive enough, but nothing to really inspire.

According to legend, Wong Tai Sin was a shepherd living in a remote section of Zhejiang Province in the 3rd century AD. At the age of 15 he apprenticed to an immortal and through his studies concocted a medicine that cured all illnesses. Not surprisingly he is worshipped by those concerned about their health. The statue of Wong Tai Sin, located in the main temple, was brought to Hong Kong from China and installed in its present site in 1921.

Like most Chinese temples, this one is an explosion of colour, with red pillars, bright yellow roofs and blue latticework all around. Behind the main temple are the Good Wish Gardens, replete with colourful (though concrete) pavilions, curved pathways and an artificial waterway. Adjacent to the temple is an arcade filled with dozens of booths operated by fortune tellers. Some of them speak good English, so if you really want to know

GLENN BEANLAND

GLENN BEANLAND

Top: Jade Market, Yaumatei
Bottom: Wong Tai Sin Temple, Kowloon

what fate has in store for you, this is your chance to find out. Just off to one side of the arcade is a small open area where you can look up and get a magnificent view of Lion Rock, one of Hong Kong's prominent natural landmarks.

The temple is open daily from 7 am to 5.30 pm. The busiest times are around the Chinese New Year, Wong Tai Sin's birthday and most Sundays. There is no admission fee for visiting this or any other temple in Hong Kong, but they've become used to tourists dropping a few coins (HK$1 will do) into the donation box by the entrance. Getting there is easy. Take the MTR to Wong Tai Sin station then follow the signs.

Sung Dynasty Village This was once part of Lai-chikok Amusement Park before it was hyped up as an authentic re-creation of a Chinese village from 10 centuries ago. How authentic is subject to question: it's highly doubtful ancient China was anywhere near this clean and orderly.

The village is a type of Chinese Disneyland-supermarket where craftspeople and other villagers walk around in period costumes, engaging in Sung Dynasty (960-1279AD) pursuits such as fortune-telling, black-smithing, woodcarving and getting married. It also houses Hong Kong's largest wax museum. Candy and pastries can be bought with coupons made to look like Sung money, but if you want a kimono, paperweight or other souvenir from the village shop you'll have to have 20th century cash.

Sung Dynasty Village (☎ 2741-5111) is open from 10 am to 8.30 pm daily. Admission is HK$120 for adults, HK$65 for children. The HKTA and some hotels can book you on a tour if you're so inclined. These cost HK$165, and for a higher tariff (HK$210 to HK$290) a snack or meal is thrown in. The tour includes transport from Tsimshatsui or Central plus the services of a guide.

You can, of course, get there by using the MTR or bus. From the Kowloon Star Ferry Bus Terminal in Tsimshatsui take bus No 6A, which terminates near the Sung Dynasty Village. From Hong Kong Island, take the vehicular ferry to the Jordan Ferry Bus Terminal in Yaumatei – then catch bus No 12 to the park. Alternatively, take the MTR to Mei Foo station and from there head north along Lai Wan Rd and turn left at the junction with Mei Lai Rd. Continue down Mei Lai Rd until you get to the village. It's about a 15 minute walk.

Laichikok Amusement Park Adjacent to the Sung Dynasty Village is the hokey old Laichikok Amusement

Park. This place looks to be living on borrowed time, and some of the rides are starting to show signs of rust. Still the bumper cars, shooting galleries and balloons might be good for a laugh, and the park also has one of Hong Kong's few ice-skating rinks.

Operating hours for the park are Monday to Friday from 11.30 am to 9.30 pm, and from 10 am to 9.30 pm on weekends and holidays. Admission costs HK$15 for adults, HK$10 for kids. For transport there, see the Sung Dynasty Village section above.

Lei Cheng Uk Museum & Han Tomb This burial vault dating from the Han Dynasty (206BC-22AD) is Hong Kong's earliest historical monument. It was discovered in 1955 when workers were levelling the hillside for a housing estate. The tomb consists of four barrel-vaulted brick chambers in the form of a cross, around a domed central chamber. The tomb is estimated to be more than 1600 years old. While somewhat interesting, it's kind of a long way to come for an anti-climactic peek through plexiglass.

The museum (☎ 2386-2863), a branch of the Hong Kong Museum of History, is located at 41 Tonkin St, Lei Cheng Uk Estate, Shamshuipo. It is open daily (except Thursday) from 10 am to 1 pm and from 2 to 6 pm. On Sundays and most public holidays it's open 1 to 6 pm. Admission is free.

To get there, take bus No 2 from the Kowloon Star Ferry Bus Terminal in Tsimshatsui and get off at Tonkin St. The nearest MTR station is Cheung Sha Wan, a 10 minute walk from the tomb. Just follow the signs.

Lei Yue Mun East of Kai Tak airport, the little village of Lei Yu Mun is a popular spot for Hong Kong seafood lovers. The neighbourhood is somewhat quaint and very lively at night when the diners arrive en masse. Although the seafood isn't necessarily better here than anywhere else, it makes for a nice eating excursion. You can get there on bus No 14C from Kwun Tong MTR station – take it to the end of the line (Sam Ka Tsuen Terminal).

NEW TERRITORIES

This city guide focuses on Hong Kong Island and Kowloon, and does not pretend to do justice to the New Territories. However, the following museums, temples and monasteries can be reached fairly quickly from the urban area, and thus are included here. Several day trips into the New Territories are also covered in the Excursions chapter.

For a look at life among the land-owning clans of 200 years ago, check out the **Sam Tung Uk Museum** (☎ 2411-2001). The museum's 2000 sq m house a restoration of a village founded by the Chan clan in 1786. Within the museum grounds are eight fully furnished houses plus an ancestral hall. The museum is a five minute walk to the east of Tsuen Wan MTR station and is open from 9 am to 4 pm daily except Tuesday. Admission is free.

The **Chinese University Art Gallery** (☎ 2609-7416) is a four-level museum housing local collections as well as those from museums in China. There's an enormous exhibit of paintings and calligraphy by Guangdong artists from the Ming period to modern times, as well as a collection of 2000-year-old bronze seals and a large collection of jade flower carvings. The gallery is open weekdays and Saturdays from 10 am to 4.30 pm, and on Sundays and public holidays from 12.30 to 4.30 pm (closed on some public holidays). Admission is free. To get there, take the KCR to University station. A free bus outside the station runs through the campus to the top of the hill. It's easiest to take the bus uphill and then walk back down to the station.

Also on the KCR line is the **Hong Kong Railway Museum** (☎ 2653-3339), which is housed in a restored 1913 railway station. Inside there are photos and illustrated explanations dating back to the start of rail travel in the colony and China. Lined up outdoors are a series of old trains dating back as far as 1911. The museum is open daily (except Tuesdays) from 9 am to 4 pm. Admission is free. The museum is a 10 minute walk north-west along the KCR tracks from Tai Po Market station. There are signs pointing the way.

The New Territories offer the chance to see a few working monasteries as well as some nicely appointed temples. One of the most impressive is the **Chuk Lam Sim Yuen**, or 'bamboo forest monastery'. Founded in 1927, it boasts three of the largest Buddha statues in Hong Kong. There are also a couple of smaller monasteries nearby. Two are on the hillside just above Chuk Lam Sim Yuen, and a third – Tung Lam Nien Temple – is across the road. To reach the monastery and temple complex, take green minibus No 85 from Shiu Wo St, two blocks south of Tsuen Wan MTR station.

Just 1.5 km north-east of the MTR station is the **Yuen Yuen Institute**, a large complex with Taoist, Buddhist and Confucian temples. The main building is a replica of the Temple of Heaven in Beijing. There is also a vegetarian restaurant. To get there, take green minibus

No 81 from Shui Wo St. Alternatively, take a taxi, which is not expensive. It would be possible to walk except that there seems to be no way for a pedestrian to get across Cheung Pei Shan Rd, which is basically a superhighway.

If you're big on Buddhas, head for the **Ten Thousand Buddha Monastery**, which sits on a hillside about 500m west of Shatin. Built in the 1950s, it actually has 12,800 miniature Buddha statues, all of similar heights but striking slightly different poses along the walls of the main temple. There is a nine level pagoda and larger than life statues of Buddha's followers in front of the temple. From the main monastery area, walk up more steps to find a smaller temple housing the embalmed body of the founding monk who died in 1965. His body was encased in gold leaf and is now on display behind a glass case. It is considered polite to put a donation in the box next to the display case to help pay for the temple's upkeep. The temple is open from 8 am to 6.30 pm. It's easy to reach: just take the KCR to Shatin station and go through the left-hand exit, following the signs. However from here on you'll need some strong legs to climb the 400 odd steps up to the complex.

If you're up in Tai Po to visit the railway museum, there is a **Man Mo temple** about 200m away on Fu Shin St. Like the Man Mo temple in Sheung Wan, Hong Kong Island, this place is dedicated to two Taoist deities representing the pen and the sword.

Further up the KCR line, at Fanling, you'll find the **Fung Ying Sin Kwun Temple**, a Taoist temple for the dead. The ashes of the departed are deposited here in what might be described as miniature tombs. It's an interesting place to look around, but be respectful of worshippers. The temple is located across from Fanling KCR station.

ACTIVITIES

Participatory Sports

Hong Kong may be a sea of concrete and asphalt, but there are a surprising number of ways to keep fit and have fun. One excellent all-round option is the South China Athletic Association (☎ 2577-6932), 88 Caroline Hill Rd, Causeway Bay (Map 7). The SCAA has numerous indoor facilities for billiards, bowling, tennis, squash, ping pong, gymnastics, fencing, yoga, judo, karate and dancing. Outdoor activities include golf, and there is also a women's activities section. Membership is very cheap and there is a discounted short-term membership available for visitors. Another excellent place you can contact is the Hong Kong Amateur Athletic

Association (☎ 2574-6845), Room 913, Queen Elizabeth Stadium, 18 Oi Kwan Rd, Wanchai (Map 6). All sorts of sports clubs have activities or hold members meetings here.

In general, gyms and fitness centres have prohibitively expensive membership fees and there's often a long wait to join (one exception is the SCAA). So if your exercise routine involves fitness training, you may want to find an alternative, unless your hotel has a gym.

For information on martial arts, see the following Courses section.

Billiards & Snooker Snooker is more prevalent, though you may be able to shoot a game of eight-ball in some places. In Tsimshatsui East, try the Peninsula Billiards Club (☎ 2739-0638), Peninsula Centre, and the Castle Billiards Club (☎ 2367-9071), Houston Centre. In Wanchai, there are two good places, Jim Mei White Snooker (☎ 2833-6628), 339 Jaffe Rd, and Winsor Billiard Company (☎ 2575-5505), 10 Canal Rd West. Also in Wanchai, Ridgeways (☎ 2866-6608) has eight-ball tables. In Causeway Bay there is Kent Billiard & Snooker Association (☎ 2833-5665), Elizabeth House, Jaffe Rd and Percival St.

Cricket This most British of sports is also increasingly popular with locals, and club waiting lists are very long. On Hong Kong Island, north of Deep Water Bay, is the Hong Kong Cricket Club (☎ 2574-6266). On the other side of Victoria Harbour is the Kowloon Cricket Club (☎ 2367-4141) in Yaumatei. Additional information may be obtained by contacting the Hong Kong Cricket Association (☎ 2859-2414).

Cycling There are bicycle paths in the New Territories, mostly around Tolo Harbour. The paths run from Shatin to Tai Po and continue up to Tai Mei Tuk. You can rent cycles in these three places, but they get very crowded on weekends. On a weekday you may have the paths to yourself. Bicycle rentals are also available at Shek O on Hong Kong Island, and Mui Wo on Lantau Island. Try contacting the Hong Kong Cycling Association (☎ 2573-3861) in Wanchai or the Hong Kong Cyclist Club (☎ 2788-3898) in Shamshuipo. To find out about good mountain biking areas, try asking the staff at Flying Ball Bicycle Co (☎ 2381-3661) in Mongkok.

Fishing Sport-fishing from small-sized yachts is a popular activity for expats and locals alike. To organise a trip, contact the Hong Kong Amateur Fishing Society (☎ 2730-0442), Yaumatei. While there are virtually no restrictions on sea fishing, it's a different story with fishing at freshwater reservoirs. There are limits on the quantity and size of fish taken from reservoirs, and the fishing season is from September through March. A licence (HK$20) is required, which can be obtained from the Water Supplies Department (☎ 2829-4500), Wanchai.

Football (Soccer) Soccer has caught the imagination of the Chinese, so competition for playing fields is keen. If you want to get serious about competing in matches, contact the Football Association (☎ 2712-9122), Kowloon. The association also maintains a women's division.

Golf There are five golf courses in Hong Kong. Green fees vary, but average around HK$800 for visitors. Fees can fall to around HK$300 if you're signed in by a member. On weekends, the courses are crowded and you pay more. The Royal Hong Kong Golf Club has two courses. The less expensive one is the nine hole course at Deep Water Bay (☎ 2812-7070), on the south side of Hong Kong Island. Considerably nicer is the course at Fanling (☎ 2670-1211) in the New Territories. The Discovery Bay Golf Club (☎ 2987-7271) on Lantau Island is perched high on a hill, offering some impressive views. So does the Shek O Country Club, which sits at the south-east tip of Hong Kong Island. The Clearwater Bay Golf & Country Club (☎ 2719-5936) is on the Sai Kung Peninsula in the New Territories.

Hiking Hiking is one of Hong Kong's best outdoor activities. Scenery is beautiful and the trails, most of which are in country parks, well maintained. Lantau Island and the MacLehose Trail in the New Territories offer some outstanding hikes. The sport is quite popular so that many trails are very crowded on weekends. But on weekdays many trails are deserted.

The Government Publications Office (see the Maps section in the Facts for the Visitor chapter) has a series of excellent topographical maps. The Country Parks Authority (☎ 2733-2132) in Kowloon and the HKTA also have useful leaflets detailing good hikes. If you really want to scour the trails, consider picking up a copy of Kaarlo Schepel's *Magic Walks in Hong Kong*, which has three different volumes.

If you're planning to hike a good distance, take into account the merciless sun, high heat and humidity during spring and summer. November through March are the best months for strenuous treks. Hong Kong's countryside is also home to a variety of snakes, some poisonous. There's not a big chance that you'll run into one, especially if you stick to trails and avoid walking through dense underbrush. If you see a snake, the best thing to do is to walk away from it.

To contact hiking clubs, call the Federation of Hong Kong Hiking & Outdoor Activities Groups (☎ 2720-4042) in Mongkok. More serious climbers should try the Mountaineering Association (☎ 2391-6892), also in Mongkok; or the Mountaineering Union (☎ 2747-7003; fax 2770-7115).

Horseback Riding Hong Kong's small size limits opportunities for horseback riding. The Hong Kong Riding Union (☎ 2762-0810), Kowloon Tong, organises rides in the New Territories. You can also call the Hong Kong Equestrian Centre (☎ 2607-3131), in the New Territories. Some very limited riding is possible at the Lantau Tea Gardens (☎ 2985-5718) at Ngong Ping on Lantau Island. On Hong Kong Island, riding lessons are available at the Pokfulam Riding School (☎ 2550-1359).

Parachuting It's not the cheapest of sports, but you can't beat it for thrills. If you get your jollies by diving out of aircraft, contact the Hong Kong Parachute Club (☎ 2891-5447) on Hong Kong Island. Jumps take place almost any day when the weather is good.

Paragliding If floating on air appeals to you, the place to contact is the Hong Kong Paragliding Association (☎ 2803-2779). The club has three sites for regular meets: Big Wave Bay on Hong Kong Island, nearby Dragon's Back at Shek O and Sunset Peak on Lantau Island. A four-day training course is required for beginners, which costs HK$1500 and is held in Tai Po in the New Territories.

Running If you'd like a morning jog with spectacular views, nothing beats the path around Victoria Peak on Harlech and Lugard Rds. Part of this is a 'fitness trail' with various exercise machines (parallel bars and the like). Almost as spectacular is the jog along Bowen Rd, which is closed to traffic and runs in an east-west direction in the hills above Wanchai. As long as there are no races at the time, the horse-racing track at Happy Valley is an excellent place to run. There is also a running track in Victoria Park in Causeway Bay. If you like easy runs followed by beer and company, consider joining Hash House Harriers (☎ 2376-2299). On the Kowloon side, a popular place to run is the waterfront Promenade in

Tsimshatsui East. The problem here is that it's not a very long run, but the views are good and it's close to many of the hotels.

The Hong Kong International Marathon is held on the second day of the Chinese New Year. This has become a cross-border event, with part of the running course passing through China. The Coast of China Marathon is held in March. Contact the HKTA for more information on upcoming marathons.

Sauna & Massage OK, so it's not much of a sport. But it's a great way to relax following any activity, whether it's been a strenuous hike through the hills or a frantic day of dodging fellow shoppers in Causeway Bay. Sauna baths are popular in Hong Kong and many offer a legitimate massage service. Most are only for men, but the hotels and a few of the saunas have facilities for women as well. Prices typically range from around HK$190 to HK$250 for a sauna, steambath and one hour massage.

On Hong Kong Island one of the biggest places is the New Paradise Health Club (☎ 2574-8404), 414 Lockhart Rd, Wanchai. Services include sauna, steambath, jacuzzi and massage for both men and women. Nearby the elaborate Sunny Paradise Sauna (☎ 2831-0123), 339-347 Lockhart Rd, only takes men, but it's legitimate. One of the oldest places in town is the funky Hong Kong Sauna (☎ 2572-8325) at 388 Jaffe Rd, Wanchai. This place is tiny and looks really seedy, but it's on the up and up. Again, it only takes men.

Over in Kowloon, another reputable establishment is Crystal Spa (☎ 2722-6600), Basement 2, Harbour Crystal Centre, 100 Granville Rd, Tsimshatsui. In pricey Tsimshatsui East is VIP Sauna (☎ 2311-2288), 13th floor, Autoplaza, 65 Mody Rd.

Scuba Diving Diving in Hong Kong is not very rewarding as pollution has killed off most of the interesting sea life and muddied the water. But there are organisations which put together dives near reefs and islands further out from Hong Kong. Try the Hong Kong Underwater Association (☎ 2572-3792) in Wanchai. An alternative is the Sea Dragons Skin Diving Club (☎ 2891-2113). Bunn's Diving Equipment (☎ 2893-7899) in Wanchai organises dives every Sunday from 9 am to 4.30 pm at a cost of HK$280. Bunn's also has another branch (☎ 2380-5344) in Mongkok.

Squash There are about 600 public squash courts in Hong Kong. These become totally full in the evening or on holidays. The most modern facilities are to be found at the Hong Kong Squash Centre (☎ 2869-0611), next to Hong Kong Park in Central. Book in advance. This is also the home of the Hong Kong Squash Rackets Association, which has done much to promote the sport. There are also squash courts in the Queen Elizabeth Stadium in Wanchai. In Shatin in the New Territories, you can play squash at the Jubilee Sports Centre (☎ 2605-1212).

Swimming Except for Kowloon and the north side of Hong Kong Island, there are good beaches spread throughout the territory. The most accessible beaches are on the south side of Hong Kong Island but some of these are becoming increasingly polluted. The best beaches can be found on the Outlying Islands and in the New Territories. The longest beach in Hong Kong is Cheung Sha on Lantau Island.

There is an official swimming season from 1 April to 31 October. At this time, the 42 gazetted public beaches in Hong Kong are staffed with lifeguards. When the swimming season is officially declared finished, the beaches become deserted no matter how hot the weather. Conversely, from the first day of the official swimming season until the last, expect the beaches to be chock-a-block on weekends and holidays. On weekdays, it's not bad at all. At most of the beaches you will find toilets, showers, changing rooms, refreshment stalls and sometimes restaurants.

Hong Kong's Urban Council also operates 13 public swimming pools. There are particularly excellent pools in Kowloon Park (Tsimshatsui) and Victoria Park (Causeway Bay).

Tennis The Hong Kong Tennis Centre (☎ 2574-9122) is at Wong Nai Chung Gap, a spectacular pass in the hills between Happy Valley and Deep Water Bay on Hong Kong Island. It's open from 7 am until 11 pm, but it's only easy to get a court during working hours.

There are 13 courts in Victoria Park (☎ 2570-6186) in Causeway Bay which can be booked and are open from 6 am until 11 pm. There are four courts open from 6 am until 7 pm at Bowen Road Sports Ground (☎ 2528-2983) in the Mid-Levels. The South China Athletic Association (☎ 2577-6932) also operates the tennis courts at King's Park, Yaumatei.

Other facilities in Kowloon are at Tin Kwong Rd Playground in Kowloon City and at Kowloon Tsai Park in Shek Kip Mei. In the New Territories, you can play tennis at the Jubilee Sports Centre (☎ 2605-1212) in Shatin.

The Hong Kong Tennis Association (☎ 2890-1132) is in Victoria Park. This is the place to ask questions about available facilities and upcoming events. Spectators may be interested in the Hong Kong Open Tennis Championship, held every September. In October, there's the Hong Kong Tennis Classic in Victoria Park.

Waterskiing The main venues for waterskiing are on the south side of Hong Kong Island at Deep Water Bay, Repulse Bay, Stanley and Tai Tam. The south side of Lamma Island also attracts waterskiers. Ski rental and boat hire is around HK$300 per hour.

Places to contact include the Deep Water Bay Speedboat Company (☎ 2812-0391) and Hong Kong Waterski Association (☎ 2431-2290).

Windsurfing The best months for windsurfing are September through December when a steady north-east monsoon blows. Windsurfing during a typhoon is *not* recommended! Rental fees are typically from HK$50 to HK$80 per hour. Around December, Stanley Beach becomes the venue of the Hong Kong Open Windsurfing Championship. At Stanley Main Beach on Hong Kong Island you can try the Pro Shop (2723-6816) and the Stanley Windsurfing Centre (☎ 2813-9937). Shek O is another good place on Hong Kong Island for windsurfing.

Equipment rentals are available in the New Territories at the Windsurfing Centre (☎ 2792-5605), Sha Ha (just past Sai Kung). Also check out Tai Po Sailboard Centre in Tai Po. On Cheung Chau Island try the Cheung Chau Windsurfing Centre (☎ 2981-8316), Tungwan Beach. The place to ring for more information is the Windsurfing Association of Hong Kong (☎ 2866-3232), Wanchai.

Yachting & Sailing With water all around, it makes sense that this is an extremely popular activity in Hong Kong. Bearing witness to this are seven major yacht clubs. Most prominent among these is the august Royal Hong Kong Yacht Club, which has facilities throughout the territory. Even if you're not a member, you can check with any of the following clubs to see if any races are being held and whether an afternoon's sail aboard one of the entrant vessels is possible: Aberdeen Boat Club (☎ 2552-8182), Aberdeen Marina Club (☎ 2555-8321), Discovery Bay Marina Club (☎ 2987-9591), Hebe Haven Yacht Club (☎ 2719-9682), Royal Hong Kong Yacht Club

(☎ 2832-2817) and Hong Kong Yachting Association
(☎ 2574-2639).

If smaller sailboats or hobie cats are more your style,
you may be able to rent one down at St Stephen's Beach,
near Stanley. Hobies rent for around HK$150 to HK$200
per hour, depending on the size.

If there is a group of you, you may also want to
consider hiring a junk for the day or evening. This is a
great way to see the Outlying Islands and New Territories. Or sail out to Lamma or Lantau islands for
seafood lunches or dinners. A 16m junk can accommodate around 28 persons and costs HK$2500 to HK$2800
per day (eight hours). Costs tend to be higher on weekends and holidays. Junks nowadays are rather
mundane-looking diesel-powered boats, though they're
still largely made of wood. Outfits that rent junks
include: Charterboats Ltd (☎ 2555-8377), Aberdeen; The
Boatique (☎ 2555-9355), Aberdeen; Rent-A-Junk
(☎ 2780-0387), Mongkok.

COURSES

Hong Kong is not a bad place to brush up on your
Chinese culture, be it learning how to make a decent pot
of hot-and-sour soup, paint a classic landscape or jabber
away in Cantonese. The following list includes some
options for study. If you can't find what you're looking
for, the Community Advice Bureau (☎ 2524-5444) is a
volunteer-staffed operation that puts people together
with the organisations they seek. Also, the YMCA
(☎ 2369-2211) and YWCA (☎ 2522-3101) both offer a
broad range of cultural classes. For the visual arts, check
with the Hong Kong Museum of Art (☎ 2734-2167), the
Hong Kong Visual Arts Centre (☎ 2521-3008) and the
Hong Kong Arts Centre (☎ 2582-0219).

Calligraphy Most calligraphy courses in Hong Kong
are given in Chinese, but the Hong Kong Arts Centre has
some in English as well. You can also check with the
School of Professional and Continuing Education at
Hong Kong University (☎ 2547-2225).

Chinese Dancing The Jean M Wong School of Ballet
(☎ 2886-3992) has six branches across the territory where
you can study Chinese dance as well as ballet and other
western styles.

Chinese Painting Classes come and go with
demand, but you can check with the Hong Kong Arts

GLENN BEANLAND

Pleasure craft, Causeway Bay

Centre, the YWCA and the School of Professional and Continuing Education at Hong Kong University (☎ 2547-2225).

Cuisine Oddly enough, among the most regular providers of Chinese cooking lessons are two of Hong Kong's utility companies. Continuous classes in both Chinese and western cuisine are offered by the Towngas Cooking Centre (☎ 2576-1535), in Causeway Bay, and the Home Management Centre (☎ 2510-2828) in North Point. For strictly Chinese/Asian fare, try the Oriental Culinary Institute (☎ 2550-4961) in Pokfulam. In Kowloon, Chinese cooking lessons are given at the Chopsticks Cooking Centre (☎ 2336-8433) in Homantin.

Language Not too many people take the time and considerable effort needed to learn Cantonese, but there are a number of schools where you can learn. With China's economy booming, demand for Mandarin classes has soared. However, Hong Kong is a poor place to learn Mandarin, as there are few chances to use it, and if you do practice with Hong Kongers you risk picking up their atrocious accent. If you're really keen on Mandarin, head for Taiwan or China.

The Chinese University in Hong Kong offers regular courses in Cantonese and Mandarin. Classes can be arranged through the New Asia Yale centre in the China Language Institute, associated with the university. There are three terms a year – one 10-week summer term and two regular 15-week terms. Classes are also held by the

School of Professional and Continuing Education at Hong Kong University (☎ 2547-2225).

There are a number of private language schools which cater to individuals or companies. These informal schools offer more flexibility and will even dispatch a teacher to a company to teach the whole staff if need be. Considering all the native Chinese speakers in town, tuition is not cheap at these places, often running at around H$300 for one-on-one instruction. Some to consider include: Chinese Language Institute of Hong Kong (☎ 2524-8678) in Central; Chinese Language Society of Hong Kong (☎ 2529-1638) in Wanchai; Xianggang Putonghua Yanxishe Ltd (Mandarin only) (☎ 2391-7379) in Kowloon.

Martial Arts Chinese *gongfu*, or 'kungfu' as it's often called in the west, has formed the basis for many Asian martial arts. There are several organisations offering training in various schools of Chinese martial arts (*wushu*), as well as other Asian disciplines. Gongfu is related to taijiquan, the slow-motion shadow boxing used for exercise and spiritual health. Taijiquan classes are also available. Relevant addresses include:

Hong Kong Amateur Karatedo Association – Room 1006, Queen Elizabeth Stadium, 18 Oi Kwan Rd, Wanchai (☎ 2891-9705)

Hong Kong Chinese Martial Arts Association – 9th floor, 687A Nathan Rd, Kowloon (☎ 2394-4803)

Hong Kong Taekwondo Association – Room 1006, Queen Elizabeth Stadium, 18 Oi Kwan Rd, Wanchai (☎ 2891-2036)

Hong Kong Taichi Association – 11th floor, 60 Argyle St, Kowloon (☎ 2395-4884)

Hong Kong Whushu Union – 3rd floor, 62 Castle Peak Rd, Kowloon (☎ 2304-2733)

South China Athletic Association – 88 Caroline Hill Rd, Causeway Bay (☎ 2577-6932)

Wing Tsun Martial Arts Association – Block A, 8th floor, 440-442 Nathan Rd, Kowloon (☎ 2385-7115)

YMCA – 41 Salisbury Rd, Tsimshatsui (☎ 2369-2211)

Places to Stay

Though constantly flooded with visitors, Hong Kong does not have very diverse accommodation options. There are three basic categories: cramped guesthouses; adequate but uninspiring mid-range hotels; and luxury hotels, some of which are considered the world's finest.

Prices, even for budget accommodation, are higher than most other Asian cities, and you don't get a whole lot for your money, except for some of the top-end places. At the same time, within each category there is a good deal of choice, and you should be able to find a comfortable place to stay.

Dominating the lower end of the market are the so-called guesthouses, usually a block of tiny rooms squeezed into a converted apartment or two. Often there are several guesthouses operating out of the same building. Even the cheapest option, a bed at one of the youth hostels, is no bargain at HK$50. The picture brightens up a bit if there are two of you. Find a room in a clean guesthouse for around HK$200 and your accommodation cost falls to a more bearable level. And though the room may be a glorified closet, at least it's yours.

Hong Kong's mid-range hotels are as expensive as top-end places in many other cities. Prices range anywhere from HK$500 (relatively scarce) to HK$2000 for a double room. Singles are sometimes priced a bit lower. The average price you're likely to encounter is HK$1000. This will usually buy you a somewhat small room with bath and shower, TV, air-con and the other amenities. The best thing about these hotels is that there are a lot of them – several dozen in fact – so you can find one in almost any part of urban Hong Kong.

For those who can afford HK$2000 or more for a room, a stay in one of Hong Kong's luxury hotels is an experience worth savouring. Of course one must be selective: there are plenty of average hotels that charge top-end rates. But a few, such as The Peninsula, Island Shangri-La and Regent offer comfort, amenities and service that can compete with the world's finest five-star hotels.

Rates for mid-range and top-end hotels go up during the peak tourist seasons, which generally last from September through January, and March through June. The degree of increase varies widely with each hotel, but generally ranges between 10% and 30%. Prices given in this chapter represent low season, or standard, rates.

If you fly into Hong Kong needing a place to stay, the Hong Kong Hotels Association has a reservation centre at Kai Tak airport's Buffer Hall, located just outside customs. They can get you into a mid-range or luxury room cheaper than if you were to just walk in to the front desk. The centre does not handle any budget accommodation. The office is open from 7 am to midnight.

Booking hotels through a travel agent can also garner substantial discounts, sometimes as much as 40% off the walk-in price. If you're in Hong Kong and want to book either a mid-range or luxury hotel, you can call Phoenix Services (☎ 2722-7378), Room B, 6th floor, Milton Mansion, 96 Nathan Rd, Tsimshatsui. Another place that handles hotel bookings is Traveller Services (☎ 2375-2222), Room 1012, Silvercord Tower 1, 30 Canton Rd, Tsimshatsui.

The Hong Kong Tourist Association publishes a *Hotel Guide* that lists more than 80 Hong Kong hotels, complete with prices and photos. To get a hold of this before you leave home, contact the nearest HKTA overseas office (see the Facts for the Visitor chapter).

WHERE TO STAY

For the most part Central and Tsimshatsui are the most convenient for access to public transport. But between the MTR and the bus network, almost anywhere is pretty easy to get to, so this needn't be a major consideration. At any rate Central and Admiralty only have luxury hotels (with one exception), so you can pretty much rule these districts out if that's beyond your budget.

Staying in Tsimshatsui, Causeway Bay or Wanchai puts you close to a wide choice of restaurants, bars and shopping, and all have good transportation connections. Budget or room availability may push you out a bit further to areas like Mongkok, or North Point on Hong Kong Island. While these areas aren't as cosmopolitan, they have their own gritty charm, and will give you a chance to see where average Hong Kongers live.

The only time when Hong Kong's public transport network falls short is after 1 am, when the MTR shuts down and crossing the harbour becomes a bit more difficult. Serious night-owls may want to stay on Hong Kong Island, since the bars and clubs around Wanchai are open almost until sunrise. But Tsimshatsui holds its own in this department, so you'll have late-night entertainment options whichever side you stay on.

Hong Kong's budget accommodation is clustered mainly in Tsimshatsui, and to a lesser degree Causeway Bay. Mid-range hotels are all over the place, but the majority are in Kowloon, running from Tsimshatsui to Mongkok. There are also quite a few in Wanchai. It's easy to pick out Hong Kong's luxury accommodation: just look for the hotels with the fantastic harbour views.

If you need easy access to the airport, you can't get much closer than at the *Regal Airport Hotel* (☎ 2718-0333; fax 2718-4111), Sa Po Rd, Kowloon. The hotel is linked to the airport by a pedestrian overpass, so you can walk from your room right to the boarding gate. Doubles and twins range from HK$1300 to HK$2050.

PLACES TO STAY – BOTTOM END

The average double room in one of Hong Kong's guesthouses is slightly larger than a shoe box, with the bed taking up most of the floor space. Almost all rooms come with TV and air-conditioning. The price difference between singles and doubles ranges from HK$50 to HK$100. The cheapest rooms have no attached bath, and cost anywhere from HK$140 to HK$300. Rooms with a private washroom range from HK$160 to HK$550. Often the 'washroom' is not more than a shower cubicle with a sink and toilet crammed in it. Triple rooms are available in some places, and there are one or two spots that still have dormitory accommodation. If you're looking to pay HK$450 or more for a double room, consider some of the cheapest mid-range hotels: for HK$100 more you'll likely get a much better environment.

Before handing over any money, first check the room – especially the plumbing and air-con. Also, standards of cleanliness vary wildly from place to place: if one guesthouse is a dump take the time to check the next one.

In general it's safe to leave your luggage in your room provided there is a lock on the door. In some places you can keep your bags in a storage closet. But never leave valuables unattended, even for a few minutes. Another warning: be wary of touts who hang around the airport to lure backpackers with offers of cheap rooms. If they insist on escorting you to their guesthouse, it's probably best to decline. Some touts will even flash name cards of hostels and guesthouses which have been highly recommended in Lonely Planet or other guidebooks, and then they take you to some other dump. These characters also work the airport bus stops, particularly in Tsimshatsui.

Youth Hostels

The cheapest accommodation is through a member hotel of Hong Kong Youth Hostels Association (HKYHA), which charge HK$50 per night for a dorm bed.

There is only one youth hostel close to the city, the *Ma Wui Hall* (☎ 2817-5715), perched atop Mt Davis, near Kennedy Town on Hong Kong Island. From Central it's about a 20 to 30 minutes bus ride, and then a half-hour hike from the bus stop to the hostel. On the other hand this place is clean, quiet, has great views of the harbour and costs only HK$50 per night. There are cooking facilities and secure lockers. The hostel has 112 beds and is open from 7 am to 11 pm. Call ahead to make sure there's a bed before you make the trek out here.

To get to the hostel, take bus No 5B, 47 or 77 and get off at Felix Villas (the 5B terminus) on Victoria Rd. (Note: the 5B only runs from 6.50 to 10.14 am and 4.50 to 8.20 pm.) From the bus stop, walk back 100m. Look for the YHA sign and follow Mt Davis Path (not to be confused with Mt Davis Rd) – there is a shortcut which is signposted halfway up the hill. The walk takes 20 to 30 minutes. If you come from the airport, take the A2 bus to Central, then change to the 5B or 47 bus. Bus No 5B runs from Paterson St in Causeway Bay to Felix Villas. Bus No 47 starts at the Exchange Square Bus Terminus. You're least likely to use bus No 77, which runs westwards through to Aberdeen.

Dormitories

These are dwindling in number, but there are still a few left in Kowloon. The *STB Hostel* (☎ 2710-9199), operated by the Hong Kong Student Travel Bureau, has 32 single dorm beds at HK$100 each per night. It also has doubles for HK$400 to HK$450 and triples for HK$450 to HK$560. It's clean and relatively quiet, although some travellers have encountered less than friendly management in the past. The hostel is on the 2nd floor, Great Eastern Mansion, 255-261 Reclamation St, Mongkok, just to the west of Yaumatei MTR station (Map 13).

Up on the 16th floor of A Block in Chungking Mansions (see below) is the popular *Travellers' Hostel* (☎ 2368-7710), which has mixed dormitory accommodation for HK$60. Cooking facilities are available. There are also double rooms with/without attached bath for HK$140/160. This place sees a steady stream of travellers, and has a useful bulletin board.

Guesthouses

Tsimshatsui is the place to go for the cheapest guesthouses. Although the area can be noisy, at least you are close to inexpensive noodle shops and fast food places as well as several useful bus routes, airport bus stops, the MTR and the Star Ferry Terminal.

Chungking Mansions The very mention of this name can strike horror into some backpackers, while others look back with a twisted sort of fondness. Creaking with the weight of dozens of guesthouses, this enormous high-rise dump sits at 30 Nathan Rd, in the heart of Tsimshatsui (Map 16). It may not be pretty, but it's about the cheapest place to stay in Hong Kong.

Some of the guesthouses are actually quite nice inside. It's getting to them that makes for the Chungking Mansions' experience. Greeting all visitors at the Nathan Rd entrance is the ever-present pack of shiftless indolents who apparently have nothing better to do than eye you and your possessions while scheming ways to score quick cash. Make your way past rows of tiny shops – selling everything from tailored suits to trashy novels to dusty office supplies – to find the lifts labelled for the block you're headed to. This is the really fun part. There are only two tiny overworked lifts for each 17 storey block, often giving you a choice between a long line or a sweaty walk up the fire stairs. Lines for the A and B blocks are the worst. The lifts for the C, D and E blocks see much less use: the A and B blocks have the densest concentration of guesthouses, and are the most popular with travellers. Sooner or later the antiquated lifts will force you to use the fire stairs. This could be your clearest memory of Chungking Mansions: the grime, grease and trash that line some of these staircases look to predate the building itself.

Adding to the fun are occasional midnight raids by the police. Mostly they are looking for illegal immigrants – if your passport is at some embassy to get visa stamps, this could create a problem. At least try to have a photocopy of your passport and some other picture ID card. A few grams of hashish in your backpack could also win you a quick trip to jail.

There have been calls to raze Chungking Mansions because it's an eyesore and a firetrap. But the place is actually improving somewhat, though it's not in danger of losing its unique charm. After a 1993 fire, there was a crackdown on fire-safety violations, and many guesthouses were shut down. Others survived by upgrading their standards to meet the now-strict building codes.

It's usually possible to bargain for a bed, especially when business is slack. You can often negotiate a cheaper price if you stay a long time, but never do that the first night. Stay one night and find out how you like it before handing over two weeks' rent. Once you pay, there are no refunds, and be certain to get a receipt. Below is just a sampling of the dozens of Chungking Mansions guesthouses. The prices listed are only a guide and vary with the season, peaking in summer and during certain holidays such as Easter.

A Block:
Park Guesthouse – 15th floor; clean and friendly; singles range from HK$150 (bath outside) to HK$200 (attached bath) with air-con while doubles are HK$250 to HK$280 (☎ 2368-1689)

Super Guest House – 12th floor; owners are polite and the rooms very clean; singles/doubles without bath are HK$200, with bath attached HK$250 (☎ 2723-4817)

Tom's Guesthouse – 8th floor; has bright, airy rooms with attached bath starting at HK$200 (☎ 2722-4956)

London Guesthouse – 6th floor; looks a bit run down but is still clean; has larger than average rooms ranging from HK$200 to HK$220 (☎ 2366-5010)

Chungking House – 4th & 5th floors; not that friendly but has quiet singles with attached bath for HK$279, doubles HK$299 (☎ 2366-5362)

B Block:
Tom's Guesthouse (2nd branch) – 16th floor; management seems a bit lackadaisical but the rooms are clean and prices range around HK$200 (☎ 2367-9258)

Carlton Guesthouse – 15th floor; also has tidy rooms for around HK$200 (☎ 2721-0720)

Kamal Guesthouse – has very cheap rooms and even a couple of dorm beds for HK$50, but is a bit of a dump (☎ 2739-3301)

C Block:
Tom's Guesthouse (third branch) – 16th floor; clean and quiet rooms for around HK$200 (☎ 2367-9258)

Garden Guesthouse – 16th floor; excellent but more pricey; singles and doubles with private bath cost HK$200/300 (there's also one on the 7th floor) (☎ 2368-0981)

New Grand Guesthouse and *Osaka Guesthouse* – both on 13th floor, run by the same owner; not too welcoming but rooms range from HK$180 to HK$350 (☎ 2311-1702)

D & E Blocks:
Royal Plaza Inn – 5th floor, D Block; rooms with shared bath are HK$150 to HK$250 and with attached bath HK$200 to HK$450 (☎ 2367-1424)

Mandarin Guesthouse – 13th floor, E Block; clean and nice rooms though the smell of incense can get a little heavy; singles with attached bath are HK$200, doubles HK$300 (☎ 2366-0073)

Other Guesthouses If you just can't stomach the sight and stigma of staying at Chungking Mansions, don't despair. There are other options, both in Tsimshatsui and Causeway Bay.

In Tsimshatsui (Map 16), *Mirador Arcade* at 58 Nathan Rd is like a scaled-down version of Chungking Mansions, but considerably cleaner and roomier. It's on Nathan Rd between Mody and Carnarvon Rds, one block north of Chungking. A good place here is *Man Hing Lung Guest House* (☎ 2722-0678) on the 14th floor in Flat F2. All rooms come with air-con and TV and most have private baths. Singles cost HK$280 to HK$300 and doubles are HK$300 to HK$360. On the 13th floor is the *Kowloon Hotel* (☎ 2311-2523) and *New Garden Hotel* (same phone and owner). Singles or doubles with shared bath are HK$200 to HK$300. Doubles with private bath and refrigerator cost HK$300 to HK$450. Ask about discounts if you want to rent long-term. Down on the 12th floor, the *Cosmic Guest House* isn't really all that cosmic, but it's spotlessly clean and has been recently renovated. Singles with attached sink and shower (but no toilet) are HK$170 to HK$190, and doubles with private bathrooms are HK$190 to HK$240.

There are more guesthouses to be found in Tsimshatsui along Cameron Rd, near the intersection with Chatham Rd. The Lyton Building, 32-40 Mody Rd, also has several good guesthouses, all with private bath, air-con and TV.

Further north In Yaumatei, the *New Lucky Mansions* at 300 Nathan Rd (entrance on Jordan Rd) is in a fairly decent neighbourhood and has a number of places to choose from in different price ranges.

Causeway Bay (Map 7) has a number of decent guesthouses, though they are generally more expensive than those in Tsimshatsui. One which gets great reviews from travellers is the *Noble Hostel* (☎ 2808-0117), Flat A3, 17th floor, Great George Building, 27 Paterson St. Singles with private bath are HK$400; doubles with shared bath HK$320; doubles with private bath are HK$400 to HK$440. Rooms are small but very clean, and the lobby has a small lending library.

About one block north is the friendly and sparkling clean *Payless Inn* (☎ 2808-1030), Flat A, 5th floor, Fairview Mansion, 51 Paterson St. Singles/doubles without bath are HK$250/300, doubles with bath attached HK$500. One floor below is the *Jetvan Traveller's House* (☎ 2890-8133). This place isn't bad, but not as comfortable as the Payless Inn, and the beds are tiny. Singles/doubles without bath are HK$300/400.

Located on the south side of Causeway Bay is the *Causeway Bay Guest House* (☎ 2895-2013), Flat B, 1st floor, Lai Yee Building, 44A-D, Leighton Rd. With only seven rooms, it's easily booked up, but if you can get one you'll probably be happy with it. All are quite clean and have attached bathrooms. Singles are HK$350, doubles HK$450 and the sole triple HK$600. Another plus is that the guesthouse is quite near the No 10 stop of the A3 airport bus.

Nearby, the Phoenix Apartments building, 70 Lee Garden Rd, has a number of somewhat sleazier guesthouses. Most are 'love hotels' where rooms are rented by the hour. Nevertheless, they are also available for overnighters. Prices here are a bit lower than the guesthouses mentioned above, but staff are usually not that friendly either. One of the cheapest places is the *Wah Lai Villa*, on the 4th floor, where HK$200 will get you a round bed with mirror headboard for the night. On the 1st floor the *Baguio Motel* offers quite fancy rooms between HK$400 and HK$600 for the night. There are also more guesthouses/love motels in the Leishun Court building at 116 Leighton Rd, and at 14-20 Pak Sha Rd.

PLACES TO STAY – MIDDLE

Hong Kong's mid-priced accommodation consists mainly of business/tourist hotels. There is little to distinguish one from another. At the very least rooms will have a built-in bathroom with shower, bath and toilet, air-conditioning, telephone and TV. Some hotels also supply in-house cable television systems, mini refrigerators, toiletries and other small amenities. Many have business centres.

Surprisingly few of these hotels have swimming pools. If this is something you want, on Hong Kong Island check out the City Garden, Empire, Newton Hong Kong and Wharney hotels. In Kowloon, the Metropole, Miramar and Prudential are the only mid-range hotels with pools (needless to say, we're not talking Olympic size here).

In comparison with most other major cities, almost none of the mid-range hotels in Hong Kong offer good value for money. High demand and soaring property values keep accommodation costs high, and there's really no way of getting around it. There are a few places that might be considered better deals though. On Hong Kong Island, the *Newton Hotel Hong Kong* in North Point is quite nicely furnished and, once you're inside, feels a bit like a luxury hotel. It also has a rooftop pool with a great view. *The Excelsior* (run by the Mandarin Oriental group) falls at the higher end of the mid-range category, but in some ways offers similar service to the top-end hotels. Over in Kowloon, the *Eaton Hotel Hong Kong* has quite comfortable rooms and good service despite its relatively low rates. Staying at the *Kowloon Hotel* (which is run by the Peninsula group) allows you to use the fantastic pool, health club and other gorgeous facilities at the nearby Peninsula. If you can manage to book a room at the *Salisbury YMCA* you'll be rewarded with courteous, professional service, a comfortable room and excellent exercise facilities.

Within the mid-priced category are several places that deserve special mention for their low prices, all located in Kowloon. The *King's Hotel* has singles for HK$410 and doubles for HK$520 to HK$550. No class at all, but pretty much the cheapest hotel in town. The *International* and *Bangkok Royal* hotels are in the same price range.

Also fairly cheap is hostel-style accommodation offered by several non-profit organisations, such as the Salvation Army's *Booth Lodge* in Yaumatei. There is also the *Caritas Bianchi Lodge* in Yaumatei and Mongkok. The *YMCA International House* in Yaumatei and the *Anne Black Guest House (YWCA)* in Mongkok are two other options.

The hotels listed below are divided by area and in as many cases as possible are indicated on the appropriate area maps. Prices for double rooms refer to twin rooms as well. Some hotels that only have double rooms give a lower rate for single occupancy. The rates do not include the 10% service charge and 5% government tax.

Central

There is only place near this district that falls outside the luxury hotel category. The YWCA's *Garden View International House* (☎ 2877-3737; fax 2845-6263) at 1 MacDonnell Rd hovers on the border between Central and the Mid-Levels (Map 5). Twin rooms range from HK$693 to HK$814.

Wanchai & Causeway Bay

Hotels in these districts (Maps 6 & 7) tend to be a bit more expensive than their counterparts in Kowloon or eastern Hong Kong Island. This is due to their proximity to Central. If you stay here, you're paying for the location. A few of these hotels offer nice harbour views, but you have to pay for it.

Charterhouse Hotel – singles/doubles from HK$1100/1450 to HK$1800/HK$2000; 209-219 Wanchai Rd, Wanchai (☎ 2833-5566; fax 2833-5888)

Empire Hotel – doubles from HK$1000 to HK$1500; 33 Hennessy Rd, Wanchai (☎ 2866-9111; fax 2861-3121)

The Excelsior – doubles from HK$1400 to HK$2100; 281 Gloucester Rd, Causeway Bay (☎ 2894-8888; fax 2895-6459)

Harbour View International House – doubles from HK$850 to HK$1250; 4 Harbour Rd, Wanchai (☎ 2802-1111; fax 2802-9063)

Luk Kwok Hotel – singles/doubles from HK$1300/1400 to HK$1500/1600; 72 Gloucester Rd, Wanchai (☎ 2866-2166; fax 2866-2622)

New Cathay Hotel – singles HK$630, doubles HK$850 to HK$1100; 17 Tung Lo Wan Rd, Causeway Bay (☎ 2577-8211; fax 2576-9365)

New Harbour Hotel – doubles from HK$880 to HK$1300; 41-49 Hennessy Rd, Wanchai (☎ 2861-1166; fax 2865-6111)

South Pacific Hotel – singles/doubles from HK$1200/1350 to HK$1800/1800; 23 Morrison Hill Rd, Wanchai (☎ 2572-3838; fax 2893-7773)

The Wesley – singles/doubles from HK$900/1100 to HK$1500/1800; 22 Hennessy Rd, Wanchai (☎ 2866-6688; fax 2866-6633)

Wharney Hotel Hong Kong – doubles from HK$1450 to HK$1750; 57-33 Lockhart Rd, Wanchai (☎ 2861-1000; fax 2865-6023)

Eastern Hong Kong Island

There are more mid-range hotels spread between North Point and Quarry Bay. For the most part their prices aren't much cheaper than those in Wanchai or Causeway Bay, possibly because all are close to MTR stations.

City Garden Hotel – doubles from HK$1330 to HK$1830; 231 Electric Rd, North Point (Fortress Hill MTR) (☎ 2887-2888; fax 2887-1111)

Grand Plaza Hotel – doubles from HK$1100 to HK$1650; 2 Kornhill Rd, Quarry Bay (Tai Koo MTR) (☎ 2886-0011; fax 2886-1738)

Newton Hotel Hong Kong – doubles from HK$1100 to HK$2000; 218 Electric Rd, North Point (Fortress Hill MTR) (☎ 2807-2333; fax 2807-1221)

South China Hotel – doubles from HK$780 to HK$1450; 67-75 Java Rd, North Point (North Point MTR) (☎ 2503-1168; fax 2512-8698)

Tsimshatsui

This district (Map 16) almost sinks under the weight of all the hotels clustered around here. Prices are generally lower than those on Hong Kong Island, though some of the hotels are also a bit more seedy. At some of the cheaper places you may find that only the front-desk staff speak English. (Note: a few hotels list their address as Yaumatei, but are located on the border of Tsimshatsui and so are included here.)

Bangkok Royal Hotel – singles/doubles from HK$420/500 to HK$600/680; 2-12 Pilkem St, Yaumatei (Jordan MTR) (☎ 2735-9181; fax 2730-2209)

BP International House – doubles from HK$980 to HK$1700; family rooms from HK$1050 to HK$1230; 8 Austin Rd, Tsimshatsui (☎ 2376-1111; fax 2376-1333)

Guangdong Hotel – doubles from HK$1100 to HK$1400; 18 Pratt Ave, Tsimshatsui (☎ 2739-3311; fax 2721-1137)

Imperial Hotel – singles/doubles from HK$700/800 to HK$1150/1250; 30-34 Nathan Rd, Tsimshatsui (☎ 2366-2201; fax 2311-2360)

International Hotel – singles/doubles from HK$430/560 to HK$750/950; 33 Cameron Rd, Tsimshatsui (☎ 2366-3381; fax 2369-5381)

Kimberley Hotel – doubles from HK$1150 to HK$1650; 28 Kimberley Rd, Tsimshatsui (☎ 2723-3888; fax 2723-1318)

Kowloon Hotel – doubles from HK$1200 to HK$2100; 19-21 Nathan Rd, Tsimshatsui (☎ 2369-8698; fax 2739-9811)

Miramar Hotel – doubles from HK$1300 to HK$1800; 130 Nathan Rd, Tsimshatsui (☎ 2368-1111; fax 2369-1788)

New Astor Hotel – doubles from HK$980 to HK$1400; 11 Carnarvon Rd, Tsimshatsui (☎ 2366-7261; fax 2722-7122)

Park Hotel – singles/doubles/triples from HK$1200/1300/1600 to HK$1400/1500/1800; 61-65 Chatham Rd South, Tsimshatsui (☎ 2366-1371; fax 2739-7259)

Prudential Hotel – doubles from HK$1080 to HK$1630; 222 Nathan Rd, Yaumatei (Jordan MTR) (☎ 2311-8222; fax 2311-4760)

Ramada Hotel Kowloon – doubles from HK$980 to HK$1680; 73-75 Chatham Rd South, Tsimshatsui (☎ 2311-1100; fax 2311-6000)

Royal Pacific Hotel & Towers – singles HK$980, doubles HK$980 to HK$2280; 33 Canton Rd, Tsimshatsui (☎ 2736-1188; fax 2736-1212)

The Salisbury YMCA of Hong Kong – singles HK$730, doubles from HK$860 to HK$1060; 41 Salisbury Rd, Tsimshatsui (☎ 2369-2211; fax 2739-9315)

Shamrock Hotel – doubles from HK$600 to HK$950; 223 Nathan Rd, Yaumatei (Jordan MTR) (☎ 2735-2271; fax 2736-7354)

Stanford Hillview Hotel – doubles from HK$990 to HK$1500; 13-17 Observatory Rd, Tsimshatsui (☎ 2722-7822; fax 2723-3718)

Windsor Hotel – doubles from HK$1050 to HK$1400; 39-43A Kimberley Rd, Tsimshatsui (☎ 2739-5665; fax 2311-5101)

Yaumatei & Mongkok

Although further from the action, hotels in these two districts (Map 13) are not much cheaper than those in Tsimshatsui. But all of them are close to an MTR station, and put you in a fairly interesting, if gritty, part of town.

Anne Black Guest House (YWCA) – single rooms range from HK$300 to HK$500 and doubles from HK$600 to HK$650; 5 Man Fuk Rd, Mongkok (☎ 2713-9211)

Booth Lodge – spartan but comfortable doubles and twins range from HK$500 to HK$800; 11 Wing Sing Lane, Yaumatei (☎ 2771-9266)

Caritas Bianchi Lodge – singles are HK$590, doubles HK$690 and triples HK$840; 4 Cliff Rd, Yaumatei (☎ 2388-1111)

Caritas Lodge – not as fancy, but less expensive than the Bianchi with singles at HK$450, doubles/twins HK$520 and triples HK$730; 134 Boundary St, Mongkok (Prince Edward MTR) (☎ 2339-3777)

Concourse Hotel – doubles from HK$980 to HK$1580; 22 Laichikok Rd, Mongkok (☎ 2397-6683; fax 2381-3768)

Eaton Hotel Hong Kong – doubles from HK$770 to HK$1650; 380 Nathan Rd, Yaumatei (☎ 2782-1818; fax 2782-5563)

Grand Tower Hotel – doubles from HK$1050 to HK$1750; 627-641 Nathan Rd, Mongkok (☎ 2789-0011; fax 2789-0945)

King's Hotel – singles/doubles from HK$410/520 to HK$430/550; 473 Nathan Rd (☎ 2780-1281; fax 2782-1833)

Majestic Hotel Hong Kong – doubles from HK$1100 to HK$1480; 348 Nathan Rd, Yaumatei (☎ 2781-1333; fax 2781-1773)

Metropole Hotel – doubles from HK$1080 to HK$1580; 75 Waterloo Rd, Yaumatei (☎ 2761-1711; fax 2761-0769)

Nathan Hotel – singles/doubles/triples from HK$730/880/1030 to HK$800/950/1100; 378 Nathan Rd, Yaumatei (☎ 2388-5141; fax 2770-4262)

Newton Hotel Kowloon – doubles from HK$990 to HK$1390; 58-66 Boundary St, Mongkok (☎ 2787-2338; fax 2789-0688)

Pearl Seaview Hotel – singles/doubles from HK$780/850 to HK$930/1050; 262-276 Shanghai St, Yaumatei (☎ 2782-0882; fax 2388-1803)

Stanford Hotel Hong Kong – singles HK$980, doubles from HK$980 to HK$1380; 118 Soy St, Mongkok (☎ 2781-1881; fax 2388-3733)

YMCA International House has single rooms for HK$270 to HK$300, though majority of their rooms are considerably higher-priced doubles and twins ranging from HK$720 to HK$930; 23 Waterloo Rd, Yaumatei (☎ 2771-9111)

PLACES TO STAY – TOP END

Prices for Hong Kong's luxury hotels are as high as anywhere on earth. But in some cases, the money you spend brings a level of comfort and service not often matched. Hong Kong's top flight hoteliers are constantly trying to match or better their peers in Bangkok, London, New York, Paris and Tokyo. So far they're doing a fine job.

This assessment does not extend to all the hotels in the top-end category. Some merely have top-end prices: their amenities, location and service are good, but not outstanding. If you're going to spend this amount of money anyway, try and book one of the six or seven hotels that take service to that next rarefied level.

Mention Hong Kong and many people think of *The Peninsula*, which opened in 1928 and has become the patriarch of the territory's luxury hotels. Lording over the tip of the Kowloon peninsula, the place still evokes a feeling of colonial elegance, even if the lobby is often jammed with less-than-elegant hordes of tourists. The lifts quickly whisk you away from the lobby fray and take you to classic European-style rooms boasting little features like fax machines, CD players and marble bathrooms. The health facilities, including pool, sauna, steambath, jacuzzi and weightroom, are probably what Emperor Nero would have ordered were he ruling Rome today. Due to a new 20 storey addition, many more of the hotel's rooms offer spectacular views of either Hong Kong Island or Kowloon and the New Territories.

Near the Peninsula, is *The Regent*, flagship hotel of the Regal International Hotels chain. It is much more modern in feel, though like the Peninsula, it bows to a few colonial traditions, such as a fleet of Rolls-Royces. This hotel is a favourite with business travellers, and its outdoor swimming pool has an outstanding views.

Other Kowloon notables include the *New World Hotel*, which also has an outdoor pool with a spectacular view, and the *Nikko Hong Kong*, where you'll find all the amenities and attention typical of fine Japanese hotels.

The Peninsula's counterpart on Hong Kong Island is the *Mandarin Oriental*, owned by none other than Jardine Matheson, Hong Kong's most famous trading house. The Mandarin has a healthy dose of old-world charm. Styling is subdued, and in some rooms a bit outdated, and one gets the feeling that the hotel is riding a bit on its reputation. But the service, food and facilities are still excellent, and you get all the atmosphere that comes with staying at one of Hong Kong's landmarks.

Though looking a bit sterile and modern from the outside, the *Island Shangri-La* places a strong emphasis on personal service. This is the kind of hotel that will find you a guitar, your favourite book, even a pet if you really want it: staff seem genuinely interested in making your stay pleasant. This tasteful hotel has some nice touches, like a library where you can take afternoon tea, an outdoor jacuzzi and a 24 hour business centre.

Next door is the *Conrad Hong Kong*, a member of the Hilton Hotels group. While not quite as elegant as the Island Shangri-La, the hotel has gotten enthusiastic reviews for its attention to business travellers' needs.

Winning the prize for the most overblown lobby is the *Grand Hyatt Hong Kong*. A swirl of black marble, oriental rugs and palm trees, this vast foyer inspires either admiration or amusement. But the hotel itself can be taken seriously. The rooms are tastefully and comprehensively furnished, the service attentive and the recreation facilities among the most complete of any hotel.

Hong Kong used to have a Hilton Hotel that boasted one of the best locations in the city, but unfortunately it was bought by Hong Kong tycoon Li Ka-shing, who tore it down to make way for another office tower. Li also built his own luxury hotel, the *Harbour Plaza*, curiously located in Hunghom in Kowloon (though it *is* on the waterfront). Most of the former Hilton staff moved to the Harbour Plaza, but the Hilton's elegance failed to follow.

Prices for double rooms in the hotels listed below refer to twin rooms as well. Some hotels that only have double rooms give a lower rate for single occupancy. Rates are exclusive of 10% service charge and 5% government tax.

Hong Kong Island

Century Hong Kong Hotel – singles/doubles from HK$1400/1600 to HK$1900/2100; 238 Jaffe Rd, Wanchai (Map 6) (☎ 2598-8888; fax 2598-8866)

Conrad Hong Kong – doubles from HK$2250 to HK$3500; Pacific Place, 88 Queensway, Admiralty (Map 5) (☎ 2521-3838; fax 2521-3888)

Furama Kempinski Hong Kong – doubles from HK$1700 to HK$2650; 1 Connaught Rd, Central (Map 5) (☎ 2525-5111; fax 2845-9339)

Grand Hyatt Hong Kong – doubles from HK$2650 to HK$3850; 1 Harbour Rd, Wanchai (Map 6) (☎ 2588-1234; fax 2802-0677)

Island Shangri-La Hong Kong – doubles from HK$2500 to HK$3350; Pacific Place, Supreme Court Rd, Admiralty (Map 5) (☎ 2877-3838; fax 2521-8742)

JW Marriot Hotel Hong Kong – doubles from HK$2350 to HK$3300; Pacific Place, 88 Queensway, Admiralty (Map 5) (☎ 2810-8366; fax 2845-0737)

Mandarin Oriental – doubles from HK$2250 to HK$3600; 5 Connaught Rd, Central (Map 5) (☎ 2522-0111; fax 2810-6190)

New World Harbour View – singles/doubles from HK1880/2130 to HK$3080/3330; 1 Harbour Rd, Wanchai (Map 6) (☎ 2802-8888; fax 2802-8833)

Park Lane – doubles from HK$1800 to HK$3000; 310 Gloucester Rd, Causeway Bay (Map 7) (☎ 2890-3355; fax 2576-7853)

Regal Hongkong Hotel – doubles from HK$1900 to HK$2650; 88 Yee Wo St, Causeway Bay (Map 7) (☎ 2890-6633; fax 2881-0777)

Ritz-Carlton Hong Kong – singles/doubles from HK$2250 to HK$3350 (same rate for both); 3 Connaught Rd Central, Central (Map 5)

Kowloon

Grand Stanford Harbour View – singles/doubles from HK$1700/1800 to HK$3150/3250; 70 Mody Rd, Tsimshatsui East (Map 16) (☎ 2721-5161; fax 2369-5672)

THE PENINSULA

Top of the line – The Peninsula, Tsimshatsui

Harbour Plaza – singles/doubles from HK$1800 to HK$2900; 20 Tak Fung St, Hunghom (☎ 2621-3188; fax 2621-3311)

Holiday Inn Golden Mile – singles HK$1550, doubles from HK$1900 to HK$2150; 46-52 Nathan Rd, Tsimshatsui (Map 16) (☎ 2369-3111; fax 2369-8016)

Hong Kong Renaissance Hotel – doubles from HK$1950 to HK$2800; 8 Peking Rd, Tsimshatsui (Map 16) (☎ 2375-1133; fax 2375-6611)

Hyatt Regency Hong Kong – doubles from HK$1900 to HK$2500; 67 Nathan Rd, Tsimshatsui (Map 16) (☎ 2311-1234; fax 2739-8701)

Kowloon Shangri-La – doubles from HK$2150 to HK$3550; 64 Mody Rd, Tsimshatsui East (Map 16) (☎ 2721-2111; fax 2723-8686)

New World Hotel – singles/doubles from HK$1650/1850 to HK$2400/2400; 22 Salisbury Rd, Tsimshatsui (Map 16) (☎ 2369-4111; fax 2369-9387)

Nikko Hong Kong – doubles from HK$1800 to HK$2800; 72 Mody Rd, Tsimshatsui East (Map 16) (☎ 2739-1111; fax 2311-3122)

Omni The Hong Kong Hotel – doubles from HK$1900 to HK$3500; Harbour City, Canton Rd, Tsimshatsui (Map 16) (☎ 2736-0088; fax 2736-0011)

Omni Marco Polo Hotel – doubles from HK$1600 to HK$1800; Harbour City, Canton Rd, Tsimshatsui (Map 16) (☎ 2736-0888; fax 2736-0022)

Omni Prince Hotel – doubles from HK$1600 to HK$2150; Harbour City, Canton Rd, Tsimshatsui (Map 16) (☎ 2736-1888; fax 2736-0066)

The Peninsula – doubles from HK$2450 to HK$3500; Salisbury Rd, Tsimshatsui (Map 16) (☎ 2366-6251; fax 2722-4170)

Regal Kowloon Hotel – singles/doubles from HK$1000/1480 to HK$2280/2280; 71 Mody Rd, Tsimshatsui East (Map 16) (☎ 2722-1818; fax 2369-6950)

The Regent – doubles from HK$2000 to HK$3100; Salisbury Rd, Tsimshatsui (Map 16) (☎ 2721-1211; fax 2739-4546)

The Royal Garden – doubles from HK$1800 to HK$2550; 69 Mody Rd, Tsimshatsui East (Map 16) (☎ 2721-5215; fax 2369-9976)

Sheraton Hong Kong Hotel – doubles from HK$2100 to HK$3200; 20 Nathan Rd, Tsimshatsui (Map 16) (☎ 2369-1111; fax 2739-8707)

LONG TERM

Rental Accommodation

Finding an apartment in Hong Kong is usually not a lot of fun. Finding what you want for a reasonable price can take weeks of scurrying up and down lifts and stairwells, all the while beating off the promptings of your estate agent, who is used to clinching several deals daily. At the same time, it's a lot easier for foreigners here than in other Asian cities. English is more widely spoken, and there are literally thousands of real estate agencies.

You can look for a place by yourself by checking the classified sections of the English-language newspapers, or bulletin boards at expatriate associations like the Royal Hong Kong Yacht Club or Foreign Correspondent's Club. But most people end up going through an estate agent, who can scour through the reams of Chinese-language rental ads and notices. It's best to go with one of the bigger outfits, such as L&D or Centaline Property, though there are plenty of smaller agencies that are reliable as well. Check the *Commercial/Industrial Telephone Directory* for a complete listing.

The agent's fee is generally equivalent to one month's rent. Other upfront expenses will include a deposit, usually equal to two months' rent, and the first month's rental payment. This can add up to a lot of money, as rents in Hong Kong are very steep, on a par with those in New York, London and in some cases, Tokyo.

A one-bedroom apartment in the Mid-Levels will cost anywhere from HK$15,000 to HK$50,000 per month. That same flat will go for somewhat less in Tsimshatsui or Wanchai. More affordable are districts on eastern Hong Kong Island, and north-eastern or north-western Kowloon, where you may be able to find a 600 sq foot one-bedroom flat for HK$8000 per month. The most expensive place is the Peak, where rents can easily top HK$100,000 per month (nearly US$13,000).

Hong Kong people are used to living in small apartments, and unless you can spend several thousand US dollars a month on rent, you'll have to learn to adapt as well. Most places have closet-sized bathrooms, bathroom-sized kitchens and bedroom-sized living rooms. Getting the idea? Of course there are exceptions, which you may be lucky enough to stumble upon, and the further out you go from the city centre, the better your chances are. If you're willing to go as far as the Outlying Islands, such as Lamma or Lantau, or the New Territories you'll get a lot more for your money.

Serviced Apartments

If you're only going to be based in Hong Kong for several months (and the company is footing the bill) serviced apartments are worth considering. A complete list can be found in the *Commercial/Industrial Telephone Directory*. Occasionally the property sections of the English-language newspapers also carry advertisements.

Most serviced apartments are part of hotels, such as the *Royal Pacific Hotel & Towers*, *Sheraton Hong Kong Hotel & Towers* and the *Grand Plaza Apartments*, housed in the Grand Plaza Hotel. Monthly rents in these places run anywhere from HK$22,000 for a 400 sq foot studio to HK$55,000 for a two-bedroom suite. Serviced apartments are also available at the *Hong Kong Convention & Exhibition Centre* in Central and at *Parkview*, a luxury residential complex located near Wong Ngai Chung Gap on Hong Kong Island. These apartments are more luxurious, and monthly rents are well over HK$60,000.

Most serviced apartment providers require a minimum lease of one month, a deposit equivalent to one month's rent, and the first month's rent paid in advance.

Places to Eat

Hong Kong's reputation as a shopper's paradise may be in question, but there's no doubt that this place is a food-lover's heaven. The territory is said to have the world's highest per capita ratio of restaurants. Small wonder, for the Chinese truly live to eat: any night of the week you will find restaurants, banquet halls or tiny noodle shops crammed with customers. The frenetic pace and long hours of working life in Hong Kong also make eating out a necessity for many.

For the visitor this translates into an exciting range of choices. Almost all the different styles of Chinese cooking are represented in Hong Kong, as well as a dazzling number of foreign cuisines. Obviously the more you can spend, the greater the variety you will enjoy.

It's easy to eat on a budget in Hong Kong. Almost every residential and commercial neighbourhood has cheap noodle shops. During lunchtime keep an eye peeled for sidewalk signs advertising set lunches. These usually belong to Hong Kong-style western restaurants: you can get soup and entrée, dessert and tea or coffee for as low as HK$28, though HK$35 is closer to the average.

There are also some interesting options on the fast food front. In addition to international chains like McDonald's and KFC, there are several local chains that dish up passable Chinese and western food. Oliver's Super Sandwiches offer fresh, tasty sandwiches, soups and baked potatoes from HK$17 to HK$35. A more recent arrival is Genroku Sushi which has sushi for as little as HK$7. Another cheap option is Indian restaurants, although these aren't the bargain they once were. Still in some places you can get dinner for around HK$50 to HK$60.

The best hunting grounds for budget diners are the little back streets uphill from Central (such as Stanley and Wellington Sts), Sheung Wan, Wanchai, Causeway Bay and Tsimshatsui. Most of these areas have the steady flow of commuters or residents needed to support a large number of noodle shops, fast food joints and so on.

All these areas also have plenty of mid-range restaurants, and this is where Hong Kong truly comes into its own. You can also get almost any Asian or western cuisine, from African to Vietnamese. Unfortunately, like its hotels, Hong Kong's mid-priced restaurants charge more than one might expect. Lunch at a nice Chinese or western restaurant can easily cost HK$600 for three people.

Hong Kong's bent for conspicuous consumption extends to dining, and there are plenty of spots where you can spend astronomical sums indulging your palate. But as with Hong Kong's top-end hotels, only some of these high-priced restaurants can turn out a meal that is truly worth the money.

Dedicated diners may want to pick up the annual *HK Magazine Restaurant Guide*. Covering more than 500 restaurants, this is one of the best, and most lively guides to Hong Kong dining. Some of the guide's favourite picks are included in this chapter. At HK$50 a copy, it's well worth the money if you plan to really go restaurant hunting. To get a copy, call *HK Magazine's* editorial offices (☎ 2850-5065). The HKTA also puts out an *Official Dining and Entertainment Guide* which includes many of its member restaurants, but as all the 'reviews' are uniformly upbeat, it's hard to get a feel for which places are worth going to.

CHINESE FOOD

Chinese food is without doubt one of the finest aspects of this venerable culture. The diversity of flavours, cooking styles and ingredients, and the thousands of different dishes show that chefs have kept busy throughout China's 5000 year history.

The various types of Chinese cuisine are classified by region, and the ingredients tend to reflect what is available in each area. For example, northern China is suitable for raising wheat, so noodles, dumplings and other wheat-based dishes are most common. In the south, where the climate is warm and wet, rice is the basic staple. The Sichuan area, where spices grow well, is famous for fiery hot dishes.

In Hong Kong the dominant style of cooking is Cantonese and, to a lesser extent, Chiu Chow, named after a coastal area in eastern Guangdong Province. But there are also plenty of restaurants serving other types of Chinese food. In fact, Hong Kongers are proud to state that their city has the world's best Chinese food. This is debatable: Sichuan or Peking-style food is generally far better in China and Taiwan. But there's plenty of outstanding food to be had here, and if you do nothing else in Hong Kong, make it to a Chinese restaurant.

Following is a brief introduction to some of the styles of Chinese food available in Hong Kong, along with the names of a few notable dishes. Since it is the dialect of Hong Kong, the names of all regional dishes are romanised into Cantonese.

Cantonese

Originating in neighbouring Guangdong Province, Cantonese food is the most popular in the city. Flavours are more subtle than other Chinese cooking styles, and some dishes almost have a sweet taste to them. There is almost no spicy Cantonese fare. All Chinese stress the importance of fresh ingredients, but the Cantonese are almost religious about it. Thus it is common to see fish tanks in most seafood restaurants.

chà sìu 叉燒
  barbecued pork
cháu dǎumiu 炒豆苗
  stir-fried pea sprouts
chìngcháu gāilán 清炒芥蘭
  stir-fried kale (cabbage)
chìngjìng sēkbànyue 清蒸石斑魚
  steamed garoupa (fish) with soy sauce dressing
jiuyim ngaupai 椒鹽牛排
  deep-fried salt-and-pepper spareribs
sǐjìu ngauhó 豉椒牛河
  fried rice noodles with beef and green peppers
sàilanfā dāijí 西蘭花帶子
  stir-fried broccoli with scallops
sàng sìu gāp 生燒鴿
  roast pigeon
sìnning jìnyǔengài 鮮檸煎軟雞
  pan-fried lemon chicken
tāibǎk jūiyùng hā 大白醉翁蝦
  'drunken' prawns (steamed in rice wine)

Dim Sum These famous Cantonese delicacies are normally served steamed in a small bamboo basket, or on a little plate, during breakfast and lunch hours. Typically, each basket or plate contains three to four identical pieces and does the rounds of restaurant tables via a pushcart. Various stir-fried and steamed vegetable dishes, as well as some tasty sweets, are also available and nicely complement the dim sum. Though you can usually point to what you want, the following list gives you an idea of what's on offer.

chà sìu bàu 叉燒包
  barbecued pork buns
chéung fén 腸粉
  steamed rice flour rolls with shrimp, beef or pork
chìng cháu sichōi 清炒時菜
  fried green vegetable of the day
chùn gúen 春卷
  fried spring rolls

fùng jáu 鳳爪
  fried chicken's feet
fún gwó 粉果
  steamed dumplings with pork, shrimp and bamboo shoots
gàisì cháumiň 雞絲炒麵
  fried crispy noodles with shredded chicken
gòn sìu yìmiň 干燒伊麵
  dry-fried noodles
hà gáu 蝦餃
  shrimp dumplings
ham súi gōk 鹹水角
  fried rice flour triangles (usually with pork inside)
ho yìp fǎn 荷葉飯
  rice wrapped in lotus leaf
pai gwàt 排骨
  steamed spare ribs
sàn jùk ngau yók 山竹牛肉
  steamed minced beef balls
sìu mai 燒賣
  pork and shrimp dumplings
wǒo gōk 芋角
  deep-fried taro puffs

Chiu Chow

Chiu Chow dishes are in some cases lighter than Cantonese, and make heavy use of seafood. Sauces sometimes border on sweet, using orange, tangerine or sweet beans for flavour. Among the most famous specialities are shark's fin and bird's nest. But duck and goose are also popular. Chiu Chow chefs are known for their skills in carving raw vegetables into fancy floral designs.

bàkgù sàilanfà 北菇西蘭花
  stewed broccoli with black mushrooms
bìngfà gòngyìn 冰花宮燕
  cold sweet bird's nest soup (dessert)
chuenjìu gǒklunghà 川椒焗龍蝦
  baked lobster in light pepper sauce
chìngjìu ngauyóksì 清椒牛肉絲
  fried shredded beef with green pepper
dǎi yuechī tòng 大魚翅湯
  shark's fin soup
fòngyue gaīlán 方魚芥蘭
  fried kale with dried fish
gàiyung sīuchōi 雞茸紹菜
  stewed Tianjin cabbage with minced chicken
jìng hǎi 蒸蟹
  steamed crab

The Ritual of Dim Sum

The best known of Hong Kong's culinary traditions, dim sum blends China's ancient traditions of tea drinking with the Cantonese penchant for snacking. The term *dim sum* refers to 'little snacks' though more literally translated it means 'to touch the heart'.

When Cantonese go for dim sum, they often describe it as going to drink tea *(yam cha)*. Although tea does play a major role, it's the array of different, delicious little snacks which make dim sum so much fun. That, and the places where you eat it. Hong Kong dim sum restaurants are mostly huge, boisterous affairs – the scene of constant action. Diners usually go in large groups, which makes for a wider variety of snacks, and more lively conversation.

In a cavernous room where they must compete with several hundred other diners, as well as the constant crash of clearing plates and teacups from tables, the noise level has to be heard to be believed. Even the decor seems loud. But if you're in the mood for it, this is all part of the experience, for it's the sound of people relaxing and enjoying themselves. Obviously the best way to participate is to come in a group yourself. Dim sum alone is not much fun, especially because on your own you can't sample a whole range of snacks: they fill you up very quickly.

It takes time to get used to the whole ritual. Don't be afraid to wave or call over the people with the pushcarts. Each pushcart has a different selection, so take your time and order a few things from the different carts. It's estimated that there's about 2000 dim sum dishes, though a restaurant will only prepare 100 on any given day. You pay by the number of plates and baskets you order. When the cart comes by, feel free to lift up the lids to see what's underneath. It's not considered rude. If you want more tea, remove the lid and let it hang from the cord attaching it to the pot. Someone will see it, and refill the pot with hot water for you.

Usually dim sum is not expensive – HK$30 per person is about average for breakfast, or perhaps HK$50 for a decent lunch. However if you venture into one of the restaurants in the hotels, or a very traditional looking place loaded with rosewood chairs and ceiling fans, expect prices to be much higher.

Restaurants normally open about 6 am and close about 2.30 pm, with many also shutting down between 10 and 11.30 am. Arriving after lunch is probably not a good idea as the best food will be gone. This is also true of mid-morning. Operating hours are often extended on weekends and holidays, though it can also get very crowded at these times. Listing all the dim sum places in town would fill several volumes, but the places below should get you started.

Canton Court – under HK$100 per person, dim sum served from 7 am to 3 pm; Guangdong Hotel, 18 Prat Ave, Tsimshatsui (☎ 2739-3311)

Harbour View Seafood Restaurant – under HK$100 per person, dim sum served from 11 am to 5 pm; 3rd floor, Tsimshatsui Centre, West Wing, 66 Mody Rd, Tsimshatsui East (☎ 2722-5888)

Lai Ching Heen – HK$300-400 per person, dim sum served from noon to 2.30 pm; Regent Hotel, 18 Salisbury Rd, Tsimshatsui (☎ 2721-1211)

Luk Yu Teahouse – one of Hong Kong's oldest dim sum venues, prices range from HK$200-300 per person, dim sum served from 7 am to 6 pm; 26 Stanley St, Central (☎ 2523-5464)

Serenade Chinese Restaurant – HK$100-200 per person, dim sum served from 11 am to 3 pm; 1st and 2nd floors, Restaurant Block, Hong Kong Cultural Centre, 10 Salisbury Rd, Tsimshatsui (☎ 2722-0932)

Steam and Stew Inn – under HK$100 per person, dim sum served from 11.30 am to 3 pm; ground floor, Hing Wong Court, 21-23 Tai Wong St East, Wanchai (☎ 2529-3913)

Summer Palace – HK$200-300 per person, dim sum served from noon to 3 pm; 5th floor, Island Shangri-La Hotel, Pacific Place, Supreme Court Rd, Admiralty (☎ 2820-8552)

Tai Woo Restaurant – under HK$100 per person, dim sum served from 10 am to 1 pm; 15-19 Wellington St, Central (☎ 2524-5618)

Yat Tung Chinese Restaurant – HK$100-200 per person, dim sum served from 11 am to 3 pm; Eaton Hotel, 380 Nathan Rd, Yaumatei (☎ 2710-1093)

Yung Kee Restaurant – HK$100-200 per person, dim sum served from 2 to 5.30 pm; 32-40 Wellington St, Central (☎ 2522-1624) ■

HKTA

jā ngʰèung ngāp　炸五香鴨
　deep-fried spiced duck
sēisèk pīngpún　四色拼盤
　cold appetiser platter of four meats/seafood

Peking (Beijing)

Peking cuisine, also referred to as northern-style food, originated in China's wheat belt, so steamed bread, dumplings and noodles figure more prominently than rice. Dishes feature stronger spices such as peppers, garlic and coriander.

The most famous speciality is Peking duck, served with pancakes and plum sauce. Another popular dish is beggar's chicken, supposedly created by a beggar who stole the emperor's chicken and then had to bury it in the ground to cook it. The chicken is stuffed with mushrooms, pickled Chinese cabbage, herbs and onions, then wrapped in lotus leaves, sealed in clay and baked all day in hot ashes.

bàkgìng tinngāp　北京填鴨
　Peking duck
bàkgìng fúngcháu làimīn　北京風炒拉麵
　noodles fried with shredded pork and bean sprouts
bàkgùpa jùnbǎkchōi　北菰扒津白菜
　Tianjin cabbage and black mushrooms
chòngyau béng　蔥油餅
　pan-fried spring onion cakes
fōogwāi gài　富貴雞
　beggar's chicken
gòncháu ngauyŏksì　干炒牛肉絲
　fried shredded beef with chilli sauce
gòngbāu dǎihà　宮爆大蝦
　sauteed prawns in chilli sauce
sàmsìn tòng　三鮮湯
　clear soup with chicken, prawn and abalone
sìnyŏk síulong bàu　鮮肉小龍包
　steamed minced pork dumplings

Shanghai

Shanghainese cooking is generally richer, sweeter and oilier than other Chinese cuisines. Seafood is widely used, as are preserved vegetables, pickles and salted meats. Like Peking food, there are a lot of dumplings on the menu.

chìngcháu dǎumiu　清炒豆苗
　sauteed pea sprouts

fěichūi yuedāi 翡翠玉帶
    sauteed scallops with vegetables
fótúi síuchōi 火腿小菜
    Shanghai cabbage with ham
hongsìu sìjítau 紅燒獅子頭
    braised minced pork balls with vegetables
jā jígài 炸子雞
    deep-fried chicken
jūi gài 醉雞
    'drunken chicken' in cold rice wine marinade
ngʰèung ngauyŏk 五香牛肉
    cold spiced beef
sĕunghói chòcháu 上海粗炒
    fried Shanghai noodles with pork
sùenlāt tòng 酸辣湯
    hot-and-sour soup
sungsúe wongyue 松鼠黃魚
    sweet-and-sour yellow croaker fish

Sichuan (Szechuan)

This area is known for having the most fiery food in China. Simmering and soaking are used more than in other Chinese cuisines, which really gives the chilli peppers time to work their way into the food. In addition to chilli, common spices include aniseed, coriander, fennel seed, garlic and peppercorns.

chìngjìu ngauyŏksì 青椒牛肉絲
    sauteed shredded beef and green pepper
dān dān mīn 擔擔麵
    noodles in spicy peanut soup
chūipei wongyuepīn 脆皮黃魚片
    fried fish in sweet-and-sour sauce
gònbin sĕigwāi dáu 干煸四季豆
    pan-fried spicy string beans
gòngbāu gàidìng 宮爆雞丁
    sauteed diced chicken and peanuts in chilli sauce
gòngbāu minghà 宮爆明蝦
    sauteed shrimp in chilli sauce
jèungcha háu ngāp 樟茶烤鴨
    duck smoked in camphor wood
mapo dāufŏo 麻婆豆腐
    'grandma's beancurd' in spicy sauce
sùenlāt tòng 酸辣湯
    peppery hot-and-sour soup with shredded meat
yuehèung kéijí 魚香茄子
    sauteed eggplant in spicy fish sauce

Other

Vegetarian The Chinese are masters at the art of adding variety to vegetarian cooking. Even if you are not a vegetarian it is worth giving one of the excellent vegetarian restaurants a try. Vegetarian food is largely based on soybean curd – but the Chinese do some miraculous things with it. 'Pork' or 'chicken' can be made by layering pieces of dried bean curd or can be fashioned from mashed taro root. It may not always taste like meat, but is sure looks real. Mushrooms are also widely used.

bòlo cháufān 菠蘿炒飯
   fried rice with diced pineapple
chìngdūn bàkgù tòng 清燉北菇湯
   black mushroom soup
chùn gúen 春卷
   spring rolls
fŏopei gúen 腐皮卷
   spicy bean-curd rolls
gùmgù súnjìm 金菇筍尖
   braised bamboo shoots and black mushrooms
jàilŏuměi 齊鹵味
   mock chicken, barbecued pork or roast duck
lohōn chōi 羅漢菜
   stewed mixed vegetables
lohōnjài yìmīn 羅漢齊伊麵
   fried noodles with vegetables
yehchōi gúen 椰菜卷
   cabbage rolls

Noodles Most noodle shops have several types of soup noodles, fried noodles and a few small dishes, such as steamed vegetables with oyster sauce or shrimp dumplings. Some shops also serve congee, a savoury rice porridge usually flavoured with pork, fish and pickled egg. The more deluxe places also serve full-blown Chinese dishes like fried beef and green pepper, curry chicken rice or sauted prawns. Regular thin noodles (*min*) can be substituted with thick rice noodles (*ho fun*). A few variations are shown here (the more common dishes are listed first).

yuedán mīn 魚蛋麵
   fishball noodles
ngauyúen hó 牛丸河
   beef balls with rice noodles
sìnhà wuntùn mīn 鮮蝦雲吞麵
   shrimp dumpling noodles

chōiyúen mīn 菜遠麵
  vegetable noodles
sèungyúen hó 雙丸河
  fish and beef balls with rice noodles
hoyau yēchōi 蠔油野菜
  steamed vegetables with oyster sauce
yupīn jùk 魚片粥
  congee with fish slices
sìngjàu cháumǎi 星洲炒米
  Singapore fried noodles (spicy)
yeungjàu cháufǎn 揚州炒飯
  fried rice with egg, shrimp and spring onion
gàlěi ngauyǒk fǎn 咖喱牛肉飯
  curried beef on white rice

DRINKS

Alcoholic Drinks

Beer is by far the most popular alcoholic beverage, and there's a wide range of choice in bars, convenience stores and supermarkets. Hong Kong has two major breweries, one each owned by Carlsberg (Denmark) and San Miguel (Philippines). In addition to producing their own brands, they brew other beers under licence, including Lowenbrau and Kirin. Carlsberg and San Miguel are the two brands most widely available, which is unfortunate, since they are among the worst-tasting.

Imported beers have, however, become very popular, and most bars have all kinds, mostly in bottles but in some cases on tap as well. There are some good English bitters and ales on draught, though their taste suffers a bit from having spent several weeks in a cargo ship. And Tsingtao, China's main export beer, is sold everywhere.

Among Hong Kong's more well-heeled drinkers, Cognac is the liquor of choice. It's hard to believe, but Hong Kong accounts for nearly 11% of the worldwide market for Cognac brandy, and has the world's highest per capita consumption. Hong Kongers generally drink it neat, but rarely sip it: sometimes you'll even see a group of enthusiastic diners downing it shot-style! No wonder they go through so much of it. Supermarkets, departments stores, restaurants and bars usually have a decent selection of other spirits and wines. A luxury goods tax, however, makes them fairly expensive.

Of course if you want to try Chinese alcohol that's available too, most commonly in restaurants (few bars deal with it). Easiest on the palate is probably *siu hing jau*, more commonly known by its name in Mandarin, *shao xing jiu*. This is a yellow rice wine that is sweet,

Food Etiquette

The Chinese are by and large casual eaters, and they don't expect foreigners to understand all of their dining customs. But there are a few rules that are good to know.

Chinese meals are social events. Typically, a group of people sit at a round table and order dishes (at least one per person) from which everyone partakes. Ordering a dish just for yourself appears selfish, unless you're with close friends. Most Chinese pick food from these communal dishes with their own chopsticks. But if you notice someone carefully placing a pair next to each plate of food, then use these 'public chopsticks' to serve yourself. Some dishes will come with a serving spoon, in which case use this.

Toasts in Hong Kong are not usually the long-speech variety that occasionally befall western dinners, but are considerably more succinct. Sometimes a toast is limited to the words 'yam seng', which roughly translates to 'down the hatch!'. Raising your tea or water glass is not very respectful, so unless you have deep-rooted convictions against alcohol, it's best to drink your booze with the rest of the crowd. If you are the guest of honour at dinner, don't be surprised if you're called on to down a few glasses.

When the food is served, it's best to wait for some signal from the host before digging in. You will likely be invited to take the first piece if you are the invited guest. Often your host will serve it to you, placing a piece of meat, fish or chicken in your bowl. When eating fish, don't be surprised if the head gets placed on your plate: the head is considered to have the tastiest meat. It's all right if you decline, as someone else will gladly devour it.

Apart from the communal dishes, everyone gets an individual bowl of rice or a small soup bowl. It's considered polite to hold the bowl near your lips and shovel the contents into your mouth with chopsticks (or a spoon for soup). Soup is usually eaten at the end of a meal, rather than as an appetiser.

Eating is generally a hearty affair and often there is a big mess after the end of a meal. Restaurants are prepared for this – they change the tablecloth after each customer leaves. In Hong Kong it is also acceptable for Chinese diners – depending on the situation of course – to spit the bones from their food out on to the tablecloth.

Another good rule to remember is not to stick your chopsticks upright into your rice: this is how rice is offered to the dead, and the connotations at meal time are not pleasant for Chinese people. Chinese habitually make use of toothpicks after dinner, and even between courses. The polite way is to cover one's mouth with one hand while using the toothpick with the other.

Finally, if you absolutely can't manage chopsticks, don't be afraid to ask for a fork. Nearly all Chinese restaurants have them. Better a little humility and a full belly than intact pride and an empty stomach. ∎

tasting like a distant cousin of sherry. Other options may not go down so smoothly. Though Chinese tend to refer to all their alcohols as 'wine' in English, the majority are hard alcohols distilled from grains like rice, sorghum or millet. Most are quite potent, and some impart the pleasing sensation of having your throat and stomach lit on fire. The best known is *mao tai*, distilled from millet. Another searing delicacy is *goh leung (gao liang* in Mandarin), which is made from sorghum. Have fun with these, but if your dining companions start repeating the phrase *'gon bui'* ('drain your glass'), you may want to start scouting out escape routes.

Non-Alcoholic Drinks

A consumer's paradise, Hong Kong has a large selection of beverages. In any convenience store or supermarket you'll find a whole range of juice, soft drink and milk products. Most restaurants have cola and juice at the very least.

Of course tea is everywhere. In Chinese restaurants tea is often served free of charge, or at most you'll pay HK$2 for a large pot with endless refills of water. There are three basic types of tea: green or unfermented *(luk cha)*; fermented *(bolei)*, also known as black tea; and semi-fermented *(oolong)*. Within these categories fall dozens of varieties. One of the most well known is jasmine *(heung pin)*, a blend of tea and flowers. Chinese teas are drunk straight, without milk or sugar.

There are also some pretty good English teas to be had, though you usually must go to a nice hotel if you wish it served properly. Cheaper Chinese places also serve up western-style tea, but with a Hong Kong twist. Milk tea *(nai cha)* uses an extremely strong brew so the flavour can punch through the heavy dose of condensed milk. Lemon tea *(ningmeng cha)* is also strong, and is often served with several whole slices of fresh lemon.

Coffee is also widely available, though it's mostly of the instant variety. However there are more and more coffee shops popping up, particularly in the business districts.

In the summer Hong Kongers like to have a sweet cold drink called a 'fleecy'. These are quite tasty, and are most often made with milk and red or green beans (it tastes better than it sounds). Sometimes fruit is used instead.

PLACES TO EAT – BOTTOM END

It's easy to go budget dining in Hong Kong. Every neighbourhood has cheap spots of one sort or another to cater to workers and local residents. The most common option is the noodle shop; for the more adventurous there's the street markets.

Noodle Shops

These are absolutely everywhere, and while there are larger shops, most occupy a little hole in the wall and hold only eight to 10 tables. If you go to these places for every meal you will soon get bored: though the menus look long, the selections are basically variations on a few basic themes. Here you can usually get a bowl of soup noodles for HK$14 to HK$25, and often a plate of steamed veggies with oyster sauce for HK$10 to HK$12.

It's pretty easy to spot these places, as the noodle vats are usually right by the front window. Often shops will also have signs out front with the Chinese characters for noodles (麵) and sometimes rice (飯).

Recommending particular shops is no easy task. There are literally hundreds, if not thousands, of noodle shops in Hong Kong. The selection below represents shops that have either become quite well known in their neighbourhoods or are favoured by the author.

Chinese Delights – good Peking-style noodles and dumplings; 9B Sharp St East, Causeway Bay (Map 7)

Happy Garden Noodle & Congee Kitchen – good soup noodles and congee (HK$26-30); 76 Canton Rd, Tsimshatsui (Map 16)

Jim Chai Kee Noodle Shop – famous for king prawn dumpling noodles (HK$13-14); 98 Wellington St, Central (near Sheung Wan; Map 4) and 36 Stanley St, Central (Map 5); there's also one at 277 Temple St, Tsimshatsui

Law Fu Kee Noodle Shop Ltd – famous for dumpling noodles (HK$14); 140 Des Voeux Rd, Central (near Sheung Wan; Map 4)

Taiwan Beef Noodle – chain with good Taiwan-style beef noodles (HK$26); 78-80 Canton Rd, Tsimshatsui (Map 16), and 13 King Kwong St, Happy Valley

Wah Yuen Restaurant – reasonably priced dishes (HK$35); Minden Row, Tsimshatsui (Map 16)

Japanese Ramen Shops

This is a very tasty and relatively inexpensive option. Several shops serving Japanese ramen noodles have sprung up around town, but two in particular are highly recommended by local Japanese. In Central there is *Miyoshiya*, 39 Lyndhurst Terrace (near Sheung Wan, Map 4). The owner prepares all the ramen himself, and you can choose from either pork or soy sauce-based broth. A bowl will cost you around HK$35. Add in some appetisers and the bill should be around HK$50-60.

The other expert's choice is *Ichibantei* which has specialities like the fiery 'bomb hot noodles' loaded with chilli and garlic, as well as a wide assortment of rice dishes and appetisers. This place specialises in miso-based broth. Ramen ranges from HK$34 to HK$52 per bowl. It's located in a tiny shop at 17 Morrison Hill Rd, Wanchai (Map 6).

Vegetarian Spots

In certain pockets of town you can find the occasional cramped, narrow, cheap vegetarian restaurant. In the Central/Sheung Wan area, try *Fat Heung Lam*, on Wellington St (Map 4). *Vegi-Table* has a lengthy menu, and offers a bargain set lunch for HK$40 that is highly recommended by the good folks at *HK Magazine*. It's located at 1 Tun Wo Lane, Central. To get there walk under the Mid-Levels escalator as it cuts between Lyndhurst Terrace and Hollywood Rd. Tun Wo Lane is to the left as you walk uphill.

There are a string of budget veggie places on Jardine's Bazaar in Causeway Bay (Map 7). The *Fat Mun Lam* is said to have good dishes, but all the places look about the same. Also in Causeway Bay is the *Kung Tak Lam*, at 31 Yee Wo St. This place is a bit more expensive, closer to the mid-range category. But there are often good lunch specials, and all their vegetables are grown organically (there is a branch in Tsimshatsui at 45-47 Carnarvon Rd). The *Vegi Food Kitchen*, located off Gloucester Rd, is less of a budget option. It even has a brass sign out front forbidding anyone from carrying meat into the restaurant! Check your Big Mac at the front desk. Across Victoria Park, near Tin Hau MTR station at 102 Hing Fat St, is *Vegetarian House*. This place is said to do a good job on the mock meats: pork, chicken and so on, and prices are back in the budget range.

Indian Spots

Indian food used to be one of the great budget options in town, but Hong Kong's ridiculously high rents and stiff competition from fast food joints have taken their toll. Now a good lunch or dinner will cost between HK$35 and HK$70 at the cheaper spots. There are also some fancier Indian places: for details see the mid-priced restaurants section following.

There are a bunch of little places on the mezzanine level of Chungking Mansions in Tsimshatsui (Map 16) that still have rock-bottom prices. For a better atmosphere check out some of the restaurants upstairs in the various blocks. Prices are still fairly low, with set meals for around HK$40. The *Kashmir Club* (3rd floor, A Block) and the *Centre Point Club* (6th floor, B Block) have gotten good recommendations. Also worth trying is the *Taj Mahal Club Mess* (3rd floor, B Block) and the *Royal Club Mess* (5th floor, D Block). For Nepalese food, there's the *Everest Club* (3rd floor, D Block).

The *Koh-I-Noor* chain of restaurants also has a presence in Tsimshatsui, at 3-4 Peninsula Mansion, 1st floor, 16C Mody Rd. This place is cheaper and less stylish than its counterpart in Central, but the food is still great and the staff friendly.

On the Hong Kong Island side, there is a cluster of Indian places along Wellington St, in the Central and Sheung Wan districts. The *Spice Island Club*, 63-69 Wellington St, has good Indian and Nepali food, and prices are quite reasonable for lunch, but not so great for dinner. On the other side of the street is *Woodlands*, a favourite with many expats.

Nestled in Wing Wah Lane, next door to Club 64 in Lan Kwai Fong (Map 8), the *India Curry Club* is another cheap, longstanding expat hangout, and with good reason. The food is good value for the money and the staff always obliging. It's located on the 3rd floor of the Winner Building. Also in Lan Kwai Fong is the Central branch of the *Koh-I-Noor*, located on the 1st floor of the California Entertainment Building.

Costing a bit more but worth it is *Club Sri Lanka* (☎ 2526-6559), Basement 17, Hollywood Rd, Sheung Wan (Map 4). This place features an excellent Sri Lankan buffet for around HK$70. There's also a second vegetarian buffet that costs a bit less. You may want to call ahead to see if there's a table, as this place is quite well known.

Over in Wanchai (Map 6) are two good Indian places, though you need to order carefully if you want to stay in true budget range. *JoJo Mess Club*, at 1st floor, 86-90 Johnston Rd, suffers from somewhat dreary decor, but you can sit by the window and watch the Wanchai action while you enjoy your meal. Just down the street is the *Johnston Mess*, another expat favourite. It's located at 1st floor, 104 Johnston Rd.

Street Markets

Though not the epitome of hygiene, these streetside markets (known as *dai pai dong*) can whip up some pretty tasty dishes in no time, and prices are generally quite reasonable. Ordering is also no problem: just point at what you want. Meals are taken at folding tables set up on the sidewalk or street. These are not for everyone, but for what it's worth, the wok is subjected to such searing heat that it should kill any nasty bacteria.

Most dai pai dong don't start hopping until nighttime, but there are a few where you can grab lunch or an afternoon snack. Hong Kong's best known dai pai dong is at the north section of the Temple St market in Yaumatei (Map 13). Check the Causeway Bay, Sheung Wan, Stanley and Wanchai maps for locations of several others.

Set Lunches

One good way to fill up for relatively little is the set lunch. In areas like Sheung Wan, Wanchai and parts of Tsimshatsui you will stumble across sidewalk signs advertising soup or salad, entree, dessert and tea/coffee for anywhere between HK$28 and HK$60. Even if the sign is in Chinese you should be able to get the idea, and most of these place have English-language menus. Set lunches are a staple of Hong Kong-style western restaurants. Most also have Chinese dishes on the menu, but these are not usually part of the set lunches.

There are no places worth recommending in particular, as they all taste pretty much the same. But the food isn't all that bad, and it gives you a chance to have a little variety and a chance to sit down, relax and take your time. One of the most popular chains in this category is the *Farm House* group of restaurants. There's one in nearly every district and they are easy to recognise by their yellow and green motif.

Fast Food

The landscape is not as bleak as this name might suggest. In Hong Kong people do everything quickly, so there's a good market for places that can turn out quality food in a hurry.

Of course the usual international offenders are here: McDonald's, KFC, Hardee's etc. In fact Hong Kong has earned a special place on the McDonald's corporate map: at last count some seven of the world's 10 busiest McDonald's restaurants were in Hong Kong. If you've a craving for a Big Mac and fries, you'll have no trouble satisfying it: there are some 50 McDonald's branches spread throughout over the territory.

Hong Kong has several home-grown fast food chains, serving both western and Chinese food. Breakfast usually features congee, fried noodles or western-style ham and eggs. For lunch and dinner there is a slew of different dishes, ranging from pepper steak to home-style bean curd. Most chains also have afternoon tea sets:

a chicken leg, hot dog or fried radish cake with tea or coffee. Breakfasts average around HK$20, lunch and dinner HK$35 to HK$50 and tea sets HK$15.

The four major chains are *Cafe de Coral*, *Fairwood*, *Ka Ka Lok* and *Maxim's*. All are very similar in price and quality. It's pretty much hit-or-miss. Some of the dishes are really not bad, but every once and a while you may come across a contender for the rubbish bin.

One of the brightest spots on the fast food scene is the *Oliver's Super Sandwiches* chain. Originally started as a gourmet food store in Central, these have evolved into a network of clean, reasonably priced sandwich shops that continues to expand. Ingredients are fresh and sandwiches quite tasty, though they do tend to skimp a bit on the meat. But nonetheless you can get a good turkey sandwich on five-grain bread with lettuce, tomato, cucumbers and onions for under HK$20. They also serve real brewed coffee, soup, baked potatoes and salads. The shops are fairly easy to find in the business and tourist districts. In Central there are shops in Exchange Square, Prince's Building and Citibank Plaza. In Causeway Bay there's an Oliver's in Winsor House. For other locations, check the Sheung Wan, Tsimshatsui and Wanchai maps.

Similar to Oliver's in arrangement are several fast food places selling kebabs, meat or vegetables served with cucumber yoghurt sauce on a pita. Prices are HK$20 to HK$25, and the kebabs are quite tasty.

Clinching the trophy for most exotic fast food chain is *Genroku Sushi*. Sushi is priced from HK$7 per plate and is served on a conveyor belt. Though obviously not in the same league as the delicacies served in a good Japanese restaurant, the sushi is still OK. The only drawback is that there can be a long wait for seats, especially during the 1 to 2 pm lunch-hour. For locations of some Genroku Sushi branches, check the Central, Causeway Bay and Tsimshatsui maps.

More Japanese food can be had at *Yoshinoya Beef Bowl*, which specialises in big bowls of steamed rice with sliced beef or chicken for HK$27 to HK$35. It's tasty and quite filling – check the Wanchai and Tsimshatsui maps for locations.

Self-Catering

The most obvious target for those wishing to make their own food is one of the ubiquitous *7-Eleven* convenience stores that seem everywhere. You'll not find anything healthy here, but there are instant noodles and soup, an entire freezer full of microwavable goodies and a wide

---

Morning Coffee & High Tea

Afternoon tea as a tradition is dying out in frantic, business-crazed Hong Kong. But a few of the upmarket hotels still make a good show of these is *The Peninsula*, where silent, immaculately clad waiters painstakingly prepare your pot of tea and serve up an impressive array of finger sandwiches and pastries. The best place to enjoy this experience is on the mezzanine level, which spares you the noise and distraction of the constant crowds in the lobby.

Also in Tsimshatsui (Map 16), the *Regent Hotel* lacks the colonial air of The Peninsula, but offers nice harbour views along with your tea. In Central (Map 5), the *Mandarin Oriental* serves afternoon tea in its mezzanine level cafe, which is also a good spot to watch the mix of tourists and business types parading through the lobby below.

Coffee has undergone a renaissance in Hong Kong in the past several years, to the relief of the western and Japanese expat community, many of whom have long suffered under the tyranny of instant coffee. Most restaurants now do a much better job of brewing up fresh pots for their customers, and cappuccino/espresso machines can be found all over the place.

Best of all, coffee stands and shops offering a variety of tasty straight brews and speciality coffees have started appearing in more and more areas. They're thickest on the ground in Central, though Wanchai and Tsimshatsui are beginning to sprout their own branches. Prices vary. Among the best value is *Uncle Russ*, where a regular cup of coffee is just HK$7 to HK$10. Other places sell their regular brews for between HK$8 and HK$20. Cappuccino, café latte and espresso drinks average between HK$15 and HK$30 for the larger servings. Here's a list of some places where you can get your daily dose of caffeine. Some of these places also sell beans.

---

selection of beer, drinks and juices. Prices are higher than in the supermarkets, but at least they're open 24 hours.

If you want to get something more substantial head to one of the two supermarket chains, *Wellcome* or *Park'n Shop*. The branches in Central, Causeway Bay, Wanchai, Tsimshatsui, Happy Valley and the Peak have all kinds of western goodies that you may have missed if you've been away in Asia for a while.

More upmarket do-it-yourselfers may want to check out the basement floors of the Japanese department stores in Causeway Bay. The supermarkets here have all manner of exotic items and high-quality foods, as reflected by the prices. The basement level of the *Seibu department store*, in the Pacific Place Mall in Admiralty

Coffee Central – ground floor, Alexandra House, Central (Map 5)

Mr Bean – 2nd floor lobby, Central Plaza, Wanchai (Map 6)

Pacific Coffee Co – ground floor, Bank of America Tower, Central (Map 5)
Shop 404, Pacific Place mall, Admiralty (Map 5)
Star Ferry Terminal, Central (Map 5)
Star Ferry Terminal, Tsimshatsui (Map 16)
1st floor, Devon House, Quarry Bay

San Francisco Coffee Shop – 8 Humphrey's Ave, Tsimshatsui (Map 16)

TW Cafe – ground floor, Capitol Plaza, 2-10 Lyndhurst Terrace, Central (Map 4)
Mezzanine, 2 Queen Victoria St, Central

Uncle Russ – 32 D'Aguilar St, Central
2 Peking Rd, Tsimshatsui (Map 16)

In addition to these places, *Oliver's Super Sandwiches* (see the Fast Food section) makes an acceptable cup of brewed coffee, and has cappuccino as well. *La Rose Noire* (see French restaurants) has excellent coffee, including the best café au lait in Hong Kong. *La Trattoria*, the Italian restaurant in the Landmark shopping centre, has a fine adjacent coffee shop.

All of these places serve pastries. Some, like La Rose Noire and La Trattoria, have treats that can be addictive; others, like Uncle Russ and Pacific Coffee Co, do a good job of satisfying the sweet tooth, but that's about all. *Cova* (see Italian restaurants) has excellent pastry shops in Central, Admiralty and Tsimshatsui.

For ice cream, Haagen-Dazs is, as always, ridiculously expensive, but it's damn good. There are a few branches around town: the Exchange Square in Central; Pedder St, Central; Kingston St, Causeway Bay; and the Peak Galleria, the Peak. ■

has one of the best markets in town, with dozens of imported cheeses, meats, snacks and luxury foods.

Another place for gourmet foods is *Oliver's Food Stores*, associated with the sandwich fast food chain. Almost any type of European delicacy you seek may be found here, and the stores also have good wine selection. Prices are steep. There are Oliver's stores in the Prince's Building in Central, Harbour City in Tsimshatsui and the Repulse Bay Shopping Arcade.

PLACES TO EAT – MIDDLE

This is where you can really start to enjoy what Hong Kong has to offer. In addition to the numerous types of

Chinese restaurants, consider trying out some of the other Asian cuisines on offer. There are also plenty of western restaurants worth visiting.

Chinese

Central & Admiralty This district (Map 5) is on the whole better for non-Chinese food, but there are a few places worth recommending. Most are packed to the walls during the weekday 1 to 2 pm lunch-hour, but if you go around noon to 12.30 pm you should be able to get a table.

Noble House (☎ 2877-3993), in the basement of the Standard Chartered Bank Building, suffers from a clichéd name, but the Cantonese food is outstanding and the service attentive. The fried pork chop Noble House-style comes highly recommended. Prices are higher, but for your money you also get an elaborate decor.

Sitting between the towers of Exchange Square, on the 3rd floor of the Forum shopping mall, is *Hunan Garden* (☎ 2868-2880). This elegant, somewhat expensive place specialises in spicy Hunanese cuisine. Their seafood dishes are particularly good, and the setting, looking out over the harbour or the heart of Central, adds to the atmosphere.

Hunan Garden is part of a chain run by Maxim's, a local restaurant and food service company. The names usually reflect the style of Chinese cuisine. There's a *Chiu Chow Garden* (☎ 2525-8246) in the basement of Jardine House (and another one on the ground floor of the Lippo Centre), a *Shanghai Garden* (☎ 2524-8181) on the first floor of Hutchison House and a *Peking Garden* (☎ 2526-6456) in the basement of Alexandra House. Buried on the ground floor of the Pacific Place shopping mall is *Sichuan Garden* (☎ 2845-8433). There are exceptions to the regional names: *Jade Garden* (☎ 2526-3031) is a Cantonese restaurant on the 1st floor of Swire House. Food at all of these is usually quite tasty, and presentation, while perhaps not unforgettable, is well done. Hunan Garden is pretty much the most expensive: prices at the others tend to be quite reasonable.

Near Lan Kwai Fong on Wellington St (Map 8) is the reigning patriarch of Cantonese restaurants, the *Yung Kee* (☎ 2522-1624). The food is consistently good, and with seating for over 1000 diners spread over five floors, it's always an interesting dining experience. The roast goose here has been the talk of the town for 50 years, and the dim sum is also excellent. Across the street is the *Tai Woo Restaurant* (☎ 2524-5688). This is part of a chain, but don't let that put you off. The seafood here has won praise from diners and critics alike, and the food overall is great value for the money.

Sheung Wan The province of cheap eats and noodle shops, this area (Map 4) also has a few good mid-priced spots. For the full aircraft-hanger Cantonese restaurant experience, try the *Hsin Kuang Restaurant* (☎ 2542-0338), a multi-storey affair sitting next to Western Market. The food isn't all that memorable, but the atmosphere is pure Hong Kong.

In the same area, at 7 On Tai St, is the *Golden Snow Garden Restaurant* (☎ 2545-7779), at the end of the street, just past the Western Market. The name may make you chuckle, but there's an English menu, good variety and helpful waiters.

Despite its trite name, *Mythical China* (☎ 2815-3212) is actually a pretty good spot. Located on the 2nd floor of the Western Market, the place has a nice historical feel that is complemented by the restaurant's styling, made to echo a 1920s teahouse. In addition to Cantonese food and dim sum, the restaurant serves a variety of regional cuisines, including Peking and Shanghai. It's worth ordering one of the tasty noodle side dishes.

If Peking food is what you're after, you can try the *Silver Moon Peking Restaurant* (☎ 2803-7202) at 26-30 Des Voeux Rd West, also near the Western Market. The food is said to be consistently good, especially the hot pot and the dumplings.

A more off-beat meal can be had at the *Yat Chau Health Restaurant* (☎ 2545-8688), near Sheung Wan MTR station. This place actually has Chinese doctors who check you out and then suggest dishes to bolster your particular constitution. It's a bit tricky to do this if you don't speak Cantonese, and the food is pretty expensive, but if you're in quirky mood this might do the trick.

Decent Shanghai food is available at the *South and North Restaurant* (☎ 2816-6421) at 480 Queen's Rd West, west of Sheung Wan. The place is little more than a hole in the wall, with only four tables that are usually full. But there are lots of tasty little treats on offer: the Shanghai dumplings are especially good, as are the filling pork chop soup noodles. Although the sign out front is in English, the menu is not, so be prepared to point. Another good Shanghai spot is the *Hong Qiao Deli* (☎ 2858-6683), on the 3rd floor of the Shun Tak Centre (Macau Ferry Terminal).

Wanchai & Causeway Bay Both these districts (Maps 6 & 7) are brimming with all types of restaurants.

Johnston Rd in Wanchai has a couple of really traditional spots that always seemed packed: the *Lung Moon Restaurant* (☎ 2572-9888) and the *Sheung Hei Teahouse* (☎ 2575-7723). Eating in these places is probably similar to what it was like in the 1950s here, and the prices, while not at 1950s levels, are still pretty reasonable. Not a lot of English is spoken at these places.

Nearby, the *Steam and Stew Inn* (☎ 2529-3913) serves up 'homestyle' Cantonese food, most of which is steamed, stewed or boiled. The food is good, but you may want to ask a waiter for some advice, as there are some Cantonese delicacies (read 'guts' and 'innards') that may not appeal. The place is popular, so it may be a good idea to call ahead.

If you don't mind a steeper bill, *One Harbour Road* (☎ 2588-1234) is a beautifully designed Cantonese restaurant in the Grand Hyatt Hotel. In addition to a harbour view, you can choose from six pages of gourmet dishes. Not a bad combination. Another good hotel restaurant for Cantonese fare is *Dynasty* (☎ 2802-8888), located in the New World Harbour View. The dim sum here is outstanding, and the minced pigeon in lettuce was rated by *HK Magazine* as among the best in Hong Kong.

For Chiu Chow food, the *Carriana Chiu Chow Restaurant* (☎ 2511-1282) rates right up there. Try their pork with tofu, or Chiujiew chicken for a subtle taste treat. The restaurant is almost constantly crowded, but there are a lot of tables, so there shouldn't be much of a wait.

This is the part of town for Sichuan food. One of the best places is the *Yin King Lau Restaurant* (☎ 2520-0106), which is tucked away on the 2nd floor of a grimy building on Lockhart Rd. The atmosphere is purely utilitarian, but for some reason this makes it even more fun to sit back, down a few cold beers and order up some spicy dishes. The sizzling chilli prawns are one of house specialities, and shouldn't be missed. Way down at the other end of Lockhart Rd in Causeway Bay is another contender for the top Sichuan spot. The *Sze Cheun Lau Restaurant* (☎ 2891-9027) is even more authentic: this is where you can get some dishes so hot you'll be crying into your rice. The duck smoked with camphor is a favourite.

Spicy food lovers may also want to try the *Yunnan Kitchen* (☎ 2506-3309), located in a vertical food court (you'll understand when you see it) on the 12th floor of the Times Square shopping complex. This place does a pretty good job of capturing the taste of Yunnan cuisine: specialities include Yunnan ham, fried vermicelli Dali-style and fresh prawns stuffed in bamboo. Like all the restaurants in Times Square, this one's a bit pricey, but the food does not disappoint.

At the *Shanghai Village* (☎ 2894-9705), at 9 Lan Fang Rd, Causeway Bay, the chef, who comes from Hangzhou in China, knows her business. Though often crowded, the restaurant has a quiet back room where you can sometimes escape the masses. More pedestrian Shanghai fare can be had at the *3.6.9. Restaurants*, a chain of sorts. Service is not inspiring but the food is usually reliable, and fairly priced. There are two branches in Wanchai: one on O'Brien Rd and the other on Queen's Rd East, across from Hopewell Centre.

Finally, the one place in town to go for Taiwanese food is *Forever Green* (☎ 2890-3448) on Leighton Rd in Causeway Bay. This place does a good job with traditional Taiwanese specialities like oyster omelette, fried bean curd and three-cup chicken (sanbeiji). Prices are fairly high.

Aberdeen Restaurants have pretty much made Aberdeen (Map 10) world famous. Not because the food there is exceptionally good (it's not), but rather where you go to eat it. This little harbour city is home to three of the largest, gaudiest and most unique eateries anywhere: the floating restaurants. Chief of these is the *Jumbo* (☎ 2553-9111), a massive four-storey blaze of neon, gold lettering and ersatz pagoda roofing. Inside looks like Beijing's Imperial Palace crossbred with a Las Vegas casino. The Jumbo has played host to dignitaries from around the world, has featured in several movies (including one James Bond film) and has fed tourists for three decades. It's not so much a restaurant as an institution. That's how you should view it if you go to eat there, because the food can be disappointing. The neighbouring *Jumbo Palace* does a better job on the food, but is also considerably more expensive. On the other side is the *Tai Pak*, which has prices and standards similar to the Jumbo. Dinner for four persons without drinks should run around HK$800 to HK$1200, more at the Jumbo Palace.

Transport to and from the restaurants is via boats, which regularly run between piers at the Aberdeen Promenade and next to the Aberdeen Marina Club.

If dining on water-borne warehouses is not for you, there are also a few good Chinese and Thai restaurants on Old Main St. For details on getting to Aberdeen, see the Things to See & Do chapter.

Southern Hong Kong Island There's not much in the way of notable Chinese restaurants on the south side of the island. If you're in Repulse Bay and in the mood for dim sum or a fancy Cantonese meal you can try the

Hei Fung Terrace Chinese Restaurant (☎ 2812-2622), 1st floor, Repulse Bay Shopping Arcade.

In Stanley (Map 11), *Stanley's Oriental* (☎ 2813-9988), 90B, Stanley Main St, has some decent Chinese dishes, as well as other Asian cuisine. The best part about this place is its waterfront location, which makes for a pleasant afternoon snack or sunset cocktail.

If you've made it all the way out to Shek O, you can try the *Welcome Garden* (☎ 2809-2836), a little Sichuan place that, while roofed, has a pleasant open-air feel to it. The food is generally well prepared and prices reasonable. The restaurant is on the left side of the main road as you enter town. Across the street, the *Shek O Chinese-Thai Seafood Restaurant* (☎ 2809-4426) does a booming trade, but is known more for its Thai dishes than Chinese cuisine.

Tsimshatsui This area (Map 16) is inundated with Cantonese restaurants, and once you get away from Nathan Rd, a lot of them are quite good. Prices are generally a bit lower than on Hong Kong Island.

Siu Lam Kung Seafood Restaurant (☎ 2721-6168), at 17-21 Minden Ave, has long been a local favourite and is known for its shellfish specialities. This place is a bit more expensive than most, but that doesn't deter the crowds, so you may want to call ahead. Also frequented by local seafood lovers is the *North Sea Fishing Village Restaurant* (☎ 2723-6843), located in the 1st basement of the Auto Plaza, 65 Mody Rd, Tsimshatsui East. Don't worry about the cheesy nautical decor: this place really is all right. They also do a good dim sum here.

For a good but reasonably priced Cantonese meal, try the *Canton Court* (☎ 2739-3311) in the Guangdong Hotel, 18 Prat Ave, Tsimshatsui. The staff don't speak much English, but the food is usually good. That, and the prices, explain why this place is frequented by visitors from mainland China. A few blocks away at 20 Granville Rd is a branch (☎ 2739-8813) of the reliable *Tai Woo Restaurant* chain. Also not a bad deal for the money is the *Jade Garden Restaurant* (☎ 2730-6888), 4th floor, Star House (right across from the Tsimshatsui Star Ferry Terminal).

For harbour views that won't send your meal price sky-high, try the *Oriental Harbour Chinese Restaurant* (☎ 2723-3885), 2nd floor, Tsimshatsui Centre, 66 Mody Rd, Tsimshatsui East. There are good set lunches here, allowing you to concentrate on the view instead of ordering. Also on the 2nd floor of the Tsimshatsui Centre is the Kowloon branch (☎ 2368-7266) of Maxim's *Chiu Chow Garden*, where you can taste this lighter, more subtle variation on Cantonese cooking for a modest sum. Just east of the Guangdong Hotel, the *Delicious Food Co Chiu Chow Restaurant* also looks worth trying, though the decor is a bit more basic.

Next door is the *Shanghai Restaurant* (☎ 2739-7083), which presents its food the authentic Shanghai way: heavy with lots of oil. If you don't mind that, and a somewhat high bill, it's probably worth trying. One door over, the *Great Shanghai Restaurant* (☎ 2366-8158), which while a bit more touristy and less authentic, is also somewhat cheaper and easier to negotiate for non-Chinese speakers.

Tsimshatsui is home to what is probably Hong Kong's most famous Peking restaurant, the *Spring Deer* (☎ 2366-4012). Tucked away in a nondescript building at 42 Mody Rd, this place serves some of the crispiest Peking duck in town. At HK$250 for a whole bird, it's not exactly budget dining, but won't break the bank either. This place is extremely popular, so you may have to book several days in advance. If you can't get in here, try the *Tai Fung Lau Peking Restaurant* (☎ 2366-2494), 29 Chatham Rd, Tsimshatsui, which also does a fine job on the northern specialities.

Yaumatei & Mongkok Most of the mid-range places around here (Map 13) are very local seafood restaurants that don't have English menus. If you're feeling adventurous, stroll the streets west of Nathan Rd and take a chance. If you don't feel like battling the language barrier, some of the hotel restaurants are worth a shot. The *Yat Tung Chinese Restaurant* (☎ 2710-1093) in the Eaton Hotel has an interesting menu, and the service is usually friendly and attentive. The *Nathan Restaurant* (☎ 2388-5141), in the Nathan Hotel, is known for its seafood set dinners. For a slightly more refined atmosphere, try the wood-panelled *House of Tang* (☎ 2761-1711) in the Metropole Hotel, which serves a mix of traditional and nouveau Cantonese cuisine.

International
African The only spot that comes close is the *Afrikan Cafe and Wine Bar* (☎ 2868-9299), 7 Glenealy St, Central (Map 5). The menu and atmosphere make for a pretty westernised version of Africa, but this is still a pleasant, relaxing place to enjoy a fine meal and some good wine.

American The 1990s saw an eruption of American restaurants in Hong Kong. There are now so many it's almost ludicrous, but they all have one thing in common:

high prices. The first, and still one of the best places is *Dan Ryan's Chicago Grill*. There are two branches, the original (☎ 2845-4600) in the Pacific Place shopping mall in Admiralty (Map 5), and a newer Tsimshatsui counterpart (☎ 2735-6111) at Ocean Terminal (Map 16). The food is consistently good, the portions huge and the service excellent. The burgers have been voted the best in Hong Kong four years running by readers of *HK Magazine*.

GLENN BEANLAND

Outdoor dining, Temple Street, Yaumatei

One of the other top picks is *American Pie* (☎ 2877-9779), hidden away on the 4th floor of the California Entertainment Building in Lan Kwai Fong (Map 8). Featuring more home-style dishes like turkey with gravy, fresh salads and even meatloaf, this place has become so popular you almost always need to book a table in advance. Try their Sunday brunch, a real bargain. If you're craving a fat slab of ribs, hit *Tony Roma's* (☎ 2512-0292), next door on the 1st floor of the California Tower.

In Tsimshatsui East, *King Lobster* (☎ 2724-8101), 1st floor, Toyo Mall, 94 Granville Rd, is developing a loyal following, despite its fairly steep prices. For your money you get succulent steaks and expertly prepared lobster, along with other goodies like shark fin and lobster bisque.

Similar in both quality and price is the *San Francisco Steak House* (☎ 2735-7576), 7 Ashley Rd, Tsimshatsui, which specialises in surf-and-turf, using only US corn-fed certified Angus beef, no less. On the Hong Kong Island side, *Trio's* (☎ 2877-9773), on Wo On Lane near Lan Kwai Fong (Map 8), also serves up a fine Maine lobster. The place is cosy, but tiny, so reservations are recommended.

US pop culture elbowed its way into the restaurant scene with the arrival of *Planet Hollywood* and the *Hard Rock Cafe*. Planet Hollywood (☎ 2377-7888), located near the bottom of Canton Rd in Tsimshatsui, is the more entertaining of the two, with better food, better service and lower prices. The Hard Rock Cafe makes you feel like you're paying for the decor, because the food is nothing special. There is one branch (☎ 2377-8168) at Swire House, Chater Rd, Central (Map 5) and another branch (☎ 2377-8118) at 100 Canton Rd, Tsimshatsui (Map 16). Of the two the Central restaurant is better: the Kowloon branch doubles as a dance club and the service suffers for it.

Australian Far off in the eastern Hong Kong Island district of Quarry Bay is *The Continental* (☎ 2563-2209), which *HK Magazine* considers one of the territory's best restaurants. The varied menu changes frequently, and the freshness of the ingredients comes through delightfully in the food. The restaurant is on the ground floor, 2 Hoi Wan St. To get there, take the MTR to Quarry Bay, take the exit to Tong Chong St and Devon House. Hoi Wan St is near the end of Tong Chong St on the left.

Brett's Seafood Restaurant (☎ 2866-6608) at 72 Lockhart Rd, Wanchai (Map 6) is nothing fancy: formica and fish and chips are the order of the day. But it's a good spot to take a breather and inhale some speedy seafood.

British Pubs are everywhere, though many have 'gone native'. One place that stays true to its roots is the *Bull and Bear Pub* (☎ 2525-7436) on the ground floor of Hutchison House in Central (Map 5). All the standards are on the menu, at prices even the English should be able to stomach. More expensive is *Bentley's Seafood Restaurant and Oyster Bar* (☎ 2868-0881) firmly rooted in the basement of the Prince's Building in Central (Map 5). Try the fish or meat pies, or the bread and butter pudding.

For Hong Kong's best fish and chips, there's really no contender to *Harry Ramsden's* (☎ 2832-9626), at 213 Queen's Rd East, Wanchai (Map 6). The place is cheery and the food consistently good, at least in the main dining area; quality at the take-away section varies, but the prices are cheaper.

Burmese The only show in town is the *Rangoon Restaurant* (☎ 2893-2281), located at 265 Gloucester Rd, near the corner of Cannon St, in Causeway Bay. The decor is nothing special, but the menu is extensive, and has a good vegetarian selection. Don't worry, the food looks better than the photos on the menu.

Continental Dozens of nondescript places fall under this moniker, which means 'European-style cuisine, but not from anywhere in particular'. One of the oldest names in this genre is *Jimmy's Kitchen* (☎ 2526-5293), at 1 Wyndham St, Central (Map 5), which at 60 years of age has become a Hong Kong institution. The dishes are always good and the menu, which has a strong emphasis on British fare, doesn't change, which is good as Jimmy's die-hard fans would probably riot. There's also a Tsimshatsui branch (☎ 2376-0327) at 1st floor, Kowloon Centre, 29 Ashley Rd (Map 16).

Camargue (☎ 2525-7997) offers both outstanding meals and the chance to look down on Central from the 24th floor of the Regent Centre, 88 Queen's Rd (near the Mid-Levels escalator link). *HK Magazine* gives this place its highest 'not to be missed' rating, so perhaps you should take their advice. Prices are on the high side.

Under this category also falls one of Hong Kong's most relaxing, laid-back cafe/restaurants, *Post 97* (☎ 2810-9333), 1st floor, 9 Lan Kwai Fong (Map 8). Truth be told, the food and service can disappoint sometimes. But good music, plush comfy couches and chairs and muted decor make it easy to sip your wine, read a book and contemplate a nice relaxing nap, although during lunch, dinner and weekend nights it gets pretty lively.

French There are a fair number of French places in town, but most fall into the 'Things to Eat – Astronomical End' category. *Le Fauchon* (☎ 2526-2136) at 6 Staunton St near Central won't require a bank loan to pay the bill, and the food and mood are almost certain to satisfy. Dinner for two, however, can easily run to near HK$1000. Friendlier to the wallet and just as nice to the palate is *Papillon* (☎ 2526-5965) hidden near the end of Wo On Lane, next to Lan Kwai Fong (Map 8). The place has a relaxed feel to it and the food is excellent. The lunchtime set is good value, but you may need to book a table in advance.

For breakfast, it's hard to beat a bowl (that's right, bowl) of café au lait and pastries at *La Rose Noire Patisserie* (☎ 2877-0118) on the 3rd floor of the Pacific Place shopping mall in Admiralty (Map 5). Lunch and dinner menus feature pleasant light fare like salads and pastas, as well as more traditional, and heavier, meat dishes. The wine list offers some good value, at least for Hong Kong. There is another branch in Tsimshatsui (☎ 2956-1222), on the ground floor of the Gateway at 254 Canton Rd. If you're in Pacific Place, you can also check out *La Cite*, a bistro of sorts located on the basement level. The fixed luncheon menu is a good deal, and the cappuccino a fine reason to sit back and rest your feet.

Returning to the high-priced, high-class establishments, a trip to Stanley on southern Hong Kong Island will bring you to *Stanley's French* (☎ 2813-8873), 86 Stanley Main St (Map 11). The seaside setting, the attentive staff and above all the fine food can more than justify the trip out here.

German/Austrian If you're yearning for a good bockwurst and maybe even some German conversation, there are places on both sides of the harbour that can oblige. In Lan Kwai Fong (Map 8) both *Schnurrbart* (☎ 2523-4700) and *Bit Point* (☎ 2523-7436) serve up hearty bierstube fare, and there's always at least one German behind the bar to guide you through the menu. They are bars however, and the cigarette smoke can get pretty thick at times. If so, hike up Glenealy St to *Mozart Stub'n* (☎ 2522-1763) in Central (Map 5), a cosy little Austrian spot with good food and wines and a delightful atmosphere.

In Tsimshatsui more German pub grub is available at the *Biergarten* (☎ 2721-2302), 8 Hanoi Rd, and the Kowloon branch of *Schnurrbart* (☎ 2366-2986), at 9 Prat Ave (Map 16). If you're near the Star Ferry Terminal, a fine pfannengebratener fleischkase awaits at *Weinstube* (☎ 2376-1800), on the 1st floor of the Honeytex Building, 22 Ashley Rd.

Indian While most of Hong Kong's Indian restaurants fall into the budget price range (see above) there are a some places that offer a more refined setting. Perched above Lan Kwai Fong on Wyndham St (Map 8) is a string of such spots. Two that get good reviews are *Ashoka* (☎ 2524-9623) at ground floor, 57 Wyndham St, and *The Village* which is at the same address but on the basement level. The Ashoka is a bit more elegant and expensive, while the Village has a warm, cosy feel to it. Both serve curries that will warm your belly and ignite your palate.

Tandoor (☎ 2845-2299), 3rd floor, On Hing Building, 1-9 On Hing Terrace (Map 5), is another local favourite, and has an open kitchen so you can see how it's all done. Prices are a bit high, but not unreasonable.

For northern Indian cuisine, there's the *Bombay Palace* (☎ 2527-0115) located on the ground floor (west side) of the Far East Finance Centre in Admiralty (Map 5). This is part of an international chain, and has a popular lunchtime buffet.

The venerable *Gaylord Restaurant* (☎ 2376-1001) in Ashley St, Tsimshatsui (Map 16), has been going strong since 1972. Dim lighting, booth seating and live Indian music create a fine mood for appreciating old favourites like lamb vindaloo and chicken masala. This is one of the priciest Indian eateries in town, but few seem to mind.

Indonesian If you don't mind a bit of formica and fake wood panelling, go for an authentic meal at the *Indonesian Restaurant* (☎ 2577-9981), 28 Leighton Rd, Causeway Bay (Map 7). The service won't have you jumping for joy, but the fried chicken and super-spicy roasted fish with chilli might. There are also a couple of Indonesian hole-in-the-wall places on Lockhart Rd, just west of the Sogo department store, that may be worth a try.

Over in Wanchai, the *Shinta* (☎ 2527-4874) is a dimly-lit, laid-back spot that serves up a pretty good nasi goreng. It's located on the 1st floor of the Kar Yau Building, 36-44 Queen's Rd East, near the intersection with Hennessy Rd.

If you're in Tsimshatsui, the *Java Rijsttafel* (☎ 2367-1230), at 38 Hankow Rd, packs a lot of restaurant into a tiny room. The menu is extensive, but if you get overwhelmed just order the rijsttafel, which gives you 16 tasty dishes for under HK$150.

Irish *Delaney's* is about as close to real Irish pub grub and silky smooth Guinness draught as you're going to get outside of Dublin. There are two branches: in Wanchai (☎ 2804-2880), 2nd floor, One Capital Place, 18 Luard Rd (Map 6); and in Tsimshatsui (☎ 2301-3980), 3-7 Prat Ave (Map 16). The Tsimshatsui version, which has an impressive long bar that stretches the length of the restaurant, has the better atmosphere. But food in both places is always reliable. Also on tap is Delaney's Irish Ale, which is specially brewed for the bar by the South China Brewing Co.

Italian Along with American restaurants, a bevy of new Italian places have flooded onto the scene in recent years. Most aren't bad, but there are only a few that really justify the money you have to shell out for a taste of old Italy. One of the best bets is *Va Bene* (☎ 2845-5577), located at the top end of Lan Kwai Fong (Map 8). Elegantly appointed, with pastel walls and wooden venetian blinds, this place has some great northern Italian dishes.

Also in Lan Kwai Fong, *Tutto Meglio* (☎ 2869-7833) is also beautifully decorated, and the food excellent, albeit a bit more down to earth than the sophisticated specialities of Va Bene. Tutto Meglio has a sister restaurant in the northern section of Tsimshatsui: *Tutto Bene* (☎ 2316-2116) at 7 Knutsford Terrace (Map 16). This spot has the added benefit of outdoor seating under giant umbrellas: throw in a nice spring day and you could be in Florence.

In the Landmark shopping centre in Central (Map 5) is *La Trattoria* (☎ 2524-0111). Coming here for dinner can get really expensive, but your money buys you some of the best-prepared and exotic Italian dishes in town.

Cova Caffe (☎ 2523-5225) on the ground floor of Swire House in Central (Map 5) really feels like an elegant little eatery in Italy, no doubt due to the tireless efforts of its Italian manager. Cova is a great place to come for lunch and insulate yourself from the constant bustle of Central. Their lunch specials are not a bad deal, and their pastries divine. Cova also has pastry shops in Times Square and the World Trade Centre (Causeway Bay), Pacific Place (Admiralty) and Ocean Terminal (Tsimshatsui).

If you're on more of a budget, *Ristorante Romano* (☎ 2506-0988) on the 13th floor of Times Square (Map 7) has an all-you-can-eat lunch special for around HK$100. In addition to a soup and salad bar, there's a pasta table where you pick your own noodles, ingredients and sauce, which is then cooked up while you wait. In Wanchai, *La Bella Donna* (☎ 2802-9907) is another lower-cost option. Again the food is not spectacular, but you should walk away full and happy. It's located on the 1st floor of the Shui On Centre, 6-9 Harbour Rd (Map 6).

Japanese There are countless numbers of Japanese places to choose from, the best of which are, not surprisingly, run by native Japanese. These restaurants support a large and growing Japanese expatriate community, so you stand a good chance of getting a high-quality authentic meal, though you will pay for it. Some Japanese venture that Hong Kong's Japan fare is sometimes more expensive than Tokyo's in terms of what you get for your money. One way around this is to go for the set luncheons. There are priced at around HK$100 to HK150, and include soup, pickles and other appetisers, all served together. Go at night, start enjoying the sake, and your bill can easily soar past HK$1000.

Two great places for lunch in Central are *Hanagushi* and *Fukuki*, both in the Lan Kwai Fong area (Map 8). Hanagushi (☎ 2521-0868) is a bit cramped and really fills up from 1 to 2 pm on weekdays, but the skewered yakitori, soba noodles and sushi are all crowd-pleasers.

Fukuki (☎ 2877-6668) is more refined, with *tatami* mats and private dining enclaves: it also costs more. This place has a particularly good reputation with local Japanese. Two other decent lunch spots in Central (Map 5) are *Sakaegawa* (☎ 2877-6666) in the basement of the Ritz-Carlton and *Agehan* (☎ 2525-5111), in the basement of the Furama Kempinski Hotel.

For a more down-to-earth atmosphere, try *Ichiban* (☎ 2890-7589), 21 Lan Fong Rd, Causeway Bay (Map 7). The mood here is more like an *izakaya*, Japan's ubiquitous pubs. Though the service can be a bit negligent, the food does not disappoint and the atmosphere lends itself to enthusiastic bouts of sake drinking.

Trek over to Tsimshatsui East (Map 16), and in the basement of the Kowloon Shangri-La you'll find *Nadaman* (☎ 2721-2111), which is usually filled with Japanese business people during the lunch-hour taking advantage of the set meals, which are good value.

It's also worth checking out the basement levels of the Japanese department stores Daimaru, Matsuzakaya, Mitsukoshi, Seibu and Sogo. With the exception of Seibu, located in the Pacific Place shopping mall in Admiralty, all these stores are clustered together in Causeway Bay. The restaurants are usually pretty authentic and have good set lunches.

Korean If you don't mind hiking over to Sheung Wan (Map 4), you can eat where the local Korean expats do. In the Korean Centre Building, 119-21 Connaught Rd, you'll find the *Korea House Restaurant* (☎ 2544-0007), acknowledged as having some of the most authentic Korean barbecue, kimchi and appetiser plates in Hong Kong. Prices are very reasonable too. Enter from Man Wa Lane. In the same building, the *Korea Garden* also seems to draw a steady crowd of Korean diners.

On the other side of the harbour in Tsimshatsui, the *Arirang Korean Restaurant* (☎ 2956-3288) has been around for 10 years, though it just moved into sparkling new digs at the Gateway on Canton Rd.

Mediterranean *Bacchus* (☎ 2529-9032), Basement, 8 Hennessy Rd, Wanchai (Map 6), is a place to go and have a good time: the food is deliciously different and the service friendly and upbeat. Some nights there is live entertainment. The experience will cost you, but it's almost always worth it.

Mexican Several places in town claim to serve Mexican food. With the following exceptions, they should all be given a wide berth, unless you enjoy flushing money down the toilet. In Lan Kwai Fong (Map 8) *Zona Rosa* (☎ 2801-5885) has impressed serious Mexican food fans. The food is fresh, the sauces and chillies quite hot, but the high prices may cool you down a bit. Another tasty but expensive option is *JW's California Grill* (☎ 2810-8366), located in the JW Marriot Hotel in Admiralty (Map 5). It's a bright airy place with innovative Tex-Mex dishes, and the menu changes regularly.

You can go a bit cheaper with a trip to the *Mexican Association* (☎ 2367-4535) a tiny place hidden on the 11th floor of the Hankow Centre, 1C Middle Rd, Tsimshatsui (Map 16). For licensing and tax reasons, this place is a members-only club, meaning you need to hand over HK$10 for a temporary membership card. This allows you to order burritos, quesadillas and other acceptable dishes at reasonable prices.

Nepalese It might be worth making the trek up to Staunton St in Sheung Wan (Map 4) to pay a visit to *Nepal* (☎ 2521-9108), for steamed vegetable dumplings, yak cheese and Nepali barbecued chicken, among others. Service, while a bit haphazard, is polite and the prices aren't too steep.

Pan-Asian/East Meets West King of the pan-Asian genre is the *Peak Cafe* (☎ 2849-7868), which sits across the top end of the Peak Tram (Map 9). The food is always delicious, including Chinese, Indian, Thai and some western dishes (the Indian food is usually the best pick). But what really makes this place is its amazing setting, vaulted ceiling, elegant decor and one of Hong Kong's best looking bars. If you're on the Peak, this is your best choice, hands down.

Across the road, housed in the hulking Peak Galleria, is the *Cafe Deco Bar and Grill* (☎ 2849-5111). This place also does the pan-Asian/east-west thing, though with neither the class nor the warmth of the Peak Cafe. Still the food is good, if overpriced, and you can't argue with the jaw-dropping view of Hong Kong and Kowloon.

Another place with a great setting and fairly good food is *Stanley's Oriental* (☎ 2813-9988), 90B Stanley Main St, Stanley (Map 11). Again, you're paying as much for the view, this time of peaceful Stanley Bay. It's a good place to relax with a drink, though it may take some time before it's brought to you.

One of the great bargains in town is the lunch/dinner buffet at *Salisbury's Dining Room* (☎ 2369-2211) on the 4th floor of the Salisbury YMCA in Tsimshatsui (Map 16).

GLENN BEANLAND

Dining out in Lan Kwai Fong

The food is not exquisite, but for around HK$70 you can make as many trips as you wish to the table. Add in the cheery atmosphere and the prime location over Salisbury Rd, and this place is hard to beat for the money.

Kublai's is a fast growing chain of places that does a refined version of Mongolian barbecue. Head to the food counter, pick out whatever meat, veggies, spices and sauces you want (there's a lot to choose from), hand it through a hole in the wall to the cook, and return to your table to await your creation. It's all you can eat for HK$118, and for the taste and the experience, this is a fine price. It's best if you can go with a group, as it's a very social atmosphere. Diners are allotted time blocks (two hours after 9.30 pm) due to the high demand, so call ahead to book your spot. There are four branches: 151 Lockhart Rd, Wanchai (☎ 2511-2287); 3rd floor, One Capital Place, 18 Luard Rd (☎ 2529-9117); 1 Keswick St, Causeway Bay; and 55 Kimberley Rd, Tsimshatsui (☎ 2722-0733).

Portuguese If you don't have the time to make it to Macau, you might consider the *Casa Lisboa* (☎ 2869-9631), at 20 Staunton St near the Central/Sheung Wan border (Map 4). They do all the favourites, like African chicken, ribs and baked seafood rice. It costs a lot more than a Portuguese meal in Macau, but then you don't have to buy a ferry ticket either.

South-East Asian Amidst all the glitter and lights of Central's Pacific Place shopping mall (Map 5) is *Tiger's* (☎ 2537-4682). The decor is a bit off-beat, but the food is right on target. The extensive menu does a good job of covering the region, and each tasty dish is identified by country.

Considerably less refined, but also delicious, is a meal at *Man Fai Food of South-East Asia* (☎ 2543-8468), ground floor, 243 Des Voeux Rd Central, Sheung Wan (Map 4). The menu takes you through Cambodia, Malaysia, Singapore, Thailand and Vietnam. In addition to the main courses, there are all sorts of tasty fruit drinks made with beans and coconut.

Spanish A long-time favourite with expats, *El Cid* (☎ 2312-1989), 14 Knutsford Terrace, Tsimshatsui (Map 16), does justice to classics such as paella and fritas, and has an excellent assortment of tapas (appetiser plates that go great with drinking). The decor does seem a bit overdone, but the effect is fairly cosy.

A Lan Kwai Fong (Map 8) landmark for years, *La Bodega* (☎ 2877-5482) recently was reborn and expanded to fill two floors. Though the remodelling pushed up prices somewhat, the food is as good as ever. The bottom floor is given over to a tapas and wine bar.

Thai People in Hong Kong tend to differ over which is the best Thai place in town. *Chili Club* (☎ 2527-2872) was voted 'best Thai' by *HK Magazine* readers in 1995. You can decide for yourself, but you'd be wise to book a table: this place is always packed. It's located on the 1st floor, 88 Lockhart Rd, Wanchai. Nearby at 44 Hennessy Rd (Map 6), *Thai Delicacy* (☎ 2527-2598) certainly has some of Hong Kong's most authentic tasting Thai food, and at prices that few other places can match. The decor is strictly utilitarian, but you'll probably be too busy feasting to notice.

Lan Kwai Fong (Map 8) has two Thai places that have only one thing in common: good food. At the bottom-end in terms of price is *Good Luck Thai* (☎ 2877-2971), a no-frills place that spills out onto Wing Wah Lane, which churns out truly tasty standbys like phat Thai, coconut tum yam kung and shaved beef soup noodles. Some of the fried dishes are a bit greasy, but the prices and the outdoor seating more than make up for it. At the other end of the spectrum is *Supatra's* (☎ 2522-5073), 50 D'Aguilar St. This place is super trendy, but all of the food is done right. It gets a bit loud when the after-work crowd starts flowing in, but the mood is cheerful enough.

Outdoor dining of a more refined nature is available at *Her Thai* (☎ 2735-8898), Promenade Level, Tower One, China Hong Kong City, Tsimshatsui (Map 16). The green

curry and roast chicken come highly recommended, so
it's probably worth the walk up here. Less distinct, but
more conveniently located is the upbeat *Sawadee*
(☎ 2376-3299), 6 Ichang St, Tsimshatsui. Dishes are
served without much fanfare, but that's probably
because the staff are desperately trying to keep up with
the constant influx of customers.

If you're down in Shek O, try and stop by the semi
open-air *Shek O Chinese-Thai Seafood Restaurant* (☎ 2809-
4426), just down from the bus stop. For many people this
is Hong Kong's best Thai place, not so much for the food
as for the laid-back mood and proximity to the beach.
The Thai appetiser platter really is good.

You can also have Thai food under the sun, or stars,
at *Sampan East* (☎ 2812-1618), in Deep Water Bay. This is
primarily a place to have a drink and watch the day slip
away, but if you get hungry the food is decent.

Vietnamese There's good Vietnamese food to be had
in Hong Kong thanks to a large community of overseas
Chinese from Vietnam. One of the best and most well-
known places is *Saigon Beach* (☎ 2529-7823) at 66 Lockhart
Rd, Wanchai (Map 6). You'll find in and say 'what a
dump!' and you'll be right. If it's crowded and there are
only one or two of you, chances are you'll be sharing your
table with strangers. Don't worry: it's all worth it. Prices
are higher than you might expect for a place of this size
and appearance, but if you don't want to pay it, there are
plenty of others who will grab your seat.

Another little gem of a place is the *Yuet Hing Yuen*
(☎ 2832-2863), jammed between the storefronts along
Cannon St in Causeway Bay (Map 7). The speciality here
is fried beef balls, but all their dishes are lip-smacking
good, and you can't really complain about the prices
either. Like Saigon Beach, the main drawback here is that
this place is packed.

The pickings are leaner on Kowloon side. *W's Paris
13th* (☎ 2723-6369), Toyo Mall, 94 Granville Rd, Tsimshatsui East, wins no points for decor, but the food is
delicious, and the prices should make you happy as well.
Closer to the Star Ferry Terminal at Level 1, No 17, New
World Centre, Salisbury Rd, the *Golden Bull* (☎ 2369-6417)
used to be pretty good, but has slid downhill.

PLACES TO EAT – TOP END

Oftentimes in Hong Kong the price difference between
a top-end meal and a mid-range one is a matter of what
you order on the menu. There are numerous restaurants

in the preceding section where dinner for two can cost HK$1000 or more. Likewise, in the places listed below, you may be able to get out for less than HK$1000 for two. But not if you really want to go for it, which after all is what top-end dining should be all about.

Many of Hong Kong's finest restaurants are in the luxury hotels. Those staying in one of the five-stars will also find more top-end restaurants without having to even venture outside. The following is a fairly selective list that includes a few of the top picks.

Chinese

There aren't too many really high-priced Chinese places, perhaps because there's so much good food already available for less money. At the few really expensive restaurants you're usually paying more for the setting, decor or reputation, rather than the food.

At the *Golden East Lake Chinese Cuisine Restaurant* (☎ 2576-2008) you will find yourself surrounded by carved wooden screens, frosted glass, small trees and fountains. The idea is to put your mind and body at ease, and focus all your attention on the elaborate Cantonese seafood dishes that the chefs have laboured over. The restaurant is located on the ground and 1st floors of the Eton Tower, 8 Hysan Ave, Causeway Bay.

Long one of Hong Kong's top Cantonese restaurants, the *Fook Lam Moon* makes sure you're taken care of from the minute you walk in the door, with *cheong-sam* clad hostesses escorting you in and out of the elevator that brings you to the dining room. Once you've been comfortably seated you will be faced with an intimidating menu that's designed for shock value, by listing prices for shark's fin on the first page. Sample the pan-fried lobster balls, the house speciality. Portions are not very large, but they are filled with flavour. There are two branches: 35 Johnston Rd, Wanchai (☎ 2866-0663); and 1st floor, 53 Kimberley Rd, Tsimshatsui (☎ 2366-0286).

For conspicuous consumption, it's hard to beat the *Sun Tung Long Shark's Fin Restaurant*. This is where business executives go to celebrate big deals or the very wealthy for wedding receptions. The speciality, shark's fin, comes in a variety of different gradings and prices. The most basic shark's fin soup runs around HK$500 for a single serving bowl. The decor feels a bit sterile, though maybe this is because all the staff wear white gloves. The restaurant has two locations: ground and 1st floors, Sunning Plaza, 1 Sunning Rd, Causeway Bay (☎ 2882-2899); and Shop 63, ground floor, Ocean Galleries, Harbour City, Tsimshatsui (☎ 2730-0288).

It may not win any awards for its name, but *The Chinese Restaurant* (☎ 2311-1234) has a good reputation for its Cantonese dishes. Again seafood is the speciality, but the high ceilings and traditional booth seating make for an unusual dining experience. The design is based on Chinese teahouses of the 1920s. The restaurant is on the 2nd floor, Hyatt Regency Hong Kong, 67 Nathan Rd, Tsimshatsui (Map 16).

Sitting on the harbour side of the Regent Hotel in Tsimshatsui (Map 16), the *Lai Ching Heen* (☎ 2721-1211) has repeatedly won awards for its refined Cantonese cuisine (although the elegant interior and stunning view must have influenced the judges somewhat). The menu changes with each lunar month, and if the selections get confusing there's always a waiter hovering nearby to act as a guide.

International

Undeniably the territory's most fantastic restaurant setting, both inside and out, is at *Felix* (☎ 2366-6251), which takes in nearly all of Hong Kong from high atop The Peninsula (Map 16). High ceilings, vast windows and hulking copper-clad columns surround the Art Deco table settings. At either end of the dining room are what look to be giant metal washtubs, within which you will find a bar, a mini disco and a wine-tasting room. Then there are the bathrooms, which are still the talk of Hong Kong (you can find out for yourself). Somehow it all fits together, and even if you're not taken with the interior, you'd have to be made of stone to resist the simply stunning views out every corner of every window. The food, if you even notice it, is east meets west. It is of course quite tasty, but portions are not generous. At least your eyes won't go away hungry. Felix is open from 6 pm to 1 am daily.

For 30 years *Gaddi's* (☎ 2366-6251) has managed to hold onto its reputation as *the* French restaurant in Hong Kong, though there is now a challenger to the title (see below). Also located in The Peninsula, this place has boasted virtually the same menu (and some of the same staff) for its entire three decades. Obviously the system doesn't need fixing. The atmosphere is a bit stiff, making it hard to relax, but then again the food will probably keep you pretty excited anyway.

Doing its best to unseat Gaddi's is *Petrus*, sitting near the clouds on the 56th floor of the Island Shangri-La Hotel in Central (Map 5). On the whole the setting is more relaxing than Gaddi's: even the ever-attentive waiters manage to seem unobtrusive. Many diners opt for the eight-course set dinner (HK$750), probably because this lets them focus on the view and the extensive wine list. Petrus is open for lunch and dinner daily, except Sundays when only dinner is served.

Sabatini (☎ 2721-5215) is a direct copy of its namesake in Rome, with designs painted on the walls and ceilings and a polished tile floor. Even classic Italian heavyweights like fettuccine carbonara come across as light but filling, leaving room to sample the exquisite appetisers. The wine list should keep you entertained, and if you can't find what you want you're just not trying. The restaurant is on the 3rd floor, Royal Garden Hotel, 69 Mody Rd, Tsimshatsui East (Map 16).

No one seems to have a bad thing to say about *M at the Fringe* (☎ 2877-4000), which is hidden in the basement of the Fringe Club at 2 Lower Albert Rd, Central (Map 8). The continental menus change with the season, and are usually as much fun to read as to order from. The soups here are excellent, and people in the know recommend the Mediterranean mezze. It's worth saving room for dessert, if you have that kind of self-restraint. Reservations are must.

Over on the south side of the island in Stanley (Map 11), *Tables 88* (☎ 2813-6262) is housed in what used to be the local police station. Though the building dates from 1854, you wouldn't know it from the hip decor inside. However, the effect is not unpleasant, and once you settle in it starts to feel quite inviting. The menu is continental, and the food is worth the price. The restaurant is located at 88 Stanley Village Rd, diagonally opposite the Stanley bus station.

HONG KONG RESTAURANT INDEX
Chinese Cuisine

CENTRAL & ADMIRALTY	**Maps 5 & 8**
Cantonese	Jade Garden, Noble House, Tai Woo, Yung Kee
Chiu Chow	Chiu Chow Garden
Hunan	Hunan Garden
Peking	Peking Garden
Shanghai	Shanghai Garden
Sichuan	Sichuan Garden

SHEUNG WAN	**Map 4**
Cantonese	Golden Snow Garden, Hsin Kuang, Mythical China, Yat Chau
Peking	Silver Moon
Shanghai	South and North, Hong Qiao
Vegetarian	Fat Heung Lam, Vegi-Table

WANCHAI & CAUSEWAY BAY   Maps 6 & 7

Cantonese	Dynasty, Fook Lam Moon, Golden East Lake, Lung Moon, One Harbour Rd, Sheung Hei, Steam & Stew, Sun Tung Long Shark's Fin
Chiu Chow	Carriana Chiu Chow
Shanghai	3.6.9., Shanghai Village
Sichuan	Sze Cheun Lau, Yin King Lau
Taiwan	Forever Green
Vegetarian	Fat Mun Lam, Kung Tak Lam, Vegi Food Kitchen, Vegetarian House
Yunnan	Yunnan Kitchen

ABERDEEN   Map 10

Cantonese	Jumbo, Jumbo Palace, Tai Pak

HONG KONG ISLAND SOUTH

Cantonese	Hei Fung Terrace (Repulse Bay), Shek O Chinese-Thai (Shek O)
Sichuan	Welcome Garden (Shek O)

TSIMSHATSUI   Map 16

Cantonese	Canton Court, The Chinese Restaurant, Fook Lam Moon, Jade Garden, Lai Ching Heen, North Sea Fishing Village, Oriental Harbour, Siu Lam Kung, Sun Tung Long Shark's Fin, Tai Woo
Chiu Chow	Chiu Chow Garden, Delicious Food Co Chiu Chow
Peking	Spring Deer, Tai Fung Lau
Shanghai	Shanghai Restaurant, Great Shanghai
Vegetarian	Kung Tak Lam

YAUMATEI & MONGKOK   Map 13

Cantonese	House of Tang, Nathan, Yat Tung

International Cuisine

CENTRAL & ADMIRALTY   Maps 5 & 8

African	Afrikan Cafe and Wine Bar
American	American Pie, Dan Ryan's, Hard Rock Cafe, Tony Roma's, Trio's
British	Bull and Bear Pub, Bentley's Seafood
Continental	Jimmy's Kitchen, M at the Fringe, Post 97
French	La Cite, Le Fauchon, Papillion, Petrus, La Rose Noire
German/ Austrian	Bit Point, Mozart Stub'n, Schnurrbart
Indian	Ashoka, Bombay Palace, India Curry Club, Koh-I-Noor, Spice Island Club, Tandoor, The Village, Woodlands
Italian	Cova Caffe, La Trattoria, Tutto Meglio, Va Bene
Japanese	Agehan, Genroku Sushi, Fukuki, Hanagushi, Sakaegawa
Mexican	JW's California Grill, Zona Rosa
SE-Asian	Tiger's
Spanish	La Bodega
Thai	Good Luck Thai, Supatra's

SHEUNG WAN   Map 4

Continental	Camargue
Indian	Club Sri Lanka
Japanese	Miyoshiya
Korean	Korea House, Korea Garden
Nepalese	Nepal
Portugese	Casa Lisboa
SE-Asian	Man Fai Food of South East Asia

WANCHAI & CAUSEWAY BAY   Maps 6 & 7

Australian	Brett's Seafood
British	Harry Ramsden's
Burmese	Rangoon Restaurant
Indian	JoJo Mess Club, Johnston Mess
Indonesian	Indonesian, Shinta
Irish	Delaney's
Italian	La Bella Donna, Ristorante Romano
Japanese	Genroku Sushi, Ichiban, Ichibantei, Yoshinoya
Mediterranean	Bacchus
Pan-Asian	Kublai's
Thai	Chili Club, Thai Delicacy
Vietnamese	Saigon Beach, Yuet Hing Yuen

THE PEAK   Map 9

Pan-Asian	Cafe Deco, Peak Cafe

HONG KONG ISLAND EAST/SOUTH

Australian	The Continental (Quarry Bay)
Continental	Tables 88 (Stanley – Map 11)
French	Stanley's French (Stanley – Map 11)
Pan-Asian	Stanley's Oriental (Stanley – Map 11)
Thai	Sampan East (Deep Water Bay), Shek O Chinese-Thai (Shek O)

TSIMSHATSUI   Map 16

American	Dan Ryan's, Hard Rock Cafe, King Lobster, Planet Hollywood, San Francisco Steak House
Continental	Jimmy's Kitchen
French	Gaddi's, La Rose Noire,
German	Biergarten, Schnurrbart, Weinstube
Indian	Centre Point Club, Everest Club (Nepalese), Gaylord, Kashmir Club, Koh-I-Noor, Royal Club Mess, Taj Mahal Club Mess
Indonesian	Java Rijsttafel
Irish	Delaney's
Italian	Sabatini, Tutto Bene
Japanese	Genroku Sushi, Nadaman, Yoshinoya
Korean	Arirang
Mexican	Mexican Association
Pan-Asian	Felix, Kublai's, Salisbury's Dining Room
Spanish	El Cid
Thai	Her Thai, Sawadee
Vietnamese	Golden Bull, W's Paris 13th

Note: Not all entries are shown on maps. Check text under district headings for addresses and directions.

Entertainment

CINEMAS

Hong Kong films are shown in Cantonese, but almost always have English-language subtitles, as well as Chinese characters. The latter is for export markets: Chinese audiences in Taiwan, China and South-East Asia may not understand a word of Cantonese, but they'll be able to read the characters.

Foreign films are mostly screened in their original language. If the film is in a language other than English, there will often be English subtitles as well as Chinese. Some of the more popular foreign films, particularly of the action genre, are dubbed into Cantonese, but generally these are only shown in neighbourhoods where foreigners are few and far between.

Foreign movies tend to arrive in Hong Kong within one to three months after being screened in their home market. Nearly all the major releases make it here, so if you've been travelling for a while Hong Kong is a good place to catch up.

Many cinemas have assigned seating. You pick up your seats at the ticket window, which explains why the queues move so slowly. Hong Kongers are crazy about movies and cinemas are often packed, especially on the weekends. Most places offer three days' advance booking services at the ticket office. This not only ensures you get a ticket, but increases your chances for a better seat. Several places have advance telephone booking, though the lines are often busy.

For a complete list of cinema phone numbers and addresses, check *HK Magazine's* 'HK2' section, which also has reviews of current films and where they are showing. To see what's playing that day it's best to check one of the local English-language newspapers. *HK Magazine* is a weekly, and most movies (especially foreign films) come and go so quickly in Hong Kong that it can't really keep up.

While most theatres only screen the mainstream stuff, you can catch some more off-beat or artistic offerings at *Columbia Classics* (☎ 2827-8291), ground floor, Great Eagle Centre, Wanchai (Map 6). In Kowloon, *Astor Classics* (☎ 2781-1833), 380 Nathan Rd, Jordan, has a similar selection. Another good place to try is *Cine-Art House* (☎ 2827-4778), ground floor, Sun Hung Kai Centre, Wanchai. Also in Wanchai, the *Hong Kong Arts Centre*

(☎ 2877-1000), which places strong emphasis on cinematic art, nearly always has some film show or festival going on. In terms of screen and sound quality, the United Artists (UA) theatres are the most advanced technologically, though others are now catching up.

PERFORMING ARTS

To see what's on and where, check the weekly *HK Magazine*. The 'HK2' section has complete listings for western music, dance and theatre as well for Chinese traditional music and other performances. The HKTA has two free handouts that are also helpful: the more comprehensive *Hong Kong Diary*, issued weekly; and the monthly *Official Hong Kong Guide*. All these publications give information on performance venues, times and prices. The local English-language daily papers are also worth checking, though they tend to miss some events.

Most major events are staged at the *Hong Kong Cultural Centre* (☎ 2734-2010) in Tsimshatsui (Map 16); *City Hall* (☎ 2921-2840) in Central (Map 5); the *Hong Kong Academy for Performing Arts* (☎ 2584-8514) and the *Hong Kong Arts Centre* (☎ 2877-1000), both in Wanchai (Map 6). Sometimes performances also make it out to various civic centres and town halls in the New Territories.

Bookings for most high-culture happenings can be made by telephone through URBTIX (☎ 2734-9009) between 10 am and 8 pm. Tickets can either be reserved with ID card or passport numbers (and picked up within three days of ordering), or paid for in advance by credit card. You can collect tickets at one of the many URBTIX outlets throughout the city. Bring your passport or ID for proof of identity. There are URBTIX windows at the City Hall in Central, the Hong Kong Arts Centre in Wanchai and the Hong Kong Cultural Centre in Tsimshatsui. Some Tom Lee Music stores also have URBTIX facilities. *HK Magazine* also lists all URBTIX outlets.

Chinese Opera

Among the best times to see Chinese opera are during the annual Hong Kong Arts Festival, held in February/March, or the Festival of Asian Arts, which takes place every other year in October/November. The HKTA has leaflets giving full details of the festivals, and *HK Magazine* also gives them good coverage.

Cantonese opera can also be seen throughout the year at the *Sunbeam Theatre* (☎ 2563-2959), 423 King's Rd, North Point. Performances usually run for about a week, and are usually in the evening, though sometimes there are matinees. Ticket prices run anywhere from HK$60 to HK$230. This place does not deal with many foreigners, and very little English is spoken, nor is there usually any English-language summary of the opera being performed. If you can't reach an English speaker at the theatre, call the HKTA hotline (☎ 2807-6177). They usually have an idea of what's playing, and if not should be willing to help you find out. To get to the Sunbeam Theatre, take the MTR to North Point station. The theatre is right above the station, on the north side of King's Rd, near the intersection with Shu Kuk St. Just look for the garish Chinese opera posters.

Opera performances are sometimes held at the *City Hall*. Check the HKTA's *Hong Kong Diary* or the local English-language newspapers for details on performance times and venues.

Theatre

Local theatre groups mostly perform at the *Hong Kong Arts Centre*, the *Academy for Performing Arts* or the *Hong Kong Cultural Centre*. Performances are mostly in Cantonese, though summaries in English are usually handed out. Tickets range between HK$60 and HK$200, depending on the seats and the venue.

Smaller theatre companies occasionally stage plays at the *Fringe Club* (☎ 2521-7251), 2 Lower Albert Rd, Central (Map 8). Most deal with local themes and feature amateur actors. It's not always great theatre, but it's usually an interesting experience.

Arts Festivals

Hong Kong hosts several of these each year. Exact dates vary, so if you want to time your visit to coincide with any of these events it would be wise to first contact the HKTA overseas office nearest you. Some of the large events include:

Hong Kong Arts Festival – a month of music, performing arts and exhibitions by hundreds of local and international artists; held in February/March

Hong Kong Festival Fringe – the Fringe Club sponsors three weeks of performances by an eclectic mix of up-and-coming artists and performers from Hong Kong and overseas; held in late January/early February

Hong Kong International Film Festival – brings in hundreds of films from around the world, and is used to showcase new local and regional productions; held in March or April

International Arts Carnival – features mime, puppetry, visual
theatre dance and children's drama; held in July or
August

Festival of Asian Arts – one of Asia's major cultural events,
bringing in musicians, dancers, opera singers and other
performance groups from all over the region; held every
other year in October/November

Hong Kong Folk Festival – the Hong Kong Folk Society brings
together well known international acts and local musicians; held in November

CLASSICAL MUSIC

Hong Kong holds it own in this department. There are
performances every week, often featuring foreign ensembles. Less frequent are Chinese classical or folk music
concerts. *HK Magazine*, the HKTA's *Hong Kong Diary* and
the entertainment sections of the English-language newspapers all have details on venues, performance times,
ticket prices and booking. Many of these performances are
held at the *Hong Kong Cultural Centre* (☎ 2734-2010) in
Tsimshatsui (Map 16), so it might be worth stopping by
there to pick up their monthly schedule.

In general, it's cheaper to go to performances by local
ensembles like the Hong Kong Philharmonic or the
Hong Kong Chinese Orchestra. But the Hong Kong
government subsidises the cost of bringing in foreign
acts, so prices are sometimes pretty reasonable. Tickets
range from as low as HK$50 for a seat in the back at a
local performance to HK$300 for something like the
English Chamber Orchestra.

In addition to the Hong Kong Cultural Centre, classical music concerts are often held at two other
venues:*City Hall* (☎ 2921-2840) in Central (Map 5)
and the *Hong Kong Academy for Performing Arts*
(☎ 2584-8514) in Wanchai (Map 6).

ROCK/JAZZ

To describe Hong Kong's rock and progressive music
scene as pitiful might be going overboard, but only just.
When the big stars from Europe or the USA come touring
in Asia, most only see Hong Kong from the plane, on
their way from Tokyo to Bangkok. This is largely due to
a lack of suitable venues. This territory has stadiums, but
none large enough to pack in the numbers needed by
profit-conscious band managers. The few foreign acts
that do make it are usually rewarded with wild shows
of enthusiasm and gratitude from music-starved fans.

Hong Kong pop stars are another matter of course, and concerts by singer/idols like Leon Lai, Jackie Cheung and Faye Wong are relatively frequent. But in all truth, unless you're a part of the Cantonese community you won't likely find 'Canto-pop' much to your liking. At any rate, it certainly can't be classified as rock.

Occasionally China's nascent rock-n-roll scene sends a delegate or two down to Hong Kong. With names like Tang Dynasty, Dou Wei and He Yong, these acts sometimes come up with some surprisingly original (and refreshingly hard-edged) music. Led Zep it is not, but it makes for a nice change from the shallow strains of Canto-pop.

A few bars, most notably the Jazz Club, bring in well known artists from time to time. Most of these are jazz musicians, but other types slip through as well.

The local scene is a bit more lively. There are usually a couple of decent rock bands playing around town, and there are numerous bars with house bands that play dance tunes. Hong Kong is not really a friendly environment for musicians. The few bars that dare to book original bands are usually too small or lack a decent sound system. And with rents in the bar districts as high as they are, you can be sure a lot of musicians are up there for little, if any, pay. Things do seem to be picking up a bit: more and more bars have live music, and local audiences are increasingly receptive to bands that play something other than pop tunes or classic rock.

To find out what's going on, pick up a copy of *HK Magazine*. The 'HK2' pullout section lists who's playing where in the Music section. Another good source of information is the free monthly *BC Magazine*, which has a good live music guide.

Live Venues

At lot of places have on-again, off-again live music, but there are a few spots that have bands nearly every night.

Heading up this list is the *Jazz Club* (☎ 2845-8477), 2nd floor, California Entertainment Building, Lan Kwai Fong, Central (Map 8). This has long been the sole salvation for true music lovers, and many of jazz greats have stood on its stage. But the club also books rock, blues, folk and other kinds of acts, both local and foreign. The club is not very big, so it helps to book tickets well in advance for the bigger names. Drinks are expensive, but no more so than other bars that have live music, and there's a 2-for-1 happy hour from 6 to 9 pm that helps soften the blow. Tickets for local acts are around HK$100, for overseas bands usually anywhere from HK$200 to HK$350.

The *Hard Rock Cafe* (☎ 2377-8118), 100 Canton Rd, Tsimshatsui (Map 16), brings in the occasional foreign band, and has a house band that plays a rock/soul mix five nights a week. It's probably not a bad spot to go dancing, but if a popular foreign act is playing there, don't even bother: this is one of the worst music venues going.

To see what local Hong Kong bands have to offer, stop by *Amoeba* (☎ 2376-0389), ground floor, 22 Ashley Rd, also in Tsimshatsui. This is one of the few places that gives Hong Kong's aspiring rock stars a chance to win some fans. If you're in a frivolous mood, try one of their neon-coloured test tube shots: HK$28 for one, or HK$150 for a rack of six.

Ashley Rd has its own little time warp in the form of *Ned Kelly's Last Stand* (☎ 2376-0562), 11A Ashley Rd, Tsimshatsui. Step through the door and into a blast of brash Dixieland jazz and the pungent aroma of several decades worth of spilled beer. Ken Bennett and his Kowloon Honkers have been churning out that big band Dixie sound every night for years now, and they never fail to draw a crowd.

For years *The Wanch* (☎ 2861-1621) in Wanchai (Map 6) was one of the few venues for live bands. There's a lot more competition now, but The Wanch still has live music seven nights a week. The selection centres mainly on rock and folk, with the occasional solo singer/guitarist thrown in. Prices here are better than most places, and are discounted during their particularly good happy hours, which run from 3 to 9 pm daily and 1 to 4 am Friday and Saturday nights.

Except for the Jazz Club, Lan Kwai Fong (Map 8) doesn't have any other really serious music venues. *F-Stop* (☎ 2868-9607) is a tiny place at 14 Lan Kwai Fong that squeezes bands onto its minuscule stage Thursday, Friday and Saturday nights. *Mad Dogs* (☎ 2810-1000), a rollicking British-style pub at 1 D'Aguilar St, has music three or four nights a week, usually in the form of a solo singer/guitarist. The bar has a counterpart in Tsimshatsui (Map 16), *Mad Dogs Kowloon* (☎ 2301-2222), which also has music occasionally.

Up on Lower Albert Rd, just on the border of the Lan Kwai Fong quadrant (Map 8), is the *Fringe Club* (☎ 2521-7251). There is live music in the bar area here Friday nights, a Saturday night 'open mike' and occasionally acts during the week as well. The Fringe Club was originally designed to give local artists a friendly venue to display their talents. Times have changed, and the place has gone more upmarket and commercial, though most nights are still free.

One spot that is decidedly not commercial is the *Music Union* (☎ 2312-2688), Flat F, 1st floor, Comfort Building, 88 Nathan Rd, Tsimshatsui. From its unlikely spot in a grimy commercial block, this place runs Hong Kong's only real music club. Gigs are held regularly in a little lounge that resembles a low-key jazz bar, all featuring local, usually Cantonese, performers. Though it's not a bar, juice and beer are served during live performances. You can also buy CDs put out by local artists here. There is a 10,000 CD lending library, but it's only open to members. There's also a local musicians' bulletin board that makes for interesting reading. To find out if anything's going on while you're in town, give them a call. Music Union gigs are also sometimes listed in *HK Magazine*.

There are a number of other bars that have live music on a more occasional basis, usually one or two nights a week. For more details, see the Pubs/Bars section below.

Concerts

Big concerts are usually held at one of four venues. The most commonly used is the *Hong Kong Coliseum* (☎ 2355-7233), 9 Cheong Wan Rd, Hunghom (Map 16). This is a 12,500 seat indoor facility next to Kowloon KCR station. The sound here is abysmal, but if someone like Eric Clapton or Santana comes to town, this is probably where you'll have to come to see them.

Smaller acts are sometimes booked into the *Ko Shan Theatre* (☎ 2334-2331) on Ko Shan Rd, Hunghom. This is actually not a bad venue. The sound isn't great, but the back portion of the seating area is open-air, and the theatre is fairly small, so that most seats give you a good view.

Known mainly as the site of the wildly popular Hong Kong Rugby Sevens, the *Hong Kong Stadium* (☎ 2839-7300) at So Kan Po (near Happy Valley) was expanded several years ago and can now seat 40,000. The main reason was to house more rugby fans, but the government also figured it would be a good way to attract big-name music acts from abroad as well. But the planners didn't take into account the local residents, who after the first few concerts raised a tremendous stink about the noise and crowds. Bureaucrats scrambled to find a solution, since this threw revenue projections right out the window. At one point someone suggested turning off the stage speakers and issuing concert-goers with earphones!

The only other big place to see a band is *Queen Elizabeth Stadium* (☎ 2591-1347), 18 Oi Kwan Rd, Wanchai. This is not bad for sporting events, but it's one lousy place to see a concert: you'd get better acoustics in an empty aircraft hanger.

CLUBS/DISCOS

Hong Kong has developed a pretty active club scene, and more and more bars have started offering dancing and thematic club nights à la London and New York, with names like 'Listen to Chill', 'Massive Attack' and 'Club Royale'. This evolution has been aided by the arrival of some talented, professional DJs whose sole mission is dream up ever more seamless, innovative mixes to keep people on their feet. Most of the club nights take place on Fridays and Saturdays, but there are some mid-week as well. Cover charges range from HK$50 to HK$150. As with most bars and clubs in Hong Kong, beer and drinks range from HK$30 up to HK$70 at the really expensive places.

Both *HK Magazine* and *BC Magazine* have club night listings, and the latter also boasts a regular column on the subject, 'Club Scene'. It's a good idea to check these as things are pretty fluid: club nights come and go, and venues fall in and out of fashion.

For the non-raver, there are also plenty of straightforward discos where you can dance till you drop, or the sun rises, whichever comes first.

Central & Admiralty

One place with particular staying power in Central (Map 5) is *Judgement AD* (☎ 2521-0309), a dark, cavernous multi-level place in the basement of the Bank of America Tower. You can get lost in here: there are two bars and two dance areas with soundproofed walls so that live music and dance parties can peacefully coexist. Though it's been around for years, this place is still super trendy (and super expensive – a beer will cost you around HK$70).

It's hard to know what Peter the Great would think of it, but *Cossacks* (☎ 2869-0328), a 'Russian' theme bar in the basement of the Ritz-Carlton, has decided that more than 30 different types of vodka was not enough. Last time we checked, this place had three different club nights a week. What with the kitschy pseudo-Russian decor (a cupola above the bar for instance) and the petite bourgeoisie furniture, it's a pretty funky place to dance the night away.

An unlikely venue is *Bank Bar at Portico* (☎ 2523-8893), in the basement of Citibank Plaza. This place is a sea of suits from Monday to Friday, but on Saturday hosts some very late night rave parties. Leave your suit at home.

In Admiralty (Map 5), the *LA Cafe* (☎ 2526-6863), ground floor, Lippo Centre, has hosted some very successful club nights, and they continue to come up with new ideas to try and keep things fresh. On non-club nights it reverts to its original persona: an entertaining pseudo-American bar with lots of chrome and flashy neon lights, as well as the obligatory Harley hanging from the ceiling.

Considering the number of bars, there's not all that much dancing going down in Lan Kwai Fong (Map 8). *Club Yes* (☎ 2877-8233) is dark and very loud (you can evaluate the music from out in the street). Across the way the exclusive *Club 1997* (☎ 2586-1103) has a strictly enforced members-only policy, which is perhaps why it can survive with a dance floor the size of a postage stamp. You may be able to take a peek inside when it's not too busy, but otherwise you have to be a guest of a member. *California* (☎ 2521-1345) is a bit pretentious, but really packs in the crowds, especially when the tables are cleared off the dance floor. Both California and Club Yes bar entry to anyone wearing shorts, non-collared shirts or sandals.

Wanchai

If dress codes don't sit well with you, head over to Wanchai (Map 6), where you can dance and be comfortably dressed. This is where the late night crowd settles in for the wee hours. It's also one of the first destinations for naval sailors stopping in Hong Kong for a little R&R.

Already becoming a Wanchai institution is the venerable *Neptune Disco* (☎ 2528-3808), Basement, 54 Lockhart Rd. Slightly seedy, decidedly down-market and completely unpretentious, Neptune is the kind of place you find yourself at 3 am, when eight hours of partying still doesn't seem like enough. People mainly come to dance, and if you're not dancing you have no right being here. Officially there's an HK$70 minimum charge, but it's sporadically enforced.

Over at 98 Jaffe Rd, *Neptune II* (☎ 2865-2238) lacks the character of its progenitor, but is open just as late (until around 7 am). There's an HK$140 cover for men that includes one drink. Women need only pay HK$50. In the same league as Neptune is *Big Apple* (☎ 2529-3461), Basement, 20 Luard Rd, which alternates between a live dance band and a DJ. Dancing here is totally uninhibited: boogie to your heart's content. There's a post 9 pm cover of HK$70 for men, HK$45 for women, but it's not always enforced.

Looking for something a bit more down-market? You can't do much better than the *New Makati* (☎ 2527-8188), a sleazy pickup joint at 100 Lockhart Rd. If you go in and decide to take a seat in one of the dimly lit booths, make sure you don't plop down on top of a groping couple. Cover charge is HK$70 for men, HK$40 for women, and includes one drink.

As long as you're wearing a collared shirt, you should have no trouble getting into *Joe Banana's* (☎ 2529-1811), 23 Luard Rd. JB's is a source of contention: some people rave about it, while others blast it as the trendiest, yuppiest meat market in town. There's a cover charge of HK$100 Fridays and Saturdays after 9 pm for men, after 1 am for women.

Rick's Cafe (☎ 2528-1812), at 78 Jaffe Rd, has a branch in Wanchai that seems just as popular as the original in Tsimshatsui (see below). Though smaller, the arrangement here seems more roomy, but otherwise it's pretty much the same crowd, same atmosphere. A cover charge of HK$100 is levied on men Fridays and Saturdays. There is no cover for women.

Carnegie's (☎ 2866-6289), 55 Lockhart Rd, bills itself as 'the spirit of rock', and drapes guitars and other musical paraphernalia around the bar to shore up the image. There actually seems to be a bit of an identity crisis going on here, because dance tunes and hip-hop seem to be playing more often than rock-n-roll. However, when the band or DJ do their job right, folks start dancing wherever they can get a foothold, including on top of the bar (they've got photos to prove it). There's an HK$70 cover here Friday and Saturday nights.

Westworld (☎ 2824-0380) mainly draws a Cantonese crowd, and is an ever-so-slightly subdued version of Catwalk (see below). Strobe lights, smoke machines and techno-pop set the scene. Westworld is located in the New World Harbour View Hotel in Wanchai (Map 6). Cover charge is HK$88 Sunday through Thursday, HK$140 Friday and Saturday, and includes one drink.

Just a block or two away, *JJ's* (☎ 2588-1234), in the Grand Hyatt Hotel, has a house band playing five to six nights a week. The band changes periodically, but whoever is playing, they're usually quite good. This is one of those spots where the beautiful people come to play. It's also expensive: there's a cover charge of HK$120 after 8.30 pm Mondays through Thursdays, and HK$170 Friday and Saturday nights.

You might not think there would be dancing at *Jimmy's Sports Bar* (☎ 2882-2165), an American beer, burger and football joint next to Hong Kong Stadium, 55 Eastern Hospital Rd, So Kon Po (near Happy Valley). But people come here to bop, and this place even has club nights. Why? Because it's huge: there's a lot of space for dancing and moshing.

Tsimshatsui

Tsimshatsui (Map 16) has it's own fair share of spots to shuffle your feet. One of the better known is *Rick's Cafe* (☎ 2367-2939), 4 Hart Ave. The decor is cheesy Casablanca, complete with palm trees and Bogie and Bergman photos slapped on the walls. Opinions are fairly divided on this place: some people always have a great time here, while others see it as little more than an over-priced pickup joint. There's an HK$100 cover charge for men only Friday and Saturday after 10 pm.

On the other hand, almost everyone loves *Bahama Mama's Coconut Bar* (☎ 2368-2121), 4-5 Knutsford Terrace. The theme here is (can you guess) tropical isle, complete with palm trees and surf boards. It really is a friendly spot, and somehow stands apart from most of the other late night watering holes. On Friday and Saturday nights there is a DJ spinning eminently danceable reggae tunes. There's an HK$100 minimum after 11 pm Friday and Saturday nights.

Though a bit far from the rest of the action, Knutsford Terrace is slowly turning into an alternative to Lan Kwai Fong. At the time of writing this little lane had Spanish and Italian restaurant/bars (El Cid, Tutto Bene), Bahama Mama's and, nearby in the Kimberley Hotel, the *Memphis Cotton Club* (☎ 2723-8811), an upmarket live music and dance bar. Another bar was under construction near Bahama Mama's as well, so it's probably worth making the trek up here to see what's up.

Catwalk (☎ 2369-4111), in the New World Hotel, 22 Salisbury Rd, is the hot spot for Hong Kong's young wealth. There's live music (usually quite good) in one section, disco in another (and we mean disco) and yes, karaoke in several other areas. Mobile phones, designer watches and Cognac are the order of the day. Catwalk also features one of Hong Kong's highest cover charges: HK$200 on Fridays and Saturdays, though this does include two drinks. The fee falls to HK$120 Sunday through Thursday for men, and it's free admittance for women.

Nearby in the Regent Hotel, the posh *Club Shanghai* (☎ 2721-1211) usually has an American house band cranking out dance tunes five to six nights a week. The place is decked out à la 1930s Shanghai, down to opium pipes (not filled) on each table. Cover is HK$120 Sunday through Thursday, and HK$150 Friday and Saturday.

Bringing Hand-Crafted Beers to Hong Kong

It all began when a young American named David Haines ordered what he thought was a draught beer in a Hong Kong bar. 'They brought me a can: that's no way to serve a good beer', he recalls with a pained expression.

Haines' discontent was heightened by developments back in the USA, where beer has experienced a renaissance with the advent of microbreweries. Stressing quality and taste over mass-production volumes, microbrewed beers have taken the USA by storm. While Hong Kong drinkers have a good variety of beers to choose from, most brews are imported, meaning they are four to six weeks old by the time they reach local bars.

Haines wasn't the first westerner to gripe about the lack of high-quality, fresh beer in Hong Kong. But he was the first to do something about it. With the help of some other investors, he opened up South China Brewing Company in July 1995. Using equipment imported from the USA, South China operates out of a factory tower in the industrial town of Wong Chuk Hang, near Aberdeen on Hong Kong Island. Current capacity is 260 cases of beer per day, and South China expects to reach maximum production by mid-1996.

Within five months of South China's opening, nearly 70 bars and restaurants in town were serving its flagship brew, Crooked Island Ale. Two local pubs, Delaney's and BB's, have already commissioned the fledgling outfit to brew 'private label' beers, which are available only from their respective taps. And Haines expects Crooked Island to be available in retail shops by early 1996.

More varieties are on the way of course. Given Crooked Island's popularity, finding these new brews should be no problem. South China (☎ 2580-2506) also has tours, which naturally include a taste of Hong Kong's first truly home-grown beer. ∎

Though a miserable venue for big-name gigs, the *Hard Rock Cafe* (☎ 2377-8118) in Tsimshatsui is not a bad spot to hit the dance floor. All the guitars and rock memorabilia spice up the place a bit, and there is usually a live band playing. Otherwise there's a DJ working the tunes from about 10.30 pm onward. Cover is HK$80 for men, women get in free.

PUBS/BARS

Drinking is a larger part of Hong Kong social life than in many other Chinese societies. Though there are still many Chinese who either don't touch or only occasionally sip alcohol, the influence of western culture and

Hong Konger's increasing affluence have made alcohol more popular. Bars, though alien to traditional Chinese culture, can be found everywhere in Hong Kong, and are fairly well patronised, especially by younger Chinese men and business executives. Adhering to custom, most Chinese women don't drink, though there are more and more exceptions among the younger generations.

Hong Kong's expatriates show no such shyness toward libation. Hordes of western professionals descend on Lan Kwai Fong in Central, Wanchai and Tsimshatsui on Friday and Saturday nights to engage in what cynics call Hong Kong's number one form of expatriate recreation. It's not a cheap sport: a beer or standard cocktail will routinely cost HK$30 to HK$50, making it easy to part with HK$500 to HK$600 on a good night. However, the endemic popularity of happy hours has helped soften the blow, although to really get your money's worth you need to kick off the evening in the late afternoon. Most happy hours last from around 5 to 9 pm, but a few places offer breaks for late-nighters as well, usually from 1 to 2 am. Aside from the 2-for-1 deals, reduced prices for drinks usually range from 20% to 50% off.

There's no way to list all of Hong Kong's bars here, nor any reason to. Many are quite similar, if not in decor, then in atmosphere, as one evening in Lan Kwai Fong will demonstrate. The following are places that many people in Hong Kong feel have a little extra to offer, for better or for worse. In addition to these, check out the music and dancing venues listed: all of them also function as bars, and some are quite good at it.

Lan Kwai Fong

Central's Lan Kwai Fong (Map 8) has the densest concentration of bars in Hong Kong. Though still in many ways a foreigner's drinking ghetto, there are more and more Chinese heading here for a night on the town as well. Most of the bars are clustered around the four streets that make up the Lan Kwai Fong quadrant (fong means 'square' in Cantonese), but there are a few, like the aforementioned Fringe Club and Mad Dogs, which sit on the periphery.

Some of the bars around here are pretty pretentious (they're easy to spot). One place that bucks this trend is Club 64 (☎ 2523-2801), 12 Wing Wah Lane. Inside the design is unique but simple, and really feels like homegrown Hong Kong. Club 64 also has one of Hong Kong's better happy hours: from 10 am to 8 pm, pints of draught beer are HK$19, bottles HK$17.

GLENN BEANLAND

One of Lan Kwai Fong's many bars

On D'Aguilar St near the entrance to Wing Wah Lane, *Acropolis* (☎ 2877-3668) is a good spot to watch the crowds go by, whether from the wide open ground floor or the comfortable windowsills upstairs. On Friday and Saturday nights this place can really rage, but it's also a good spot for a laid-back afternoon cocktail. Credit cards aren't accepted here.

If you're a fan of German beer, both *Schnurrbart* (☎ 2523-7436) and *Bit Point* (☎ 2523-4700) take the time and effort to draw you a brew the right way. Most of the draught beers are Pilseners, but both have a fine selection of bottled brews too. Schnurrbart also has a dizzying choice of German and Austrian schnapps (ask for the special menu).

Across the street in California Tower, *Sherman's Bar and Grill* (☎ 2801-4946) doesn't seem like anything special, but there's something about the warm, woody decor that keeps you comfortably rooted to your chair or barstool. The only drawback is the lack of a happy hour.

If your aim is to slam down a lot of drinks in as little time as possible, you'll be in good company in either Hardy's or Yeltz Inn. With frequent live (and occasionally talented) music acts, *Hardy's* (☎ 2526-7184) is more for rowdy beer-swillers, some of whom will jump on stage to share their abilities (or lack thereof) with the crowd. *Yeltz Inn* (☎ 2524-7790), with its moody colours, pictures of prominent communists and blaring tunes, is more the environment for shots, which you'll see plenty of people doing here. If neither of these are silly enough for you, try *Al's Diner* (☎ 2521-8714) where you can do booze jello shots (now that's silly).

The *Cactus Club* (☎ 2525-6732) is usually a pretty upbeat hang, probably due to the Latin music playing. They have a decent selection of tequila (for Hong Kong), but stay away from the nachos, which are pathetically skimpy.

Just down the street, *La Dolce Vita* is nearly as trendy as they come, but the grappa comes highly recommended, and it's another good people-watching spot. *Oscar's* (☎ 2804-6561), the place with the surging mob out front, *is* as trendy as they come, and proud of it. Some people love this place, others abhor it.

Up at the top of the hill, just outside Lan Kwai Fong proper is *La Bodega* (☎ 2877-5472). Though also a fully fledged, sit-down restaurant, this place has nice tapas and a wine bar in the basement.

Central & Admiralty

A lot of the bars outside Lan Kwai Fong in Central and Admiralty (Map 5) tend be a bit more stuffy and corporate, which is understandable given that they are in the heart of Hong Kong's major business district. The epitome of this image is the *Captain's Bar* (☎ 2522-0111), on the ground floor of the Mandarin Oriental Hotel. After 5 pm you can't enter wearing either jeans or a collarless shirt, and truth be told, you'd really be most comfortable wearing a suit. But if you've got the right attire (and plenty of money) it's worth coming in here just to drink an ice cold draught beer from one of the Mandarin's chilled silver mugs.

For the view, you can't beat the *Harlequin Bar,* on the Mandarin Oriental's 24th floor, especially at night. See Victoria Harbour in all its lighted glory while sipping your HK$65 drink. Still, the money buys not only the drink and the view but some outstanding service as well.

This is a good place to go when you feel like being pampered.

At the other end of the scale in Hutchison House lies the *Bull and Bear Pub*, probably the closest thing to a real British pub in Hong Kong. All the standard pub fare (bangers and mash, mushy peas, meat pies) are available, along with a decent selection of bitters and lagers. Although a lot of your fellow patrons may be wearing suits, you don't need to worry about a dress code.

Also heavily favoured by the after-work crowd is *Pomeroy's*, which has two locations. The one in Central (☎ 2810-1162), on 9 On Hing Terrace, really gets packed and after 5 pm on a weekday is a sea of dark blue and pinstripe. But the long bar and good service mean you don't have to wait long for your drink, despite the masses. The original Pomeroy's is on Level 3 of the Pacific Place shopping mall in Admiralty. This got its start as a somewhat out-of-the-way wine bar, and it still retains a more refined feel than its Central sibling.

A fun place to escape to is the *China Tee Club* (☎ 2521-0233), hidden away on the 1st floor of the Pedder Building, 12 Pedder St. It has all the appearance and feel of a low-key colonial watering hole, and is one of Central's better spots for a having bit of libation with your conversation. Officially this place is members only, but they're usually pretty flexible.

If you want to go really high-end in more ways than one, *Cyrano* (☎ 2877-3838) on the 56th floor of the Island Shangri-La can oblige with fantastic views and equally impressive prices. The bartenders do their best to make up any type of drink you require, and their skills are often put to the test by the demanding upper-crust types who frequent this spot.

Wanchai

Most of the bars are located along Jaffe and Lockhart Rds on the western end of Wanchai (Map 6). Like Lan Kwai Fong, on Friday and Saturday night this area is crawling with partiers looking for a place to drink or dance, or both. It's also fairly happening during the week.

Knowledgeable beer drinkers will probably like *BB's* (☎ 2529-7702), which has on tap several beers custom-brewed for it by Hong Kong's only microbrewery, the South China Brewing Company. The beer is outstanding, and in addition they have an enviable collection of bottled imports from around the world. The bar is located at 114 Lockhart Rd.

Also serving up truly memorable draughts is *Delaney's* (☎ 2804-2880), an authentic Irish pub incongruously located on the 2nd floor of the shiny One Capital Place building, 18 Luard Rd. This place is immensely popular, so you'll probably have to battle pressing crowds, deafening noise and a fog of cigarette smoke to get to the bar. But it's worth the effort, for here you can order a draught Guinness Stout poured with the care and expertise it deserves. You could drink these all day if it weren't for the cost, HK$50 a pint (ouch). They also have their own house brew, Delaney's Irish Ale, made specially for them by the South China Brewing Company.

Nearby is the *Flying Pig* (☎ 2865-3730), 2nd floor, 81 Lockhart Rd, an entertaining little placed all decked out in aviation memorabilia, including airliner seats. This is another bar that's always packed. Downstairs from the Flying Pig is *Ridgeways* (☎ 2866-6608), a bar/pool hall where you can play a game of eight ball, if you don't mind a long wait.

Scattered around the area are several Tudor-style pubs with names like the *Horse & Groom, Royal Arms, Horse & Carriage,* and so on. They are all remarkably similar, looking like Hong Kong movie sets of an English pub. They certainly don't feel English, but they're good enough for a (relatively) cheap beer and perhaps a plate of greasy chips. The only one that stands out from the rest is the *Old China Hand*, which is usually filled with, you guessed it, old China hands, who now seem to spend most of their time in this place. Interesting, but not a lively scene.

For those who came to see the Wanchai of Suzie Wong, there are a few girlie bars where you can shell out HK$50 for a Carlsberg and watch the dancers do their thing. It's pretty tame around here, and topless places are more the exception than the rule. The most popular of the lot is probably *Country Club 88*, which seems to always fill every stool around its circular bar. Other spots include *Crossroads, New Pussy Cat* and *Popeye*.

Finally, if you want to spend lots of money on drinks, head over to the *Champagne Bar* (☎ 2588-1234) at the Grand Hyatt Hotel in Wanchai North (Map 6). You really should only come here if you've a reason to celebrate, or if someone else is buying. How else can you justify spending HK$120 to HK$400 for a single glass of champagne?

Causeway Bay

Things start to thin out around here (Map 7), but there are still some bars that do a thriving business, supported in part by those who are sick of hanging out in Lan Kwai Fong and Wanchai.

The Jump (☎ 2832-9007) bills itself as an American-style bar, but let's hope not all Americans are as filled with attitude as the bottle-flipping youngsters behind the bar. To be fair, there must be a fair number of people in Hong Kong who like this place, because on weekends it's always hopping. There is a HK$100 cover charge Friday and Saturday nights after 11 pm, which includes one free drink. It's located on the 7th floor, Causeway Bay Plaza 2, 463 Lockhart Rd.

There are a few bars located in the Times Square shopping complex that also seem able to draw a steady crowd. *Roy's* at the new China Max (☎ 2506-2282), on the 11th floor, works hard to keep its customers entertained and often has live music. There's a cover charge of HK$100 Friday and Saturday nights after 10 pm, unless you've had dinner there, in which case the charge is waived. In Times Square, *La Placita* (☎ 2506-3308) is also big on entertainment, with an eight-piece band and more unique offerings like Brazilian dance shows (you don't see much of that in Hong Kong...).

Considerably more subdued, but also fairly unusual, is *Brecht's* (☎ 2577-9636), 123 Leighton Rd, an arty kind of place given more to intimate, cerebral conversation than serious raging. The decor is pseudo-German, and includes oversized busts of Mao and Hitler. If you're looking for a different country theme, you can try the *Dubliner Bar* (☎ 2890-8830), a pleasant, low-key Irish-style pub located in the Lee Theatre Plaza.

Back to the mainstream now with the *King's Arms* (☎ 2895-6557). Squeezed in between two glass and steel office blocks at Sunning Plaza, this indoor-outdoor place is an old standby for many a resident. The service can be pretty frosty, but it's still easy to stay here for several hours.

Another favourite expat hangout, for some reason, is the *Dicken's Bar* (☎ 2894-8888), located in the basement of the Excelsior Hotel. Perhaps people like it because it never seems to change. Some nights there's live music, and there is always free popcorn (maybe that's the draw).

Lastly, just in case you missed the Tudor-style pubs in Wanchai, there are two more tucked away on Cannon St: *Royal's Pub* and *Shakespeare Pub*. These are mainly the domain of Hong Kong Chinese, but foreigners are made to feel welcome.

Tsimshatsui

Bars are more spread out in Tsimshatsui (Map 16), but there are three basic clusters: along Ashley Rd; within the triangle formed by Hanoi, Prat and Chatham Rds; and up by Knutsford Terrace. In addition to the bars listed below (and those under Live Venues in the Rock/Jazz section) there are other nondescript watering holes scattered about. Should you decide to go exploring, bear in mind that a few of the smaller places are more for Hong Kong Chinese than foreigners. If you're treated to chilly welcome just continue on to another bar: there are plenty of options out there.

If you want to see one of Hong Kong's more humorous local bars, check out *Jouster II* (☎ 2723-0022), 19 Hart Ave. Made up to look like a medieval castle, down to a knight in armour and a miniature drawbridge, it's a pretty amusing place. The crowd is mostly Chinese, and the volume can get deafening when several tables all start in on the drinking games. Across the street is the *Waltzing Matilda* pub, a decrepit dive that occasionally plays host to extremely drunk hordes of expats.

Up on Prat Ave is the Kowloon branch of *Delaney's* (☎ 2301-3980). This one seems even more authentically Irish than the original in Wanchai: lots of dark wood, green felt and a long bar that you can really settle into for the long haul. Just up the street a bit is *Schnurrbart* (☎ 2366-2986), which is smaller and somewhat more restrained than its counterpart in Lan Kwai Fong. The beer is just as good though. *Biergarten* (☎ 2721-2302), 8 Hanoi Rd, is another low-key German style pub, which also has several excellent beers on tap. In addition to night crawling, any of these places would make for a fine afternoon breather from shopping or sightseeing. Across the street from Delaney's is a place called *Harry's Bar*, which despite the name has absolutely no relation to the famous Harry's Bar in New York.

The *Watering Hole* (☎ 2312-2288), Basement, 1A Mody Rd, is a kind of grotty, salt-of-the-earth spot where locals expats sometimes congregate for a swilling session. Along similar lines is the *White Stag* (☎ 2375-1951) on Canton Rd, a Tsimshatsui incarnation of the Tudor lookalike pubs of Wanchai. Actually this place looks a bit more upscale, and is not a bad spot for at least a pint or two.

Sitting up at the northern end of Ashley Rd is the infamous *Kangaroo Pub* (☎ 2376-0083), bane of those Australian expats struggling to prove that not all their countrymen are lager louts. This place gets pretty lively, and there are some decent Aussie brews like Cooper's and VB.

Finally, for you James Bond fans, there's *Bottoms Up* (☎ 2367-5696), Basement, 14 Hankow Rd. Duty brought 007 here on one of his Asian sojourns, and the club is still milking it for all its worth. Just because Mr Bond made it here doesn't mean you have to, however; this place is a true sleazepit.

Gay Bars

Hong Kong used to have only one gay bar, the Yin Yang Club, up on Ice House St in Central. At the time of writing the Yin Yang appeared to have closed its doors for good. The only place that really rages now is *Propaganda* (☎ 2868-1316), 30 Wyndham St. The music mix here hasn't earned much praise, but it's a monopoly of sorts, and the club is packed every night. As Propaganda's ads are proud to proclaim, this is Hong Kong's premier gay meat market. Cover charges get steeper as the week goes on: HK$40 Monday to Wednesday, HK$60 Thursday, HK$80 Friday and HK$100 Saturday. *Club 1997* (☎ 2586-1103) in Lan Kwai Fong (Map 8), does have a gay night on Fridays, but unless you can find a member to sign you in you're pretty much out of luck.

Considerably more subdued is *Petticoat Lane* (☎ 2973-0642), 2 Tun Wo Lane, Central (where the Mid-Levels escalator cuts between Lyndhurst Terrace and Hollywood Rd). It's a small place with French decor, and is more suited to chatting than bopping. The same is true for *Wally Matt* (☎ 2367-6874), 9 Cornwall Ave, Tsimshatsui. It's a bit more chic, with gay art adorning the walls and such, but is still basically a place for a few relaxed beers.

HOSTESS CLUBS

At least in monetary terms, this is the very top end of Hong Kong nightlife. The territory boasts some of the world's largest and most elaborate hostess clubs, where you pay through the nose to have young women in revealing outfits sit, talk and dance with you. Whether things go further than that probably depends on the club. Even at the lower-end hostess clubs a restrained evening can easily cost US$500. At some of the top spots the bill quickly shoots up into the thousands. The ritziest places are mostly in Tsimshatsui East; somewhat less exorbitant options are in Wanchai.

SPECTATOR SPORTS

There's not much variety to spectator sports in Hong Kong. This may change after 1997, when Hong Kongers may gradually be infected with the sports-mania that has longed gripped a large chunk of the Chinese population. Some of the mainstream sports that people in Hong Kong watch are listed below. For sports you play yourself, see the Activities section of the Things to See & Do chapter.

Horse-Racing

Hong Kong's racing season lasts from mid-September to early June and there are usually 65 meets per season. Normally, races at the *Shatin track* in the New Territories are held on Saturdays from 1 to 6 pm. At *Happy Valley*, on Hong Kong Island, races are normally on Wednesday evenings from about 7 to 11 pm, though some races are also held on Saturday. The HKTA can provide you with a schedule for the season. You can also check the sports section of the English-language newspapers.

Admission charges include: infield enclosure HK$2; public enclosure HK$10; pavilion stand HK$30, tourist and member's guest tickets HK$50. The tourist ticket entitles you to a visitor's badge and a seat in the members' box. These badges can be purchased at the gate on race day, or up to two days in advance at any of

---

A Flutter on the Ponies

This is not merely a spectator sport, it's an obsession. On Wednesdays and Saturdays during the racing season about one-third of Hong Kong's population drops what it's doing and either tunes in to, or attends, the races. Of Hong Kong's 40 or so Chinese-language newspapers, around a dozen are devoting solely to covering the ponies.

What's all the excitement for? In a word, gambling. Horse-racing is the only legal way to place bets in Hong Kong, and the Chinese love of gambling has sent demand to unprecedented heights. Over the 69 race meets of the 1994-95 racing season Hong Kongers wagered HK$72 billion (a bit under US$10 billion), easily the highest amount of money for any racing establishment on earth.

The whole system is run by the Royal Hong Kong Jockey Club, which has to be the world's most well-heeled charity organisation. From its luxurious headquarters next to the Happy Valley Horse Racing Track, the club runs two race tracks, 125 off-course betting centres and handles over 500,000 telephone betting accounts. A good portion of the betting revenue goes to charitable causes, and many of Hong Kong's museums, medical clinics, parks, recreation venues and social welfare centres have the Jockey Club stamp on them. But the tremendous inflow of cash has also allowed the club to develop state-of-the-art facilities and a computerised betting system that handles up to six million wagers per race meet. Horses are housed in multi-million dollar air-conditioned stables complete with swimming pools and piped-in music. With all its accountants, engineers, turf experts, administrative staff, waiters and stable boys, the Jockey Club is the second largest employer in Hong Kong after the government.

the Royal Hong Kong Jockey Club's off-track betting centres, which are everywhere. For visitors, two of the most conveniently located ones are at 39-41 Hankow Rd in Tsimshatsui and 64 Connaught Rd in Central. You'll need your passport to prove you are only visiting.

During race meets, extra buses and trams serve the Happy Valley race track from all over Hong Kong Island. Alternatively you can take the MTR to Causeway Bay station, exit through Times Square and walk about 15 minutes to get there. The KCR has special trains that go directly to the Shatin track on race days only.

Another option is to sign up for the HKTA's 'Come Horseracing Tour'. HK$490 per person buys transportation to and from the track, a seat in the members' box, lunch or dinner before the meet, guide service and ample information on betting procedures. For more information call HKTA tour operations (☎ 2807-6390).

Horse-racing in Hong Kong harks back to 1841, when some of the colonials used to hold meets in Macau. In 1846 a makeshift track was opened in the swampy area of Happy Valley. With a only a few interruptions, the races have continued down to this day. It was strictly an amateur affair until the 1970s when repeated race-fixing scams were uncovered. The Jockey Club decided it was time for change and brought in professional jockeys and trainers. Now punters go to the two all-weather tracks at Happy Valley and Shatin, each of which can seat around 70,000. This is the place to go if you want to see the *real* Hong Kong. Cab drivers, stock brokers, shopkeepers and CEOs: all the different strata of society can be seen here – resolutely betting away. ∎

NICKO GONCHAROFF

Horses on their way to Happy Valley

Rugby Sevens

The only other sporting event that sparks the same kind of enthusiasm is the Seven-A-Side Rugby Tournament, popularly known as the Rugby Sevens. Teams from all over the world come together in Hong Kong every March (or early April) for three days of lightning fast 15-minute matches. Even non-rugby fans scramble in the rush to get the scarce tickets, for in addition to the sport, there's a lot of action in the stands. For many, the Rugby Sevens is a giant, international three day party.

Getting tickets is the hard part, as many are reserved for members of rugby clubs from overseas. Hong Kong companies, public relations firms and society's upper-crust also get sizeable allocations, leaving little for ordinary fans. The situation may improve following the expansion of *Hong Kong Stadium*, where the matches are held. But judging from the monster queues that form the night before tickets go on sale, the competition will still be stiff. Information on ticket sales is carried in the local newspapers, usually sometime in mid-February.

For details on the tournament and buying tickets, you can contact the Hong Kong Rugby Football Union (☎ 2504-8300), Room 2004, Sports House, 1 Stadium Path, So Kon Po, Causeway Bay. The HKTA's overseas offices may also be able to provide you with information as well.

Soccer

Hong Kong has a fairly lively amateur soccer league. Games are played on the pitches inside the *Happy Valley Horse Racing Track* and at *Mongkok Stadium*. The sports sections of the English-language papers carry information on when and where matches are held. Alternatively you can contact the Hong Kong Football Association (☎ 2712-9122), 55 Fat Kwong St, Homantin, Kowloon.

Tennis

There are several international tennis tournaments held annually in Hong Kong. The largest are the Salem Open, held in April, and the Marlboro Championship, which takes place toward the end of the year, usually in October. They have drawn some fairly big names in the past, including Michael Chang, Ivan Lendl and Ilie Nastase. The tournaments are held in *Victoria Park* in Causeway Bay. Check the local English-language news-papers for information on times and ticket availability.

Shopping

Hong Kong still rides on its reputation as one of the world's top spots to shop. But times have changed. Prices have gone up across the board here, even for the bottom-end items. Moreover a lot of goods that people used to come to Hong Kong for, such as electronics and garments, are now available in many other places, often for less money. New York, for example, is a much better place to buy a camera, computer or camcorder, Bangkok has cheaper clothing and silks, and Chinese souvenirs and some antiques cost far less just across the border in Guangdong Province.

What hasn't changed is the variety. If anything, Hong Kong has a wider array of things to buy than ever before. So if you've come here to shop, you'll find plenty to keep you occupied. But to find the real bargains you're probably going to have to pound a lot of pavement.

Sitting adjacent to China's vast pool of manual labour, Hong Kong offers some good deals on clothing, footwear, luggage and other items that require little technology to produce. But even here prices are on the rise as China's rampant inflation continues to drive up workers' wages and other production costs.

There are no hard and fast shopping hours in Hong Kong, but generally, shops in the major districts are open as follows: Central and Western from 10 am to 6 pm; Causeway Bay and Wanchai from 10 am to 10 pm; Tsimshatsui, Yaumatei and Mongkok from 10 am to 9 pm; and Tsimshatsui East from 10 am to 7.30 pm. Causeway Bay is the best part of town for late-night shopping.

Most shops are open seven days a week, but on Sundays or holidays many only open from 1 to 5 pm. Street markets are open every day and well into the night. Almost everything closes for two or three days during the Chinese New Year holiday period. However, just before the Chinese New Year is the best time to go on a spree – everything goes on sale at that time because the stores want to clear out old stock.

SHOPPING TIPS

Hong Kong has more than its fair share of unscrupulous stores and shopkeepers. Even in the honest places there is often little concept of post-sale service. Of course not every place is out to get you, and there's a good chance you'll never come across anything dishonest. But a little preparation can avert of lot of misery down the line, so here are some basic Hong Kong shopping tips to keep in mind before you start spending your hard-earned cash.

Guarantees

When buying things like cameras or electronics, it's best to get something that comes with an international warranty: a local one won't do you much good once you get home. Every guarantee should carry a complete description of the item (including model and serial number) as well as the date of purchase, the name and address of the shop it was purchased from and the shop's official stamp. If the shop won't give you a warranty, chances are you're dealing with grey-market equipment (ie imported by somebody other than the official local agent), which usually either comes with no guarantee at all, or one which is only valid in the country of manufacture. The HKTA's *Official Shopping Guide* has the addresses and phone numbers of most of Hong Kong's sole agents and distributors.

Refunds & Exchanges

Many shops will exchange goods if they are defective, or in the case of clothing, if the garment simply doesn't fit. Be sure to keep receipts and go back to the store as soon as possible.

Refunds are almost never given in Hong Kong, but most stores will give you credit towards another purchase. Usually there is no need to put a deposit on anything unless it is being custom-made for you, like a fitted suit or a pair of eyeglasses. Some shops might ask for a deposit if you're ordering an unusual item that they normally wouldn't stock, but this isn't all that common.

Rip-Offs

While most shops are honest, there are also some pretty shady stores in Hong Kong, most of which prey solely on tourists. The HKTA recommends that you only shop in stores which display the HKTA membership sign, a red Chinese junk sailing against a white background. This sounds like great advice except that a lot of good stores are not HKTA members. Furthermore, many of the dubious camera and video shops in Tsimshatsui are HKTA members, so this may not be any guarantee.

The most common way to cheat tourists is to simply overcharge. In the tourist shopping district of Tsimshatsui, you'll rarely find price tags on anything.

Checking prices in several stores therefore becomes essential. However, shopkeepers know that tourists compare prices in several locations before buying, so they will often quote a reasonable or ridiculously low price on a big ticket item, only to get the money back by overcharging on small items or accessories. You may be quoted a reasonable price on a camera, only to be gouged on the lens cap, neck strap, case, batteries and flash.

Using a more sneaky approach, some dishonest shopowners may remove components that should have been included free (like the connecting cords for the speakers on a stereo system) and demand more money when you return to the shop. The truly vicious ones may even take your purchase into the back room to 'box it up', using the opportunity to remove essential items that you've already paid for. Another tactic is to replace some of the good components with cheap or defective ones. Also be alert for signs of wear and tear – the equipment could be secondhand. Insist on getting an itemised receipt and avoid handing over the cash until you have the goods in hand and they've written a receipt.

Fake Goods

Watch out for counterfeit brand goods. Fake labels on clothes are the most obvious example, but there are fake Rolex watches, CDs and tapes, Gucci leather bags, jade, jewellery, and even fake herbal medicines. Hong Kong's customs agents have been cracking down hard on fake electronics and cameras, so this is not as big a problem. However, counterfeit brandname watches are everywhere. If you discover that you've been sold a fake brandname watch when you thought you were buying the genuine article, it would be worthwhile to contact the police or customs as this is definitely illegal. Also beware of factory rejects.

Getting Help

There isn't much you can do if a shop simply overcharges. However, if you discover that the goods are defective or something is missing, return to the shop immediately with the goods and receipt. Sometimes it really is an honest mistake and they will clear the problem up at once. Honest shopkeepers will give you an exchange on defective goods or replace missing components. On the other hand, if the shop intentionally cheated you, expect a bitter argument.

If you feel that you were defrauded there are a few agencies that might be able to help you. The first place to try is the HKTA (☎ 2807-6177): if the shop is one of their members they can lean on them, but don't expect miracles. If not, they can at least advise you on who to contact for more help. Another place to try is the Hong Kong Consumer Council's complaints and advice hotline (☎ 2929-2222).

Shipping Goods

Goods can be sent home by post, and some stores will package and post the goods for you, but you may want to check costs before you go and buy that antique couch.

Sometimes doing it yourself can save some money, though it may not be worth the hassle. Smaller items can be shipped from the post office. United Parcel Service (UPS) also offers services from Hong Kong to 40 other countries. It ships by air and accepts parcels weighing up to 30 kg. UPS (☎ 2735-3535) has an office in the World Finance Centre, Canton Rd, Tsimshatsui.

In Hong Kong, there are many shipping companies that transport larger items by sea freight. One of the biggest is Orient Consolidation Service (☎ 2368-7206). If you want to ship heavier goods by air, there are many air cargo companies with offices at Kai Tak airport. Among the better known companies are DHL (☎ 2765-8111) and Jacky Maeder (☎ 2715-9611). Check the *Yellow Pages Commercial/Industrial Guide* for some listings.

WHERE TO SHOP

The three major shopping districts are Causeway Bay, Tsimshatsui and Mongkok. Each one has something different to offer, though they all have one thing in common: constant, dense crowds.

Causeway Bay has perhaps the broadest spectrum in terms of price. The high-end is well represented by numerous designer clothing shops and a cluster of Japanese department stores. There are also plenty of places selling medium-priced clothing, electronics, sporting goods and household items. Jardine's Bazaar and the area behind it are home to stalls and shops peddling cheap clothing, luggage and footwear.

Tsimshatsui is mostly geared toward tourists, and is probably the worst part of town for bargain hunters, who often fall prey to shady shopkeepers. But for those interested in high-quality and luxury items, there are lots of designer and signature shops. Some of these lie along Nathan Rd, but the bulk are to be found in Harbour City, an enormous labyrinth of a shopping complex that stretches nearly one km from the Star Ferry

Terminal north along Canton Rd. For middle and low-priced clothing you can try the back streets east of Nathan Rd.

Mongkok caters mostly to local shoppers, and there are some good prices to be found here on clothing, sporting goods, camping gear, footwear and daily necessities. There's nothing very exotic to be found, but for everyday items it's a popular spot.

Of course there is plenty to shopping outside these three areas as well. Hong Kong's finest luxury offerings are mostly found in the glittering shopping malls in Central and Admiralty. The Landmark, Galleria and Pacific Place, among others, have branches of most international luxury retailers as well as some homegrown varieties. Some of Hong Kong's top jewellery and accessories shops are also in these districts. Tsimshatsui East has a string of mostly upscale shopping malls, the biggest being the Tsimshatsui Centre at 66 Mody Rd.

For antiques, head over to Hollywood Rd in Sheung Wan, where there is a long string of shops selling Chinese and Asian items. Some of the really good spots have genuine finds, but be careful what you buy.

Wanchai is another good spot for medium and low-priced clothing, sporting goods and footwear. For these types of items, it may be worth also checking out the shopping malls on eastern Hong Kong Island, northern Kowloon or even the New Territories. Being further from the main business districts, these malls charge retailers lower rents, which can translate into lower prices for consumers. And during the weekdays, they're less crowded than the central districts. One of the biggest of these is Cityplaza, an enormous shopping complex in Quarry Bay at Tai Koo MTR station. Up in the New Territories the Shatin New Town Plaza is another mammoth mall, and can be easily reached by taking the KCR to Shatin station.

If you're targeting the bottom end, there's no better place to start than one of Hong Kong's street markets. Hong Kong's biggest market is held on Temple St, which basically runs parallel to Nathan Rd in Yaumatei. If it's cheap (and in many cases shoddy) it's on sale here: clothes, cassettes, watches, pens, alarm clocks, radios, knives, cheap jewellery, naughty postcards, potions, lotions and hundreds of other down-market items. There's also a night market here where you can grab a bite in between purchases. For more details see the Things to See & Do chapter. The market runs roughly from 6 pm to midnight.

The Tung Choi St market, two blocks east of Mongkok MTR station, is pretty similar. People start setting up their stalls as early as noon, but it's better to get here between 6 and 10 pm, when there's a lot more on offer. Another bustling market is the one on Apliu St (noon to 9 pm) in Shamshuipo, one block west of Shamshuipo MTR station. If you're looking strictly for clothing, you can also try Jardine's Bazaar in Causeway Bay. The majority is women's clothing, but there are some male garments toward the back. A bit more upscale is the Stanley market, located in the village of Stanley on southern Hong Kong Island. Here you'll find brand-name clothing, sports shoes, lower grade jewellery and art, and lots of little trinkets.

At any of these markets, it's good to check out the shops on the sides of the street, which are hidden behind all the street stalls. Often the real bargains, if there are any, can be found here, and staff are generally a bit less pushy as well.

Another possible bargain option is going to one of Hong Kong's factory outlets. Most of these deal in ready-to-wear garments, but there are a few that also sell carpets, shoes, leather goods, jewellery and imitation antique pieces. But often prices aren't that much less than in retail shops. It's important to always check purchases carefully, since at most outlets all sales are final. If you decide to go factory-outlet hopping, it's highly advisable to invest HK$69 in a copy of *The Complete Guide to Hong Kong Factory Bargains* by Dana Goetz & Caroline Radin, sold in most bookshops. This gives a thorough rundown on what to expect and could save you a lot of time. The HKTA also has a useful handout on factory outlets.

Shopping is still one of Hong Kong's biggest tourist draws, and the HKTA does what it can to make it easier for foreign shoppers. Its *Official Shopping Guide* has brief rundowns on various consumer goods with addresses and phone numbers of HKTA member stores that sell them. The HKTA also publishes a number of free special-interest pamphlets such as the *Shopping Guide to Consumer Electronics* and the *Shopping Guide to Jewellery*.

WHAT TO BUY

Arts, Crafts & Antiques

For Chinese arts and crafts the main places to go are the large China-run department stores scattered throughout the territory. You can get all sorts of hand-carved wood pieces, ceramics, paintings, calligraphy, silk garments and even bolts of silk. Prices are much higher than in

GLENN BEANLAND

Cat Street antique stall, Sheung Wan

China, but are fairly reasonable by Hong Kong standards, and the selection is usually pretty good.

One of the biggest chains is Chinese Arts & Crafts, which is also the most upmarket of these type of stores: you can actually find some pretty valuable pieces at these places. Branch stores include: Admiralty (☎ 2523-3933), Unit 230, Pacific Place Shopping Mall, 88 Queensway (Map 5); Central (☎ 2845-0092), ground floor, Prince's Building, 3 Des Voeux Rd Central (Map 5); Tsimshatsui: Star House (☎ 2735-4061), 3 Salisbury Rd, and Silvercord Shopping Centre (☎ 2375-0155), 30 Canton Rd (both Map 16); Wanchai (☎ 2827-6667), ground floor, Lower Block, China Resources Building, 26 Harbour Rd (Map 6).

A bit more pedestrian are the Yue Hwa Chinese Products Emporium stores, where in addition to the art and crafts you can also buy clothing, appliances, books etc. This is a great place to pick up little gifts for friends back home. The largest branch (☎ 2384-0084) is at 301 Nathan Rd, Yaumatei (Map 13). Others are in the Mirador Mansion, 54 Nathan Rd, and Park Lane Shopper's Boulevard, 143 Nathan Rd (near Kowloon Park).

Similar in quality and selection are CRC department stores. There are three branches on Hong Kong Island: 92 Queen's Rd Central, Central (☎ 2524-1051); and 488 Hennessy Rd (☎ 2577-0222) and Lok Sing Centre (☎ 2890-8321), 31 Yee Wo St, both in Causeway Bay.

For folk crafts, one of the nicest stores in town is Mountain Folkcraft (☎ 2523-2817), 12 Wo On Lane, Central, near Lan Kwai Fong (Map 8). This place has batiks, clothing, wood carvings and lacquerware made by ethnic minorities in China and other Asian countries. The shop attendants are friendly, and prices, while not cheap, are not outrageous either.

Most of Hong Kong's antique shops are bunched along Hollywood Rd in Sheung Wan (Map 4). It's difficult to recommend a particular shop, since finding what you want is really a matter of hunting around. The shops at the western end of Hollywood Rd tend to be cheaper in price and carry more dubious antiques.

The more reputable places should have price tags on all their items that also state the antique's name, age and whether any restoration work has been done. Most of these are up around the Man Mo Temple area and on Upper Lascar Row (Cat St). Some more well known places include: Hobbs & Bishop Fine Art Ltd (☎ 2537-9838), 28 Hollywood Rd; Chui Wah Co (☎ 2547-6251), 122 Hollywood Rd; and Tang's Fine Antiques & Arts (☎ 2543-8022), 161 Hollywood Rd.

There are also a few antique shops in the Ocean Terminal/Harbour City complex in Tsimshatsui (Map 16), but getting a good price there is said to be considerably more difficult.

If you're serious about your antique shopping, you may want to pick up a copy of *Hong Kong Antique, Fine Art and Carpet Galleries* by Barbara Anderson. Available at most bookstores, this 1993 volume is a bit dated but is still a comprehensive pocket guide that should prove useful. The authors solicited help from local art professionals in writing the guide, which tells which shops have what. In a refreshing note of candour, they admit that finding the bargains is still up to the reader.

Collectors may also want to check with the local auction houses. Even if you don't end up buying anything, the spectacle of an auction, with wealthy speculators jetting in from all around Asia, is worth seeing. The three main auction houses, all in Central, are: Christie's Swire (☎ 2521-5396), 28th floor, Alexandra House, 16-20 Chater Rd; Lammert Brothers (☎ 2522-3208), 9th floor, Malahon Centre, 10 Stanley St; and Sotheby's Hong Kong Ltd (☎ 2524-8121), Tower Two, Exchange Square.

Bookshops

Hong Kong has a great selection of books, though they're generally way overpriced. One of the biggest and best bookshops is Swindon Books (☎ 2366-8001), 13 Lock Rd, Tsimshatsui (Map 16). There are also smaller branches in Tsimshatsui at Shop 346, 3rd floor, Ocean Terminal and at the Star Ferry Terminal.

Times Books (☎ 2311-0301) gives its address as Shop C, 96 Nathan Rd, but the entrance is around the corner on Granville Rd in Tsimshatsui. There is also a branch (☎ 2525-8797) located on the ground floor of the Hong Kong Club Building at 3 Jackson Rd across from Statue Square in Central (Map 5). Bookazine has a fairly good selection, though their prices tend to be higher than other stores. There are two branches in Central: one is on the lift lobby of Alexandra House (☎ 2524-9914) on Chater Rd, the other on the south-west corner of Hutchison House (☎ 2501-5926).

There is a *South China Morning Post* bookshop (☎ 2801-4423) at the Star Ferry Terminal in Central (Map 5). There is another in Times Square, Matheson St, Causeway Bay (Map 7). On the Kowloon side there is a branch on the 3rd floor, Ocean Terminal, Tsimshatsui (Map 16) and on the ground floor, Tung Ying Building, Granville Rd.

Joint Publishing Company (☎ 2525-0105), 9 Queen Victoria St (opposite the Central Market) in Central, is an outstanding store to find books about China or books and tapes for studying the Chinese language. Another good shop for China-related works is Cosmos Books Ltd (☎ 2528-3605), 30 Johnston Rd, Wanchai (Map 6). For books in French, visit Parenthese (☎ 2526-9215) at 4th floor, Duke of Wellington House, Wellington St, Central.

Books related to the arts can be found at the Arts Bookshop (☎ 2802-4582) on the 2nd floor of the Hong Kong Arts Centre in Wanchai (Map 6) and at the Performing Arts Shop (☎ 2734-2091) in the Hong Kong Cultural Centre in Tsimshatsui (Map 16).

The Government Publications Office (☎ 2537-1910), located at Government Office Building, Queensway Government Offices, 88 Queensway, Admiralty (Map 5), is open 9 am to 4 pm daily, and 9 am to 1 pm on Saturdays.

Cameras & Film

Stanley St in Central (Map 5) is one of the best spots in Hong Kong for buying photographic equipment – there are several camera shops in a row and competition is keen. Everything carries price tags, though some low-level bargaining might be possible.

Photo Scientific (☎ 2522-1903), 6 Stanley St, is the favourite of Hong Kong's resident professional photographers. You might find equipment elsewhere for less, but Photo Scientific has a rock-solid reputation – labelled prices, no bargaining, no arguing and no cheating. Almost next door is Color Six (☎ 2526-0123), 18A Stanley St, which has the best photoprocessing in town. Colour slides can be professionally processed in just three hours. Many special types of film are on sale here which can be bought nowhere else in Hong Kong, and all the film is kept refrigerated. Prices aren't perhaps the lowest in town, but the quality is excellent. If you just need prints done quickly, there is a little place on the ground floor of the Prince's Building in Central that will process 36 exposures for HK$15. There are also plenty of one hour developing places all over the city.

Despite the endless number of shops selling cameras, Tsimshatsui is probably the worst place to buy a camera. Many shops blatantly overcharge and otherwise cheat tourists. This particularly applies to Nathan Rd. No shops here put price tags on the equipment and charging double or more is standard. One place that seems pretty reputable, and does use price tags, is Kimberley Camera Company (☎ 2721-2308), Champagne Court, 16 Kimberley Rd. This place sells used equipment also. A specialist at repairing broken cameras is Sun-Ant Camera Repair (☎ 2722-4966), Room 1010, 5-11 Granville Circuit, also in Tsimshatsui.

Camping & Travel Gear

There are a number of stores in Mongkok (Map 13) where you can buy all sorts of useful items for travelling or camping, such as backpacks, sleeping bags, water bottles, Swiss Army knives etc. If you need a backpack, check out some of the local brands, like Nikko, Podia and Rhino. Some of their products are very well designed and the prices are great. Some stores worth checking out include: Chamonix Alpine Equipment (☎ 2388-3626), 395 Shanghai St; Mountaineer Supermarket (☎ 2397-0585), 395 Portland St; Well Mount Sports Co (☎ 2391-9256), 56 Tung Choi St; and Wise Mount Sports Co (☎ 2787-3011), 75 Sai Yee St.

For travel garments, there is an outstanding group of stores called Pro Cam-Fis. It's a local outfit that designs and manufactures items like travel vests, Gore-Tex raingear, hiking shirts and two-in-one travel pants which unzip to become shorts. These items are definitely more upmarket than what you'll find in Mongkok, but they are also high quality and durable. Pro Cam-Fis locations include: Shop 265 (☎ 2736-9866), Ocean Centre, Tsimshatsui; Shop 61 (☎ 2302-0000), Park Lane Shopper's Boulevard, Nathan Rd, Tsimshatsui; Shop 611 (☎ 2506-2211), Times Square, Causeway Bay.

Carpets & Rugs

These are not really that cheap in Hong Kong, but there is a good selection. Imported carpets from China, Paki-

stan, India, Iran and Turkey are widely available. The
bulk of Hong Kong's carpet and rug shops are clustered
on Wyndham St in Central. There are also a few places
in Ocean Terminal, Tsimshatsui. You can custom order
from Hong Kong's own Tai Ping Carpets Ltd, which has
its main showroom (☎ 2522-7138) on the ground floor of
Hutchison House, 10 Harcourt Rd, Central.

Clothes & Shoes

This is what the vast majority of Hong Kong's stores sell.
It seems impossible that so many clothing and fashion
shops could survive. But Hong Kongers are very fashion
conscious and steady business from both western and
Asian tourists helps keep these places afloat.

For bargain basement clothes shopping, one of the
best known places is Granville Rd in Tsimshatsui. The
eastern end is not much more than a row of down-
market shops with bins and racks of discount clothing,
including a fair amount of factory rejects. Clothes are
definitely cheap, but the selection from store to store isn't
great, and you need to check carefully for any flaws. In
general the stores with permanent signs carry better
stock, and this is where you'll have a better chance of
getting something that is really good value for money.
Also take the effort to check the upstairs shops: some of
these places have good deals on silk garments. There are
also some cheap places on Nathan Rd, but veteran Hong
Kong shoppers avoid them. Most of the brand name
items are fakes, and even fall apart after several washes.

On Hong Kong Island, Jardine's Bazaar in Causeway
Bay (Map 7) has stall after stall of low-cost garments,
though it may take some hunting to find anything
decent. If you can't, try Lee Garden Rd, where there are
several sample shops and some places to pick up cheap
jeans. Another place to look is Li Yuen St in Central.

The street markets at Temple St (Yaumatei), Tung Choi
St (Mongkok) and Apliu St (Shamshuipo) have some of
the cheapest clothes anywhere, both in terms of price
and quality. These not bad places to pick up T-shirts and
you may find something else you like, especially in the
stores that are hidden behind the stalls. Tung Choi St and
adjacent Sai Yeung Choi St South are also good places to
hunt for sports shoes and hiking boots.

For mid-priced items, Causeway Bay and Tsimshatsui, particularly east of Nathan Rd, are good hunting
grounds. Take the time to pop into one of the dozens of
Bossini, Giordano or U2 clothing chain stores. Quality at
these places is good, and prices are often very reasonable. All these places tend to stock fairly similar items,

but it's worth checking a few of them: most have frequent sales, and if stock is sold out at one shop you may find it at another.

The section of Lockhart Rd near the Sogo department store in Causeway Bay (Map 7) is a good place to look for footwear: there are a lot of shops around here, and the competition makes for pretty good value. Check around though, as some places have considerably better prices than others for the same product. It's also worth taking a stroll down Johnston Rd in Wanchai, which has lots of mid-priced and bottom-end clothing outlets.

For the high-end, head to the shopping malls in Central and Tsimshatsui and the Japanese department stores in Causeway Bay. Nearly all the world's top international designers are represented in Hong Kong, and there are some interesting local fashions as well.

In Central (Map 5), the best places for top-end garments, accessories and footwear are the Landmark, the Galleria, the Prince's Building and the Pedder Building. In Admiralty the Pacific Place shopping mall has an impressive array of top-end shops, as well as some good mid-range offerings. In Tsimshatsui (Map 16) the Ocean Terminal/Harbour City complex has so many clothing and shoe stores that it would probably take a year to go through them all. Locals say that in general the shops in Central, while expensive, generally give better value for money than those in Ocean Terminal/Harbour City.

In Central, you might want to duck into Shanghai Tang (☎ 2525-7333), located on the ground floor of the Pedder Building. Started up by David Tang, a flamboyant Hong Kong businessman, this one store sparked something of a fashion wave in Hong Kong with its updated versions of traditional Chinese garments. What's on offer isn't cheap, but the designs are unique and generally tasteful. Custom tailoring is available.

Although people still flock to Hong Kong's tailors, getting a suit or dress made here is not the great bargain it used to be. For a quality piece of work you'll probably pay close to what you would in New York or London. An exception might be some of the Indian tailors who flag you down on the streets of Tsimshatsui, but just remember that you usually get what you pay for. Bear in mind that most tailors will require a 50% non-refundable deposit. And the more fittings you go to, the more comfortable you will feel. For men's suits, the Pacific Custom Tailors (☎ 2845-5466) in Pacific Place in Central do an outstanding job, though prices are fairly high. Women interested in getting a traditional Chinese cheong-sam dress made may want to inquire at Linva Tailor (☎ 2544-2456), 38 Cochrane St, Central.

Computers

Hong Kong is not a bad place to buy computers, unless you're coming from the USA, in which case shop at home. There is a good selection, and prices are not bad, at least for Asia. The highest markups are on smaller items like floppy disks and printer cartridges.

One of better places to go is Star Computer City, on the 2nd floor in Star House, 3 Salisbury Rd, Tsimshatsui (Map 16). There are around 20 stores up here, so you can probably find what you need. Though it's less conveniently located, you may be able to get better deals at Mongkok Computer Centre, at the intersection of Nelson and Fa Yuen Sts in Mongkok. It's mostly patronised by locals, but you can usually find someone who speaks English fairly well.

The Golden Shopping Centre, basement and 1st floor, 146-152 Fuk Wah St, Shamshuipo, has the cheapest collection of desktop computers, accessories and components in Hong Kong. The speciality here is generic computers – machines assembled from various components by the shops themselves. This place is also the centre of Hong Kong's notorious trade in pirated software. To get there, take the MTR to Shamshuipo station and follow the signs.

Most people buy computers on the Kowloon side, for the variety and lower prices. But Hong Kong Island does have one reasonable computer arcade (Computer 88), located in Winsor House, Causeway Bay (Map 7).

Computers are prone to breakdowns, so when choosing a shop don't go by price alone: evaluate the service and the kind of warranty offered. Before leaving Hong Kong it's also a good idea to run the computer continuously for several days to make sure it is free of defects.

Electronics

Shamshuipo is a good neighbourhood to search for electronic items. You can even buy (and sell) secondhand goods here. If you take any of the west exits from the MTR at Shamshuipo station, you'll find yourself on Apliu St. This is one of the best areas in Hong Kong to go searching for the numerous permutations of plug adapters you'll need if you plan to use your purchase in Hong Kong, or are heading for China.

Mongkok is another good neighbourhood to look for electronic gadgetry. Starting from Argyle St and heading south, explore all the side streets running parallel to Nathan Rd, such as Canton Rd, Tung Choi, Sai Yeung Choi, Portland, Shanghai and Reclamation Sts.

There are also quite a few electronics shops in Causeway Bay, with windows stuffed full of camcorders, CD players and other goodies. Locals generally avoid these places: apparently many of them are under the same ownership, ensuring that prices are kept high across the various stores in the area. Also, it's probably best to avoid the shops in Tsimshatsui, many of which are skilled at fleecing foreign shoppers.

Though the selection isn't as good, the Fortress group of stores is quite reliable, and will always give you a warranty with your purchase. There are branches all over Hong Kong, including Central, Causeway Bay, Sheung Wan, Tsimshatsui and Wanchai.

Remember that most electrical appliances in Hong Kong are designed to work with 220V. Some manufacturers now equip their computers, stereos and video machines with an international power facility that automatically senses the voltage and adapts to it – others include a little switch for 110/220V operation. Also make sure you have the correct plug for wherever you plan to use your equipment.

Ivory

Ivory jewellery, chopsticks and ornaments used to be big sellers in Hong Kong, fuelling the demand for tusks and contributing to the slaughter of Africa's already depleted elephant population. In 1989, the Hong Kong government signed the CITES (Convention on International Trade in Endangered Species) treaty which effectively bans the import of raw ivory.

GLENN BEANLAND

Shopping for a bargain, Li Yuen Street, Central

In the meantime, the only carved ivory products being sold in Hong Kong are those which were supposedly manufactured before the ban went into effect. Any ivory retailers need to have all sorts of documentation proving where and when the goods were made. Many countries now ban the importation of ivory altogether, no matter how it was manufactured.

Jade

The Chinese attribute various spiritual qualities to jade, including the power to prevent ageing and keep evil spirits away. It's very popular in Hong Kong and commands a high price, which may be an incentive to think about buying it somewhere else. The other problem is a high number of shifty jade dealers who delight at the thought of skimming extra profits off tourists.

There are two different minerals which can be called jade: jadeite from Myanmar (Burma) and nephrite (commonly from Canada, China, New Zealand and Taiwan). While the colour green is usually associated with jade, the milk-white shade is also highly prized. Shades of pink, red, yellow, brown, mauve and turquoise come in between. Most so-called Chinese jade sold in Hong Kong actually comes from South Africa, New Zealand, Australia and the USA.

Unfortunately Hong Kong also does a thriving trade in fake jade. The deep green colour associated with some jade pieces can be achieved with a dye pot, as can the white, green, red, lavender and brown of other pieces. Green soapstone and plastic can be passed off as jade too. One trick of dishonest merchants is to sell a supposedly solid piece of jade jewellery which is actually a thin slice of jade backed by green glue and quartz.

If you're interested in looking at and possibly purchasing some jade, head on up to the jade market in Yaumatei (Map 13), about 10 minutes walk from Yaumatei MTR station. Unless you're fairly knowledgeable about jade already, it's probably wise to limit yourself to fairly modest purchases. The jade market is open daily from 10 am to 3.30 pm. For more details, see the Yaumatei section of the Things to See & Do chapter.

Jewellery

Jewellery stores do an amazingly brisk trade in Hong Kong, aided by the traditional Chinese desire for gold and other non-cash investments. Care should be taken when visiting these shops, since visitors are often tempting targets for the less reputable retailers.

King Fook and Tse Sui Luen are two chain stores which guarantee to buy back any jewellery they sell to you at its current wholesale price. Of course, be sure you get the certificate and keep in mind that you need to be in Hong Kong to take advantage of the buy-back plan. One of the most fantastic-looking branches is King Fook at 30 Des Voeux Rd, Central, worth checking out for its sheer garishness. Other branches include: Shop 216, Pacific Place Shopping Mall, Admiralty; ground floor, Hong Kong Mansion, 1 Yee Wo St, Causeway Bay; and Hotel Miramar Shopping Plaza, 118 Nathan Rd, Tsimshatsui. Tse Sui Luen shops can be found at: Commercial House, 35 Queen's Rd, Central; 141 Johnston Rd, Wanchai; 467 Hennessy Rd, Causeway Bay; and 132 Nathan Rd, Tsimshatsui. There is also a factory outlet (☎ 2878-2618) at ground floor, Wah Ming Building, 34 Wong Chuk Hang Rd, Aberdeen.

Music

Hong Kong music stores were long cursed with a paltry selection of quality CDs and tapes, but the scene has brightened considerably with the arrival of several international chains. Prices are comparable to other major cities, and sometimes there are some good sales. Some of the best places to check out are the HMV Records stores in Central (Swire House), Causeway Bay (Winsor House) and Tsimshatsui, and Tower Records in Causeway Bay (Times Square). Also worth looking at are the KPS video rental shops, some of which also have a pretty good range of CDs for sale. The best one is in the Silvercord Shopping Centre on Canton Rd in Tsimshatsui (Map 16); the branch on Jaffe Rd in Wanchai (Map 6) isn't bad either. You can also buy CDs at the street markets on Temple St, Yaumatei, and Tung Choi St, Mongkok, but these are usually pirated and the sound quality poor.

Unless you really must, don't bother buying any musical instruments in Hong Kong. There's not a great selection, and prices are truly outrageous (care for a Martin D-28 guitar for US$3000?). If you absolutely need something, your best bet is Tom Lee music stores, with branches in Causeway Bay, Tsimshatsui and Wanchai.

If you're looking to buy Chinese instruments, again Hong Kong is not a great place. There are a few shops along Wanchai Rd between Johnston and Morrison Hill Rds in Wanchai, but what they offer is generally not good value for money. It might even be cheaper to buy a train ticket up to Guangzhou in neighbouring Guangdong Province and buy something there.

Excursions

For those who have the time, it's definitely worth taking a day to explore 'the other Hong Kong' of the New Territories and Outlying Islands. In addition to some great scenery, visiting these places will give you a much more balanced view of the territory as a whole. Life in the more rural parts of Hong Kong is so relaxed it's hard to believe that the frantic urban sprawl is only a bus or boat ride away.

Wedged between China and urban Hong Kong, the New Territories has lost a lot of its rural character, especially in the western half, where the bulk of the New Towns are located. But the eastern section, most notably the area around Sai Kung, has some of Hong Kong's most beautiful scenery and hiking trails.

If you only have one day to get out and about though, it would probably best be spent checking out one of the Outlying Islands. Get up early, grab a ferry, sit out on the back deck and enjoy the sun and the stunning views. The islands are where Hong Kong's roots as a society of farmers and fishers can still be seen. And there's something about getting there by boat that makes the city slip out of mind, if not always out of sight.

The other option is to make the journey over to Macau, the historic Portuguese enclave 65 km to the west. Dating back to the 1500s, Macau is a different world from Hong Kong. Although nearly as crowded, it moves at a much slower, more relaxed pace. In some parts there's a European feel that somehow blends with the omnipresent signs of Chinese culture. There are ancient churches and temples, cobbled streets and Chinese gardens. And perhaps most importantly, some truly amazing Portuguese food. Macau is only about one hour away by jetfoil or jet boat, although immigration at both ends adds another 40 minutes or so to the journey. Still, it's easy to do the trip in one day, though there are plenty of places to stay if you want to do some more exploring and fit in a few more meals.

NEW TERRITORIES

Tai Mo Shan

At 957m Tai Mo Shan is Hong Kong's highest mountain, and is also one of the closet to the urban area. There is a road leading up most of the way, though unless you have your own car you will have to walk from the bus stop, a hike of about four km. Views from the top are quite impressive if the weather is clear, and there are numerous hiking trails in and around the peak. There is no food or water available, so bring some along.

(Refer to Map 1 for the location of this and some of the other New Territories sights listed below.)

Getting There & Away Take the MTR to the Tsuen Wan terminus, and from there catch the No 51 bus. The bus stop is on the overpass above the station. The bus heads up Route Twisk. The bus stop for Tai Mo Shan is at the top of the pass: just tell the bus driver 'Tai Mo Shan' and he'll let you off there. If you're starting off from Central you can also take the hoverferry to Tsuen Wan from Pier 6 at the Outlying Islands ferry piers (Map 5). The catch bus No 51 from the Tsuen Wan Ferry Pier.

Kam Tin

This small town contains the walled village of Kat Hing Wai, where the Tang Clan put down roots in the 10th century after migrating from what is now Guangdong Province. The village that stands today was built in the 16th century and is still home to several hundred descendants of the Tang, which was the first of the Cantonese 'Five Great Clans' to make the move down to what would become Hong Kong. Inside, the village has many trappings of 20th century Hong Kong, but the six-metre-high walls still stand, surrounded by a moat. Within, there is a small main street with a series of little alleys. The main thoroughfare is packed with souvenir stands, so don't go here expecting to be transported back to ancient China. Visitors are expected to make a 'donation' of HK$5 when entering the village.

Getting There & Away Take the MTR to the Tsuen Wan terminus, and then catch the No 51 bus, which also passes by Tai Mo Shan. Kam Tim is the last stop on the route. You can also take a hoverferry from Central to Tsuen Wan and catch the No 51 there (see above).

Sai Kung Peninsula

This is arguably the most unspoiled part of the New Territories, though the area around Sai Kung Town is quite built up. But north of the town are terrific hiking trails and nice beaches, though the latter are sadly no longer the pristine stretches of white sand that greeted hikers just a few years ago.

Sai Kung Town was originally a fishing village, and though it's now more of a suburb, some of the original port feel remains. Fishing boats still put in an occasional appearance, and down on the waterfront are a string of seafood restaurants that draw patrons from all around the territory, despite their high prices.

North of the town lies the sprawling **Sai Kung Country Park**. From the Park Visitor Centre at Pak Tam Chung there are trails out to High Island Reservoir and the beautiful beaches at Tai Long Wan. These hiking paths form part of the 100 km **MacLehose Trail** that stretches from east to west across the New Territories. Getting to either the reservoir or the beaches and back will take up most of the day, although sometimes you can hitch a ride on park service trucks that will take you part of the way. If you're in the mood for something less strenuous, the **Sheung Yiu Folk Museum**, a restored 200 year old Hakka home, is just 30 minutes walk from the Park Visitor Centre. To get to Pak Tam Chung, take the No 94 bus, which leaves hourly from Sai Kung Town.

After Pak Tam Chung the bus continues on to terminate at the Wong Shek boat pier. It's possible to get off midway, access Stage Two of the MacLehose Trail and take it down to the beaches at **Tai Long Wan**. (Tell the driver you want to go to Chek Keng, which is a little village mid-way between the road and the beaches.) It's a good two hour hike, but the views en route are great and there are little restaurants at the beaches where you can reward yourself with a beer and a plate of fried noodles. Don't forget to leave the beaches early enough to catch a bus back. The last bus leaves Wong Shek Pier at 7.35 pm, passing by the trailhead about eight to 10 minutes later. There is also a ferry that leaves Chek Keng for Wong Shek around 4 to 5 pm in the afternoon.

This is a rewarding hike, but the logistics are a bit tricky. It's highly advisable to first buy one of the countryside series maps of the Sai Kung Country Park area from the Government Publications Office (see the Maps section of the Facts for the Visitor chapter). For more information, contact the Country Parks Division of the Agriculture & Fisheries Department (☎ 2733-2132).

Places to Eat Of the seafood restaurants in Sai Kung, the *Tung Kee* (☎ 2792-7453), 96 Man Nin St, has the best reputation. You pick your own fish or shellfish from the tanks and the cooks take it back into the kitchen to work their magic with it. This place is often packed, and it's not cheap either, but should be worth the effort.

If it's western food you crave, try *Pepperoni's* (☎ 2813-8605) located on Po Tung Rd, just off Hiram's Highway, the main road leading through town. This little indoor-outdoor place serves up surprisingly good pasta and pizza.

There are also a bunch of noodle shops and a few Chinese and western restaurants in the heart of Sai Kung Town. It's small enough that you should be able to size up all your options after a 20 minutes walk.

Getting There & Away Take the MTR to Choi Hung station, and exit where the sign says 'Clearwater Bay Road North'. Here you can catch either the No 92 bus or the more frequent No 1 green minibus. The bus costs HK$3.50 and takes around 35 minutes, the minibus HK$6.80 and around 20 minutes.

CHEUNG CHAU ISLAND

At one time a refuge for pirates, and later an exclusive retreat for British colonials, Cheung Chau is now the most populous of the Outlying Islands. Some 22,000 people, many of them commuters, are crammed onto Chueng Chau's 2.5 sq km. There is also a sizeable fishing community here, part of which resides on the junks and sampans anchored in the typhoon shelter surrounding the ferry pier.

Cheung Chau Village has become quite built up, but is still fun to explore, with narrow alleys, old creaking homes and shops, burning incense and drying fish. There are also some pleasant walks around the northern and southern ends of the island. Cheung Chau, along with Lamma Island, has no motorised transport (save for a few small tractors), which adds to the casual atmosphere. However, the island becomes a zoo on weekends when thousands of city dwellers come out to feast on seafood or play at the beach. Many of them rent vacation homes overnight and there's even a hotel, the Warwick. Prices are quite high during the weekend. Like all the Outlying Islands, Cheung Chau can very easily be done as a day trip so there's no need to overnight here unless you really like the place.

Beaches

The main beach is **Tung Wan**, about 10 minutes walk from the ferry pier, straight across the narrow isthmus of the island. There are lots of little restaurants and shops around here, and you can also rent windsurfing equipment. A quieter spot is **Tai Kwai Wan**, a small sandy beach on the north-west part of the island. On the north-east side is **Tung Wan Tsai**, which is smaller still and also a bit rocky.

Kwun Yum Wan Beach is located just south of Tung Wan, and is named after a temple dedicated to the Goddess of Mercy (Kwun Yum) located at the top of a hill near the end of the beach. You can also continue up the footpath to Fa Peng Knoll and walk along Don Bosco Rd to get to **Nam Tam Wan**. This beach is a bit rocky, but the scenery along the way here makes for a nice walk.

Finally if you take Peak Rd, which leads past the island's cemetery, you'll come to **Pak Tso Wan**, an isolated sandy beach which has good swimming. Peak Rd continues onto Sai Wan (West Bay), from where you can either walk or catch a sampan back to Cheung Chau Village.

Temples & Other Sights

Probably the most interesting of these is the **Pak Tai Temple**, built in 1783 to honour a Taoist deity who vanquished the Demon King and his allies, the tortoise and the serpent. Pak Tai has become the patron god of Cheung Chau, and is the leading deity in the annual Cheung Chau Bun Festival (see the Festivals section in the Facts about Hong Kong chapter). Inside the temple is a sword said to date from the Song Dynasty (960-1279AD) – recovered from the sea by fishermen over 100 years ago – and a 100 year old sedan chair used to carry Pak Tai's image around in festival processions. Note that all the statues of Pak Tai have a defeated serpent under one foot and a beaten tortoise under the other.

There are several temples dedicated to **Tin Hau**, the patron goddess of fisherfolk. There is one just north of the Pak Tai Temple, and another at the southern end of Cheung Chau Village, along the waterfront. The third is located at Sai Wan, at the southern tip of the island. You can either walk or take a sampan marked 'Sai Wan' from the main ferry pier. The five minute ride costs around HK$5 and takes you through the fishing junks moored in the harbour. Near the temple is **Cheung Po Tsai Cave**, said to have been a hiding place for a ruthless, bloodthirsty 19th century pirate.

Lastly there's the **Kwun Yum Temple**, which sits on a hill overlooking Kwun Yum Wan Beach.

Places to Eat

There are lots of little sidewalk restaurants along the waterfront where you can choose your own seafood. On Tung Wan Rd there are two Chinese restaurants, the *Bor Kee* and the *East Lake*, which are quite popular with both locals and expats, especially in the evening when there are often outdoor tables set up. The *Garden Cafe* (☎ 2981-4610) is a pleasant western-style pub and restaurant that has become the watering hole for Cheung Chau's expat community.

Getting There & Away

Ferries to Cheung Chau leave hourly between 6.25 am and 12.30 am from Pier 7 at the Outlying Islands ferry piers in Central (Map 5). The last boat back to Central from Cheung Chau leaves at 11.30 pm.

The ride takes about one hour, and the adult one-way fare is HK$9 Monday through Saturday morning, and HK$16 Saturday afternoon, Sunday and public holidays. The fare is halved for children twelve and under and seniors. Fares for deluxe class, which lets you sit on the open-air back deck, are HK$16 and HK$30 respectively. During the weekdays there are also several hoverferry sailings in the morning and afternoon. The fare is HK$22. Tea, coffee, soft drinks, beer and some basic snacks are available onboard.

LAMMA ISLAND

Known mainly for its seafood restaurants, Lamma Island (Map 12) also has some good beaches, beautiful hikes and even a few decent pubs. The third-largest island, after Lantau and Hong Kong, Lamma is home to Chinese fishers, farmers and commuters, and the hills above the main village, Yung Shue Wan, are littered with small homes and apartment blocks. The village itself is a haphazard cluster of old homes, restaurants and tiny shops spreading out from the narrow main street. The name 'Lamma' is an approximation of the Cantonese words for 'southern Y' which describes both the island's shape and its location relative to Hong Kong.

Yung Shue Wan is also where you'll find the closest thing Hong Kong has to an alternative lifestyle community, made up mostly of western expats. Though many of these people still commute to Hong Kong for work, long hair and tie-dye shirts are just as prevalent, if not more so, than suits. Regardless of what they wear, however, nearly everyone here feels that the only way to survive in Hong Kong is to retreat at the end of the day to this quiet haven of tree-lined paths and low-rise homes. The second largest village is Sok Kwu Wan, which lies mid-way down the island on the eastern shore. Its livelihood is derived from a nearby quarry and a string of extremely popular seafood restaurants that cater to a steady stream of 'mainlanders'. Ferries serve both villages, though boats to Sok Kwu Wan are fairly infrequent. There are no cars on Lamma, as everything is close enough to walk to.

NICKO GONCHAROFF

Shade Pavilion, Lamma Island

One very popular pastime in Hong Kong is to hire a pleasure junk and cruise out to either Yung Shue Wan or Sok Kwu Wan for a seafood lunch or dinner. On the weekends, junks can also be seen moored off the beaches on Lamma's western shore. Aside from the wide selection of restaurants, Lamma is popular for these trips because of its proximity to Hong Kong Island. By ferry it's only a 45 minute journey, by junk around two hours. Unless there are a lot of you it's not very economical to come by junk, as the rental rate for eight hours is HK$2500 to HK$2800. For details on junk rental, see the Activities section of the Things to See & Do chapter.

Even the longest hikes on Lamma can easily be done in one day. Should you decide to make a few days of it, there is accommodation in Yung Shue Wan in the form of several basic hotels and vacation guesthouses. There is also a fairly expensive hotel at Hung Shing Ye Beach.

Like the other islands, it's best to avoid Lamma on the weekends, when it gets quite crowded with city visitors.

Beaches

The easiest beach to access is the one at **Hung Shing Ye**, about 25 minutes walk from the Yung Shue Wan ferry pier. This is also the most popular beach on Lamma, and there's usually a fair number of people down here. There are a few restaurants and drink stands nearby, as well as the Concerto Inn, a hotel that also serves hot and cold drinks, as well as some mediocre western food.

The nicest beach on Lamma is probably at **Lo So Shing**, down towards the southern part of the island on the western shore. The beach is not that big, but it's charming and at the back has a nice cover of shade trees, which come in handy during the height of summer. During the April-October swimming season there is a small snack stand and lifeguard/first aid stations in operation here. From Sok Kwu Wan, turn right from the ferry pier and follow signs initially for the youth hostel before turning left for the beach. Walking time is about 30 minutes. From Yung Shue Wan it takes around 1½ hours following the Yung Shue Wan-Sok Kwu Wan pathway and then veering right for the beach.

Twenty minutes walk east of Sok Kwu Wan there is a fairly isolated beach at **Mo Tat Wan**, behind which lies a village that dates back 400 years, one of the oldest in Hong Kong. To get there, turn left from the ferry pier at Sok Kwu Wan and just keep walking. Occasionally sampans will take you there before continuing on to Aberdeen, but these are fairly infrequent.

If you want to get even more remote, continue past Mo Tat Wan to the south-east tip of the island, where there are beaches at **Shek Pai Wan** and **Shum Wan**.

Hikes

A popular hike on Lamma is to walk from **Yung Shue Wan** to **Sok Kwu Wan**, or vice-versa. It takes about 1½ hours and affords some good views of the ocean, Lamma's barren, rocky hillsides and Hong Kong Island. If you start off from Yung Shue Wan it's good to first check the Sok Kwu Wan ferry schedule to avoid a long wait at the other end. From the Yung Shue Wan ferry pier take the main road through town, out past Hung Shing Ye Beach and keep following the signs. It's a concrete path and there's little chance of you getting lost.

A shorter but equally scenic walk is out to **Pak Kok**, at the north-east tip of the island. From the Yung Shue Wan ferry pier, take the steep set of stairs on the right, near the Man Lai Wah Hotel, and follow the signs.

If you're feeling really ambitious you can tackle **Mt Stenhouse**, a 353m peak that dominates the southern end of the island. From Sok Kwu Wan the hike to the top and back takes around two hours, longer if it's a hot day. It's a steep climb and the trails are often not well defined, so allow for some extra time. If you start from Yung Shue Wan, the entire trip will probably take around five hours.

The whole of Lamma is crisscrossed with little hiking trails that make for great exploring. If you're interested it would be wise to first buy one of the countryside series maps for Lamma Island, which are available at the Government Publications Office.

Places to Eat

Both Yung Shue Wan and Sok Kwu Wan have rows of seafood restaurants, and you can't really go wrong at any of them. But for what it's worth, in Sok Kwu Wan the *Rainbow Seafood Restaurant* (☎ 2982-8100) and the *Genuine Lamma Hilton* (☎ 2982-8220) (no connection with the hotel group) are both quite good. Both these and all the other restaurants are located right along the waterfront on either side of the ferry pier. Prices aren't much cheaper than in Hong Kong, so be prepared.

In Sok Kwu Wan, remember to carefully check the bill at the end of meal, as some of the restaurants have been known to overcharge. This doesn't always mean they're trying to rip you off: it may be an honest mix-up as there are usually a lot of tables all simultaneously clamouring for service.

If you want to get away from the bright lights and crowds at Sok Kwu Wan, you can hike around 20 minutes east to the *Coral Seafood Restaurant* (☎ 2982-8328) in Mo Tat Wan. The menu is pretty much the same as those in Sok Kwu Wan, but the setting is quieter and prices a bit lower.

In Yung Shue Wan one of the most popular seafood places is the *Lancombe* (☎ 2982-0881), 47 Main St. They have some nice outside tables at the back, and though service is often quite slow, it gives you a chance to relax and enjoy the scenery. The deep-fried salt-and-pepper squid is excellent, as are the steamed prawns. Prices are also very reasonable.

On the way into town from the ferry pier you'll pass by the *Man Fung Seafood Restaurant* (☎ 2982-1112) and the *Sampan Seafood Restaurant* (☎ 2982-2388). These places are not bad, but they are used to dealing with tourists and service is not all that friendly. In addition hordes of people troop past your tables every time a ferry docks.

If you feel like a stroll, walk down to the *Han Lok Yuen Pigeon Restaurant* (☎ 2982-0680) which sits on a hillside looking down over Hung Shing Ye Beach. In addition to succulent roast pigeon, this place also serves up excellent seafood, well worth the walk. The views are quite nice too, and most seating is outdoors. The restaurant is closed Sundays and Mondays, and you need to call ahead to order pigeon.

There are several western restaurants: the one with the most character is the *Deli Lamma* (☎ 2982-1538), which serves continental fare with a Mediterranean influence. This place also doubles as one of Yung Shue Wan's most popular watering holes, and there is a good selection of beer and wine available.

Nearby is the *Capital Restaurant* (☎ 2982-0631) which, oddly enough, specialises in fondue. It's OK, but nothing fantastic. Down near where the main street makes a sharp left is the *Waterfront* (☎ 2982-0914), Lamma's most refined eatery. There are sea views from nearly every table on its three levels, and the ambience is quite inviting. The menu includes everything from British pub grub to Thai curries and Italian pasta. It's a bit expensive, but the overall effect is very pleasant.

If you want to pick up some snacks or food for a hiking trip, stop by the *Green Cottage*, a little bakery on the main road coming into town from the ferry pier. Their fresh-baked goodies are tasty, and they also make some pretty good sandwiches.

Getting There & Away

Ferries to Lamma leave at some strange intervals, so it's best to pick up a copy of the latest ferry schedule from the information centre of the Hong Kong & Yaumatei Ferry Co (HYF) near the Outlying Islands ferry piers in Central (Map 5). Ferries leave from Pier 6.

Ferries to Yung Shue Wan leave approximately every hour from 6.45 am to 12.30 am, but a few intervals last almost two hours. The last boat to Central from Yung Shue Wan leaves at 10.35 pm. There are seven sailings a day to Sok Kwu Wan between 8 am and 11 pm. The last boat from Sok Kwu Wan back to Central sails at 10 pm.

The adult fare is HK$8.50 Monday through Saturday morning, and HK$11.50 Saturday afternoon, Sunday and public holidays. Children and senior fares are HK$4.30 for weekdays, HK$6 for weekends and public holidays. Deluxe class fares are HK$16 and HK$30 respectively, but unless it's a big boat with an open-air back deck, it's not really worth the money. Tea, coffee, soft drinks and beer can be bought on board, along with some basic snacks.

LANTAU ISLAND

With more than 140 sq km of peaks, valleys, beaches and fields, Lantau is pretty much the most pristine chunk of Hong Kong (see Map 1). There are several good mountain hikes, some interesting villages and a few monasteries, the largest of which is the Po Lin Monastery, site of a 26m-high Buddha statue.

This is a particularly good place to get away from the city. Spend the day hiking Sunset or Lantau Peak: even though urban Hong Kong can be clearly seen from the top, you'll feel like the city is in another world. Or head down to the fishing village of Tai O and check out street scenes that have changed fairly little from 50 years ago.

More than half of the island has been designated country parkland, and there are over 70 km of walking and hiking trails, as well as camping and barbecue sites. Despite its size Lantau doesn't have too many beaches, and getting to most of them requires some hiking.

The main village is **Mui Wo**, also known as Silvermine Bay because of the old silver mines in the vicinity. This is where the ferries from Central dock, and where you can catch buses to other parts of the island. The back streets of the town, about 300m inland from the ferry pier, are mildly interesting to walk around. There is a small beach here, but the water is usually quite foul, so it's not much good for swimming. There are also a few run-down hotels and holiday homes, but there's no need to overnight on Lantau unless the mood strikes you.

Lantau is also home to a modern residential community called **Discovery Bay**, which is located on the north-east end of the island. There is no road between Disco Bay (as it's locally known) and the rest of Lantau, and it generally functions apart, having its own ferry service to Central. Unless you have friends to visit, there's really no reason to go see Discovery Bay.

Lantau is served by eight bus routes and a small fleet of taxis. Buses leave the Mui Wo ferry pier about 10 to 15 minutes after ferries arrive, so if you want to hang around the town for a while you'll have to wait about an hour before you can catch another bus. Taxis come and go sporadically. Like Cheung Chan and Lamma, Lantau is swamped on the weekends with urbanites, and both buses and taxis are in high demand. It's far better to come here during the week when there are no crowds, except at the Po Lin Monastery.

Po Lin Monastery

Sitting atop the 520m-high Ngong Ping plateau, this monastery and its enormous bronze Buddha statue are Lantau's main tourist draw. Established in 1928, Po Lin (Precious Lotus) has become the largest Buddhist monastery in Hong Kong. The main temple hall has undergone numerous renovations over the years, and the older buildings are now mostly hidden behind newer structures.

On a hill above the monastery sits the **Buddha statue**, forged in China and funded through charity. Tourist literature notes that it is 'the world's largest, seated, outdoor bronze Buddha'. There are bigger Buddhas out there (notably the 71m-high Grand Buddha in Leshan, China), but apparently they're not sitting, outdoors, or made of bronze. Even if it's not the biggest, Po Lin's Buddha is certainly impressive, and it's worth hiking up the steps to get a closer look at him, as well as the surrounding scenery.

Nearby the monastery are the **Lantau Tea Gardens**. These are not much more than a tourist attraction, as the weary-looking shrubs don't produce much tea any more. The best part is the little tea house, where you can enjoy a cup of the homegrown blend. There is also a miniature horse stable and corral where horses can be rented, either for photos or brief rides.

Just east of the of the tea gardens is the trailhead for **Lantau Peak**, which at 934m is the second highest in Hong Kong. This approach is quite steep. For more information, see the section on hikes below.

Places to Stay & Eat You can stay overnight around here if you wish. The *monastery* (☎ 2985-5113) has separate dormitory accommodation for men and women at around HK$200 per night, which includes three vegetarian meals. There is a *vegetarian restaurant* in the monastery complex that lets you sample what the monks eat. A plate of spring rolls, vegetables and rice costs around HK$40.

The *Lantau Tea Gardens* (☎ 2985-5161) has a few tiny rooms starting at HK$200 during the week and HK$300 on weekends. About ten minutes walk east of the tea gardens is the *SG Davis Youth Hostel* (☎ 2985-5610), which has dormitory beds and several campsites. Beds are HK$25 per night, campsites HK$15, and you must be a YHA member to stay there.

Getting There & Away The No 2 bus connects Mui Wo with the Po Lin Monastery. Departures are approximately hourly from 8.20 am to 6.50 pm. The last bus back to Mui Wo leaves Po Lin at 7.30 pm Monday to Saturday and 7.10 pm on Sunday and public holidays. The fare is HK$8.50 Monday to Saturday and HK$14.50 on Sunday and public holidays. Air-conditioned buses are HK$13 and HK$22.50 respectively. The ride takes around 40 minutes.

Tai O

One hundred years ago this village used to be an important trading and fishing port, exporting salt and fish to China. The export trade has all but died, and residents now make their living off farming, fishing and processing shrimp paste and dried fish, which gives the town a rather pungent air. Tai O is built half on Lantau and half on an island a few metres from the shore – two women pull a rope-drawn boat across the creek. This 'ferry service' is symbolic of the town's atmosphere. While there are plenty of modern conveniences around, in many ways life goes on as it has for decades. It's a great place to spend a few hours just walking around. Stilt houses connected by precarious wooden walkways line the shore, and everywhere there are intriguing little alley ways. There are also a few good seafood restaurants in town, most of which have no name. Try your luck!

Getting There & Away The No 1 bus connects Mui Wo with Tai O. Departures are approximately half-hourly from 6 am to 1.30 am. The last bus back to Mui Wo leaves Tai O at 9 pm, except for Saturdays when there's also a 10.15 pm bus. The fare is HK$6.80 Monday to Saturday and HK$11 on Sunday and public holidays. Air-conditioned buses are HK$10 and HK$16 respectively.

Tung Chung

Another formerly important port, Tung Chung became a sleepy farming and fishing village whose only claim to fame was the 19th century Tung Chung Fort, which the Chinese Imperial Army used to guard the approaches to the Pearl River. The fort is still there, and Tung Chung is an interesting place to poke around. However it won't be for much longer, as it sits opposite the massive construction site for Hong Kong's new airport at Chek Lap Kok. Once the airport is complete the old buildings will be razed to make way for another sterile housing block. You might want to check with the HKTA about the status of Tung Chung before venturing over here. If the old parts are still intact it's worth the visit, and the fort makes for an interesting detour.

Getting There & Away Bus No 3 connects Mui Wo with Tung Chung. The first bus leaves Mui Wo at 7.50 am and then hourly between 9.35 to 11.35 am and from 1.35 to 4.35 pm. The last bus to Tung Chung leaves at 6.35 pm and to Mui Wo at 7.15 pm. The fare is HK$6 Monday to Saturday, HK$9.60 Sunday and public holidays.

Beaches

The only decent beach that's easily accessible is **Cheung Sha**, which stretches along the southern part of the island. There are changing and first aid facilities as well as basic snacks and drinks available during the April through October swimming season. Bus Nos 1, 2, 4 and 5 all pass by here.

One of Lantau's nicest beaches is at **Fan Lau**, a tiny hamlet at the western tip of the island. However, getting here requires an eight km hike (see below). Both Cheung Sha and Fan Lau generally have clean water, although sometimes rubbish from the nearby shipping channels washes up on shore (this is still Hong Kong, remember).

Hikes

One of the nicest hikes on the island is up to **Sunset Peak** (869m). Starting from Mui Wo the ascent is gradual, and brings you up through rolling hills and meadows. You can also catch a bus from Mui Wo and get off at the trailhead at Nam Shan, about two km up the road. Any bus will do but No 7, bound for Pui O, is the cheapest. From the trailhead, the hike is about 6.5 km and at a leisurely pace takes around three hours. The trail will take you down to the road leading to Tung Chung. From here you can either wait for an infrequent bus, or walk down to the main road and Cheung Sha beach, where buses come by more often.

If you're in good shape and feeling ambitious, you might consider continuing on to **Lantau Peak**. Although it's only about four km from the Tung Chung road to the Po Lin Monastery on the other side of the peak, it's pretty steep going, and there are some concrete steps along the way that pound the soles of your feet. For your efforts you will be rewarded with great views from the summit. Unfortunately, many Hong Kongers are still careless with waste disposal, and the summit is awash with plastic and paper wrappers, styrofoam containers and drink cans. From the Po Lin Monastery there are frequent buses back to Mui Wo. You can also do this hike in the reverse, starting from Po Lin, though it's even steeper uphill going in this direction.

The trails across Sunset and Lantau Peaks form part of the 70 km **Lantau Trail**, which starts at Mui Wo, cuts across the island to Tai O and then loops back along the southern shore. Any of the 12 sections will take you through beautiful scenery. One particularly nice combination is sections 8 and 7, from Shek Pik Reservoir, around the western tip of the island through the hamlet of Fan Lau and on up the coast to Tai O. It's a long one at 16 km, but most of the going is flat and on a weekday you may not see another person on the trail.

The HKTA may be able to supply you with some government pamphlets on Lantau's country parks and the Lantau Trail. If not, contact the Country Parks Division of the Agriculture & Fisheries Department (☎ 2733-2132) in Tsimshatsui. Maps of both Lantau and the Lantau Trail are also available at the Government Publications Office.

Getting There & Away

Ferries to Mui Wo leave approximately hourly between 7 am and 12.20 am from Pier 7 at the Outlying Islands ferry piers in Central (Map 5). The journey time is around 50 minutes, but some ferries stop at the neighbouring island of Peng Chau, which stretches the trip out 20 minutes longer. The last boat from Mui Wo to Central leaves at 11.10 pm.

The adult one-way fare is HK$9 Monday to Saturday morning, and HK$16 Saturday afternoon, Sunday and public holidays. The fare is halved for children twelve and under and seniors. Fares for deluxe class, which gives you access to the open-air back deck, are HK$16 and HK$30 respectively. During the weekdays there are also several hoverferry sailings in the morning and afternoon. The fare is HK$22. As with other HYF ferries, hot and cold drinks, beer and snacks are available.

MACAU

Although there's plenty to see in Hong Kong, you've much to gain and little to lose from spending at least a day cruising around the fascinating backstreets of Macau (Map 14), the oldest surviving European settlement in Asia. Though it's only an hour's journey, a trip to Macau takes you to a very different world. Instead of the order and efficiency so evident in Hong Kong, one finds here a relaxed, almost hands-off attitude to administration. Portuguese and Chinese societies have mixed here in a way that was never possible in a class-conscious British colony. And while people here are also busy making money, they seem able to find the time to take a break now and then, sip a glass of wine or a cup of tea, and just watch the world pass them by for a little while.

The one time when Macau is not relaxed is during the weekend, when the population seems to double with Hong Kongers over for a weekend of gambling and dining. Do everything you can to come here during the week. On the weekend, ferry tickets are difficult to buy, hotel rates go up across the board, and catching a taxi becomes nearly impossible.

The following information should get you through a day or two in Macau. Lonely Planet's *Hong Kong, Macau & Guangzhou – travel survival kit* takes a much more detailed look at the enclave.

History

In the early 16th century Portugal embarked on an aggressive campaign to cash in on Asia's lucrative trade routes. After forcefully securing footholds in Goa (India) and Malacca (modern-day Malaysia), the Portuguese set their sights on China. In typical fashion, the Chinese imperial court brushed off the entreaties of these western barbarians. But Portuguese persistence won out, and in the mid-1550s they were allowed to rent a small peninsula on the southern coast, possibly in exchange for wiping out a band of local pirates. This area, known variously as Aomen, Amagao or Macau, was quickly developed, despite that fact that China never formally ceded it to Portugal.

Macau became a key link in Portugal's major Asian trade routes, and Portuguese traders became export agents for the Chinese, who were forbidden to go abroad on pain of death. This gave Portugal a near monopoly on all large-scale commerce with China. Macau also served as the staging point for Jesuit missionaries charged with spreading the word of God in the 'Middle Kingdom'.

Macau successfully fought off encroachment by the Dutch in the early 17th century, but Portugal's subsequent decline as a world power weighed heavily on the enclave. It still managed to struggle on as an outpost for Europeans trading with China. The British annexation of Hong Kong in 1841 changed that, and Macau gradually became a backwater. The problem of keeping the place financially viable, however, was solved by Governor Isidoro Francisco Guimaraes (1851-63) who introduced legalised gambling, which is still the enclave's main source of revenue.

Although Portugal was actually ready to give Macau up in the mid-1970s, the Chinese apparently were content to maintain the status quo. It wasn't until 1987 – after Hong Kong's return to China had been decided – that a Sino-Portuguese pact was signed, handing Macau back to China on 20 December 1999. It will then become, like Hong Kong, a 'Special Administrative Region' and enjoy a 'high degree of autonomy' in all matters except defence and foreign affairs.

Even now China's relationship with Macau is quite close, and thousands of people cross the border daily going to and from work on the other side. One gets the feeling that, unlike Hong Kong, Macau won't change much after 1999, except for the flags flying over the government offices.

Tourist Offices

The Macau Government Tourist Office (☎ 315-566) has a branch on the 2nd floor of the ferry terminal, on the right side as you exit immigration. The office can provide you with all sorts of useful information including maps, hotel and restaurant lists, a great pamphlet on walking tours and details on transportation. There is also an office in Hong Kong (☎ 2857-2287), 37th floor, Shun Tak Centre, 200 Connaught Rd, Sheung Wan.

Money

Macau has its own currency, the pataca. However, its value is only a few cents less than that of the Hong Kong dollar, which circulates freely in Macau, so there really is no need to change money. Sometimes taxi drivers, restaurants and smaller stores may give you change in patacas, but all accept the Hong Kong currency and the bigger places give change in it as well.

Things to See & Do

Macau is much smaller than Hong Kong in both size (23.5 sq km) and population (500,000, of which 95% are Chinese). This means it's possible to walk to most of the sights, except for those on the outlying islands of Taipa and Coloane, which can be easily reached by bus or taxi.

Peninsular Macau A good number of the sights on the peninsula are located near Centro, the central business and government area. The main street running through here is Avenida de Almeida Ribeiro which, along with Avenida Infante D'Henrique, cuts across the width of the peninsula.

Mid-way along Avenida de Almeida Ribeiro is the **Leal Senado**, which houses the municipal government offices. It's a classical structure that looks out over a public square and a large fountain. This whole area was recently renovated, and looks like a page from a Portugal guidebook. Behind the Leal Senado is **St Augustine's Church**, which has foundations dating back to 1586, although the present church was built in 1814.

TONY WHEELER

Facade detail, St Paul's Cathedral, Macau

Wind your way up the path at the north end of the Leal Senado public square and you will come across **St Dominic's Church**, a beautiful 17th century baroque cathedral. It is only open in the afternoon.

Continuing up the cobbled main street will take you to Macau's most famous landmark, the **facade of St Paul's Cathedral**. This magnificent facade, along with the steps leading up to it and the mosaic floor behind it, are the only remains of what was once considered the finest church in Asia. Built by Jesuits in 1602, the church caught fire during a major typhoon in 1835. The facade has been described as a 'sermon in stone', recording some of Christianity's major events in its beautiful stone carvings.

On the hill overlooking St Paul's is **Monte Fort**, which was built by the Jesuits around the same time. In 1622 the fort's cannons (which are still there) destroyed a Dutch warship, helping to dissuade the Dutch from further attempts to take over Macau. From on top of the fort there are sweeping views of Macau and, across the river, China.

A few blocks north, near the modern Church of St Anthony is the **Luis de Camoes Museum**. Once the head-quarters of the British East India Co, this building now houses early Chinese terracotta, enamel ware and pottery, paintings, old weapons, and paintings and sketches of old Macau and Guangzhou (formerly Canton). The museum is open daily from 11 am to 5 pm except Wednesdays and public holidays. Admission is M$1.

Behind the museum is the **Camoes Grotto & Gardens**, which house a memorial to the 16th century Portuguese poet Luis de Camoes. There is some dispute as to whether Camoes ever even made it to Macau, but never mind: the gardens are quite pleasant and are popular with the local Chinese, some of whom you might see playing checkers. Nearby the museum is the **Old Protestant Cemetery**, resting place of the numerous non-Portuguese who made their way to Macau.

North of Centro, on Ferreira de Almeida, are the restful **Lou Lim Ieoc Gardens**. The gardens and the ornate mansion adjacent (which is now a school) once belonged to the wealthy Chinese Lou family. The gardens are a mixture of European and Chinese plantings, with huge shady trees, lotus ponds, pavilions, bamboo groves, grottoes and strangely shaped doorways. The twisting pathways are said to be modelled after the famous gardens of Suzhou in eastern China.

Around the corner from the Lou Lim Ieoc Gardens, at the junction of Avenida da Sidonio Pais and Rua de Silva Mendes, is the **Sun Yatsen Memorial Home**, dedicated to the revolutionary who inspired China after the fall of the Qing Dynasty. Sun practised medicine in Macau before turning to revolution. The house was built as a memorial to Sun, and replaces the original, which blew up when it was being used as an explosives store. Inside there are flags, photos and other relics of Sun's life. The

GLENN BEANLAND

Monte Fort, Macau

museum is open daily except Tuesdays, but only in the morning during the week. On weekends it's also open from 3 to 5 pm.

Sitting on the highest point on the peninsula is the **Guía Lighthouse**, which was first lit in 1865. The complex is still used as a meteorological station, and offers terrific views.

It's a bit of out of the way, lying up on Avenida do Coronel Mesquita, but if you like temples, the **Kun Iam Temple** complex is pretty interesting. The Kun Iam (Goddess of Mercy) Temple dates back 400 years, though the original temple on the site was probably built more than 600 years ago. It's also where the first treaty of trade and friendship between the USA and China was signed, in 1844. This area is a popular spot for fortune-tellers.

At the southern tip of the peninsula is the **A-Ma Temple**, which dates back to the 17th century. A-Ma (more popularly known by her Hong Kong pseudonym Tin Hau) became A-Ma-Gao to the Portuguese, and they named their colony after it. The temple consists of several shrines from the Ming Dynasty.

Opposite the A-Ma Temple is the outstanding **Maritime Museum**, which has a rich collection of boats and other artefacts related to Macau's seafaring past. It's open from 10 am to 5.30 pm daily except Tuesdays.

Moving up along the east side of the Peninsula is **Rua da Praia Grande**, one of the most scenic streets in the city. Here you find the pink **Governor's Residence**, which you may only admire from outside. On the hill behind it is **St Lawrence's Church**, a fairly ascetic cathedral that enjoys great views of the surrounding area.

Gambling is the main activity on Macau; but even if you're not interested in casinos, it's worth checking out the kitschy architecture of the **Lisboa Hotel**. It's just above the large traffic junction on the airport road, near the Bank of China.

Taipa & Coloane There are two outlying islands in Macau: Taipa and Coloane. The former has been overrun by amazingly ugly high-rise apartments, and there's not a whole lot to see here. **Taipa Village** has managed to resist being totally re-made, and its narrow streets are fairly interesting to scout around. In the village, the **Taipa House Museum** is a good example of what life looked like at the beginning of this century. It's open every day except Monday from 9.30 am to 1 pm and from 3 to 5.30 pm.

Coloane is larger and boasts a few nice beaches, something Taipa lacks. The northern sides of both islands have been carved away to make room for a power plant and Macau's new airport and deep-water port complex. But the southern side of Coloane is still fairly peaceful, and even has a few nice hiking trails.

Coloane Park is about one km south of the causeway leading to Taipa. Its 20 hectares contain a fountain, some nicely kept gardens and an aviary. The park is open from 9 am to 7 pm daily and admission is M$5. The aviary costs another M$5. Behind the park are two hiking trails. The **Coloane Trail** makes an 8.6 km loop around the island, while the **North-East Coloane Trail** takes in the north-east section only and stretches 6.2 km.

Coloane Village is a picturesque hamlet with a few temples, some nice restaurants and a lazy, relaxing feel to it. The main attraction here is the **Chapel of St Francis Xavier**, built in 1928, which contains a piece of the right arm bone from the missionary of the same name, who died on nearby Shang Ch'an Island in 1552. At the southern end of town there is a **Tin Hau temple**.

On the south side of the island is Coloane's claim to fame, **Hac Sa Beach**. Hac Sa means 'black sand', and the sand here does have a grey to black colour. This can make the water look very polluted, but actually it's perfectly clean and fine for swimming. The area is beautiful, with lots of pine trees to provide shade, and on weekends people swarm here. On a really clear day you can see the mountains on Hong Kong's Lantau Island. Hac Sa is also the site of the incredible Fernando's Restaurant (see Places to Eat below).

Places to Stay

Macau is littered with hotels, giving you plenty of options should you decide to stay overnight. However, nearly all of them are booked up on Friday and Saturday nights, so it's best to come during the week. Rates for Friday and Saturday nights are generally around 40% higher as well. This partial list will give you idea of what's available. The Macau Government Tourist Office at the ferry terminal can provide you with complete details for all price levels of accommodation in Macau.

Most people from Hong Kong book their hotels in advance, often at the booking offices in the Shun Tak Centre in Sheung Wan, where the ferries to Macau leave. Doing this saves a considerable amount off the walk-in rate. If you haven't booked a place already, however, there are several counters at the arrivals level of the ferry terminal in Macau where you can get the same prices. Some touts may also approach you offering discounts for hotels. Don't worry: they're usually reliable and are just trying to drum up business during the slow mid-week period.

Macau's true budget accommodation is clustered around the wharf area (Barra), which can be reached by taking the No 3A bus to its terminus. The cheapest spot without doubt is the *Hotel Ung Ieong* (☎ 573-814) at No 17 Rua de Bocage. The sign on the door (if you can even make it out) says 'Restaurante Ung Ieong'. The rooms here are huge, and though the place is pretty run-down, it's a cheap M$52 for a double with bath attached. You might want to check the rooms first though. There are also some cheap guesthouses nearby.

Costing a bit more but well worth it is the *East Asia Hotel* (☎ 922-433), 1A Rua da Madeira. The hotel is housed in a classic colonial-style building, and though it's been remodelled has lost none of its charm. Spacious doubles with private bath start at M$290. There's a fine restaurant on the 2nd floor that serves dim sum for extremely reasonable prices. A few other hotels with similar prices are located around here, but none can compare in terms of value for money.

If you want to be right near the centre of town, there's the *Hotel Sintra* (☎ 710-111), Avenida Dom Joao IV. This is a standard mid-range Macau hotel, with standard rates: M$440 per night for a double (if reserved through a booking office). It's nothing special, but is comfortable enough. Another centrally located place is the *Metropole* (☎ 388-166), 62 Rua da Praia Grande. Doubles here are around M$500 if booking through an agent.

For the high end, there are really only three places worth considering. The *Bela Vista* (☎ 965-333) is a colonial hotel that was going to seed until it was bought by Hong Kong's Mandarin Oriental Hotel Group several years ago. It has been painstakingly restored and has regained all of its former elegance. There are only eight rooms and suites, ranging from M$1800 to M$4850 per night. It may be expensive, but if you want to indulge in colonial luxury, there's no better place than this. The hotel is located on Rua Comendador Kou Ho Neng.

Built into the remains of an old fortress, the *Pousada de Sao Tiago* (☎ 378-111) is right up there with the Bela Vista in terms of character, if not quite as luxurious. Sitting above the Avenida de Republica, the hotel commands a splendid view of the harbour, and the interior decor, with its flagstones and wooden raftered ceilings, is just as enjoyable. Even if you don't stay here, it's worth stopping by for a drink on the terrace. Doubles range from M$1080 to M$1380.

Perched on the southern shore of Coloane Island is the massive *Westin Resort* (☎ 871-111), Estrada de Hac Sa. Though not quite as elegant, it has all the amenities one expects of a five-star hotel, and the setting is fantastic.

GLENN BEANLAND

GLENN BEANLAND

Top: Colonial architecture, Macau
Bottom: Taking a break, Largo do Senado, Macau

All rooms have large, private balconies where you can sip your coffee or wine and contemplate the South China Sea. There is a beautiful outdoor swimming pool, a golf course and a full suite of indoor recreational facilities. Doubles range from M$1300 to M$1650.

Places to Eat

This topic deserves its own separate volume, and this book doesn't pretend to do it justice. Suffice to say that if you exhaust these few places there are a lot of other great options out there.

Macau's Chinese food is quite good, but it's the Portuguese food that makes coming here such a culinary delight. One place not to be missed is the legendary *Fernando's* (☎ 882-531), 9 Hac Sa Beach, Coloane. The original part of the restaurant, a graffiti-filled hole in the wall, doesn't look like much, but head out the back to the main brick dining hall and prepare yourself for a slice of heaven. Must-order dishes include roast chicken, clams, fried shrimp and the simple but outstanding salad. This place is always crowded, and you can't make reservations, but there's a bar area where you can sip cappuccino or Sangria while you wait for a table. Prices are quite reasonable. Credit cards are not accepted. It's located at the far end of the Hac Sa Beach parking lot. Look for a little wooden sign that says 'Fernando'.

One of Macau's most authentic Portuguese places is also on Coloane, this one in Coloane Village. *Cacorola* (☎ 882-226) looks like a piece of Portugal was beamed over to Macau, customers and all. It serves up a fabulous variety of nouvelle cuisine, Portuguese-style. Specialities include tuna and black bean salad, beef steak with garlic and rabbit stew. This friendly restaurant is closed Mondays. It's located just off the main square.

On the Macau Peninsula, *Comida A Portuguesa Carlos* (☎ 300-315) has some of the warmest service in town, as well as outstanding food: it's the kind of place where the owner comes over and chats with you over a glass of wine. It's located at 28 Rua Bispo Medeiros, near the Lou Lim Ieoc Gardens. Credit cards are not accepted. Another highly recommended place is *A Lorcha* (☎ 313-193), 289 Rue do Almirante Sergio, just around the corner from the A-Ma Temple and the Maritime Museum at the southern tip of the peninsula.

Right next to the ferry terminal is yet another outstanding restaurant, this one Italian. *Pizzeria Toscana* (☎ 726-637) does everything right, from the pizza to the pasta to the cappuccino. It's also a good place to pick up some snacks for the ferry ride back to Hong Kong. It's located down at the end of the spectacularly ugly long building across from the ferry terminal. Look for the leaning tower of Pizza sign.

Getting There & Away

Macau and Hong Kong are linked by an interesting selection of jet-powered ferries, which make it possible to do the 65 km trip in around one hour. Departures in Hong Kong are from the Macau Ferry Terminal, near the Shun Tak Centre, 200 Connaught Rd, Sheung Wan (Map 4). The terminal is connected by underground walkway to Sheung Wan MTR station. The Hong Kong & Yaumatei Ferry Co also has ferries to Macau from the China Hong Kong City terminal in Tsimshatsui (Map 16).

There are several different ferry services. The fastest and most stable are the Far East Jetfoils, twin-decked hydrofoils powered by Boeing jet engines. These make the trip in around 50 minutes, and are by far the most popular. The service runs 24 hours a day, catering to the late-night gamblers and partiers. Sailings are every 15 to 30 minutes during the day, but the frequency drops to hourly from around 1 am to 6 am. There are economy and 1st class sections, but the difference is minimal: 1st class gives you a slightly better view. Ticket prices during the week are HK$123 for economy and HK$136 for 1st class. During the weekend the price goes up to HK$134 and HK$146 respectively. Late-night sailings cost HK$152 and HK$166.

Far East Jetfoils recently introduced a larger vessel called the Foilcat, which is a bit roomier and slightly faster. Ticket prices are HK$10 higher than those quoted above. Jetfoil tickets can be purchased up to 28 days in advance in Hong Kong at the Shun Tak Centre or booked by phone (☎ 2859-6956) if you have a credit card. Pick them up at the advance ticket window on the 1st floor of the Shun Tak Centre.

The next most popular option is the Turbo Cat, a more spacious and luxurious jet-powered catamaran that makes the journey in about 70 minutes. The interior is more pleasant than the jetfoils, but because it rides on the surface of the water, not above it, the Turbo Cat tends to jump around a lot more. If you're prone to seasickness, take the jetfoil. The Turbo Cat service runs approximately half-hourly from 8 am to 5 pm, and then hourly from 5.30 pm to 10.30 pm. Weekday ticket prices are HK$123 for economy and HK$219 for 1st class. Weekend prices are HK$130 and HK$230 respectively.

HYF's service from the China Hong Kong City terminal in Tsimshatsui uses the same kind of boats as the

Turbo Cat. Sailings are hourly from 8.30 am to 8 pm and ticket prices are similar to those for Turbo Cat.

If you're interested in the 'slow boat' to Macau, there's always the ironically named High-Speed Ferries. These look like scaled-down cruise ships, and they make the trip in about one hour and 40 minutes, which is actually fairly quick. The best thing about these is the back deck, which is an enjoyable palce to sit if the weather is good. The price is also nice: from HK$61 to HK$97 (1st class) weekdays and HK$84 to HK$121 on weekends. Sailings from Hong Kong are at 9.30 am, 3 and 8 pm. From Macau, departures are 12.15, 5.30 and 10.30 pm.

Unless you are going during the weekend there's little need to buy a round-trip ticket. With all the ferry departures, it's fairly easy to get a ticket in Macau.

For those who can afford HK$1200 for a one-way flight, there is a helicopter service between Hong Kong and Macau. The flight takes just 20 minutes, but immigration at both ends adds up so that you only save around 40 minutes compared with taking a jetfoil. However, you can't beat the view. There are 10 to 12 flights daily in each direction. For more information call East Asia Airlines (☎ 2859-3359) at the Shun Tak Centre.

You will be required to go through immigration formalities in both Hong Kong and Macau, so remember to bring your passport. Enjoy your trip!

Getting Around

Macau is fairly well served by buses. Fares range from M$2 to M$4 and you pay when you board. The most important routes for visitors are as follows:

No 3 – runs from Jetfoil (ferry) pier past Hotel Lisboa onto Avenida Almeida Ribeiro in the Centro district

No 3A – runs from Jetfoil pier down to Avenida de Almeida Ribeiro over to wharf and floating casino and budget hotel area

No 25 – runs from Barrier Gate through Centro on Avenida do Infante D'Henrique, over to Taipa and on to Hac Sa Beach in Coloane

No 28C – runs from Jetfoil pier past Hotel Lisboa, then north to Lou Lim Ieoc Gardens, Kun Iam Temple and ends up at Barrier Gate (border with China)

Taxis are pretty easy to find except on weekends, when Macau is swarming with visitors from Hong Kong. Flagfall is M$8 and each additional 0.25 km costs M$1. There are surcharges of M$5 and M$10 for rides to Taipa and Coloane islands, respectively.

Glossary

amah – a servant, usually a woman, who cleans house and looks after the children. Older Chinese women from the countryside used to find work as amahs, but in Hong Kong now the job is mostly done by Filipinas and other South-East Asian migrant workers.

cheong sam – originating in Shanghai, a fashionable, tight-fitting Chinese dress with a slit up the side. Often worn on special occasions, it's also the favoured gown for a bride departing on her honeymoon.

dai pong dong – open-air street stalls; great places to enjoy some tasty dishes from a sidewalk folding table, especially at night.

fung shui – literally meaning 'wind-water', the Chinese art of geomancy which aims to balance the elements of nature.

godown – a warehouse, usually located on or near the waterfront.

gongfu – a form of Chinese martial arts, usually called 'kungfu' in the west; see also *taijiquan*.

gwailo – a foreigner, particularly a westerner. In Cantonese the term means 'ghost person' or 'foreign devil' and stems from the 19th century when westerners began to come to China in force. Hong Kongers claim the term no longer has any negative connotation, though some foreigners are less than fond of the name.

gwaipo – a female foreigner, particularly a westerner. *'Gwai'* means 'devil' or 'ghost', *'po'* is Cantonese for woman.

hong – a company, usually engaged in trade. Often used to refer to Hong Kong's original trading houses, such as Jardine Matheson or Swire, which have grown to become major conglomerates.

junk – originally referred to Chinese fishing and war vessels with square sails. Now applies to the diesel-powered, wooden pleasure yachts which can be frequently seen on Hong Kong's harbour.

kaido – small to medium-sized ferry which makes short runs on the open sea, usually used for non-scheduled service between small islands and fishing villages.

karaoke – a system that allows you to sing along to the recorded melody of popular songs. A popular social activity among the Chinese, it takes place in bars, specialised 'karaoke lounges' and private homes. The word 'karaoke' ('empty music') was borrowed from Japan, which bears responsibility for its invention...

mahjong – popular Chinese-style 'card game' played among four with tiles engraved with Chinese characters.

sampan – motorised wooden launch capable of only carrying a few people, used mostly for inter-harbour tranport.

shroff – an Anglo-Indian word meaning 'cashier'.

taijiquan – slow-motion shadow boxing, a form of exercise; commonly shortened to taiji ('tai chi' in the west).

taipan – the 'big boss', usually of a large company.

triad – Chinese secret society. Were originally founded to protect Chinese culture from the influence of usurping Manchurians, but their modern-day members are little more than secretive gangsters. Hong Kong's triads are mainly involved in drug-running, prostitution and protection rackets.

ACRONYMS

CMB – China Motor Bus
EXCO – Executive Council
HKTA – Hong Kong Tourist Association
KCR – Kowloon-Canton Railway
KMB – Kowloon Motor Bus
LEGCO – Legislative Council
LRT – Light Rail Transit
MTR – Mass Transit Railway
SAR – Special Administrative Region

Index

MAP 4

To Western & Aberdeen

Connaught Road West

Sutherland St

Des Voeux Road West

Queen Street

Tram

New Market Street

Ko Shing Street

Wing Lok Street

Queen's Street

Bonham Strand West

Bonham Strand

Queen's Road West

Hollywood Park

Possession Street

Bonham Strand

New Street

Hollywood Road

Hospital Road

To Hong Kong University

Po Yan

Po Hing Fong

Pound Lane

13

14

12

Upper Station Street

Sai Street

Tai Ping Shan Street

Tung Street

Lok Ku Road

Upper Lascar Row

15

Square Street

Blake Garden

Kut In Fong

Ladder Street

Bonham Road

Breezy Path

Caine Lane

Caine Road

Seymour Road

Robinson Road

Castle Road

Conduit Road

MID-LEVELS

Sheung Wan

0   100   200 m

• • • • • • •   Sheung Wan Walking Tour

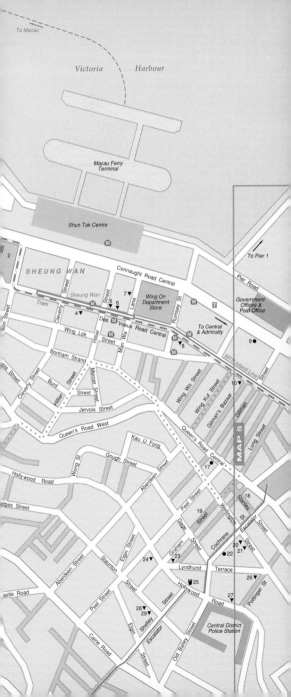

To Macau

Victoria   Harbour

Macau Ferry
Terminal

Shun Tak Centre

SHEUNG WAN

Connaught Road Central

Pier Road

To Pier 1

Government
Offices &
Post Office

Sheung Wan
Tram

7 ▼

Wing On
Department
Store

Rumsey St

7

9 ●

6
4 ▼

Des Voeux Road Central

Wing Lok   Street

Man Wa Lane

To Central
& Admiralty

8

MTR Island Line

Bonham Strand

Mercer Street

Wing Wo Street

Wing Kut Street

Gilman's Bazaar

10 ▼

Gilman

Burd Street

Jervois Street

Queen's Road West

Lung Street

Cleverly Street

Hillier Street

Kau U Fong

Queen's Road Central

MAP 5

Gough Street

Wong St

Aberdeen Street

17 ●

18

Stanley St

Hollywood   Road

dges Street

Peel Street

19

Wellington St

Escalator Street

Graham Street

Cochrane

20 ▼
21 ▼

24 ▼

23 ▼

● 22

26 ▼

Aberdeen Street

Staunton Street

Elgin Street

Lyndhurst   Terrace

25

27

Pottinger St

astle Road

Peel Street

Shelley Street

28 ▼
29 ▼

Hollywood   Road

Central District
Police Station

Caine Road

Elgin Street

Escalator
Street

Old Bailey Street

MAP 5

Reclamation
(Work in Progress)

Central & Admiralty

0   100   200 m

Pier
Road
1

To Sheung Wan   7

Bus
Terminus

Hong Kong
Yaumatei Fe
Informatio
Booth

MAP 4

Connaught Road Central

Jubilee
Street
6

Harbour View Street   7

8

9

10

11

General
Post
Office

Connaught Place

Jardine
House
12

Tram

Central Market

Queen Victoria

Man Yee Lane

Pottinger

Li Yuen St West

Li Yuen St East

Douglas Lane

Chiu Lung Street

Queen's Road

Theatre Lane

Des Voeux

Road Central

Escalator

Stanley Street

Wellington Street

22
21
23
24
25
26
27

20

19

Central

M

M

M

M

Swire
House

Ice House Street

Mandarin
Oriental
Hotel

Statue
Square

Chater Road

Statue
Square

D'Aguilar
Street

28

Wyndham Street

Wyndham Street

MAP 8

34
35
36

37

Pedder
Building

Pedder

30
29
32
33

31

Prince's
Building

Legislative
Council
Building

Zetland Street

Duddell Street

Battery Path

Ice House Street

38
39
40
41

Queen's Road Central

Bank St

CENTRAL

Beaconsfield Hou
Post Office

Glenealy
Street

42
43
44

45

Government
House

St John's
Cathedral

Cit
P

Zoological &
Botanical Gardens

Upper Albert Road

Upper Albert

Road

Lower Albert Road

Garden

Road

Zoological &
Botanical Gardens

Albany Road

Peak Tram
Terminus

Garden

Road

Robinson Road

Garden Road

46

Cotton Tree Drive

Peak Tram

Kennedy Road

Magazine Gap Road

MacDonnell Road

Victoria Harbour

Queen's Pier

Edinburgh Place

14

HMS Tamar

Connaught Road Central

17 16

Hutchison House
15
Bank of America Tower

Lambeth Walk

Murray Road

MTR Tsuen Wan Line

MTR Island Line

Far East Finance Centre

Drake Street

Ice Street

Harcourt Road

To Wanchai & Causeway Bay

Bank of China Tower

Lippo Centre

Admiralty

Tamar Street

7

MAP 6

Cotton Tree Drive

Flagstaff House Museum

Supreme Court

Queensway Plaza

United Centre

Rodney Street

Harcourt Garden

Hong Kong Park

Queensway

47
Queensway Government Offices

48

Tram

JW Marriot Hotel

Supreme Court Road

Island Shangri-La Hotel

Conrad Hotel

Justice Drive

Kennedy Road

Borrett Road

Bowen Road

To Discovery Bay

To Tsimshatsui East

To Tinshatsui

To ...ghom

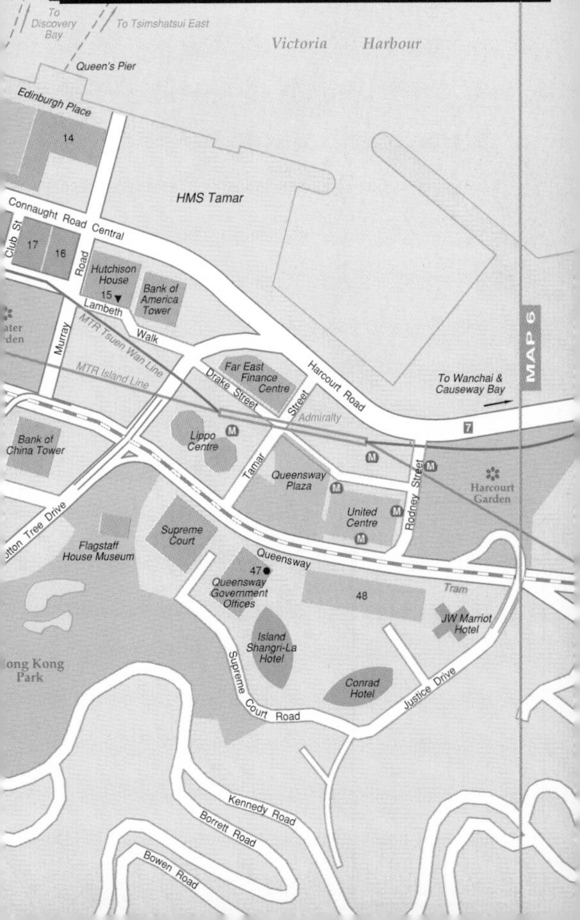

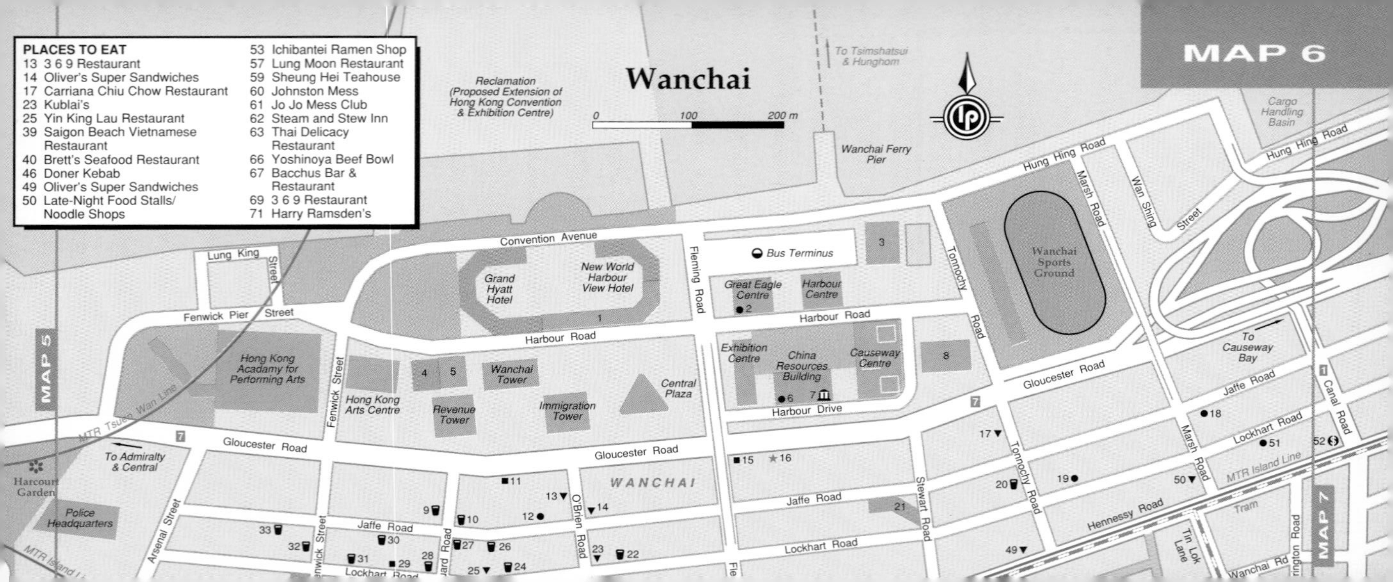

MAP 6

Wanchai

0   100   200 m

To Tsimshatsui & Hunghom

To Causeway Bay

To Admiralty & Central

Reclamation of Proposed Extension of Hong Kong Convention & Exhibition Centre)

Cargo Working Basin

Hung Hing Road

Canal Road

Jaffe Road

Lockhart Road

Marsh Road

Gloucester Road

Tonnochy Road

Hennessy Road

Tin Lok Lane

Wan Shing Street

Hung Hing Road

Marsh Road

Tonnochy Road

Stewart Road

Jaffe Road

Lockhart Road

Wanchai Sports Ground

Gloucester Road

Wanchai Ferry Pier

Harbour Road

Bus Terminus

China Resources Building

Harbour Drive

Great Eagle Centre

Harbour Centre

Causeway Centre

Exhibition Centre

Convention Avenue

Fleming Road

New World Harbour View Hotel

Central Plaza

Gloucester Road

WANCHAI

Grand Hyatt Hotel

Harbour Road

Wanchai Tower

Immigration Tower

O'Brien Road

Revenue Tower

Hong Kong Arts Centre

Jaffe Road

Lockhart Road

Fenwick Pier Street

Lung King Street

Fenwick Street

Hong Kong Academy for Performing Arts

Gloucester Road

Jaffe Road

Lockhart Road

Arsenal Street

Police Headquarters

Harcourt Garden

MTR Island Line Train

PLACES TO EAT

13	3 6 9 Restaurant
14	Oliver's Super Sandwiches
17	Carriana Chiu Chow Restaurant
23	Kublai's
25	Yin King Lau Restaurant
39	Saigon Beach Vietnamese Restaurant
40	Brett's Seafood Restaurant
46	Doner Kebab
49	Oliver's Super Sandwiches
50	Late-Night Food Stalls/ Noodle Shops
53	Ichibantei Ramen Shop
57	Lung Moon Restaurant
59	Sheung Hei Teahouse
60	Johnston Mess
61	Jo Jo Mess Club
62	Steam and Stew Inn
63	Thai Delicacy Restaurant
66	Yoshinoya Beef Bowl
67	Bacchus Bar & Restaurant
69	3 6 9 Restaurant
71	Harry Ramsden's

MAP 7

MAP 5

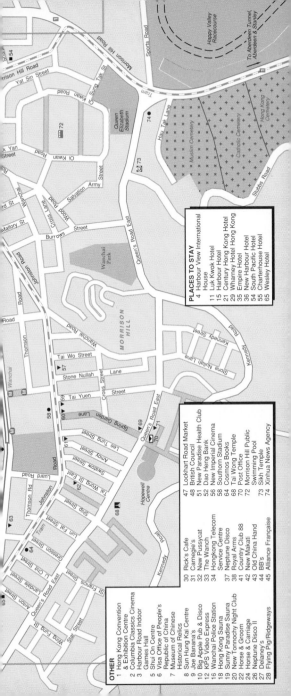

PLACES TO STAY

4 Harbour View International House
11 Luk Kwok Hotel
15 Harbour Hotel
21 Century Hong Kong Hotel
29 Wharney Hotel Hong Kong
35 Empire Hotel
54 New Harbour Hotel
55 South Pacific Hotel
65 Charterhouse Hotel
65 Wesley Hotel

OTHER

1 Heng Kong Convention & Exhibition Centre
2 Columbia Classics Cinema
3 Harbour Road Indoor Games Hall
5 Shui On Centre
6 Visa Office of People's Republic of China
7 Museum of Chinese Historical Relics
8 Sun Hung Kai Centre
9 Joe Banana's
10 Big Apple Pub & Disco
12 KPS Video Express
16 Wanchai Police Station
18 Hong Kong Sauna
19 Sunny Paradise Sauna
20 New Tonnochy Night Club
22 Horse & Groom
24 Horse & Carriage
26 Neptune Disco II
27 Delaney's
28 Flying Pig/Ridgeways
30 Rick's Cafe
31 Carnegie's
32 The Wanch
33 New Pussycat
34 Hongkong Telecom Service Centre
37 Neptune Disco
38 Royal Arms
41 Country Club 88
42 New Makati
43 Old China Hand
44 BB's
45 Alliance Française
47 Lockhart Road Market
48 British Council
51 New Paradise Health Club
52 Dao Heng Bank
56 New Imperial Cinema
58 Southorn Stadium
64 Cosmos Books
68 Tai Wong Temple
70 Post Office
72 Morrison Hill Public Swimming Pool
73 Sikh Temple
74 Xinhua News Agency

MAP 7

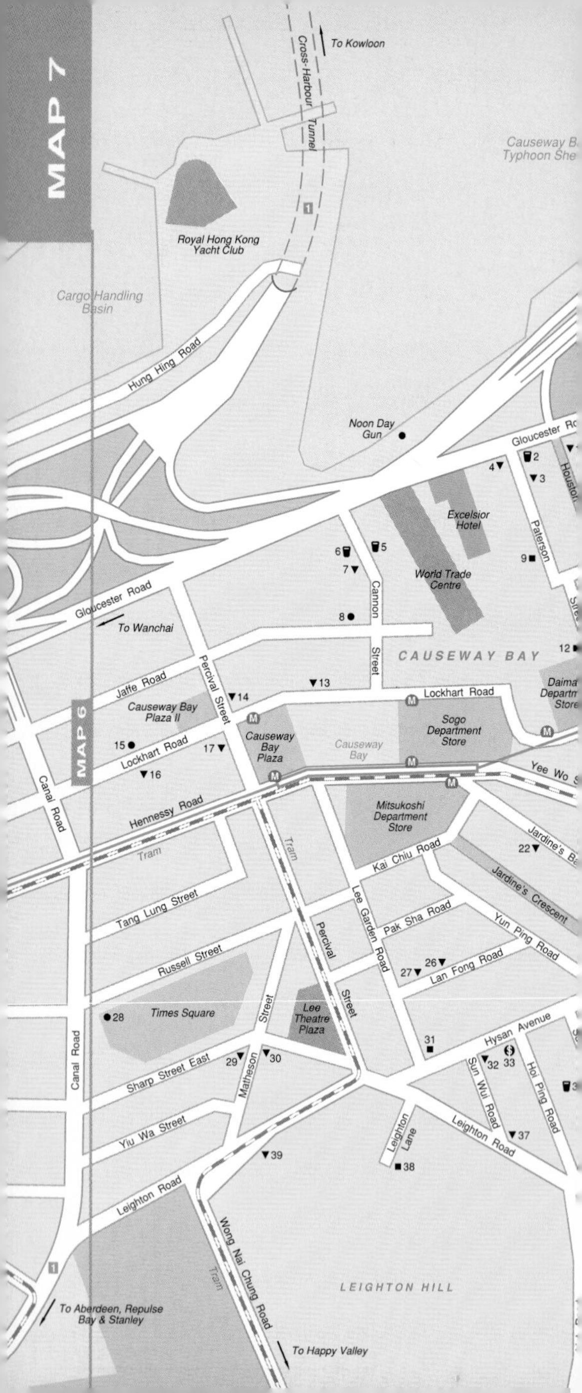

To Kowloon

Cross-Harbour Tunnel

Causeway B.
Typhoon She

Royal Hong Kong
Yacht Club

Cargo Handling
Basin

Hung Hing Road

1

Noon Day
Gun ●

Gloucester Ro

4 ▼   ▮ 2
▼ 3

Housto

Excelsior
Hotel

Paterson

6 ▮   ▮ 5
▼ 7
9 ▮

Gloucester Road

To Wanchai

World Trade
Centre

Cannon Street

8 ●

12 ▮

CAUSEWAY BAY

Daima
Departm
Store

Jaffe Road

▼ 14

▼ 13

Lockhart Road

M

Causeway Bay
Plaza II

M

Sogo
Department
Store

15 ●
17 ▼

Causeway Bay
Plaza

Causeway
Bay

M

Yee Wo S

Lockhart Road

Perceval Street

▼ 16

M

Hennessy Road

Mitsukoshi
Department
Store

Jardine's Ba

Tram

Kai Chiu Road

22 ▼

Jardine's Crescent

Tang Lung Street

Lee Garden Road

Pak Sha Road

Yun Ping Road

Russell Street

Percival Street

26 ▼

Lan Fong Road

27 ▼

● 28

Times Square

Lee
Theatre
Plaza

31 ▮

Hysan Avenue

32 ▮ 33

Canal Road

Sharp Street East

29 ▼   ▼ 30

Matheson Street

Sun Wui Road

Ho Ping Road

▼ 37

Yiu Wa Street

Leighton Lane

Leighton Road

▮ 38

▼ 39

Leighton Road

Wong Nai Chung Road

1

Tram

LEIGHTON HILL

To Aberdeen, Repulse
Bay & Stanley

To Happy Valley

MAP 6

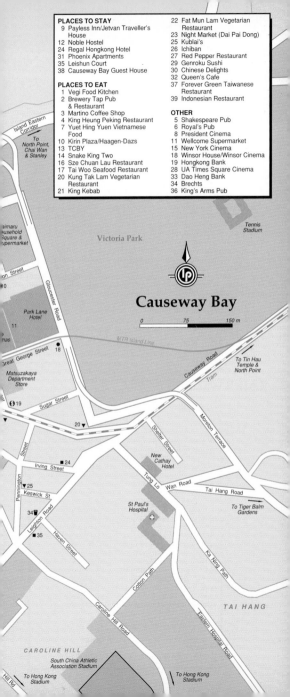

PLACES TO STAY
9 Payless Inn/Jetvan Traveller's House
12 Noble Hostel
24 Regal Hongkong Hotel
31 Phoenix Apartments
35 Leishun Court
38 Causeway Bay Guest House

PLACES TO EAT
1 Vegi Food Kitchen
2 Brewery Tap Pub & Restaurant
3 Martino Coffee Shop
4 King Heung Peking Restaurant
7 Yuet Hing Yuen Vietnamese Food
10 Kirin Plaza/Haagen-Dazs
13 TCBY
14 Snake King Two
16 Sze Chuan Lau Restaurant
17 Tai Woo Seafood Restaurant
20 Kung Tak Lam Vegetarian Restaurant
21 King Kebab

22 Fat Mun Lam Vegetarian Restaurant
23 Night Market (Dai Pai Dong)
25 Kublai's
26 Ichiban
27 Red Pepper Restaurant
29 Genroku Sushi
30 Chinese Delights
32 Queen's Cafe
37 Forever Green Taiwanese Restaurant
39 Indonesian Restaurant

OTHER
5 Shakespeare Pub
6 Royal's Pub
8 President Cinema
11 Wellcome Supermarket
15 New York Cinema
18 Winsor House/Winsor Cinema
19 Hongkong Bank
28 UA Times Square Cinema
33 Dao Heng Bank
34 Brechts
36 King's Arms Pub

Island Eastern Corridor

To North Point, Chai Wan & Stanley

aimaru
usehold
Square &
upermarket

Victoria Park

Tennis Stadium

Causeway Bay

0   75   150 m

on Street

0

Gloucester Road

Park Lane Hotel

1as

MTR Island Line

To Tin Hau Temple & North Point

Great George Street

18

Causeway Road

Tram

Matsuzakaya Department Store

19

Sugar Street

Street

20

Shelter Street

Moreton Terrace

Pennington

24

Irving Street

New Cathay Hotel

Tung Lo Wan Road

Tai Hang Road

To Tiger Balm Gardens

25

Keswick St

34

Leighton Road

35

St Paul's Hospital

Ka Ning Path

Haven Street

Cotton Path

TAI HANG

Caroline Hill Road

Eastern Hospital Road

CAROLINE HILL

South China Athletic Association Stadium

To Hong Kong Stadium

To Hong Kong Stadium

Hill Rd

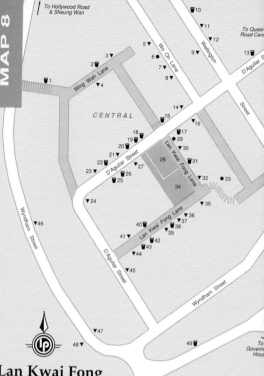

MAP 8

To Hollywood Road & Sheung Wan

To Queen's Road Central

Wo On Lane

Wellington

To D'Aguilar Street

CENTRAL

Wing Wah Lane

Lan Kwai Fong

Lan Kwai Fong Lane

D'Aguilar Street

Wyndham Street

Lan Kwai Fong Lane

D'Aguilar Street

Wyndham Street

To Governor's House

Lan Kwai Fong

0   25   50 m

To Zoological & Botanical Gardens

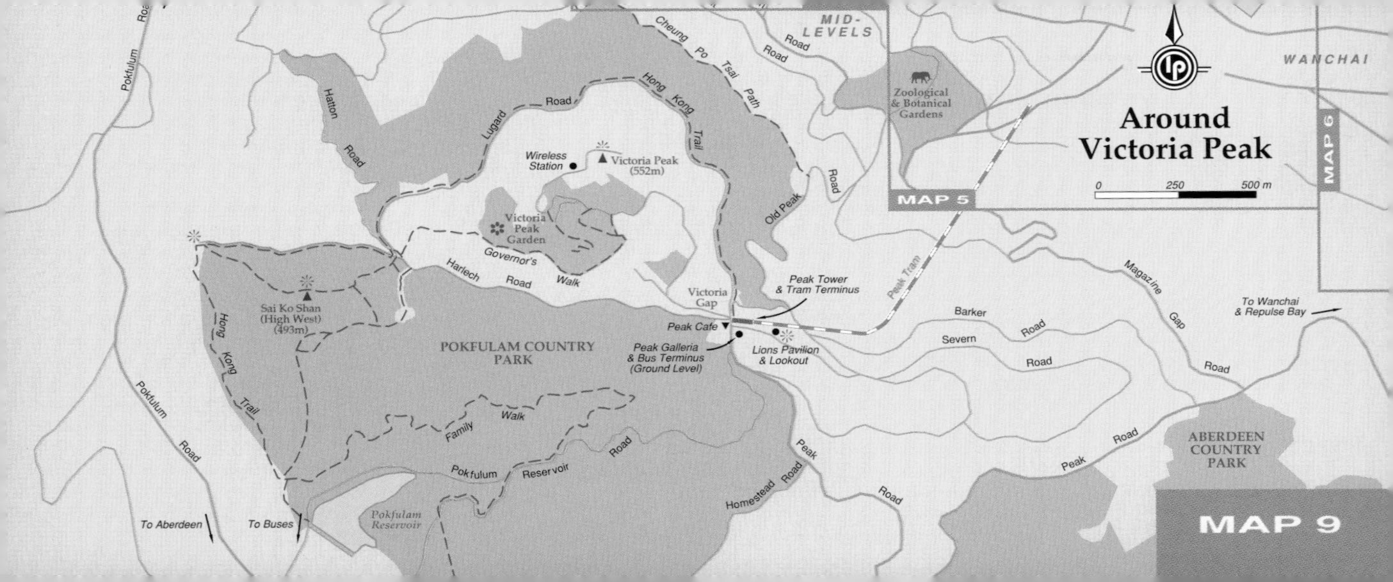

MAP 9

MAP 6

WANCHAI

Around Victoria Peak

0   250   500 m

MAP 5

ABERDEEN COUNTRY PARK

To Wanchai & Repulse Bay

Magazine Gap Road

Peak Road

Barker Road

Severn Road

Peak Road

Homestead Road

MID-LEVELS

Zoological & Botanical Gardens

Peak Tram

Old Peak Road

Road

Cheung Po Tsai Path

Hong Kong Trail

Peak Tower & Tram Terminus

Lions Pavilion & Lookout

Victoria Gap

Peak Cafe

Peak Galleria & Bus Terminus (Ground Level)

Victoria Peak (552m)

Wireless Station

Victoria Peak Garden

Governor's Walk

Harlech Road

Lugard Road

POKFULAM COUNTRY PARK

Reservoir Road

Pokfulam Reservoir

Family Walk

Hatton Road

Sai Ku Shan (High West) (493m)

Hong Kong Trail

Pokfulam Reservoir

To Buses

Pokfulam Road

To Aberdeen

Pokfulam Road

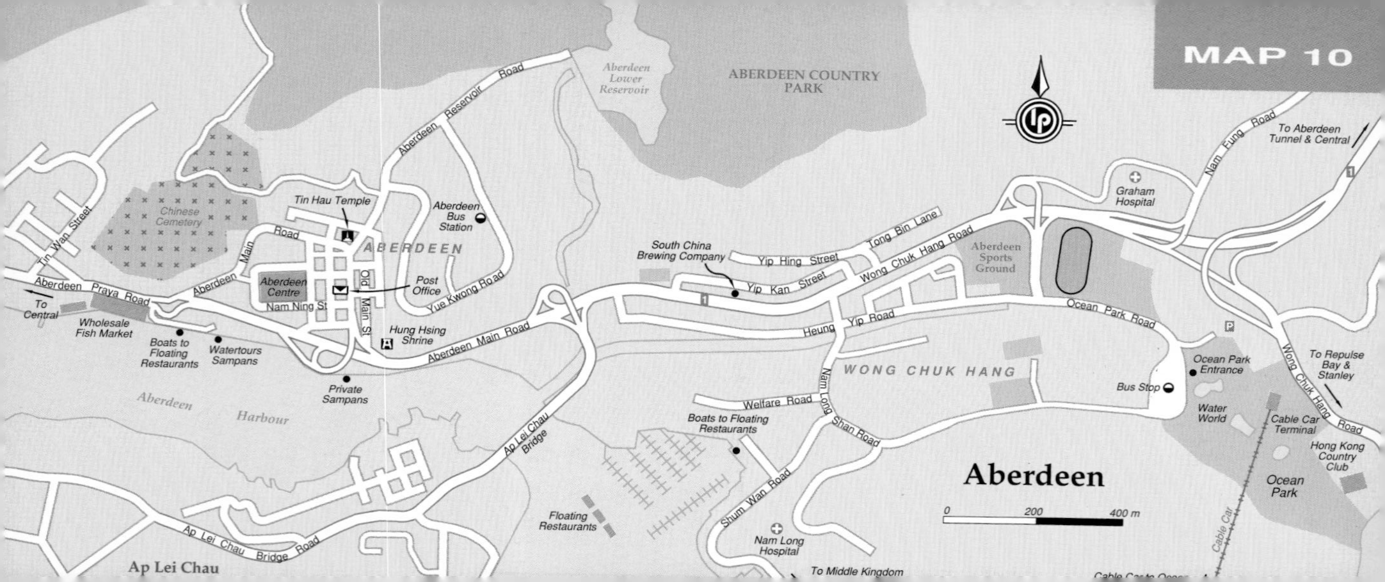

MAP 10

Aberdeen

0   200   400 m

To Aberdeen Tunnel & Central

Nam Fung Road

Graham Hospital

ABERDEEN COUNTRY PARK

Aberdeen Lower Reservoir

Tang Bin Lane

Yip Hing Street

Yip Kan Street

South China Brewing Company

Aberdeen Sports Ground

Ocean Park Road

To Repulse Bay & Stanley

Wong Chuk Hang

Hong Kong Country Club

Cable Car Terminal

Ocean Park

Ocean Park Entrance

Water World

Bus Stop

Cable Car

WONG CHUK HANG

Wong Chuk Hang Road

Heung Road

Yip Road

Nam Long

Welfare Road

Nam Long Shan Road

Boats to Floating Restaurants

Shum Wan Road

Nam Long Hospital

To Middle Kingdom

Cable Crade Crain

Floating Restaurants

Ap Lei Bridge

Reservoir Road

Brewin Path

Aberdeen Bus Station

Post Office

Old Main St

Hung Hsing Shrine

Via Kwong Road

Aberdeen Main Road

ABERDEEN

Tin Hau Temple

Aberdeen Centre

Nam Ning St

Main

Chinese Cemetery

Boats to Floating Restaurants

Wholesale Fish Market

Tin Wan Street

Aberdeen Praya Road

To Central

Waterfront Sampans

Private Sampans

Aberdeen Harbour

Ap Lei Chau Bridge

Ap Lei Chau

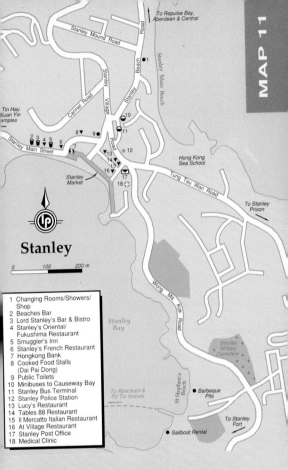

MAP 11

Stanley

0   100   200 m

1 Changing Rooms/Showers/
   Shop
2 Beaches Bar
3 Lord Stanley's Bar & Bistro
4 Stanley's Oriental/
   Fukushima Restaurant
5 Smuggler's Inn
6 Stanley's French Restaurant
7 Hongkong Bank
8 Cooked Food Stalls
   (Dai Pai Dong)
9 Public Toilets
10 Minibuses to Causeway Bay
11 Stanley Bus Terminal
12 Stanley Police Station
13 Lucy's Restaurant
14 Tables 88 Restaurant
15 Il Mercatto Italian Restaurant
16 At Village Restaurant
17 Stanley Post Office
18 Medical Clinic

NICKO GONCHAROFF

Boat building yards, Aberdeen

MAP 12

To Central

Pak Kok Shan
(138m)

Pak Kok
Kau Tsuen

Pak Kok

Luk Chau W

Tai Peng

See Enlargement

Yung Shue Wan

Tin Hau
Temple

Power
Station

Hung
Shing Ye
Beach

Lamma
Youth
Camp

Tit Sha Long

Ha Mei Wan

Lo So Shing

Lo So Shing
Beach

Mt Stenhou
(353m)

PLACES TO STAY
2 Man Lai Wah Hotel
14 Lamma Vacation House

PLACES TO EAT
4 Man Fung Seafood
    Restaurant
6 Green Cottage Bakery
7 Sampan Seafood
    Restaurant
10 Lung Wah Seafood
    Restaurant
11 Banyan Cafe
12 Capital Restaurant
13 Man Kee Restuarant
15 Sau Kee Restuarant
16 Lancombe Restaurant
17 Tai Hing Restaurant
18 Waterfront Bar
    & Restaurant

OTHER
1 Public Library
3 Yung Shue Wan Post
    Office
5 Island Bar
8 Hongkong Bank
9 Fountain Head Bar

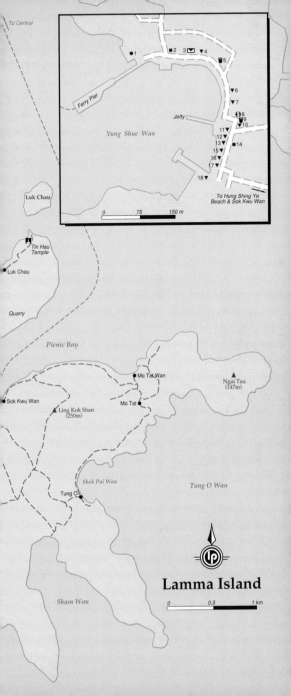

Luk Chau

Tin Hau
Temple

Luk Chau

Quarry

Picnic Bay

Mo Tat Wan

Mo Tat

Ngai Tau
(147m)

Sok Kwu Wan

Ling Kok Shan
(250m)

Shek Pai Wan

Tung O Wan

Tung O

Sham Wan

Lamma Island

0   0.5   1 km

MAP 13

Yaumatei & Mongkok

Tin Kwong Road

MATAUWAI

Argyle Street

Tweed Road

Dundas Street

Shek Ku Street

Pui Ching Road

Duball Road

Public Square Street

Kowloon Hospital

Man Fuk Road

Man Wan Rd

Waterloo Road

Prince Edward Road West

Boundary Street

Kadoorie Avenue

9

Soares Avenue

Ho M

Waterloo Road

Victory Avenue

Embankment Road

Peace Avenue

10

Mongkok Stadium

KCR

Mongkok

Yim Po Fong Street

13

Luen Wan Street

Boundary Street Sports Ground

Flower Market Road

Sai Yee Street

8

Prince Edward Road West

Fa Yuen Street

Argyle Street

Nelson Street

Sai Ming Street

Soy Street

6

7

11

Tung Choi Street

Nathan Road

Boundary Street

Playing Field Rd

Prince Edward Road

Sai Yeung Choi Street South

MTR (Kwun Tong Line)

12

Prince Edward

Nathan Road

MTR Tsuen Wan Line

Sai Yeung Choi Street

2

1

4

5

Portland Street

Portland Street

Mongkok Road

Fife Street

Mongkok

3

Shanghai Street

MONGKOK

Arran Street

Bute Street

Reclamation Street

Yu Chau St

Ki Lung Street

Tai Nan Street

Shanghai Street

Canton Road

Laichikok Road

Tong Mi Road

Palm Street

Bedford Road

Larch Street

Fuk Tsun Street

Ivy Street

Anchor Street

Cherry Street

Tung Chau Street

Tai Kok Tsui Road

Reclamation

Kok Cheung Street

To Tsuen Wan & New Territories

0   200   400 m

PLACES TO STAY
1 Newton Hotel Kowloon
2 Concourse Hotel
5 Grand Tower Hotel
9 Metropole Hotel
10 Anne Black Guest House (YWCA)
13 Stanford Hotel
14 STB Hostel
16 YMCA International House
18 King's Hotel
19 Booth Lodge (Salvation Army)
20 Caritas Bianchi Lodge
21 Pearl Seaview Hotel
25 Eaton Hotel
26 Nathan Hotel
27 Majestic Hotel

OTHER
3 Bird Market
4 Rex Cinema
6 Well Mount Sporting
   Goods Shop
7 Wise Mount Sporting
   Goods Shop
8 China Travel Service
11 Tung Choi Street Market
12 Broadway Cinema
15 Chamonix Alpine Equipment
17 Temple Street Night Market
   (North Section)
22 Tin Hau Temple
23 Jade Market
24 Kowloon Central Post Office
28 Cooked Food Stalls
29 Temple Street Night Market
   (South Section)
30 Yue Hwa Chinese Products
   Emporium
31 Jordan Ferry Bus Terminus

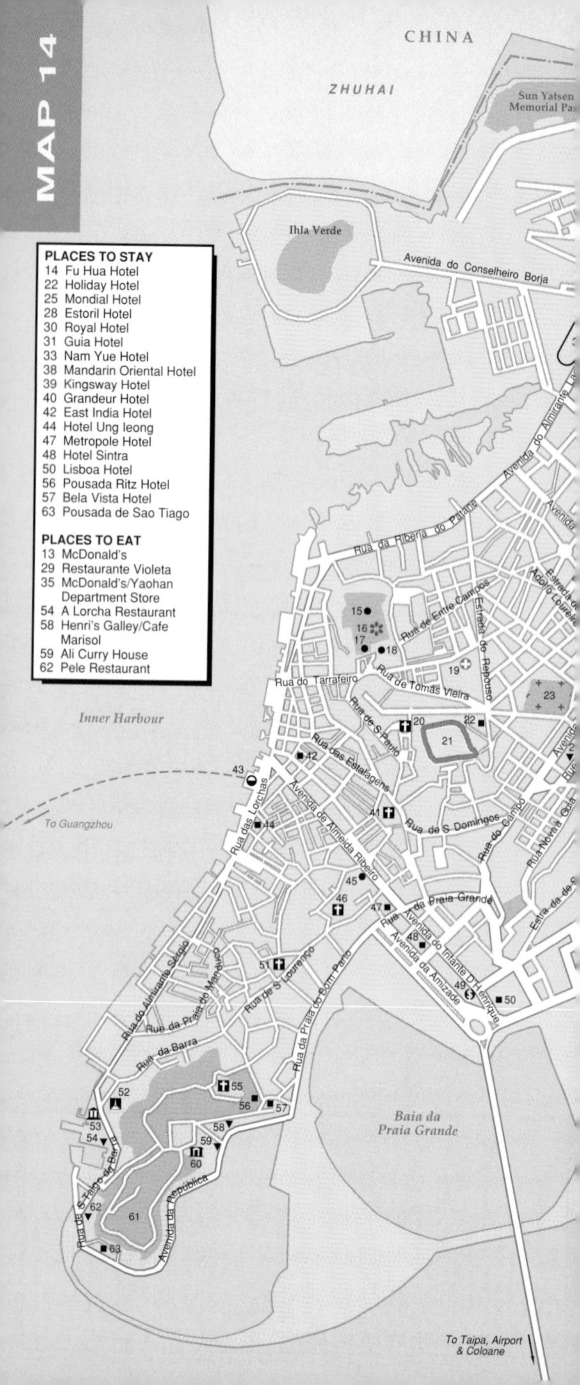

MAP 14

CHINA

ZHUHAI

Sun Yatsen
Memorial Par

Ilha Verde

Avenida do Conselheiro Borja

PLACES TO STAY
14 Fu Hua Hotel
22 Holiday Hotel
25 Mondial Hotel
28 Estoril Hotel
30 Royal Hotel
31 Guia Hotel
33 Nam Yue Hotel
38 Mandarin Oriental Hotel
39 Kingsway Hotel
40 Grandeur Hotel
42 East India Hotel
44 Hotel Ung Ieong
47 Metropole Hotel
48 Hotel Sintra
50 Lisboa Hotel
56 Pousada Ritz Hotel
57 Bela Vista Hotel
63 Pousada de Sao Tiago

PLACES TO EAT
13 McDonald's
29 Restaurante Violeta
35 McDonald's/Yaohan
   Department Store
54 A Lorcha Restaurant
58 Henri's Galley/Cafe
   Marisol
59 Ali Curry House
62 Pele Restaurant

Inner Harbour

Rua da Ribeira do Patane

Rua de Entre Campos

Estrada do Repouso

15
16
17
18
19
23
Rua do Tarrafeiro
Rua de Tomás Vieira
Rua de S Paulo
20
22
21
Rua das Estalagens
42
To Guangzhou
43
Rua das Lorchas
Avenida de Almeida Ribeiro
44
Rua de S Domingos
Rua Norte do
46
Rua de Preia Grande
Avenida do Infante D H
Rua da Praia do Manduco
Avenida da Amizade
51
48
50
Rua de S Lourenço
Rua da Praia do Bom Parto
Rua da Almirante Sérgio
Rua da Barra
Rua da Praia de Santiago

52
53
54
55
56
57
58
59
60
62
61
63
Avenida da República
Rua de Felipe de Oliv

Baia da
Praia Grande

To Taipa, Airport
& Coloane

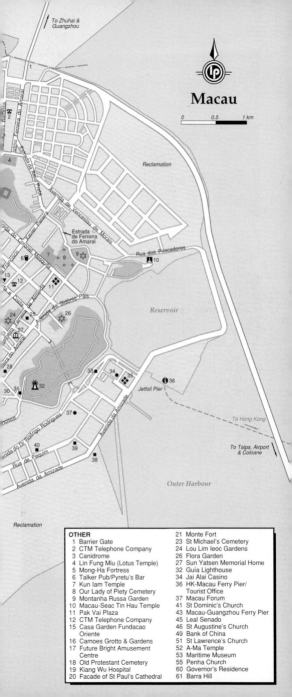

Macau

To Zhuhai &
Guangzhou

Reclamation

To Hong Kong

To Taipa, Airport
& Coloane

Reclamation

0   0.5   1 km

Estrada
de Ferreira
do Amaral

Rua dos Pescadores

Reservoir

Jetfoil Pier

Outer Harbour

Top: Antique shop, Sheung Wan
Bottom: Quiet street, Macau